Maclean's publicity poster, 1948
National Archives of Canada, C 140414; courtesy Maclean Hunter Limited

DAVID MACKENZIE

Arthur Irwin

A Biography

UNIVERSITY OF TORONTO PRESS
Toronto Buffalo London

©University of Toronto Press Incorporated 1993
Toronto Buffalo London
Printed in Canada

ISBN 0-8020-2632-x

∞

Printed on acid-free paper

Canadian Cataloguing in Publication Data

MacKenzie, David (David Clark), 1953–
Arthur Irwin: a biography

Includes index.
ISBN 0-8020-2632-X

1. Irwin, Arthur, 1898– . 2. Periodical editors – Canada – Biography. 3. Diplomats – Canada – Biography. 4. Maclean's "Canada's national magazine." I. Title.

PN4913.I79M3 1993   070.92   C93-093699-X

This book has been published with the help of a grant from the Social Science Federation of Canada, using funds provided by the Social Sciences and Humanities Research Council of Canada.

For Claire

Contents

Foreword by Pierre Berton   ix

Preface   xiii
Introduction / 3

PART ONE: 1898–1926
1 'From Darkness to Light' / 7
2 Gunner Irwin / 17
3 Cub Reporter / 30
4 The 'Smoke' of Liberalism / 43
5 Canada's National Magazine / 63

PART TWO: 1926–1940
6 'The Horse Work' / 79
7 Getting Down to Brass Tacks / 103
8 The Bren Gun Scandal / 116
9 The Campaign / 131

PART THREE: 1940–1950
10 The War Years / 151
11 The 'Real Meaning' of Destruction / 171

12 The Man Who Made *Maclean's* / 182
13 'The Editor' and His Magazine / 199
14 The Last Year / 213

PART FOUR: 1950–
15 'Mad Ministers, Rioting Reds, and Posh Parties' / 229
16 'Going to Bat' for the NFB / 243
17 'The Canadian Was *Simpatico*' / 263
18 *Pax* Victoria / 279

Abbreviations 286
Notes 287
A Note on Sources 311
Index 315

Foreword

It's high time that Arthur Irwin be given his due. As 'the man who made *Maclean's*,' he trained a generation of writers to his own exacting standards and the ripple effects are still being felt. It is not too much to say that the astonishing renaissance in non-fiction writing in Canada since the end of the Second World War – a renaissance reflected in today's best seller lists – is due in a very large part to him.

Arthur Irwin taught me my craft, but he did more than that. He turned me into a Canadian nationalist. When I arrived at *Maclean's* in 1947 I was a brash provincialist, the worst kind of B.C. booster. The magazine was to me a way point on a journey which, I hoped, would lead me to the fertile fields of *Life* or the *Saturday Evening Post*. It didn't happen because Irwin seduced me. Years later, when the Time-Life organization offered me a job, I turned it down without a second thought.

Irwin had two qualities that made him a great editor. One was a tough mind. He could spot a weak sentence or an unqualified generalization and pounce on it like an owl with a rodent. I use the simile advisedly for Irwin was owlish. When he peered out at you over his glasses, pencil in hand, you knew you were in for it. You couldn't put anything past him. He wanted evidence for every statement you made. He could tear an article apart and show you how to put it together so it made more sense. I learned structure from Irwin and I also learned about research. If you didn't do your homework, he treated you kindly but as an errant schoolchild.

His second strength was his ability to spot talent. An entire generation of writers, both freelance and staff, cut their teeth on *Maclean's*: Blair Fraser, June Callwood, Trent Frayne, Sydney Katz, Clyde Gilmour, Fred Bodsworth, Barbara Moon, James Bannerman – the list goes on and on.

And, of course, Ralph Allen, his brilliant successor, who absorbed the Irwin tradition and carried it on to train such writers as Peter Gzowski and Peter Newman. Under Allen, *Maclean's* entered its golden age; but it was Irwin who laid the groundwork. They were quite different personalities. Allen, a former sports writer and war correspondent, was a social animal who became a brilliant editor under Irwin's tutelage. But, unlike Irwin, he made no plans for his own succession. As a result, when he departed, the magazine suffered.

In building his own staff, Irwin moved at a pace that many considered glacial. He could not be hurried, for he was not a man who made snap judgments. He agonized for weeks, conducting exhausting research, before hiring a new editor. He phoned an old professor of mine before taking me on. The professor told Irwin that I might have been a brilliant scholar if hadn't spent so much time on the college paper. P.S.: I got the job.

He had his flaws. To say he wasn't given to small talk is an understatement. Even today, when I visit him in Victoria, he greets me, not with the usual pleasantries about the weather, but with a direct and blunt question. 'What's happening to the country, Pierre?' he'll say.

Magazine fiction did not interest him and here, perhaps, he was before his time. The kind of short story *Maclean's* used to publish is no more. I suspect Irwin saw it coming. He hired W.O. Mitchell as fiction editor, but irked Mitchell by turning down many of Mitchell's favourite authors.

On the other hand he had a vision of the magazine and a vision of the country (which he shared with his friend Bruce Hutchison) that helped touch off a new wave of nationalism in this country. *Maclean's* task, in Irwin's credo, was to 'interpret Canada to Canadians.' Having emerged from the shadow of a silly-ass Englishman, Napier Moore, he proceeded to do just that. Under Irwin, Canadians learned about themselves – about their cities, about their small towns, about their politics, about the relations with the world at large.

Maclean's covers, especially those by Franklin Arbuckle, showed the land itself in all its variety and its mystery. *Maclean's* profiles – from George McCullagh to Barbara Ann Scott, from a young evangelist named Charles Templeton to a veteran hockey player named King Clancy – told Canadians that this country could produce men and women of quality, character, and prestige. It was a celebration of Canadian values and Canadian ideals. Everybody wanted to be part of it – Hugh MacLennan, Morley Callaghan, Gordon Sinclair, Yousuf Karsh, Bruce Hutchison.

Under Irwin, *Maclean's* began to cover the significant postwar developments – continuing stories that were unfolding under our noses. He sent one man to report on the new oil discoveries at Leduc, another to Labrador to write about the great iron ore find. He sent me up the Alaska Highway before it was opened to tourists.

Few understood that another story was unfolding, a development as important as oil or iron: the creation of an important Canadian resource, a hidden vein of magazine journalists whom he taught to think nationally and interpret the country to a new generation of readers.

If he has only now been given his due it is because he has always been self-effacing. Irwin didn't seek publicity and didn't get it. I had to prod the *Canadian Encyclopedia* to include in its second edition a brief paragraph of tribute to him. It is proper and more than just that this imbalance is now being restored with the publication of his biography. For without Arthur Irwin, the country would have been the poorer.

Pierre Berton
Toronto, April 1993

Preface

The primary source for this biography was the large collection of personal papers held by Arthur Irwin at his home in Victoria, B.C. It was the existence of these previously unmined papers that first interested me in this project, and without them this book could not have been written. These papers are now stored in the National Archives in Ottawa and will soon be open to the public. In addition to working with the papers at Irwin's home and in collections in archives in Ottawa, Toronto, and Montreal, I was able to spend many long afternoons interviewing Irwin, his wife and family, and dozens of former colleagues and friends.

Irwin is a very private individual, and while he was open and talked freely with me over several years, there is a relative lack of personal material in his papers. The ensuing difficulties in uncovering Irwin's personal life and probing his inner thoughts are obvious. As Robert Gittings writes, the biographer is really an artist, but an artist under oath, while the art of biography is the 'welding of scientific observation with imaginative art.'[1] In order for the imagination to run free, however, the biographer must have a solid scientific foundation. Irwin's papers provide only a partial picture of his private world, and I have been reluctant to fill in the gaps by delving too deeply into speculation or into the imaginative non-fiction that has become increasingly popular in recent years.

Irwin and I signed an agreement giving me complete access to his personal papers. A biographer can never be certain that his subject has not hidden or destroyed – by accident or design – some unflattering or discomforting material; nor can he can be sure that his subject has revealed all his private secrets and hidden fears. But after getting to know Irwin as well as I have over the past six years, I feel confident that he has given me access to all extant material in his possession. The one exception was a short file of letters from a close friend who is still living and might be embarrassed if they were made public; this file Irwin sealed in an envelope. In return for the access he gave me, I have allowed him to read the manuscript and to make comments and suggestions on it. I found many of his comments helpful, but otherwise he has had no say or control over any aspect or content of this biography.

The research and writing of this book was undertaken while I was a SSHRC Canada Research Fellow in the Department of History at the University of Toronto, and I would like to thank the university and the Social Sciences and Humanities Research Council for their financial support. My thanks also to Arthur and Pat Irwin for opening their home to me during my visits to Victoria, and for their kindness and hospitality which made the task of research a pleasant and memorable one. Parts of chapters 8 and 9 have appeared in a slightly revised form in the *Journal of Canadian Studies* and my thanks to the editor for permission to reprint this material. Thanks also to Claire Pratt for permission to quote from two E.J. Pratt poems, 'Dunkirk' and 'They are Returning.' I would also like to express my appreciation to Robert Bothwell and the anonymous readers of the Social Science Federation of Canada for their helpful comments on an earlier draft of the manuscript.

A special thanks to my editor Virgil Duff of the University of Toronto Press for guiding this book through to publication and for his encouragement along the way, and to Mary McDougall Maude for copy-editing the manuscript. Finally, an acknowledgment here can only partially express my gratitude to my wife Terry for her patience and support over the years, and to my daughter Claire to whom the book is dedicated.

Irwin's birthplace, Ayr, Ontario, 1899; left, Alexander;
right, Amelia (holding Irwin)
Irwin Family Private Collection

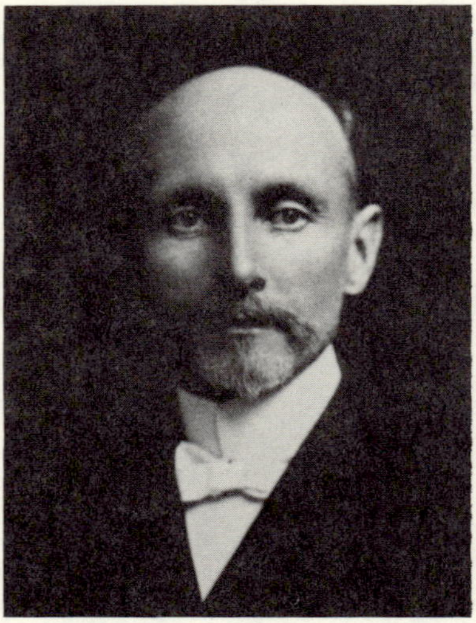

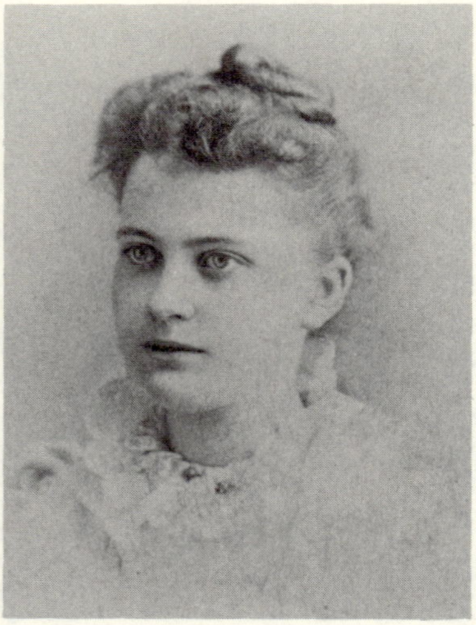

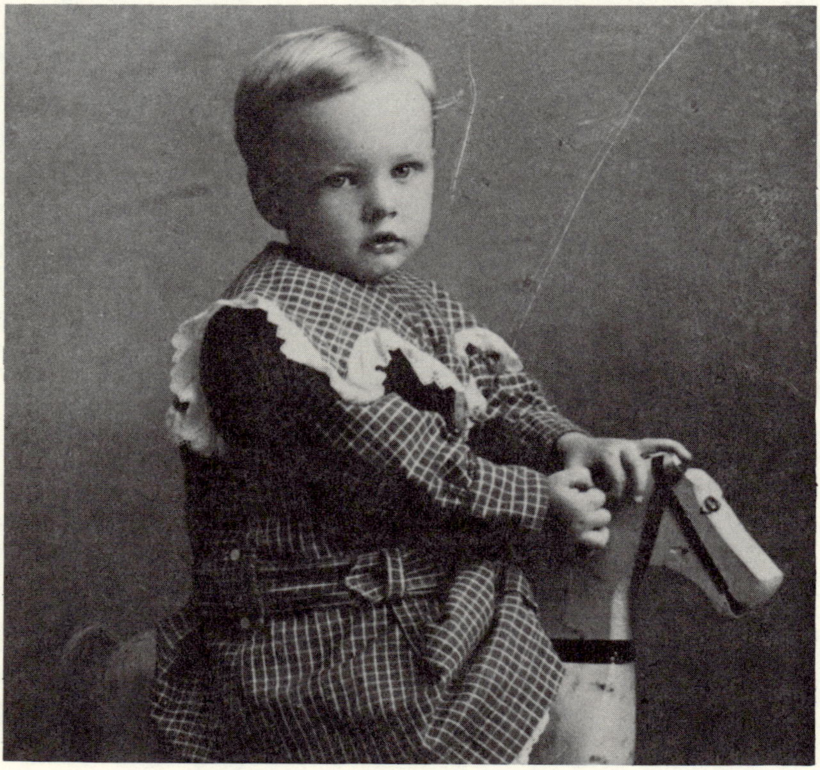

Top left, Irwin's father, Alexander Irwin, at Norfolk, Ontario, 1902–6; top right, Irwin's mother, Amelia Jane Hassard, 1890; bottom, Irwin at age two, 1900
Irwin Family Private Collection

Winnipeg, 1930; left to right, Arnold, Arthur, Harvey, Helen, Harold
Irwin Family Private Collection

Top, Gunner Irwin, 1917
Irwin Family Private Collection

Bottom, cub reporter c. 1925
National Archives of Canada, PA 186276

Jean Irwin c. 1930   *Irwin Family Private Collection*

Colonel J.B. Maclean, 1928   *Archives of Ontario, AO 1455*

Irwin camping c. 1924
Irwin Family Private Collection

Irwin c. 1935   *National Archives of Canada PA 186275*

Top, Horace T. Hunter (undated)
Archives of Ontario, AO 1454

Bottom, Floyd Chalmers c. 1941
Archives of Ontario, AO 1456

Maclean's staff meeting c. 1949; left to right, John Clare, Barbara Moon, Jerry Anglin, D.M. Battersby, Leslie Hannon, Katie Croyston, Eva-Lis Wuorio; seated, Irwin
Irwin Family Private Collection

Irwin at his desk, 29 January 1943
National Archives of Canada, PA 186278

Film commissioner Irwin c. 1950
(Reproduced by permission of the National Film Board)

National Film Board c. 1951; left to right, Stewart Keate, A.L. Caldwell, Irwin, Gratien Gélinas, Albert Trueman, Charles Band
National Archives of Canada, PA 186277

Irwin's presentation of credentials, Rio de Janeiro; left, Irwin; right, President Kubitschek of Brazil   *Irwin Family Private Collection*

P.K. Page (Irwin) c. 1955. Photograph by L.J. Dwyer
Irwin Family Private Collection

Arthur and Pat in Victoria, 1988
Irwin Family Private Collection

PART ONE

1898–1926

Introduction

In August 1941, during the second full year of the war, Arthur Irwin, associate editor of *Maclean's Magazine,* collapsed in his hotel room at the Lord Elgin Hotel in Ottawa. He had been 'invited' to Ottawa by Lieutenant-General H.D.G. Crerar, the chief of the general staff, and after 1942 the commander of the 1st Canadian Corps, to defend his magazine over some recent articles it had published, in particular a story criticizing how Canadian soldiers were trained. After his conversation with Crerar, Irwin returned to his hotel where he suffered a duodenal haemorrhage, and lost an unusual amount of blood. Few Canadians would have noticed the dropping of his name from the masthead of *Maclean's* had he died in Ottawa that summer evening in 1941. But the country would have lost one of its foremost editors and one of its staunchest nationalists. And a generation of Canadian non-fiction writers would have lost a man who was part mentor, teacher, colleague, and friend.

From 1925 to 1950 Arthur Irwin was the driving force behind the success of *Maclean's Magazine,* first as associate editor, then managing editor, and finally as editor. He had a strong feeling for the country, and strong views on what it meant to be Canadian. He exhibited a dynamic and definite brand of Canadian nationalism, and over a quarter of a century moulded, shaped, and cajoled *Maclean's* into a successful and important player in Canadian life.

Irwin's early years as associate editor were symbolized by his struggle with Napier Moore, the editor of *Maclean's,* over editorial content and the future direction of the magazine. The English-born Moore embodied the imperial sensibilities of an earlier age; his nationalism was filtered through a British lens; the land of his adopted home was warmed by the same imperial sun as the land of his birth. In Irwin's mind Moore represented everything that was old, conservative, and colonial about Canada's past. Irwin was very much a part of a new generation of middle-class Canadians that came of age during the First World War and had returned from the war with a stronger North American outlook; the belief that the Canadian experience could be better understood in American rather than British terms. Canada was unlike any European nation; it was a new society, a nation of immigrants, with a frontier heritage and a linguistic duality; it was an American nation that must look for its values, ideas, and the solutions for its problems here, on this continent. His struggle with Moore was not to make *Maclean's* a 'Canadian' magazine; it was more over how that 'Canadianism' would be portrayed. Nor was it personal; it was, rather, an encounter of ideas, played out in the offices and pages of *Maclean's Magazine*.

A highlight of his years as associate editor occurred in the months following the publication of the famous 'Canada's Armament Mystery' article, written by George Drew, which sparked the best-known defence contract scandal in Canadian history. Although he did not write the story, Irwin originated and pursued the idea, edited the article prior to publication, and then embarked on an intensive cross-country fact-finding mission to gather more material on defence contracts. The fruits of this investigation were condensed into a series of muckraking articles for *The Financial Post* from which was launched the Maclean company's moral assault on the Liberal government of Mackenzie King. It was a turning-point in his career.

During the Second World War Irwin became managing editor of *Maclean's* and thus acquired its editorial direction. He was then able to introduce changes that he had been advocating for more than a decade: to bring the focus and 'feel' of *Maclean's* articles more in line with contemporary Canadian life, and to expand the staff to include a new generation of writers from all parts of the country. Irwin believed that it was possible to have a positive impact on national affairs, and during the war and after he endeavoured to use *Maclean's* not only to entertain but also to inform and stimulate, and to reflect the ever-changing views and interests of his audience. Here his own views on what was important came into play, and increasingly the articles in *Maclean's* came to reflect his own interests in national politics, international affairs, scientific and technological change, and, above all, the Canadian dimension.

The second part of his plan was to recruit a new generation of writers and then train them in the art and business of producing a mass-circulation magazine. With some insight and an uncanny knack for spotting talent, he hired and trained in less than three years a cast of writers many of whom went on to have distinguished careers of their own, including, among others, Ralph Allen, Blair Fraser, Pierre Berton, Scott Young, W.O. Mitchell, Eva-Lis Wuorio, Jerry Anglin, Arthur Mayse, and John Clare. He had the good sense to let them develop their own talents, and by the late 1940s *Maclean's Magazine* was a very different magazine than during the Moore years. It was unique in Canada at that time, thanks largely to Irwin and to what has come to be regarded widely as the best editorial staff of any magazine in Canadian history.

Running throughout Irwin's life was a keen interest in Canadian external affairs, and after leaving *Maclean's* he went on to a second career in the public service: as film commissioner at the National Film Board (NFB), high commissioner in Australia, and ambassador to Brazil and Mexico. Irwin was appointed to the NFB at a time when that institution's survival was threatened by allegations of espionage and subversion. His impact on the film industry or cultural politics in Canada was relatively small, but as a public servant he was left to deal with the NFB's 'red scare' and, afterwards, he reorganized the board and moved its operations to Montreal. He finished his varied career as a newspaper publisher in Victoria, B.C., and has spent his retirement years there.

Irwin's character, his intellectual interests, as well as his sense of country, were shaped by a number of forces: by his anglo-Canadian heritage and language; by his strict Methodist upbringing which left a permanent stamp on his personality; by his central-Canadian roots from which his view of the country developed; and by his war experience which helped define his uniqueness as a Canadian. He was a product of his time, his place, and his class. Today scholars would add race and gender to that list: he was a white middle-class male imbued with the Protestant work ethic and the tenets of Methodist thought – discipline, modesty, thrift, sobriety, and moral stamina. His understanding of the country and his approach to his work were shaped by these forces too. Although his views were common to a great many others of similar age and background, in a country of such linguistic, cultural, and geographical diversity it is not surprising that his brand of nationalism was not shared by all of his fellow citizens.

For Irwin an important moment came in 1919, only a few months after the end of the Great War. It was early May when his troop-train filled with returning soldiers rambled through northern New Brunswick. At first he was disappointed with what he saw from the train: ice patches covered many of the lakes, the trees were barren, and the world seemed drab and lifeless. 'Is this the country we're coming home to?' he asked himself. But his spirits rose as the train wound its way along the St Lawrence River towards Quebec. The late afternoon sun shimmered above the river and city, and the old capital stood like a welcoming beacon to a majestic land. He nodded with approval: this was his country, he thought, and he was home at last.

ONE

'From Darkness to Light'

William Arthur Irwin was born on 27 May 1898 in Ayr, Ontario, a small village on the banks of the Nith River in Waterloo County. This is central Canada – the heartland of southwestern Ontario and the basin of the St Lawrence River. This land and this river, cutting halfway through a continent on its way to the sea, made a permanent impression on Irwin and the way he viewed his country and his world. When he came to look back on his life years later, he would call himself 'a St Lawrence man.'

Irwin's earliest memories were more recollections of his environment than of people: the blazing heat of the summer sun and the bone-chilling cold of an Ontario winter. Looking out to the horizon he could see 'moving silhouettes of horses and sleighs on an elevated ice road.' The faces are obscured; his destination unknown. 'The ice harvest. Soft white silence. Hand held by grown up. Presumably father. Urinating at shore line bush. Urine on woollen mittens frozen stiff.'[1]

Having a Methodist minister for a father meant that Arthur and his family moved frequently from one parsonage to another. The year after he was born the Irwins were posted to Port Colborne, a small town of 1200 people on the shores of Lake Erie. Another move came in 1902, this time to Norwich in Oxford County, about 25 kilometres south of Woodstock.

For Arthur, life in Norwich revolved around the parsonage, a square, white-brick, two-storey house on a small lot adjacent to the church. Through the front door in the hall stood the hatstand and mirror, and to one side sat a wooden chest for overshoes and a stone jar for umbrellas and walking sticks. The parlour was filled with stiff-backed Victorian furniture and the walls were adorned with his mother's copies of famous paintings. To one side was the upright Gerhard-Heintzman piano, around which the family often gathered. On less formal occasions the mahogany piano stool with its adjustable seat served as Arthur's 'dizzy machine' – to lie on, stomach-down, and twist and whirl until the walls were spinning and his head was reeling.

Across the hall his father had his study: his retreat from the noise of a growing family, a sanctuary where he could work in peace on his sermons. Along the walls were permanent bookshelves, but the rest of the furniture he had made himself: an oak roll-top desk, portable bookcases, and an adjustable dictionary stand. The centre-piece of the room was his large wooden chest which served as a filing cabinet, with its three-inch drawers, each subdivided, indexed, and filled with sermon notes.

Towards the back of the house was the kitchen, from which the sweet smells of chocolate fudge and boiling syrup wafted upstairs into the children's bedrooms. Water for the kitchen sink was brought up by pump from a cistern in the basement, milk was delivered by the milkman with his horse-cart and poured into a kitchen pail. The kitchen was the centre of household activity, where meals were prepared, fruits and jams preserved and cooled before being stored in the cellar, and where the days were measured in banging doors and running children and punctuated by raids on mother's nutcake box.

Before long, young Arthur began to experience the outside world: the fascination of the town powerhouse, the sweet tasting nectar of the local apple cider plant, a picnic at Port Dover on Lake Erie, where the waves so terrified him he refused to go on a boat ride and had to be left on shore. And his first trip to Toronto, shortly after the great fire of 1904, when, from a young boy's perspective, the great metropolis resembled little more than a vast sea of charred rubble: 'whole city blocks of desolate ruins, great piles of rubble and jagged naked walls against the skyline.' Years later, in 1945, when he travelled to the bombed-out cities of Europe, he would remember this first visit to Toronto.

◆

The Irwin family was of Scots-Protestant stock and had migrated to Ireland in the seventeenth century. In 1850, after almost two hundred years in Ireland's Sligo County, one branch of the family emigrated to British North America. They established themselves on several lots of land near Markdale, Ontario, and, by any standards of pioneer life, prospered in their new environment. Arthur's grandfather, William Irwin, arrived in Upper Canada as a boy of fourteen. He began preaching after a religious experience at a revival meeting and in 1861 was ordained a minister of the Wesleyan Methodist Church. That same year he married Jane James, whose family had also emigrated from Ireland, and the couple had eight children.

One of those children – Alexander James Irwin – was born at Invermay, near the town of Tara in Bruce County, Ontario, in 1866. Orphaned at the age of twelve, Alexander went to live with relatives and family friends, including a Quaker family in Oxford County, until he entered university at the age of eighteen. His adolescent years were solitary ones, as he sought both friendship in this world and a spiritual relationship with God. He contemplated joining the ministry like his father before him, but that road seemed blocked until he heard the call:

I went to Brantford and I lived as I had lived before. After six months I was back working on the Quaker farm for the two months' holiday. The inner skies were very dark. It seemed unbearable. I stopped the old roan mare at the end of the row of corn I was cultivating and went over to the picket fence and kneeled down. I had prayed, it seemed, only for a moment when an illumination and a freedom and a joy possessed me. I had seemingly passed from darkness to light.

The next Sabbath afternoon several of the gang of boys I had formerly associated with gathered in our drive house. A remark that was obscene or profane was made – I don't remember it. I said nothing but apparently my looks betrayed me. One of the boys looked up and said: 'Irwin's converted.' I said, 'Yes. I am.'

That was my first testimony for Christ.[2]

In 1885 Alexander Irwin entered Victoria College in Cobourg where he thrived on the rigours of athletic and intellectual life, and where he found the companionship he had missed as a boy. He took to preaching during these years, and graduated in 1893 with a bachelor of divinity. He was ordained a minister that same year, and his first appointment was to the town of Norval, near Georgetown. After three years he was moved to Ayr. The following year, on 17 July 1897, he married Amelia Jane Hassard, the daughter of the Reverend Richard Hassard and Lucinda Ann Van Valkenburg of Orangeville.

Like the Irwins, the Hassard family emigrated from Ireland, arriving in Upper Canada via New York around 1860. Richard Hassard was ordained at Kingston in 1865 and the following year he married twenty-three-year-old Lucinda (Lucy), a native of Morpeth, Ontario. The couple had six children, five sons, and one daughter – Amelia Jane, or Millie, as she was called. Millie was born in 1872 in Drumbo, in the heart of southwestern Ontario. She was raised in various small Ontario towns and, as part of a deeply religious family, she was imbued with the values and morals of late nineteenth-century Methodism. Her father was a strong believer in education for his children, and Millie attended the Ontario Ladies College in Whitby, graduating in 1891. How she met Alexander Irwin is uncertain, but her brother was a classmate of his at Victoria College, some forty miles east of Whitby.[3] Alexander and Millie in turn had six children: their first – Arthur – was born less than a year after their marriage. A daughter, Helen, was born in 1900, and then four more boys: Harvey (1903), Gordon (b. 1908, d. 1909), Arnold (1909), and Harold (1912).

Alexander was a sober man with a drooping moustache and thin beard, under a balding head and closely trimmed sideburns. He had 'a challenging face, serious and almost stern,' Arthur later wrote, 'with wide-set penetrating eyes, long straight nose and high-domed forehead.' He was an intellectual by nature and gained a reputation in the church for being something of a radical. A schism had developed in the Methodist Church in the late nineteenth century between fundamentalists, who accepted the Bible totally and without question as the inspired word of God, and the 'higher critics,' who refused to accept the literal interpretation and brought new scholarship to their re-examination of the biblical text. Alexander Irwin was 'tainted with the higher criticism,' and over the years his support for this radical theology would lead him into several ecclesiastical battles.

In 1905, for example, while living in Norwich, Reverend Irwin and a colleague embarked on a speaking tour of southern Ontario to preach the new theology. The tour was a success at the local level, but it was not well received by the church authorities on the Stationing Committee. Shortly thereafter, Irwin was dispatched to the village of Tara, in Bruce County, which was only half the size of Norwich. 'In terms of ecclesiastical hierarchy,' Arthur recalled years later, such a posting was 'equivalent to being sent to Siberia.'

Arthur was less concerned with the subtleties of church politics than he was in exploring his new world. Tara's parsonage was not dissimilar to the one in Norwich, a two-storey brick house with veranda and high-gabled roof. At the side of the house was the vegetable garden, the woodpile, and chicken-houses. There, too, was the brick stable, where Arthur's natural curiosity overtook his good sense when he poured water over the hind heels of the family horse – just to see how it would react. Only when he woke up, moment's later, splayed against the stable's back wall with the flattened water can beside him, did he realize the folly of his action.

There always was plenty for Arthur to do around the house. Depending on his age (and the availability of siblings), his chores included feeding the chickens, cleaning the chicken-house and gathering eggs; in the summer there was work to be done in the vegetable garden; in the winter there was snow shovelling. Inside, he helped in the kitchen: washing dishes, bringing in wood for the fire, and taking out the ashes afterwards.

Alexander Irwin did not believe that his children should begin school before the age of eight, so Arthur's earliest education was undertaken at home. Thanks to his father's supervision and an old school reader, Arthur could read by the time his formal education began in Tara's red-brick schoolhouse. His late start was more than compensated for by his home-schooling, and he passed six grades in the space of three years.

It is difficult not to envisage Irwin's early years as a Canadian version of a Norman Rockwell illustration or Frank Capra film. Summers were long and hot, filled with barefoot children running along the banks of the Sauble River and swimming in the cool, shimmering pond above the dam. Picture the excitement of a boy's first fishing rod and his first catch; the lazy sounds and smells floating from the bulrush marsh; endless days and long, languid evenings. In the wintertime the pond froze and was transformed into the village skating rink, open to all who cared to strap on a pair of skates. The early freeze-ups were the best – when the water froze so quickly and hard that it was almost transparent. To the boys and girls of Tara it was like skating on clear water. The sound of bells on a farmer's sleigh riding on an icy road, the crunch of hard-packed snow underfoot, the scent of wax candles hung on the freshly cut spruce Christmas tree – these were the sights and sounds of Tara.

Crossing the steel truss bridge over the Sauble River brought you from the Irwin house to Main Street, where Tara's two hotels, Van Dusen's Hardware, Wong Lee's Laundry, and Tobey's General Store were found. Up the steep stairs above Tobey's was a combined tailor shop and public library. Passing through the door into the small book-crammed room, Arthur soon discovered the works of Mark Twain and James Fenimore Cooper, G.A. Henty's *Under Drake's Flag* and *With Clive in India*, the animal stories of Charles G.D. Roberts and Ernest Thompson Seton, the adventure novels of Kipling and Defoe, Robert Louis Stevenson's *Treasure Island*, and R.M. Ballantyne's *The Young Fur Trader*. Later, Arthur would rely on libraries for forbidden books, such as the Horatio Alger adventures which Alexander believed were filled with 'false values and too materialistic.' For Arthur, as for so many other children of his age, those books were like keys that opened doors to other more exciting worlds.

At the age of ten Arthur was a shy boy of average height and build, with fair hair and blue eyes. He liked school and found the work relatively easy to grasp. He enjoyed the outdoors more, however, and relished the sports and competitions that a small town had to offer, although he was an active child rather than an athletic one. He was always eager to make friends with the other children in town, but because the family moved so often he developed few lifelong friendships as a boy.

After only three years in Tara, the family returned from exile with a new posting to Mount Forest, Ontario. Moving had almost become routine: the packing cases were retrieved from storage, valuables were carefully wrapped, and Alexander's books were boxed. The portable bookcases and chicken-houses were dismantled. The piano was of particular concern and had its own special container. Once all the trunks were filled, the family's possessions were taken to the train station on a horse-drawn dray and loaded onto a freight car for transportation to the new town.

In 1909, Mount Forest was a bustling town with a population of close to 1900. Like the other towns, Mount Forest was a self-contained community, attached to the outside world by railway and telegraph but otherwise very much a world of its own. For the Irwins, the family piano and 'dizzy machine,' father's desk, mother's paintings, and Victorian furniture gave the new parsonage a comfortable sense of the familiar and made the transition to a new home a little easier. The house had all the modern conveniences: electric lights and, even more exhilarating, a telephone. No more long walks to the telephone office.

Not too long afterwards, Arthur saw his first automobile, a 'mechanized buggy' that sputtered and stalled in a strong wind in front of the church.

Arthur finished grade school and started high school in Mount Forest. He was an excellent speller, regularly winning his class spelling bee, and he won a medal for arithmetic. He also read voraciously. One Ontario reader made a lasting impression, with its Union Jack and motto – 'One flag, one fleet, one throne' – on the fly-leaf, and, on the first page, Kipling:

> O Motherland, we pledge to thee,
> Head, heart and hand, through years to be.

This was, after all, a part of the world that basked in the splendour of the British empire, where a holiday honouring Queen Victoria's birthday had been celebrated since 1845. The pioneers had built a 'North American' nation on the rock of the Canadian Shield, but it was through the British empire that it would achieve greatness. In 1911, Mount Forest joined in the celebration of the coronation of George V by decorating the main street with flags and bunting. The Irwins played their part too, decorating the pillars on the veranda and upstairs balcony with the royal colours. There were uniquely Canadian overtones to this imperial enthusiasm, of course, but for most Ontarians the glory of the empire was their glory too.

◆

Arthur grew up in an atmosphere 'soaked in Methodism.'[4] Quite naturally, his parents were involved in local community affairs, church functions, various leagues and socials, and other volunteer work. This sense of public service was passed on to Arthur: 'It was part of living,' he said later, 'you had your responsibilities.'[5] Around the house the mood was reserved ('Victorian' is the word we would use today) and the Irwins were restrained in their displays of affection. Moreover, there was a coolness in Alexander and Millie's relationship, suggesting that their life together was founded more on a sense of duty and a strong moral code than anything else.

The church was the focus of much family attention: two services on Sundays, Wednesday night prayer meetings, and, of course, Sunday school in the church basement for the children. Alexander insisted on family participation; after all, it would not do for the minister's children to shirk their duties. And the Reverend also harboured desires for his eldest son to join the ministry himself. Arthur was not an enthusiastic convert, and often volunteered to stay home and cook the family's noon dinner in order to avoid the first of the two Sunday services.

The church also dictated the rhythm of life at home. Domestic tension mounted as Sunday approached and Alexander buried himself in his study to work on his sermon, while the rest of the family remained especially quiet. The right words never came easily to the Reverend, and he was often bothered by a nervous stomach. If he had recently returned from Toronto he would blame his gastric troubles on the city water which he claimed 'was strained through step ladders,' but as often as not he was feeling better by Sunday evening. Then, with the services out of the way, a more relaxed family would gather around the piano for a sing-along, with father's baritone leading the way through a chorus of 'Father O'Flynn.'

There was discipline in the family (although corporal punishment was rare) and a strict code of behaviour laid down by father, reflecting the taboos of traditional Methodism: drinking, gambling, and dancing were forbidden; card playing was frowned on. Attending the theatre was banned, except on rare occasions, such as the time 'Uncle Tom's Cabin' was put on in the local town hall. The circus, however, was out of the question. 'We could see the street parade and the animals,' Irwin recalled later, 'but not the three-ring circus.'

Arthur may have had a code of conduct to follow, but, like most children, he was liable on occasion to bend the rules. One favourite pastime was sneaking into the church through a loose window and playing with the motor that operated the pipe organ, or climbing up as high as possible in the rafters in the steeple. The thrill was even greater in a strong wind, when the whole steeple creaked and shook. There were other pranks as well: pushing the bench away from behind the Sunday school teacher when he was not looking; smoking cigarettes – home-made out of cedar bark – behind grandmother's house, and then having to wash his mouth out with water to mask the smell; or teasing Hummer, the family's black spaniel – one time so mercilessly that his father responded with a rare spanking.

As in most turn-of-the-century Ontario families, sex education or any discussions about sex were absent, and Arthur was left to pick up the finer points for himself from observing the local farm animals. Meeting girls was difficult, especially for a shy boy like Arthur. The regular Saturday evening skating sessions could be an endless torment as he circled round and round the partner of his choice, trying to screw up his courage to ask her to skate with him. Physical contact with the other sex was practically unheard of. Arthur's most memorable experience was getting on a toboggan behind a girl and having to wrap his legs around her. Considering that both were wearing heavy boots and thick snowsuits, most of the 'adventure' was in his imagination.[6] When Arthur went overseas in 1917, he had never kissed a girl.

There were other new fields of interest too. The visit of two of Canada's greatest Liberals – one just at the start of his career, the other entering his twilight – initiated Arthur into the world of politics. The scene was the local town hall and Arthur and a friend climbed their way to the very front to hear William Lyon Mackenzie King, freshman MP for Waterloo North and recently appointed minister of labour, expound on the virtues of Canadian Liberalism. King launched an attack on the provincial Conservative government, and, in particular, on one cabinet minister who had dealings with a prison farm near Guelph, when a loud and long hissssss!! 'stabbed the speech like an assassin's knife.' Without having to turn, Arthur knew instantly that it was the Reverend Mr Irwin making the piercing noise. A startled Mackenzie King paused, and, realizing that his audience sympathized more with his heckler than with him, backtracked and changed the topic.

The second episode occurred during the summer of 1911 at the height of the heated reciprocity election campaign when Prime Minister Sir Wilfrid Laurier made a campaign stop in Mount Forest. Even at the age of seventy Sir Wilfrid was a commanding and charismatic figure. His look and his eloquence made a lasting impression on Irwin, barely aged thirteen. As for content, Arthur recalled only three words, each choreographed with a dramatic swing of his arms: 'Canay-dyan *Pass*-if-ic Rail-way!'

Arthur was growing up, but he was not yet sure what he wanted to do with his life. One thing was certain, he would go on to university. But what then? The lure of Toronto was strong; every visit was filled with excitement, especially during the annual Canadian National Exhibition (CNE). The clang of the streetcars, the jostling crowds, the streets lined with office buildings, and the stores and shops of English Canada's burgeoning metropolis had tremendous appeal for a youngster. Choosing a career was more difficult. He felt no pull to the ministry, despite his father's wishes. Indeed he was struggling with some basic tenets of the church – he could not accept that he was born in original sin, for example. He was seeking, even longing, for a worldview that could explain or give meaning to his life, but until he could satisfy his inner doubts his path lay in the secular world.

It is possible that a few seeds were planted by one of Mount Forest's two weekly papers, the *Representative*, which was owned and operated by the Lambert family, and by one Lambert son, Norman, a *Globe* reporter whose stories regularly appeared in the Toronto paper under the byline: 'By Norman Lambert, our Special Correspondent.' There was magic in those words – they seemed so wonderfully important and cosmopolitan. Here was an honourable profession: to act as a prism through which others could catch a glimpse of the larger outside world. And glamorous too, especially when compared to Arthur's first job – filling castor oil bottles for fifty cents a day in the basement of Horace Yoeman's Drug Store.

Before Arthur finished high school, his home life took another turn. In the summer of 1913 Alexander Irwin was appointed to the pastorate at Oakville, to the west of Toronto, and the family was on the move once more. Weeks later, just as the family was settling in, Alexander was offered a post as professor of New Testament at Winnipeg's Wesley College, a small Methodist college affiliated with the University of Manitoba. Alexander left for the west in August, leaving the family temporarily behind in Oakville. Over the winter Arthur finished his last year of high school and secured his matriculation certificate which would gain him entrance into the University of Manitoba. Then, in the golden summer of 1914, while the western world teetered unknowingly on the brink of catastrophe, the family pulled up its stakes and followed Alexander to Winnipeg.

TWO

Gunner Irwin

Moving to Winnipeg was the first time Arthur Irwin left Ontario's 'golden triangle,' that area bordered by Georgian Bay and lakes Ontario, Erie, and Huron. The trip was a long one, beginning with a short train ride to Owen Sound and then a CPR passenger steamship journey through lakes Huron and Superior to Port Arthur. For the children it was a voyage of discovery. Even the steamship dining-room offered wonder and delight: 'Spotless linen, elaborately folded table napkins, gleaming silver, solicitous stewards, and enormous grapefruit in crystal bowls packed with cracked ice. Since we had never even seen a grapefruit, consuming one was a memorable gastronomical event.' The steamer docked at the Lakehead, and the family made the rest of the journey to Winnipeg by train.

The Irwins settled in a middle-class neighbourhood in Winnipeg's west end, on a street that snaked along a stretch of the Assiniboine River. Arthur was sixteen, and too young to enter university by the reckoning of his parents, so he spent his first year in Winnipeg at Kelvin Technical School. In the fall of 1915, at the age of seventeen, he entered Wesley College of the University of Manitoba.

The University of Manitoba, when it was founded in 1877, comprised three denominational colleges: Manitoba College (Presbyterian), St Boniface College (Roman Catholic), and St John's College (Anglican). The Methodist Wesley College traced its origins to the short-lived Wesleyan Institute of the 1870s, which was resurrected and affiliated with the university in 1888. In 1896 Wesley moved to a new building fronting on the north side of Portage Avenue. It was an impressive four-storey stone building with brick annex and playing fields behind.

Irwin had developed a keen interest in science, especially physics, during his later years of high school and his original intentions were to focus his studies in that direction. But because Wesley offered no specialized science program for junior students he enrolled in a general program in the arts and sciences. Having his father on the faculty of the college did not create any special problems; he did not take any of his father's courses and the two had relatively little contact at the school. He took one history course from Wesley's professor of note, Salem Bland. Bland, a small frail man with silver hair, offered his students his own recipe for writing, a recipe that Irwin took to heart: 'Fill yourself full of the subject, full to the brim and flowing over and then knock out the bung and let nature caper.'[1]

The one teacher who probably made the most significant impact on Irwin was William Talbot Allison, poet and professor of English literature. Allison suffered from asthma but was amusing and cheerful (though 'often pale and haggard'). During one class, while studying Keats' 'Ode to a Nightingale,' he stopped at the lines:

> The same that oft-times hath
> Charm'd magic casements, opening on the foam
> Of perilous seas, in faery lands forlorn

and offered a prize for the best short story or imaginative essay on them. Irwin's paper won; the prize was a copy of Allison's own book, *The Amber Arms, and Other Poems*. Later, Allison proved instrumental in securing Irwin his first newspaper job.

Despite his literature prize, Irwin's strengths as a student were more in the sciences than the arts. Hard work and a keen interest in science paid off: after his first year he received a 1A standing and a $40 scholarship in physics. He earned another 1A during his second year, along with a $60 scholarship in English, logic, economics, Latin, history, and an honorable mention in mathematics.[2] He was aided in his studies by a clear and logical mind and an ability to recall complicated theorems almost exactly. That he could also recall conversations – virtually word for word – would come in very handy in future years.

To earn a little extra money, Irwin worked on weekends and during the long summer holidays. His first summer job was in the book department of Eaton's and he continued there on Saturdays during the next school year. In the summer of 1916 he worked as a rod man on railway construction for the Canadian Northern Railway. On the social side there were plenty of things to do at Wesley: school events and dinners, clubs, sports for all seasons, and skating or toboggan parties. As a Methodist college, though, there also were restrictions; the ban on dancing, for example, was not lifted until 1930. Halloween was the occasion for a great student parade and, as in most universities in the country, was also a night for pranks and student antics. At the University of Manitoba it was something of a tradition for the medical students and members of other colleges to stage a mock attack on Wesley College on Halloween. Wesley College cherished its independence within the university and was seen in some quarters as an obstacle to the development of a unitary university. A few detractors went so far as to accuse the Wesleyans of setting themselves up as a rival to the university itself. Denominational tensions were a part of the problem, and these tensions and resentments were reflected in the student body.

On Halloween night, 1915, regular student rivalries and denominational tensions boiled over as dozens of students from the other colleges attacked the Wesleyans with rubber clubs, stones, and a makeshift battering ram. Irwin was in the middle of the ensuing mêlée and helped repulse the invaders. Fortunately no one was seriously hurt. The police arrived to break things up, and a few students were briefly detained. Damage was limited to broken windows and smashed doors.

◆

The one dominant event outside of school life was, of course, the war. Life went on at Wesley: lectures were given, exams written, courses failed or passed. The students played football and hockey, held their annual college dinner and regular toboggan parties, but there was no escaping the war. Newspapers were filled with stories from the front: reports of Canadian heroism and German barbarism, horrific tales of enemy atrocities, and the ever-increasing casualty lists. The government had introduced a total war effort and everyone at home had a role to play, ranging from buying victory bonds to growing more food or knitting socks for the men at the front.

The Methodist Church threw its entire resources behind the war effort and played a prominent role in recruiting. Christian and patriotic appeals were made to the young men of Canada and the church encouraged Canadian women to urge their men to sign up. The pressure to volunteer was enormous. One exasperated young Methodist complained to the *Christian Guardian*: 'I cannot go to a public meeting, I cannot walk down the street, I cannot go to Sunday School, League or Church, I cannot attend any of the District conventions, I cannot even go home and read *Youth and Service* or *The Guardian* without being told I am a shirker.'[3]

The students of Wesley College responded to the call. Friends and classmates began leaving for the front and many never returned. Of a total student body of only a few hundred, 330 Wesleyans had enlisted by March 1917 and 21 had died.[4] The school paper, *Vox Wesleyana*, offered up the grim details of life at the front juxtaposed to the poems of Rupert Brooke. 'Each day's newspaper carried the tally of the costs,' Irwin wrote later. 'Older classmates had fallen. The twin urge to carry on with the job they had left unfinished and respond to the challenge of upswelling national consciousness ran deep.'

Irwin was determined to play his part. He fulfilled the requirements for his lieutenant's certificate with the university's Canadian Officers' Training Corps. He wanted to volunteer, but his parents argued that he was too young and persuaded him to hold off for another year. At the end of that year, though, he would enlist. In a series of autobiographical notes written some sixty years later Irwin explained his decision to join up:

Although I was singularly lacking in martial ardour I had known for more than a year that I would enlist. The thought of sticking a bayonet into another man's belly gave me the cold shivers. But 'the war' had become life's inescapable dominant. The conventional wisdom of the time and place perceived the thrust of German autocracy as a threat to civilization itself; its denial as a crusade. We were fighting for peace with liberty, fighting a war to make the world safe for democracy, a war to end all wars. The challenge was clear; equally clear the duty of participation. No doubt other factors were in play – promise of adventure, social pressure, lure of the unknown, the seduction of danger, the ancestral call of the blood. But the sense of obligation to a just cause was primary.[5]

It is not surprising that he enlisted; indeed, it would have been far more surprising had he not.

Irwin enlisted on 15 May 1917, at the end of his second year at Wesley College and less than two weeks before his nineteenth birthday. He did not act alone, and enlisted together with Albert Cooke, a Wesleyan classmate. 'Cookie' was three years Irwin's senior and had waited to finish university before signing up. Although the two had not been close friends at Wesley, through a mutual friend they learned of a heavy artillery unit being recruited at McGill University in Montreal. 'To a mathematically and technologically inclined eighteen-year old,' Irwin recalled, a 9.2-inch howitzer 'seemed a more potent and certainly more intriguing weapon than the bayonet. We decided to join the artillery.' A request for information was sent to Montreal, and in reply the commanding officer of the new unit offered to pay their fares to Montreal.

Irwin and Cooke travelled via Minneapolis, Chicago, and Toronto and arrived in Montreal late in May. Despite his concerns that his weight and slight frame – he stood 5 foot 10 inches but weighed only 135 pounds – would prevent his acceptance into the unit, Irwin passed his medical exam and soon found himself out of 'civvies' and

swanking along Sherbrooke Sreet in stiffly moulded military cap, brass-buttoned khaki wool tunic with stiff stand-up collar, riding breeches, puttees, heavy ankle boots, spurs which never spurred a horse, white braided-cord shoulder lanyard which was never pulled, pouched shoulder bandolier which never saw a cartridge, the whole touched off by a fancy leather riding crop. As a working uniform, it was an anachronistic absurdity but we were proud of it.[6]

Irwin and Cooke enlisted in what was known as the McGill Draft. The commanding officer was Captain Sir Stopford Brunton, or 'Stoppie' as the men called him, a mining geologist and member of McGill's engineering faculty. Home for the next few weeks was the McGill Union on Sherbrooke Street overlooking the main campus. All things considered, it was a fairly pleasant introduction to military life. Training exercises and parades were conducted on the open spaces of the front campus, and in the afternoons he and Cookie had the use of a pool at the nearby YMCA. Most of the young men in the unit were university students or recent graduates, many from McGill, and although regulations and discipline were in force, the atmosphere, Irwin recalled, was less military than 'khaki collegial.' One of the recruits was a young Montreal native, Brooke Claxton, who later would be appointed minister of national defence.

Although a Montreal draft, Irwin's unit was almost totally English speaking. While he was enthralled with the 'Frenchness' of the city, he had practically no contact with French Canadians during his stay. And he could not have picked a worse time to arrive in Montreal. This was not the French Canada he had learned of in school; the ghosts of Brébeuf and Dollard were nowhere to be found. This was an angry French Canada, bristling from the injustice of restrictive language legislation in the two provinces Irwin knew best, Ontario and Manitoba. Here were French Canadians demonstrating and rioting in the streets against conscription for the war in which Irwin believed so strongly. Fearing the outbreak of more violent disturbances, his unit was put on guard duty at the Ordnance Depot on Craig (St Antoine) Street. Thus, Irwin's first taste of duty was protecting military equipment and artillery from rioters and potential saboteurs – his fellow citizens.

After about a month's training in Montreal, the McGill Draft left for Halifax, and on 25 June 1917 set sail for Liverpool. From Liverpool the McGill Draft was taken by train to the south of London, and for the rest of the year the men trained in various locations in southern England. In October, command of the unit was given to Major L.C. Ord. Ord had served for some time in France and was recalled by Claxton in his unpublished memoirs as 'opinionated and talkative,' but at that moment 'he was the only officer with us with long experience in France and he knew a good deal about gunnery.'[7] Under Ord's command the McGill Draft became the 10th Canadian Siege Battery on 22 January 1918 and was attached to the 3rd Canadian Heavy Artillery Brigade.

The long months in England gave Irwin and Cookie the opportunity to explore the English countryside and to visit London and some of the larger cities in the south. In the evenings and on weekends the two comrades often rented bicycles and escaped for day excursions to surrounding areas. Leaves were also relatively easy to obtain, and then the pair would be off on longer trips to London, Oxford, and as far as Scotland. London was everything Irwin had imagined: the Thames and Westminster Abbey, the Houses of Parliament, St James Park, all the familiar names, the architecture, the myths and legends of his boyhood. Like many Canadians of his era who came to Britain for the first time, Irwin felt very much 'at home.'

At the same time, however, his Canadianism became more pronounced. He could enjoy the cathedrals, monuments, and tombstones of historic Britain, but his encounters with the local population were few and often confused by wartime circumstance and traditional misunderstanding. His unit developed a very strong bond of comradeship which helped it function more efficiently, but this same bond fostered a sense of isolation from other units and the local community. The British were usually friendly but the Canadians inevitably resented those who slept in comfortable beds and ate comparatively well while they slept in makeshift cots and ate army rations. Irwin also felt a distance between his and the British units, which were less well paid and, in turn, resented the Canadian 'mavericks' who had invaded their country.

For Irwin there was indignation at being treated like a 'colonial.' In addition he responded with a proper, though typically Canadian, revulsion to the British 'class system.' Neither perception was completely accurate, of course, but the passion was real. Added to everything else, he was homesick. Such feelings, based as much on popular misconception as on actual experience, heightened his sense of being 'Canadian' and strengthened his perception of his country as an independent nation. Not necessarily greater or better, just different.

At long last, on 15 March 1918, the unit left for France. The 10th Canadian Siege Battery consisted of 7 officers and 187 other ranks, and the battery included six six-inch howitzers and an equal number of four-wheel drive trucks to pull them, fourteen lorries for the men, five motorcycles, and one small car. The unit was not attached to any specific division, but, rather, was moved regularly depending on need. After a few days at Le Havre the unit was stationed near the town of Arras, not far from Vimy Ridge and close to the front. By the end of the month the battery had joined in the battle and had come under enemy fire.

The 10th Siege Battery joined the Canadian Expeditionary Force (CEF) which had grown into a tough and experienced corps of four divisions rooted on the northern flank of the western front. The reputation of the CEF had been paid for in blood in the trenches of Ypres, Passchendaele, and Vimy Ridge – names already familiar to the men of the 10th Siege Battery. For almost a year a Canadian – General Sir Arthur Currie – had been in command. Shortly before the unit arrived the Germans had mounted a new offensive all along the western front, had cracked the British line near Amiens, and had broken through at Cambrai, only a few miles from where Irwin's unit was stationed.

Each of the six guns in the battery had two crews which alternated duty. The off-duty crew was anything but idle; it spent most of its time digging gun sites. An indication of the seriousness of the situation into which the battery arrived was that after only a few weeks the men had dug four rear positions. By the first week of May the unit had moved to Nine Elms, in a shallow valley close to Vimy Ridge, and here it stayed for six weeks. The men were quartered in German-built tunnels, one extending a good sixty feet below the ground. Off one of the dugouts was a trench that was transformed (by the addition of a table and a few chairs) into a room for the men to eat, read and write letters, play cards, or just relax. The men slept nearby, under a roof of corrugated iron topped with sandbags.[8]

Gunner Irwin was assigned as one of a handful of observers who functioned as battery commanders' assistants. This meant that, rather than operating one of the howitzers (and participating in endless gun drills and trench digging), he moved ahead to establish map positions of the enemy guns before returning to the battery command post. In addition, the observers were responsible for the mathematical calculations necessary for operating the guns. A number of factors were involved: wind velocity and direction, temperature, distance of target, elevation, and size of charge to be used. All these variables were taken into consideration and, with the help of a pocket-size range table, the angle of fire was determined. It was a complicated and time-consuming process and, to cut down on the time factor, Irwin, along with the other observers, made a graph with the firing sector on it, with an attached swivel ruler. With the help of this device he could visually determine the correct angle on receipt of any meteorological information.

The technique was used, with great success, by the battery, although it never received official sanction from the unit commander. Indeed, on at least one occasion it sparked a confrontation with Major Ord. Irwin's recollection of the moment was that Ord arrived unexpectedly in the post and, seeing the graph, demanded: 'What's this goddamn thing?'

'That's our graphical representation of our field of fire, it helps us to get on target quickly,' the sergeant on duty replied. 'Take the Goddamn thing out of here,' Ord barked. 'I'll not have that kind of nonsense in my fighting post!' To which the sergeant responded, 'Yes sir, yes sir,' and the graph was tossed aside. The moment Ord left, however, the graph was retrieved and put back into use.

The incident may well have been repeated on more than one occasion, with similar results. In any event, it served to reinforce one side of Irwin's character: his contempt for the arbitrary use of power by persons in authority. His contempt was directed especially at those he believed lacked the ability or character to warrant a position of responsibility. There were other examples that grated on his sensibilities: the arrogance of his unit's sergeant who insisted that one of the men bring him water every day so he could wash and shave himself; and the pomposity of Major Ord who insisted on his night-time game of bridge with the junior officers, which frequently led to delays in getting the men's mail out. He never lost this disdain for all things pretentious or his scorn for all persons self-righteous, supercilious, or patronizing.

Irwin did not fight in any hand-to-hand combat and rarely saw the enemy at close range. This distance and the mechanical aspect of artillery fire led him later in life to come to regard himself more as a technician of war than as a soldier, but at the time his attention was focused on doing his job and staying alive. Staying alive was no easy task, and although death rates in the battery never matched those on the front line, the battery had its share of casualties. The men were regularly under fire from enemy artillery and were exposed to gas attack and the odd machine-gunning from lone enemy aircraft.

The unit saw limited action through June and into July, and at one point was pulled back forty kilometres from the front to receive training in 'open warfare.' The unit returned to the line just outside of Arras, by which time the front was quiet. At the beginning of August the battery was pulled out and moved to the south and stationed at Blangy Woods, between Villers Bretonnaux and Cachy, not far from Amiens. The next few days were spent digging in and building roads from the main road to the battery. Everyone knew that something big was about to happen. At 4:20 A.M. on 8 August the guns began to fire, announcing the start of the Amiens offensive, the last great battle of the war.

For the next hundred days the unit was almost constantly in action, first in the Amiens offensive and, beginning in September, the Second Battle of Arras. It was also the time for the greatest number of injuries. On one day alone – 22 August – the unit suffered ten casualties, including two deaths. For the first time, on 7 September, parts of the battery came under direct artillery fire when stationed near the village of Villers Cagnicourt. By the beginning of October the battery was moving steadily along the Arras-Cambrai Road, under heavy shelling and regular gas attacks. By the end of the month they had reached the outskirts of Valenciennes.

Reports of breakthroughs on the German line by British, French, and American troops circulated throughout the Canadian Corps, and it was clear by the advances being made that the Germans were on the run. The news was not met with the celebrating that one might expect;

if anything it heightened fears and intensified the desire for self-preservation. Moreover, it had been raining for days and the unit was awash in a sea of mud; the men were exhausted and at least half were suffering from the flu. On 10 November, when word of the impending Armistice arrived, the battery moved into the town of Boussu, six miles from Mons, near the Belgian border.

Irwin spent the last night of the war in Boussu, 'in a feather bed in a second floor bedroom over a bakery across the square from the town hall. Forty-eight hours previously it had been occupied by a German major. Despite my lowly rank, the baker, Monsieur Dubois, and his buxom wife treated me like a prince; and her raisin rabbit stew – the unfortunate rabbit having been summarily slaughtered for the occasion – was delicious.' He rose the next morning to read the orders posted on the battery bulletin board announcing the Armistice. He later recalled his reaction:

we read them [the orders] with cool detachment, almost as if they pertained to a world beyond our experience. We realized that something deeply significant had happened and that we were involved; but there were no hurrahs, no feeling of excitement, no surge of joy, and little comment. Most of us read in silence, then walked quietly away. But each of us had to read for himself; as if to find visible assurance in a few typed words on a piece of paper that what was happening was real.[9]

The fighting had ceased but life in the ranks continued much the same as before. There were routine marches and parades, someone still had to perform the thankless kitchen duties or stand on guard, and there were the guns to be cleaned. But things were anything but calm. In his memoir notes, written years later, Irwin recalled how the men grew increasingly restive. There were rumours of riot and revolution abroad. Would the men be forced to remain here on the French-Belgian border for months, or would they be ordered to carry on into Germany? There was little enthusiasm for further action: they had done their duty and then some. Now it was time to go home.

To make matters worse, the brigade commander, Colonel Beeman, returned to the camp on 21 November, fresh from an English respite and ready for action. He found the quarters sloppy and the men's routine lax. He would see to it that discipline and order were restored. New orders were posted calling for three hours of gun drill and parade the following morning (and for every morning), beginning at 9:00 A.M.

The men were outraged. Irwin explained the feeling among his unit:

Hard-bitten veterans skilled at their trade they were inured to danger, violence, death. Temporary soldiers, not regulars – civilians at heart – they had been prepared to put up with the inevitable aberrations of arbitrary power so long as there was a job to be done. But now that the job was finished this imbecility was beyond endurance: three hours daily gun drill – three hours of the kindergarten, rote-book, movement-by numbers conditioning applied to raw recruits who didn't know a trail from a traverse, had never heard or seen a gun fired, let alone fought it through a war.[10]

Sergeant-Major Claxton was handed the order by Major Ord, and in his unpublished memoirs he recalled his astonishment. 'The men won't do it,' he stated flatly.

'I didn't think they would,' Ord replied, and then he promptly left for England.[11]

The following morning, 25 November, the bugles blew as usual and the officers arrived in the square grounds as expected, but on this day there were no troops. Representatives of the different units had met the night before and agreed that none of the men would move from their barracks when the bugles called. Faced with a possible mutiny, the officers were uncertain how to respond. After a few anxious moments, the unit sergeants went into the barracks to make peace with the men, convincing at least some of them to come out and answer roll-call. Two of the units agreed (including Irwin's) and slowly sauntered outside, but one unit remained behind in their barracks and jeered at the others, hooting 'scabs!' and other catcalls from the windows. Orders for gun drill were given, Irwin recalled, and 'the crews marched smartly to their respective stations. For perhaps thirty seconds they stood motionless contemplating the guns. Then, in an instant, the square was alive with khaki-clad figures walking quietly back to barracks. The cheer that went up from the town hall windows must have been heard for blocks.'

What had started as tired and unhappy soldiers upset at the way they were being treated now threatened to develop into a full-blown mutiny. Colonel Beeman was informed of the situation and he immediately called for a mass meeting of the men in the town hall auditorium. Irwin described the scene:

The place was packed to the walls; the tension electric. Some of the men had come equipped with rocks and bricks. The colonel appeared, accompanied by a single aide. We watched in silence as he strode to the stage, stationed himself behind a table, center front, and then very deliberately drew his revolver from its holster and laid it on the table, muzzle toward the audience. The gesture was obviously meant to intimidate. It was perceived as provocative. Tension heightened.[12]

Colonel Beeman explained that the situation remained very dangerous and that only an armistice had been reached with the Germans. There still was a job to do. He then reminded his men that they had sworn an oath of loyalty and that they were expected to fulfil their obligations. After a few moments he changed his tack slightly, acknowledging that the men had been through a lot and that he understood how they felt. In future there would be more rest and recreational activities and leave would be easier to obtain. But orders had been given and they would not be rescinded. They must be obeyed. With that he walked from the room. Within an hour orders for a five-minute gun drill the following morning were posted and the men responded. There was no mutiny. Claxton's *War Diary* recorded for 25 November: 'Bloodless revolution. Troops pacified.'[13]

Irwin and Cookie were among the earliest to receive leave. Paris was their destination and for six days early in December the two friends, like any tourists, delighted in the joys offered: the Champs Élysées and Tuileries Gardens, the Louvre, the Opéra and theatre, the grand boulevards, and Notre-Dame Cathedral. Paris, shaking off the dust of more than four years of war, was alive with victory celebrations.

President Woodrow Wilson arrived in Paris to negotiate the peace at almost the same time as the two Canadians. At that moment Wilson embodied the hopes and wishes of all Europeans and his fourteen points had been hailed as a blueprint for a more just and peaceful world. Few individuals have been received with as much goodwill as Wilson; few have been so burdened with the hopes of mankind. He drove into the city 'not as a conqueror, but as a prophet.' Crowds gathered along the Champs Élysées early, and by the time Irwin and Cookie arrived the avenue was jammed. Refusing to be disappointed they climbed a tree along the avenue, about one kilometre from the Arc de Triomphe, where they had a clear view of Wilson's open carriage as it slowly made its way into the heart of the city.

Irwin's visit to Paris was the highlight of his stay in postwar Europe, which lasted for most of the winter and spring. In March 1919 the battery was shipped to Britain. Shortage of transport ships made for long, agonizing waits and sparked numerous riots and outbreaks of violence among Canadian troops stationed in Britain. Irwin and Cookie took advantage of their stay to undertake more sightseeing trips around the country. Finally, on 5 May 1919, the 10th Siege Battery sailed from Southampton on board the SS *Mauritania*.

The unit arrived in Montreal a week later, and was discharged the following day, 12 May. A lunch was held at the McGill Union and a Battery Association was created. That night the battery danced at the Windsor Hotel. Earlier in the day, at a friend's home, Irwin changed out of his uniform into the clothes he had taken off two years before. Then, with $210 and a train ticket to Winnipeg in his pocket, he walked out into the street. He left his uniform behind. Gunner Irwin's war was over.

THREE

Cub Reporter

Irwin stopped in Toronto on his return to Winnipeg in May 1919 to meet his father. While Arthur was overseas, Alexander Irwin had become embroiled in a controversy at Wesley College, a controversy that cost him and Salem Bland their positions. The reason for their dismissal was ostensibly financial. With diminishing student enrolment the college introduced a retrenchment program, which included staff cuts. While there was much truth to Wesley's financial woes, there were other underlying reasons for the firings. Bland in particular had a number of enemies in Wesley, and in the church, over his support for the social gospel and his attempt to mix the teaching of the gospels with his zeal for reforming society. Having been dismissed from Wesley, Dr Irwin briefly sold insurance before securing a position as a preacher at a church in Brantford, Ontario. In 1919 the family returned to Toronto.

After a lengthy conversation with his father (which he later referred to as his personal 'declaration of independence'), Irwin confirmed what his father had long suspected – that he had no desire to enter the ministry. Irwin never kept a diary, and his writings from this period are few, so it is difficult to trace the evolution of his thoughts with precision.

He had left for overseas still looking for the faith, but, if anything, the war only increased his uneasiness with church doctrine. Unflattering references to the church and clergy peppered his writings: in 1925, he wrote disparagingly of one minister's 'platitudinous blubberings.'[1] On a trip to Hull, Quebec, he visited the town's largest church:

'a little less garish than some French churches I've seen but still noticeably tawdry, artificial figured marble pillars, messy paintings, etc.'[2] Incidents were burned into his memory. More than seventy years later he would recall vividly his disgust at the time he unexpectedly came upon a priest lurking behind an airplane hangar, finishing off that morning's sacramental wine.

The questioning and searching never ceased, but for the time being at least he labelled himself an agnostic. Irwin tried to convey these feelings to his father and explain why he could not enter the ministry. He could tell that his father was hurt, but he said he understood his son's views and accepted his decision.

Still, the Methodist ethos had shaped him, perhaps more than he liked to admit. He was conservative in manner and taste. He had picked up the habit of smoking while overseas, but never became a comfortable dancer, and, even after his wartime experiences, rarely swore. He was not a teetotaler by any means, and would take the occasional drink, but he often wrote of alcohol and those who consumed great quantities of it in a slightly disapproving tone. After one dinner party he wrote: 'There was plenty of liquor but surprisingly little drunkenness. With the exception of a sip or two for appearances sake I left the stuff severely alone, consequently got home about two in the morning with a clear head.'[3] On another occasion, after a day trip into Hull, he recorded critically that the 'taverns are numerous and most of them were full. So were a noticeable number of the gentlemen who boarded the street car that brought me back to Ottawa.'[4] Above all, he had accepted the Protestant work ethic, and its sense of public responsibility. As one perceptive journalist later wrote: 'Clergymen's sons may be divided into those who spend the rest of their lives reacting against their early background and those who spend it trying to live up to its standards of plain living and high thinking. Consciously or unconsciously, Irwin is one of the latter, ruling himself with unbending discipline.'[5]

If he experienced any kind of a conversion overseas, it was of a distinctly secular variety. His war experience had crystallized a sense of country, and this love for country and its people became a kind of substitute for the religious faith that he never found. On his return, his awareness of being a Canadian did not evaporate; on the contrary, it became more profound.

Arthur returned to Winnipeg a few days after his meeting with his father, still unsure over his future. He stayed with A.W. Crawford, a

University of Manitoba English professor who had been best man at his parents' wedding. He could return to Wesley and finish his studies there, but, with the family back in Toronto, his ties to Winnipeg had weakened. No matter what he decided though, he would need some money; his army pay would not see him through university. Responding to a notice pinned to the bulletin board in the college rotunda, he got a job as a book salesman.

Up to the time he returned to the west, Irwin had not given much thought to the major issue dividing Winnipegers at that moment – the general strike. The strike began on 25 May as an isolated labour dispute in Winnipeg's building and metal trades. The issues were hardly revolutionary – wages, working conditions, and collective bargaining rights – but the strike developed in a tense and electric atmosphere. A few weeks earlier in Calgary, the One Big Union was formed, and it advocated the use of the general strike as a labour weapon. And the 1917 Russian Revolution already had the city's capitalists looking for bomb-toting alien revolutionaries under their beds at night. When negotiations broke down, a general strike was called, and within days most of Winnipeg's labour force (including its public sector employees) was out on strike and the city was divided along geographic as well as economic lines.

Irwin was not really conscious at the time of what the strike was all about. He heard the rumours and had gathered some information from newspapers, but was not directly involved other than as a spectator. And it was as a spectator that he found himself one afternoon between a strikers' demonstration and a row of mounted policemen near the corner of Portage and Main. The streetcars were idle and the police were trying to clear the streets by wading, clubs in hand, into the mob. With each wave the strikers melted away, hugging close to the buildings or slipping down side-streets. Gradually they began wrenching cobblestones from the street and showering the police with stones. Around five that afternoon, just as people were leaving work and the streets were especially crowded, the police charged the mob and a near-riot broke out. To escape injury Irwin climbed a telephone pole and looked down at the unfolding scene with a burning rage over the unwarranted and malevolent actions of the police.

His sympathies were with the strikers that afternoon, not so much because he identified with their political ends but because it was to him another example of the arbitrary and reckless use of power that he had grown to despise. That night, however, he was comfortably nestled in the 'bourgeois' camp, and, in fact, took his turn standing guard on Professor Crawford's block (to protect it against an anticipated attack from roaming bands of strikers – an attack that never came).

It was here, in the establishment camp, that he really belonged intellectually. Irwin's politics fell slightly to the left but very much within the Canadian mainstream of nineteenth-century liberalism: a fundamental belief in individual rights and freedoms, tempered somewhat by the values of the social gospel movement. Irwin described himself as a small 'l' liberal, and his world-view was essentially personal; he viewed society more as a grouping of individuals than as a collection of warring classes. His sympathies lay with the underdog more often than not because, as in Winnipeg in 1919, he identified with the individual's situation, not because he aspired to any revolutionary goals.

He had developed a keen interest in politics and world affairs, especially as they affected Canada. His range of interests was quite broad, though focused primarily on the larger questions of international affairs, national power, and political change, and rather less on the pressing social questions of the day. Throughout his life he maintained his independence from active politics, never joining or campaigning for any particular party, but it is quite probable that he voted Liberal in every federal election from 1925 to 1988.

The Winnipeg General Strike did not hinder Irwin's career as a book salesman. He was obliged to complete a short introductory course on selling techniques and then was handed a sample of the book – the *Standard Dictionary of Facts* – a single-volume encyclopedia of considerable size. From that moment he was on his own. He worked on a straight commission basis and carried from door to door samples of the various bindings available. On one occasion, in an effort to move out into the countryside, he rented a horse, but the saddle had only one stirrup and was missing much of its padding. He rode only a short way until the discomfort was too great; he then dismounted and walked the horse back to town. The next day he switched to a bicycle, a more reliable source of transportation.

For the rest of the summer Irwin pedalled (in more ways than one, he later mused) around southern Manitoba, selling his encyclopedias and living out of a suitcase. In each new town or village he made his first pitch to the local schoolteacher, parson, or librarian, so that when he approached area farmers and townsfolk he could impress them with the fact that a local notable had purchased a copy or that the school would be using it. He met with considerable success – selling some 150 copies – and earned enough to pay his way through another year of university.

He found the work interesting. Often, when potential customers discovered he was a war veteran, he would be invited to dinner and, inevitably, spent hours talking with new friends, in parlours and kitchens, or out back by the barn or in the fields. He learned a good deal about politics and even more about people – often without selling any books. The long days and nights also gave him a good deal of time to ponder his own future. He decided to return to his family in Toronto.

◆

In September 1919 Irwin transferred for his third year of university to Victoria College at the University of Toronto. (Victoria, the Methodist college and his father's alma mater, had moved to Toronto from Cobourg in 1892.) Arthur entered an honours program in political science; his growing fascination with politics or the 'science of people' having overtaken his earlier interest with pure science.

Life in the family home was not that pleasant. The house on Hazelton Avenue, Irwin remembered, was rundown, dark, gloomy, and rather depressing. Relations between Arthur's mother and father had deteriorated further; Alexander's dismissal from Wesley College seemed to have been harder for Millie Irwin to accept and it became something of a sore point between them. In addition, Millie was not well. During the war she had become a semi-invalid and relied on the children more than ever to help around the house.

The bulk of the responsibility fell on Helen, the only female, but she was also a busy third-year student at the university and resented the burden thrust on her. It became a source of friction between her and Arthur for he refused to help around the house. After all, he reasoned, he was paying his own way and therefore should be exempt from 'women's work.' Besides, wasn't he a war veteran? The friction spilled over into other areas, as Arthur would have little to do with Helen's friends or classmates. One family friend later recalled how Arthur appeared cold and aloof, often walking into the house without so much as a hello and going off into another room by himself.

Arthur's brother Harvey was likewise disenchanted with his home life. Harvey eventually fled to the United States and, after lying about his age, enlisted in the American army. He served briefly in the Panama Canal Zone and then virtually disappeared. Arthur made a few attempts to contact him over the next ten years, but with no success. A 1932 letter from Harvey filled in a few of the gaps. 'I may be presuming a lot in writing to you,' the letter began, 'if [sic] fact, you may not be the W.A. Irwin who had a brat for a brother sometime ago who decided to wander off and see what he could see; also of course, you may not desire to hear anything of said brat. The remedy in either case is quite simple, consign this to the wastepaper basket and see if I give two continentals.'

Harvey had been working in Venezuela for some time (the letter was written from Caracas), and gave little indication of his future plans. 'As for heading north again I don't think so. At least not for anything more than a trip, my wildest idea just at present is to get a schooner and sail it round the world, where the mischief I get it from I don't know but I sure like the sea.' The letter barely referred to his reasons for leaving home, and he ended it with: 'In fact I don't know why I've written at all but every once in a while I think of both you and Helen altho [sic] why you I don't know we never got along but I suppose time and distance does manage to get in its softing [sic] effects. As far as the rest are concerned I dont [sic] want to bother or be bothered by them.'[6] Arthur never saw or heard from him again.

During Irwin's first year at Victoria College the family had moved to Grimsby, Ontario, across the lake from Toronto, where Alexander had been posted. Arthur stayed in Toronto and moved into the university residence. He was on his own now; the break with the family was permanent.

Two years in the service had changed Irwin more than he realized and he quickly became disillusioned with university. His grades did not suffer; his third-year transcript shows that he received firsts in political science, Roman law, and English common law, and a second in economics. He slipped a little in ethics (B), English (B), and world history (C), but overall his standing was very good. The problem was more that he felt increasingly he was stagnating at the university. He felt that he was not learning anything new and that most of his time was spent regurgitating what was being fed to him. There were a few exceptions, of course; he enjoyed his political science seminar which allowed for the discussion of political ideas and theories in a comfortable setting, and he recalled being impressed by Professor George Wrong of the history department. Otherwise, his university career was somewhat disappointing, and he decided at the end of the term to look for a job and to take only those courses that interested him.

His first idea was to look for a job as a reporter on one of Toronto's newspapers. He wanted to write for a living, and he was far more proficient at gathering facts and presenting them in a logical and persuasive manner than he was as an imaginative writer of fiction. Becoming a reporter seemed to offer the most promising career, even though the status of reporters in Canada in the 1920s was lower than it is today. Only a few years earlier one of his teachers had admonished a fellow student with: 'Ben, take that gum out of your mouth. You look like a newspaper reporter!' Nevertheless, a reporter's life had its appeal; the work would be interesting, he would be exposed to a wide variety of people and events, and he would be earning a living. There was also the hint of adventure, a powerful attraction to a young man of twenty-two.

With a list of Toronto's daily newspapers in hand, Irwin set out in search of a job. His first choice was the *Globe*, but he was turned down by the city editor, 'whose cold and baleful stare suggested he might have been dealing with a cockroach.' Next he tried the offices of the *Star* on King Street, with the same results. Standing outside on the curb, wondering where to go next, Irwin ran into William Allison, his former English professor at Wesley College. When he explained what he was doing, Allison took his arm, saying: 'Come on over to the *Mail*. I know Murdo Macdonald, the City Editor, and that might help.' Allison had worked in the newspaper business years before and had crossed paths with Macdonald.

The *Mail and Empire* building was an imposing brick structure in the heart of downtown Toronto. The two men took the elevator up to Murdoch Macdonald's floor and entered his small office to find him sitting 'behind a battered and cluttered old flat-topped oaken desk in a cubby-hole of an office on the third floor. Middle-aged, squat of figure, round-faced, he reminded me of a Scottish Buddha.' Irwin stood back slightly to allow Allison to do the talking. The old friends gossiped for a few moments and then Allison got around to the reason for his visit. He had taught young Mr Irwin and believed he had the stuff to do the job; would Macdonald take him on as a reporter?

Macdonald silently stared at Irwin for a few moments. 'Okay,' he said. 'When can you start?'

'When do you want me?' he replied.

'Well, can you be here Monday?'

Starting salary? 'It will be $30 a week,' Macdonald noted. There was no discussion. Irwin and Allison walked out of Macdonald's office. The whole interview lasted barely a few minutes. As they descended in the elevator Irwin heard Allison say that although the pay was not the greatest he was very lucky to have been taken on at all, given that he had no experience as a reporter. Fortune, indeed, smiled on Arthur Irwin that day. Aged twenty-two, not even finished school, without any newspaper experience, he had landed a good job at decent pay on an established metropolitan daily paper. He was now Arthur Irwin, cub reporter.

The Toronto *Mail* traced its origins back to 1872 when Sir John A. Macdonald backed its creation to act as a competitor to the Liberal *Globe* and to espouse the line of the Conservative party. In 1895 the *Mail* absorbed the *Empire* (another Conservative paper), to become the *Mail and Empire*. It continued to toe the Conservative line well into the twentieth century. The editor was Claude A.C. Jennings, a white-haired, distinguished-looking man.

Irwin joined the staff at a time of growing circulation and technological innovation. Headlines had gotten broader and daily editions grown fatter and heavier, with the inclusion of more entertainment features, sections for women, crossword puzzles, and so on. Competition for the growing Toronto market was fierce and papers increasingly relied on the sensational, the unusual, and the flamboyant. Editors were willing to do whatever was necessary to get the news first, to scoop the other papers, or to get an exclusive. Reporters were becoming more mobile in their search for the news. And for the new ones, learning on the job was not unusual. In fact, it was the only way – there were no schools of journalism in the country.

Irwin's first assignment was to cover churches and schools. He would report on the meetings of the board of education, annual church meetings, and so on. He was chosen for this beat ostensibly because of his church background, but, more likely, because no one else wanted to do it. On Sundays he attended a number of church services and filed a sermon report for the Monday morning edition. He could not help finding it somewhat ironical to be back attending church again on a regular basis; something he had stopped doing.

There were also special events for him to cover, ranging from luncheon speeches at the Canadian Club to the annual convention of national shoe salesmen. One of the more interesting assignments which he occasionally handled was the 'hotel and rails' beat (better known among some staffers as the 'whorehouses and boxcars' beat), which entailed snooping around the downtown hotels and Union Station to see if any interesting or distinguished individuals had arrived in town. With luck a story would turn up. Surprisingly, one usually did.

During Irwin's stay at the *Mail and Empire,* it purchased the Toronto *World,* a relatively small but lively daily, published by William McLean. The *World's* daily edition was submerged but its weekend edition, the *Sunday World,* was maintained and expanded. Both papers were produced by the *Mail and Empire* staff, which meant that some employees, like Irwin, had to work on Saturdays. The editor of the *Sunday World* was Herb Lash, remembered by Irwin as 'a roly-poly, happy-go-lucky, twinkling-eyed, gregarious little man with both drive and ambition.'[7]

One of Irwin's first articles under his own byline was published in the *Sunday World.* The subject was the Governor General's Body Guard, a Canadian cavalry regiment formed in the Toronto area in 1822. Entitled 'First Centenary of a Canadian Militia Regiment,' it revealed many of the traits that earmarked his journalistic career: clean, lucid in style, straightforward, insightful more than eloquent, historical in approach, and teeming with facts.[8] He traced the regiment's development through the series of battles and conflicts in which it participated, from the rebellion of 1837 to the First World War. Through the history of this citizen-soldier regiment ('farmers and citizens, they were gentlemen all'), and through its heroic courage in the face of adversity, he believed he had discovered something very Canadian. 'The cavalry of Toronto and York have never been pampered,' he noted. 'The regiment has suffered in seven wars, languishing under hostile ministers, defied the arm-chair critics, drilled amid the jeers of the mob and triumphed in hard-fought campaigns. It would be difficult to discover anything more characteristically Canadian.'[9]

Irwin also dabbled in fiction and verse, but only briefly. He was less suited to creative writing than journalism, and appeared more comfortable buried in facts and statistics, making sense out of the complicated. He never dedicated the time necessary to develop what talent he had, and if he wrote fiction or verse at all it was usually for fun. He loved to write, loved to play with words, and he could be witty and satirical, but he found the task of writing very hard work. One of the few examples of his verse is 'Check and Double Bind: A Binomial Ballad,' a piece of doggerel aimed at Frank Cornish, a former mayor of Winnipeg.

Cub Reporter

'Twas in the days when Winnipeg,
   Was built of clapboard shacks
And bisons roamed on Main Street
   And the railway had no tracks.

Now in that town there dwelt a man,
   Of courage and of wit,
Who took all things that came to him
   As seemly things and fit.

He ruled that town as mayor proclaimed
   And kept the place at peace,
For also he was magistrate
   And chief of 'Peg police.

His name – it really doesn't weigh,
   But if insist, you must –
Was Cornish when he sat in state
   And Frank when on the bust.

'Tis sad to tell but true to state
   He liquored rather badly,
Was fond of rye and Scotch and gin
   And rum he loved right madly.

It happened thus on one fair night
   Where Portage joins with Main
That Cornish felt the inner urge
   To drink and then raise Cain.

He did just that and bashed a hat
   That hid a head thereunder;
Said head waxed wrath and raised a row
   That roared and rolled like thunder.

Next morn the mayor of Winnipeg
   Was summoned into court
Where plaint was made and charge was laid
   Of a highly monstrous sort.

'Oyez, oyez,' the clerk, he cried,
'Come hearken all who hear,
For conduct lewd, disorderly
One Cornish must appear.'

Occasionally, a personal experience would prompt him to write a short story or vignette, and at other times he would reflect on his war experiences and include them in a piece of fiction. One untitled and unpublished draft began: 'Carpy Sludger felt cold as he sat on the pavement in front of Eaton's on Yonge Street holding up his hat in which rattled a few copper coins, – gifts of those who passed who had patted themselves on the back when they could not resist Carpy's despairing plea. Carpy had seen better days.' The reader is then taken back to Carpy's wartime regiment: doing kitchen fatigue, shining the colonel's boots, a leave in Paris, and 'hanging on the fringe' of a rioting mob, 'yelling mightily but taking careful precaution against becoming too intimately involved in what was to him a delightful protest against the suzerainty of the Red Caps and their hated discipline.' By the end of the third paragraph, Carpy was heading home: 'For the War was over, – no more Colonel's boots, no more greasy mulligan, ho[?] for the bounding billows and the land of prosperity at the setting of the western sun.'[10]

Irwin wrote few stories and published only one, a short piece entitled 'On the Street,' which he sold to Herb Lash at the *Sunday World* for two dollars. It was a story based on a woman he saw one rainy night on Yonge Street, who – very much like Carpy Sludger – was down on her luck and in trouble with the police. For a number of reasons, principally the fear of rejection, he sold it under the pseudonym Ross Ralston. With that, his career as a fiction writer ended.

Irwin moved out of the student residence after getting the *Mail and Empire* job, and moved into a small apartment on St Nicholas Street, not far from the university. He shared accommodations with two friends but rarely saw them. Most of his meals were eaten out and he worked weekends and kept odd hours, sleeping into the afternoon and then working well past midnight. It was easier to spend his free time with other newspapermen.

One lasting friendship he made at this time was with R.A. 'Bob' Farquharson, a reporter for the *Globe*. Bob and Arthur became close friends and shared a love for the outdoors. Irwin kept a sixteen-foot cedar canoe in a rented boathouse on the waterfront, and he and Bob regularly paddled around the Toronto Islands, or went swimming off Hanlan's Point. Occasionally they took canoe trips farther north, in the Muskokas, or would go on day-excursions climbing the Scarborough Bluffs. Their friendship even extended to the women in their lives; for some time they dated the same woman, alternating Saturday evenings.

Irwin had less time to devote to his studies, but, after applying for a veteran's year's standing on account of his war service, he did graduate with honours in the spring of 1921.[11] The demands of his job necessarily cut into the amount of time he could spend on school activities, but he did manage to play a little shinny and attend a few Victoria College dances. Dancing was still a Methodist taboo, so dances were held off-campus, in a rented hall on Bloor Street. At one of these dances he met another Victoria College student, Jean Olive Smith.

Jean Smith came from a background not dissimilar to Arthur's. The daughter of a missionary family, her father was a medical man and Methodist minister who spent many years serving in the Far East. Jean was born in China and, after returning to Canada, entered Victoria College as a household science major. Following graduation she took a job at Toronto's Sick Children's Hospital, and rose to become senior dietitian. Jean shared Arthur's quiet rebellion against the strictures and restrictions of her Methodist upbringing. She was also a natural athlete, excelling in sports like field hockey and tennis.

Arthur and Jean began dating regularly and, after a short engagement, were married on 31 July 1922. After a brief honeymoon canoe trip on Lake Couchiching, the newlyweds moved into an apartment on St Mary Street, in a three-storey building owned by Jean's father. Jean and Arthur took the middle flat, Jean's sister Dora lived on the main floor, while her father and stepmother occupied the third floor.

On the basis of being married he secured a raise to $35 per week. The work was going well. As he gained experience and proved himself as a reporter, Irwin was given more varied assignments. The one he enjoyed the most was the science beat, covering scientific issues, reporting on speeches, and attending scientific conventions in Toronto. Through his science reporting, Irwin came to the attention of Hector McKinnon' the rival *Globe's* city editor. McKinnon was impressed with Irwin's work and, one afternoon in the summer of 1922, dropped into the *Mail and Empire* offices and offered him a job at the *Globe*. There had been other job offers; one *Mail and Empire* reporter, for example, had left for the *Farmer's Sun* and asked Irwin to go with him. He had refused the earlier requests, but found McKinnon's offer more attractive. Irwin had no strong ties to the *Mail and Empire,* and he believed that the *Globe* was a better paper. Besides, McKinnon was offering $45 a week. He took the job.

Unexpectedly, the summer of 1922 had turned out to be an eventful one. He had married Jean in July and moved into a new home. Granted, it was not the ideal arrangement to be living with his in-laws, but it was a far cry from the domestic outpost he had been living in. And his apprenticeship in the newspaper business had come to an end; on 14 September he began a new career at the *Globe.* He had graduated from cub reporter to full-fledged journalist.

FOUR

The 'Smoke' of Liberalism

The Toronto *Globe* was an established institution when Irwin joined the staff in September 1922. Founded by George Brown in 1844 and nurtured by Brown and subsequent editors as an organ of the Liberal party, the *Globe* developed a reputation as a literate though partisan newspaper. Sporting the words 'Canada's National Newspaper' on its masthead, the *Globe* emerged in the twentieth century as a quality newspaper with a readership far outside the Toronto area.

At the time of Irwin's arrival, the ownership of the *Globe* was securely in the hands of Toronto's Jaffray family. Senator Robert Jaffray had been involved in the *Globe* since the era of George Brown and had acquired a controlling interest in it after Brown's death in 1880. After the senator's death in 1914, control of the *Globe* was assumed by his son, William Gladstone Jaffray. W.G. Jaffray served his business apprenticeship in the banking industry before embarking on a career as a stockbroker on the Toronto Stock Exchange in 1901. In 1915 he left the world of high finance for the newspaper business, assuming the role of president and publisher of the *Globe*, a position he maintained until 1936. A man of distinct views and tastes, Jaffray was what one historian charitably described as 'straight-laced.'[1] A Presbyterian of strong fundamentalist beliefs, he waged a lifelong campaign against racetrack betting and all forms of gambling.

The editor of the paper was T. Stewart Lyon, a Scottish-born reformer with strong Liberal affiliations, who had worked his way across Canada and the United States before joining the *Globe* as a news correspondent. He served in several positions on the *Globe* staff, becoming editor in 1915. A man of great vitality and integrity, he was filled with enthusiasm for his adopted country and was known to lecture on topics such as 'Canada with 40,000,000 Population, and After.'[2]

Irwin had little to do with either Jaffray or Lyon at first. Indeed, he was on the staff some months before he could even recognize Jaffray. He found the owner to be a rather mysterious figure, priggish and distant. On the surface Jaffray was a decent individual, polite and easy enough to talk to, but Irwin sensed a vindictiveness and fanaticism lurking below the surface that coloured his view of the world. In stark contrast, Stewart Lyon was both warm and gregarious, and Irwin developed a great respect and affection for him, both as an editor and as a person.

Irwin had much more contact with the other reporters on the staff, in particular his old friend Bob Farquharson. He found the atmosphere in the *Globe* offices very congenial. He enjoyed hanging around, playing cards or ping pong, waiting for the first edition to come up. Irwin always enjoyed the company of other men, and he found in the *Globe* a club-like or collegial environment. There were a number of up-and-coming journalists working on the staff at various points during his years there: A.D. 'Andy' Clarke, 'an old-fashioned, wiry nervous type,' on the news desk; Pierre Van Passen, who later established an international reputation as a foreign correspondent; and Hugh Ferguson on the city desk – 'another of these meticulous Scots' – who had a penchant for putting all unusual phrases in quotes (one time enraging Van Passen to such a degree that he submitted several pages of copy to Ferguson consisting of nothing but quotation marks). The managing editor was Harry Anderson, a competent reporter with a dramatic flair who had worked his way up through the ranks.

And there was Hector McKinnon. Only eight years Irwin's senior, McKinnon was already an established figure at the Globe in 1922. Born in Grey County, Ontario, of Scottish parents, McKinnon returned from service overseas and joined the *Globe* staff as city editor. McKinnon had the air of a rising star and Irwin was not alone in considering him as heir apparent for the editorship. He had ability and a quick mind, and he developed a close association with that other Scot at the *Globe*, Stewart Lyon. Lyon called McKinnon 'Scotsman,' and Hector did little to conceal his Scottish heritage. (Irwin later recalled McKinnon, late in the evening as the morning's paper was being put to bed, singing full throttle in Gaelic, all the while cursing that there had been no murders in town that day.)[3] Arthur and Hector's friendship was close, but they never became as good friends as Irwin and Bob Farquharson. It was more a professional relationship; they rarely, if ever, socialized outside the confines of the *Globe*.

Arthur Irwin was still a very young man. Having two years experience on the *Mail and Empire* and his recent marriage may have bolstered his self-confidence, but he remained conscious of his few years and youthful image. He was always concerned about his appearance, and took great care over the clothes he wore. On an average day he could be seen wearing his tweed suit with spats and bow tie, the latter he continued wearing years after they had gone out of style. He often walked with a cane, not because he needed it but for the effect: the cane and his slim moustache he hoped would add a touch of maturity and sophistication to his demeanour. It seemed to have some effect. Morley Callaghan, then a local college student, later recalled the first time he saw Irwin: 'Arthur dressed very, very neatly, and he somehow or other managed to look more serious on the job than the others. But he was rather aloof, as I recall, as if his mind were on bigger things.'[4]

His wardrobe sometimes caused him problems. He wanted to look sharp, but when it came time to make a decision on clothes he displayed an annoying indecisiveness. He would spend hours shopping for a particular item – trying things on, worrying over the cost – and then, at the last moment, pull back and wait. One episode he reported to Jean was not untypical: 'Saw a grey flannel with two trousers in a window at $32.50 that looked promising but decided it was too much money, and went on to another store. There I discovered a man with Palm Beach suits. Old stock, selling 'em out cheap. So he said. Cream and grey at $17.50 a piece, regular $25.' He tried both suits on and could not decide between them – 'the cream [suit] I thought too splashy and the grey too much like a preacher's outfit.' In the end he bought them both: 'why I don't know. Maybe it was a notion that the hot weather was going to last until Christmas and I could wear them week about [?], preacher one week and sport the next. And today it was so cold that I went back to tweeds. Such is life.'[5] His procrastination was applied to all things: wardrobe, career moves, where to take summer holidays or major purchases. The fashion consciousness waned over the years, but the hesitation and indecision remained.

Even with the moustache, he had a young-looking face. His hair was light brown and thin ('hair as fine as a girl's,' one barber exclaimed), and he kept it combed straight back, revealing a broad forehead.

Photographs show a thoughtful though undistinguished face: clear, intelligent eyes, with smooth cheeks coming down to a rather smallish chin. His lips were thin and tight, but set as if ready to break into a broad smile. The lips, combined with his natural shyness, could leave the impression of aloofness or arrogance. He would not open up to people until he knew them fairly well – with the predictable result, of course, that he did not get to know very many people very well. Not that he was free of vanity either. He had at times – at home, in the army, and at work – displayed the naive arrogance of youth, that self-assurance that he knew how to run things better than his elders, officers or management.

During the first years of their marriage the young couple had relatively little social life. Jean still saw a few friends from before her marriage but the Irwins entertained only occasionally. Arthur and Bob Farquharson continued their infrequent outings in the canoe, and, in the summers, Arthur and Jean took their holidays camping in the Muskokas. They could not afford an automobile in the early years, so transportation was limited to the streetcar, and, for longer journeys, the train. Arthur never took the streetcar without his book, catching a few minutes every day to read an interesting novel or book on politics. Most nights were spent at home, and once they obtained a radio it became the centre of the evening's entertainment. Arthur enjoyed all kinds of music and was self-taught and competent on the piano and recorder.

At the *Globe*, Irwin began with general kinds of work, covering local events, municipal politics, the occasional book review, and filling in for others on their beat. As promised by Hector McKinnon, he quickly graduated to writing feature articles. One, not uncharacteristic, example was a 1924 article entitled 'Toronto's 90th Birthday Slips By Without Squeak.' The story displayed the Irwin trademarks: it was knowledgeable, lucid, historical, and written in enthusiastic prose at times burdened by an excess of facts. The point of the article, moreover, was as much to shake his fellow citizens out of their lethargy as it was to inform: 'If enthusiasm in the matter of celebrating birthdays is a mark of childhood, Toronto has demonstrated her indifference to juvenile joys quite conclusively ... Big Ben, the City Fathers, the newspapers and even the oldest subscriber ignored the event completely. Not a mourner appeared to heave a sigh for the passing of the years, nor a celebrant to hail the commencement of the last decade of the city's first century.'[6]

On another occasion, he was summoned to Stewart Lyon's office shortly before a visit to Toronto of David Lloyd George, the former British prime minister. Lloyd George was booked for a speech at Massey Hall, and Lyon wanted a column on the great British statesman that he could run on the front page the day of his arrival. Irwin was chosen because he had heard Lloyd George speak in the British House of Commons in 1919, while he and Cookie were on leave in London. Irwin set to work immediately and worked through the night, submitting his copy at 7:00 A.M. the following morning. The day of Lloyd George's arrival he found his story on the editorial page, two columns wide, under a cartoon from *Punch*. He was quite pleased with himself and evidently had made an impression on Lyon. His feelings were confirmed when he discovered a dollar bill in his mail box. It was customary at the *Globe* for a reporter to receive a dollar as a reward for a scoop, and Irwin assumed it was for his Lloyd George piece. Only later did he discover his mistake: the dollar was not for his Lloyd George piece, but for an earlier scoop on a local murder story.

◆

In January 1925, Irwin was posted to the Parliamentary Press Gallery in Ottawa as the *Globe's* sessional correspondent. The posting was offered to Irwin when Hector McKinnon decided to skip the upcoming session of parliament to stay at home in Toronto. The new job was thus not exactly a promotion for Irwin, but it was impossible to regard it in any other way than as a great opportunity. The press gallery was the pinnacle achievement for a Canadian journalist in the 1920s, an opportunity to observe and report from the very heart of political power in Canada.

Reporting from the press gallery meant living away from home for an extended period and on a limited budget (he was earning $45 per week and received a $10 per week allowance for his expenses while in Ottawa). Irwin checked into Ottawa's YMCA, where he could get a room for $20 a month. 'The room here is very much like a cell,' he wrote home shortly after his arrival, 'but it appears to be clean and the showers etc. are almost across the hall.'[7] He also needed a typewriter for work, and a rental cost an additional $5 per month. For his meals he could eat in the parliamentary cafeteria (or the 'doggery' as it was called, where meals were inexpensive if not delectable) or in the more fashionable parliamentary restaurant. 'Ate twice in the H[ouse] of

C[ommons] restaurant. It's very nice but I'm not so sure I'll be able to get the sort of stuff I want. We'll see.'

The Ottawa press gallery was an association of journalists with membership drawn from across the country and a sprinkling of international representatives. It was an autonomous body, or, as one member described it, 'a jealous fraternity of strict written rules and even stricter unwritten ones.'[8] The members elected a president and other officers annually, and, although ostensibly under the direction of the speaker of the House of Commons, were left pretty much on their own. Membership came with a seat in the press gallery of the House of Commons and a desk in the press workroom, a long office in the centre block overlooking the Ottawa River. At one end of the office was the door to the lounge, a stately room that was furnished with comfortable sofas, broadloom carpets, a piano, and with a large impressive stone fireplace. The lounge had the atmosphere of a gentlemen's club – a 'Victorian elegance' in Irwin's words, 'despite the fact that it was inhabited by newspaper men.'[9] Here the reporters played cards, drank bootleg whisky, and slept it off while they waited for the day's session to come to an end.

In 1925 the press gallery consisted of some thirty journalists. It was an almost exclusively male club; the membership list for 1925 includes only one woman, listed as Mrs G. Lipsett-Skinner of the Vancouver *Sun*. John Bassett, who had been with the Montreal *Gazette* since 1910, was president of the gallery and Fulgence Charpentier of *La Presse* was vice-president. The permanent representative for the *Globe* was Fred Mears, the man who had refused Irwin a job at the *Globe* in 1920.

Others in the gallery included: H.F. Gadsby of the Montreal *Standard*, whom Irwin admired as a first-rate political reporter. C.L. 'Charlie' Bishop of the Ottawa *Citizen*, the short, hard-working veteran reporter seen by Irwin as the 'Dean of the corps' in his era; and the Ottawa *Journal's* Grattan O'Leary, another of the gallery giants, well-known for his writing skill and his close association with Arthur Meighen and the Conservative Party. Although he was not regularly in the gallery, O'Leary and Irwin developed a warm friendship that lasted many years. Mention should also be made of Grant Dexter of the *Winnipeg Free Press* only two years Irwin's senior and relatively new to the gallery. Arthur came to admire Dexter as one of the best reporters of his time, not so much for his writing ability but because of his investigative skills and his ability to use his wide range of government contacts to obtain inside information unavailable to the other reporters.

Irwin was not the only rookie member of the press gallery in the winter of 1925. The Victoria *Daily Times* had posted a new reporter to Ottawa that January – Bruce Hutchison. Hutchison was a raw, angular man, not yet twenty-five, with a mischievous face that cascaded sharply down into a pointed chin. His deeply set, penetrating eyes peering out from under a thick crop of black hair only hinted at his boundless, and sometimes explosive, energy. Irwin never failed to marvel at the ease and fluency with which he seemed to write; it all seemed so effortless. Hutchison's gift may have been all the more striking for it was in stark contrast to Irwin, who had to struggle for every word, sweat blood over every paragraph. The two men met soon after Hutchison's arrival. Hutchison later recalled the moment: Irwin 'was seated at a piano in the secret hide-out of the Ottawa press gallery ... one hand on the keys of the instrument, the other clutching a bootlegged glass of neat whisky, while he smoked a villainous-looking pipe and played Kipling's old song, 'On the Road to Mandalay,' the assembled company feeling no pain whatever and shouting out the chorus, plainly audible in the House of Commons.'[10]

In a shrewd passage in his memoirs, Hutchison described Irwin as 'a lean, silent, and superbly tailored fellow ... his opinions sunk in a deep well to spill out, with sudden vehemence, at unexpected moments. Though his desk stood next to mine, he gave me, every morning, no more than a passing nod. I thought him pompous and rather intimidating. But the real man soon emerged. Within a month we had struck up a friendship that continued for half a century while his extraordinary career of journalism and diplomacy was propelled by a rare analytical gift, a dry sense of humour, and a warmth of affection known only to his few intimates.'[11]

It did not take too long for Irwin to slip comfortably into the routine of the press gallery. 'The fellows in the gallery seem to be a decent lot – given to talking quite as much as they are in any newspaper office and quite willing to help you out so far as I could judge.' Shortly after his arrival, Fred Mears took him on a quick tour of the House of Commons and Senate, and across to the Supreme Court building. He introduced the new member to several MPs and wangled appointments to meet the three party leaders: Mackenzie King, Arthur Meighen, and Robert Forke, the leader of the Progressive party. 'King was quite friendly,' Irwin wrote home. He 'said he'd be glad to do anything he could to help me out as he realized what I could be doing for "us."' The *Globe* was still seen as a Liberal paper, of course, but the tide of partisanship had ebbed to some extent from the days when one of Irwin's predecessors in the gallery – J.S. Willison – felt it necessary to telegraph the *Globe* office for permission to accept a dinner invitation from the Conservative prime minister, Sir Charles Tupper.[12] Still, Irwin, who saw himself as independent, was stung a little by King's insinuation.

Arthur Meighen's office was more impressive than King's. So was Meighen. He clearly had a superior intellect, and he was more genuinely friendly. Meighen 'was affable.' Irwin wrote. He 'wanted to know if I had graduated from U[niversity] of T[oronto] and when. Said he graduated in same year – '21 – from another school – the premiership.' Meighen's animosity towards Mackenzie King was common knowledge, and Irwin eagerly awaited seeing them duel on the floor of the House.

Irwin grew very fond of Ottawa. He was enchanted by Parliament Hill and the natural beauty of the surrounding countryside. He brought his skates and used them often on the frozen Rideau. In the spring he began playing regular tennis matches with Grant Dexter and his wife. Once the weather warmed he took long walks and the odd canoe trip into the Gatineau Hills north of the city. He befriended Lloyd Roberts, the son of Sir Charles G.D. Roberts and the gallery member for the *Christian Science Monitor*, and on those weekends he could not return to Toronto he stayed with Roberts at his home outside Ottawa. When Jean came up to Ottawa they stayed there together. Arthur's acquaintance with Bruce Hutchison developed into a firm friendship, and in April he served as best man at Bruce's wedding. Afterwards, he spent many long, enjoyable evenings in the Hutchison's Ottawa apartment.

Judging by the comments sprinkled through his letters home, one of his biggest concerns was securing invitations to dinner. 'About five minutes ago I was boasting that I had wangled two free meals for tomorrow but now it's only one,' he informed Jean. 'Mears invited me over to dinner tomorrow night. I just phoned Crawford and he asked me to come around for dinner at one. Two minutes later Mears phoned again and asked me if I could change the time from five to one – he had forgotten he was going out, he said. So there I was completely out of luck so far as the evening is concerned.' On another occasion he wrote of a weekend more pleasant than some had been: 'I had no less than three invitations for tea tonight, but managed to distribute them to better advantage.'

There were also a few more formal social occasions, such as the press gallery dinner, the reception for the gallery hosted by the wives of the cabinet ministers, and the governor general's luncheon. Irwin never felt completely at ease at formal functions: 'you know from experience that I'm not very enthusiastic about such affairs but I suppose I should survive without serious results,' he wrote to Jean concerning one invitation. The anxiety flowed from a mixture of natural shyness, his resentment at being put in patronizing situations, and a lingering Methodist dislike for all things ostentatious.[13]

The work in the press gallery he found uninspiring. The prime function of press gallery reporter in the 1920s was to act as a conduit for information – who said what to whom. Most of his copy was straight reporting of events in the House. In this respect his timing was bad; the 1925 winter session of parliament was not one of the most memorable. Meighen was cerebral and a devastating debater, standing straight and arguing his points in a logical and precise manner. King was his antithesis, soft, pudgy, and at times excruciatingly boring. It seemed to be a mismatch. In all categories Meighen came out ahead, except where it counted most – in the polling booth. Then King's political savvy triumphed over his physical shortcomings.

For Irwin, listening from his perch up above the prime minister, the romance of parliament quickly faded, and his early anticipation of verbal jousting between the leaders evaporated. Indeed, Meighen and King's mutual antipathy soured the normally polite atmosphere of the House and dragged down everything else to ignoble depths. At night Irwin spent hours discussing international affairs and the events of the day with friends and colleagues, the political leaders seemed uninterested. Developments in Europe, especially along the Rhine, the efforts of the League of Nations to achieve a non-aggression pact, the constitutional questions raised during the Imperial Conference of 1923: What effect would these events have on Canada? Where did we stand as a country? Would the European situation lead war? Britain seemed to be playing a greater role independent of the empire in its European dealings: did this have some significance to the imperial relationship? Surely, these were the important issues that should dominate the House. Yet the political leaders droned on over estimates and points of order, in tones monotonous and incomprehensible. His frustration mounted.

The biggest story that spring was the budget debate. 'Friday night I wrote another blast about the futility of the Budget debate but they did not print a line of it,' he protested to Jean. 'It may have been too strong for them but it was well within the truth. It wasn't particularly well written, however, and may have been shoved out because of space conditions. That of course will be their excuse in any case but no matter what the excuse the reception was not calculated to arouse any great enthusiasm on my part. However, we'll see what we shall see.'

He experienced more success by poking fun at the way the House operated. Under the headline, 'Sleepy M.P.'s Snore and Sigh and Groan in Night of Talking,' he described the scene at the end of the budget debate in the House:

The cold, grey light of a rainy May morning struggles with the feeble glow of man-made illumination. Up in the Press Gallery one of a pair of newspapermen dozes with his feet on a chair. Thirty or forty members are scattered about the House in varying states of repose. One grey-headed Conservative sleeps with his head on his desk. Another leans back in his chair, eyes shut and mouth open. Was that a snore? It sounded like it. Miss Macphail is down for the finish bright and chirpy. She twirls an order paper on the end of her pencil and it flies off at a tangent in the direction of the Speaker. Over on the Liberal side there is constant muttering. Mr. Good drones on. He picks up an interesting book on economics, vintage of the early [18]40's, wants to put a chapter or so on Hansard. 'Drop it,' warns a weary voice. 'Then I'll read it.' 'No, no.' unanimous consent to dispense, and down goes the chapter on Hansard. Then a few words of wisdom from Henry George. 'Print it.' 'Shut up.' 'What do we care?' 'Exchange is a part of the productive process.'

Then comes the division bell. Fifteen minutes of constant ringing, and the round-up concludes by 8:10. Tousle-headed members blink as they flop into their chairs. A French-Canadian takes up the chorus of 'Alouette,' and for a moment the Speaker's voice is drowned in the strains of the old chanson. Then the vote, another vote, a few cheers, and it's all over at 8:45.[14]

One issue that attracted his attention concerned freight rates and the Crow's Nest Pass arrangements. He arrived in Ottawa with little knowledge of freight rates and, typically, proceeded to bury himself in the documents, studying everything he could lay his hands on, and began to write his reports as the issue was debated on the floor. Convinced that the average reader knew less than he did, he tried to convey some historical background, to explain the context of the present debate, show how the past set the precedents for the present. But the *Globe* would have none of it.

'Sometimes I am given to wonder if they have any sense left in the office at all,' he lamented to Jean. 'Before coming down here I scarcely knew the Crow's Nest agreement from a hole in the wall. Ergo, it is reasonable to argue that the average newspaper reader is not likely to know the exact significance of the agreement. It is debated in the House. I sit down and incorporate in my story of the first day's debate a bare summary of what it is, why it happened and why the House is where it is today. The Globe solemnly prints all that part of the story which talks about the Crow's Nest pact and throws the explanatory paragraphs on the floor. Now does that sound reasonable I arsks [*sic*] you? Thus does Canada's National Newspaper display the beauties of its logical faculties.'

His disdain for politics grew as the weeks passed. The June heat turned his room into a furnace, and made the already close quarters of the gallery almost unbearable. He was also having growing concerns about what was going on in the *Globe* offices. 'You may have noticed that the Globe has gone clean crazy – a religious frenzy,' he wrote to Jean on 10 June. 'That accounts for the fact that this morning I was shoved off the map.'

The House went into summer recess near the end of June, and for Irwin it was not soon enough. The end of the session was really only the beginning of a long series of events that would produce, within twelve months, two general elections and a constitutional 'crisis,' but Irwin's greatest concern was to return to Toronto for some long-overdue work in the garden and to prepare for a holiday out west. It had been a rewarding experience, even if his high regard for the Canadian political system had been bruised slightly in the process. He had learned a great deal about politics, made a few new friends, and, above all, had established a dozen or so contacts that he would rely on time and again for years to come.

◆

Jean and Arthur had been planning to take a vacation out to the West Coast for some time. Arthur had never ventured further west than he had the summer he worked as a rod man for the CNR, and he longed to see the Rockies and Pacific Ocean. At first he had hoped to mix business with pleasure by being assigned to write a feature on a reported steamship company with plans to inaugurate a line to Vancouver via the Panama Canal, but he failed to get the paper's permission. Instead, he took a leave of absence from the *Globe* and made the journey overland.

The couple were in Victoria visiting the Hutchisons when word reached them of an editorial blow-up in the *Globe*. Stewart Lyon was seriously ill, and had gone off to South Carolina for rest, leaving John Lewis as acting editor. Lewis was a veteran journalist and long-time colleague of J.S. Willison. A dyed-in-the-wool Grit, Lewis came into conflict with Jaffray over the editorial direction of the paper. Unable to accept what he considered to be Jaffray's movement away from support for the Liberal party on the eve of an election campaign, Lewis (and two other editorial staffers) resigned. The resignations created a minor sensation in the newspaper world and the reverberations were felt at the highest levels of the Liberal party. Prime Minister King closely watched the developments at the *Globe*, and was well aware of Jaffray's slipping support. 'Lewis' resignat'n has brought matters to a head and is a blessing in disguise,' King confided to his diary on 17 August. 'We have unmasked the situation, instead of having a crisis precipitated in the midst of a campaign.'[15]

Irwin's initial reaction was to do nothing; he was not an editorial writer and office politics were not his concern. Besides, he was on holiday. Still, there was a nagging curiosity. What had happened? Who was to replace Lewis and the others on the editorial team? Were more resignations to follow? He had to know. He contacted Hector McKinnon from Calgary to find out what was going on, and McKinnon suggested he return from the west.

By the time Irwin arrived back in Toronto, a state of calm reigned in the *Globe* offices. Lewis was gone – shortly to be appointed to the Senate by Mackenzie King – and the *Globe* rolled off the presses as it had in the past. Stewart Lyon had returned and published an editorial reaffirming the paper's traditional Liberal principles. It seemed that the storm had passed. But Irwin's return from the west was not uneventful. Before the dust had time to settle, Lyon dropped a bombshell: he had invited McKinnon to join the editorial staff, would Irwin like to go with him?

Irwin jumped at the offer. He owed his job at the *Globe* to Hector McKinnon, and that alone might have prompted him to accept. More important, here was an opportunity to make a real contribution to the direction of the paper and, he hoped, to have some real influence on national affairs. There was never any doubt in his mind. The editorial questions raised by Lewis's resignation were left unanswered. McKinnon and Lyon were Liberals, and undoubtedly McKinnon saw in Irwin the smoke, if not the flame, of Liberalism. Although not committed to any political party, he supported most of the platform of the Liberal party, including its policy in favour of a general reduction in tariffs.

Lyon, who remained very ill, was anxious to return to South Carolina. At his first meeting with McKinnon and Irwin, he secured a commitment from his new editorial writers to uphold the traditional policies of Canadian Liberalism. Irwin did not feel uneasy agreeing. Lyon then left the country, leaving Harry Anderson in his place as acting editor. Irwin never thought very highly of Anderson but did not anticipate any difficulties working with him. If there was to be any trouble, it would be with the owner, W.G. Jaffray.

Jaffray's latest bugbear was the bill to curb racetrack betting, introduced in the House by the Liberals, only to be allowed to wither and die in the Senate. Jaffray saw racetrack betting as one of the more serious moral sins and he held King personally accountable for the legislation's early demise. King's double-cross was only the latest in a long series of issues that had driven a wedge between them.

Irwin already knew of Jaffray's dislike for the prime minister. On his frequent returns from Ottawa during the winter and spring, Irwin often went into the office and talked to his colleagues about the Ottawa political scene. Jaffray appeared in the newsroom one time and quizzed him on the news. He was obviously interested in what Irwin had to say and the two got into an animated conversation. Irwin quickly realized that every time he made a critical or sarcastic remark concerning King and the Liberals Jaffray 'just beamed like a cheshire cat!'[16] This conversation led to invitations from Jaffray to talk politics and editorial policy in his office.

One afternoon, Irwin was sitting in Jaffray's office when the *Globe* publisher leaned over and, out of the blue, asked: 'Mr. Irwin, do you believe the Bible is the inspired word of God?'

'Why no, Mr. Jaffray,' Irwin replied, without hesitation. That was the last time he was invited to Jaffray's office.[17]

What Irwin was unaware of was that throughout the whole affair Hector McKinnon was involved in behind-the-scenes discussions with Mackenzie King concerning the possible purchase of the *Globe* by Liberal financiers. In an extraordinary letter to the prime minister, dated 22 June 1925, McKinnon wrote:

I am writing this direct to you because I know you well enough to be positive that what is said herein will not be seen by anyone else ... Indications of a coming election, not anticipated when I was talking with one or two of the Cabinet last winter, prompt me to ask whether or not something can be done toward securing for the Liberal Party control of the great paper on the staff of which I am at present.

The Globe is the greatest journalistic enterprise in Canada; that it has so remained to this day, in the face of the countless obstacles placed [in] its path by an ownership that knows nothing of newspaper work, is a tribute to the men who, day in and day out, strive to produce the finest newspaper in the Dominion, forgetting, so far as they can, the peculiarities of the man in whose hands rests their supply of daily bread. But, it is hard to go on doing this, only to see the results of long and conscientious labors go by the board at the rise of some new whim or the domination of some fresh sulk or petty spite.

McKinnon added that, with the right effort, the *Globe* 'can be bought,' and new ownership would give the *Globe* a 'chance to do what it can do almost without exerting itself – outclass editorially, financially, and in every other way every other paper in Canada. The paper and the staff can do it; all we need is a fair chance.'[18]

Clearly, McKinnon had himself in mind for the editorship of the revitalized *Globe*, and within a week he wrote a second letter. This one was short and contained a clear warning for the government.'There will appear in the Globe of tomorrow (Monday) morning,' McKinnon wrote, 'an editorial based upon the anti-Betting Bill, which will lay on the government the responsibility for its failure to pass the Senate. Unless the mood of the powers that be change *vastly* within the next few days, that editorial may, I fear, be taken as indicative of a definite anti-government turn on the part of the paper, such change of front to become open and avowed as the date of an election nears.'[19] Would Mackenzie King rise to the challenge?

King responded to McKinnon's letters on 8 July, noting that he understood the situation and was very appreciative of McKinnon's efforts on behalf of the party. 'Two or three attempts have been made' to buy the *Globe*, he continued, 'but the negotiations have been frustrated, in virtue of the very curious element in the situation which you recognize as the real problem in the equation. I am not without hope that something may yet be accomplished.'[20] Nevertheless, King was in a difficult position. He had been in office for four years and he did not dare postpone an election until the next year. But the summer of 1925 brought little good news. In June, the Liberal government of

Nova Scotia was decisively defeated at the polls (for the first time in two generations). Early in August the same fate met the Liberal government of New Brunswick. More bad news came from the west, when news leaked that the Vancouver *Sun* planned to retreat from its usual pro-Liberal stance.[21] Now all this messy *Globe* business to complicate matters further.

On 17 August, King brought together a handful of 'influential men in the Party' to discuss the purchase of the *Globe,* including Ernest Lapointe, his minister of justice and trusted French Canadian lieutenant, and the wealthy Peter Larkin, Canada's high commissioner to Great Britain, back in Ottawa for a brief holiday. The talk was wide-ranging and optimistic, and hopes were high that some arrangement could be reached. But no final decision on the *Globe* was made.

Early in September the long-expected election date was set for 29 October. King travelled to Toronto on 5 September to kick off the Liberal campaign, beginning with a speech in Richmond Hill. Earlier that day, he went to the *Globe* offices to meet with Jaffray. 'It was the horse-racing betting business that was most in his mind,' King recorded in his diary. 'I explained our difficulties, then talked of Senate Reform & explained why we could not have appealed a year sooner, which he thought we should have, talked of purpose in politics etc. and of Christian outlook. Jaffray was pleased enough but his mind has been filled with prejudice & I imagine Stewart Lyon who is now dying of cancer is in main responsible. The interview will I think do good.'[22] King's reference to Lyon is an odd one, for Lyon probably was second only to Hector McKinnon in his loyalty to King and the party. His reference to Lyon's imminent death was also a little premature; Lyon lived for another twenty-one years, dying in 1946. More important, although the talk may have helped clear the air, King had accomplished nothing by way of keeping Jaffray in the Liberal fold until after the October election. And the efforts to buy the *Globe* out from under Jaffray completely collapsed. Jaffray was a loose cannon, waiting to explode.

As the election approached, friction between Jaffray and his two new editorial writers was almost inevitable. Under Jaffray's direction the *Globe* was edging towards a state of hostile neutrality, if not a decidedly anti-Liberal stance. McKinnon and Irwin, meanwhile, had committed themselves to Lyon and his policy of traditional low-tariff Liberalism. Only by judiciously ignoring the potentially explosive issues could a confrontation be avoided; in the midst of an election campaign such a possibility was unlikely. The first hint of a crisis appeared with Irwin's editorial on the Prosperity League of Canada.

The Prosperity League was an association of central-Canadian businessmen, hastily organized prior to the election campaign, that supported the raising of Canadian tariffs to protect domestic industry. It published a number of pamphlets outlining the 'facts' on the tariff situation in Canada, which it distributed throughout the business community.[23] Supposedly non-partisan, the league was little more than a private promoter for the Conservative party in the weeks before the general election. Irwin launched a scathing editorial on the league (which he labelled one of the 'prolific producers of high protection propaganda during the present election campaign'). He collected all the pamphlets he could lay his hands on and set to work analysing the alleged facts. It was vintage Irwin: this is what the league claims; here are the facts. He raised many points of error; two examples will suffice.

The league claimed that the American tariff was three times higher than the Canadian. 'Not true,' Irwin wrote; any such assertion 'is a gross misrepresentation of the facts.' Then followed two paragraphs of statistics – import rates and values, aggregate duties' and so on – all proving that the Canadian rate was far closer to the American than the league claimed. The league also claimed that in 1923 American farmers sold $31 million more of agricultural products to Canadian cities than Canadian farmers did to American ones; the suggestion being that a higher tariff would block these imports and channel the income into the hands of Canadian farmers. 'A more barefaced misrepresentation of the facts could scarcely be imagined,' Irwin sputtered. The league had included in its figures such products as bananas, grapefruits, oranges, and a host of others that could not be produced in Canada. For the league to include them in its calculations was nothing short of silly. Indeed, Canadian farmers sold more of 'what they can produce' to the Americans than Canadians bought from the Americans. 'In their own advertising these men would adhere scrupulously to the truth,' he concluded. 'Is politics outside truth?'

Irwin made the mistake of listing the names of the league's Advisory Council – influential and respected businessmen all – several of whom were Jaffray's personal friends. Evidence of Jaffray's reaction has not surfaced, but he must have choked as he read the editorial. A tremendous row ensued. Word filtered down that he was apoplectic over Irwin's anti-protectionist tone, and enraged over the attack on his friends and the league. He hauled acting-editor Anderson in and laid down the law: there were to be no more editorials on the tariff between now and the election. Period. It was left to Anderson to inform McKinnon and Irwin.

It was an ugly situation. With Lyon in South Carolina he could neither act as a buffer between the publisher and his editorial staff nor have any influence over the course of subsequent events. But McKinnon and Irwin had given him their word concerning the *Globe's* editorial direction. Now the publisher intervened with instructions to stay clear of the tariff question – the one issue that the two editorial writers believed to be central to the campaign and central to their commitment to Lyon. What were they to do? They could toe the line and pretend that the tariff was no issue at all, but this would be tantamount to selling out on their principles and a betrayal of their commitment to Lyon. Or, they could go on as if nothing had happened and prepare their editorials as usual. If the roof caved in, so be it. They chose the latter course.

On 12 October two editorials were prepared. Hector wrote a column on the Progressive leader Robert Forke, who, McKinnon claimed, 'takes common ground with Hon. Mr. Meighen in one respect, and one alone. He places the tariff at the head of all the issues of the Federal campaign.' Although focusing on Forke's manifesto, McKinnon indirectly pricked the Liberals on the tariff issue, by implying that Forke rather than King was the stronger in his support for tariff reduction.[24] Irwin chose to attack an editorial in the Hamilton *Spectator* dealing with the tariff and its effect on produce imports. In Irwin's mind the *Spectator* editorial left the impression 'that foreign producers have something approaching a strangle-hold on the produce markets of the three cities [Toronto, Montreal, and Ottawa].' He would set the record straight. As he did with the editorial on the Prosperity League, Irwin, in an editorial entitled 'Misleading the Public,' compared what the *Spectator* claimed and what he considered to be the real facts.[25]

It was a harsh but fair editorial, an attack on a rival newspaper and its support for a particular policy. Coming in the midst of an election campaign, the editorial might well have gone unnoticed, or, at worst, been dismissed as one more partisan outburst from a Liberal organ – unwelcome, but not unexpected. But it was on the tariff, and in the *Globe* office this was now a capital offence. The editorial was withheld and the stage set for confrontation.

Anderson called McKinnon and Irwin to a conference that evening. McKinnon's editorial included references to the tariff, yes, but the main thrust of the piece concerned the Progressive party, Anderson explained, and therefore was acceptable. But Irwin's was another matter. It could not be printed in the *Globe*. McKinnon and Irwin withdrew for a moment and agreed to make their stand on this editorial. And, when Anderson refused to budge, they demanded to speak to Jaffray about it. Anderson said he would see what he could do. In the meantime, no one was to do anything foolhardy.

Jaffray's response came the following day. Irwin later recalled Anderson's 'long haggard face' as he informed them that Jaffray would not see either McKinnon or Irwin. What was going on with the staff, Jaffray had reportedly asked? Were the writers trying to establish a 'soviet' on the editorial floor? His policy dictums were not suggestions for the staff to debate or question, but rather rules to be followed. That was it. McKinnon and Irwin submitted their resignations, dated 14 October, requesting that they be relieved of their duties immediately. Anderson sputtered and choked for a few minutes. 'Put them away, put them in a drawer,' he said. 'I won't have them ...'[26] Then he accused McKinnon and Irwin of trying to ruin the paper. But it was of no use. It was over.

Jaffray remained silent until the following morning. Contacted by a reporter from the Toronto *Telegram*, he suggested that the motives of McKinnon and Irwin were personal rather than public. 'It was not a matter of the Globe's policy at all,' Jaffray explained. 'The matter of the leaving of the two members of the staff we do not think is a matter of public interest. It is simply a case of two men leaving the staff, such as may happen on your paper.' Then he took a parting shot at Irwin by questioning his credentials as an editorial writer: 'Mr. Irwin is a young man,' he explained 'a reporter, who had recently been writing editorial matter.'[27]

Irwin and McKinnon were huddled together in Irwin's apartment when a telephone call came from a *Telegram* staffer. He informed them of what Jaffray had said and asked for a statement in reply. Originally they had agreed to say nothing, but Jaffray's words were so outrageous they felt obliged to respond. A brief statement was released:

We have been informed by the Telegram that Mr. Jaffray states that our resignation, as members of the staff of the Globe, had no relation to the policy of that paper. That statement is not in accordance with the facts. While not presuming in any degree to shape the policy of the Globe, we considered that the course which was ordered to be pursued in respect of a certain political issue was not such as we could honestly condone. The matter of policy was involved, but with us principle was the primary consideration.[28]

The election campaign roared on without pause. But Irwin's perspective had changed radically; suddenly he was on the outside looking in – an observer once again. The *Globe* hoisted the flag of strict neutrality up its flagpole, and there it remained for the duration of the campaign. 'No party was ever so handicapped in its Press,' Mackenzie King moaned before the election; 'both the Free Press and the Globe have made their name & being thro' Liberalism & both are betraying the cause hourly. It would break one's heart, if it didn't fill one with scorn & contempt.'[29]

After 29 October, Mackenzie King precariously held on to power despite winning fewer seats than Meighen and the Conservatives. But his new government would last only a few months. Lyon resigned from the *Globe* early in 1926 and was replaced as editor by Harry Anderson. Meanwhile, the heir apparent – Hector McKinnon – had been dethroned, and his plans for a Liberal takeover of the *Globe* lay in ruins. For Irwin, his stand on a matter of principle brought satisfaction and a degree of admiration from colleagues, but, at the time, such sentiments were no substitute for a job. Fifty years later, digging through dusty files in the National Archives in Ottawa, he would discover that Hector McKinnon was far more involved in the events than he had imagined at the time.

◆

A few days after submitting his resignation to the *Globe*, Irwin received an unexpected telegram. It was from the prime minister. 'Have read in tonight's Star of your resignation from the *Globe*,' wrote Mackenzie King. 'I cannot acknowledge too wholeheartedly the service which in the circumstances you have rendered alike to your profession and to the Liberal Party in upholding as you have ideals of fearless independent [sic] and integrity. To avoid any concern you may have at the moment with respect to the future I shall gladly personally undertake to see that up to the end of the present year at least you are indemnified against any loss through inability to secure immediate engagement of your services at corresponding rates of remuneration.'[30]

Irwin was surprised and a bit flattered to get such an offer. (It should be noted that McKinnon received a similar offer, and King at least discussed the same kind of thing with respect to John Lewis and the others who resigned from the *Globe* in August. It is not clear, however, whether offers of financial assistance were actually made to anyone other than McKinnon and Irwin. Lewis, of course, was appointed to the Senate.) But Irwin could not accept the offer. He had acted not as a Liberal but as a journalist. To accept the money of the Liberal party would have made a mockery of his principles (even though he would have got enormous satisfaction in the unlikely event the money were to come directly from King's pocket). He wrote the prime minister rejecting his offer, but he kept King's telegram as a cherished memento. King saved Irwin's return message too, though perhaps for different reasons.

October 18, 1925
Dear Mr. King,

I thank you most sincerely for the kind words of your telegram.

Breaking with the Globe was neither easy nor pleasant but under the circumstances it seemed the only way out of a difficult situation. The chief consideration – if I may say it without appearing to be too egoistic or priggish – was my own self-respect.

Much as I appreciate your offer of assistance, I feel that I should not accept it. Fortunately, I am not in immediate financial difficulties. At the moment I do not know where I shall land but I am optimistic enough to think it won't be the discard.
Again, my thanks,

Sincerely yours,
W.A. Irwin[31]

FIVE

Canada's National Magazine

Irwin was out of work. He had not planned to end his career at the *Globe* in quite so abrupt a fashion. He had a little money set aside – not much, but some – and Jean still had her job as a dietitian at the Sick Children's Hospital, so at first their financial situation was not critical. Indeed, thanks to a quiet and frugal style of living, their monthly expenses were maintained at a manageable level. But being out of work was harder to accept emotionally. Unemployment was not a natural state for a person like Irwin to be in.

Irwin faced the future optimistically. Surely his five years of experience at the *Mail and Empire* and the *Globe* were worth something in the job market. And his *Globe* resignation did not go unnoticed. Job offers came: one from the *Advertiser* in London, Ontario, and another from as far away as Vancouver. He rejected them both. He had made Toronto his home and he wanted to continue to live and work there.

Chance once again intervened in Irwin's life, and once again in the person of Hector McKinnon. Within days of his *Globe* resignation, McKinnon was approached by J. Vernon McKenzie, the editor of *Maclean's Magazine*, with an offer for the position of associate editor. At first the job appealed to McKinnon: McKenzie already had firm plans to leave the editorship of *Maclean's* within the year for a job with *Cosmopolitan*, so acceptance of the associate editor's position came with the distinct possibility of moving up into the editor's chair in a few months. McKinnon accepted the position but a few days later he received another offer – one he found even more attractive – to head up the R.C. Smith Advertising Agency. He returned to McKenzie to back out of his commitment. McKenzie was naturally upset, and it was then that McKinnon recommended 'young Irwin' for the position.[1]

How McKenzie responded is unknown, but a few days later Irwin was offered the job as associate editor by H.V. Tyrrell, the general manager of the Maclean Publishing Company. Hector McKinnon, meanwhile, worked with the Smith Advertising Agency briefly, before being appointed secretary of the newly created Advisory Board on Tariff and Taxation, which was established by Mackenzie King, hopefully to remove the tariff debate from the centre of political life. McKinnon quickly rose through the ranks of the public service, becoming commissioner of the Tariff Board (1930) and then its chair (1940). During the war he chaired the Wartime Prices and Trade Board.

Following the initial telephone conversation, Irwin was invited to the Maclean offices to discuss the job with McKenzie and Tyrrell. The final test, however, was to meet with the approval of Colonel J.B. Maclean, owner and president of the Maclean Publishing Company. Irwin was ordered to a meeting in the colonel's office the following Saturday morning. Arriving on time, he was ushered in to encounter the piercing gaze of Maclean who was seated behind his large antique desk. Irwin later recalled the conversation. Colonel Maclean told him

that he had learned from Mr. Tyrrell that the latter wanted me for the Magazine and then went on to say that he wanted me for the Financial Post. This precipitated a debate in which I was arguing that I was too radical for the Financial Post and he argued that he was more radical than I was. The debate lasted well into the luncheon hour. The Colonel finally ordered lunch to be sent up on a tray. When it arrived, it was placed on the desk in front of him and he solemnly proceeded to satisfy his hunger while continuing the argument, leaving me foodless on the other side of the desk. This was my first contact with the old boy – then sixty-three – and while it was evident that he thought he might profit from my services, it was equally evident that he did not regard me as one worthy of the social amenities proper to his social status. He finally ended the discussion by saying that I had better go back to Mr. Tyrrell. Which I did.[2]

Irwin may have gone away hungry, but he also got the job. The meeting with Colonel Maclean was the first of many, but in a number of ways the tone of their relationship was established that first day: the colonel, comfortable and powerful as employer, demanding loyalty but lacking consideration; Irwin, hungry for work, eager to get started, but slightly resentful of the colonel's patronizing manner. He would work hard, he would sacrifice willingly to do the job well, but he'd be damned if he was going to kowtow to the old man.

Irwin took the job. Why? He had not previously contemplated moving into the magazine business; he had no experience working in the field and had never edited anything in his life. He was sure that he could learn, and the challenge of taking on a new task was part of the attraction. It was not *Maclean's* itself that was appealing; indeed, he knew little about the magazine and rarely read it. But, it was a job, the pay was decent (he negotiated a salary of $60 per week), and he could leave for greener pastures if something better turned up later. Most important, he knew from Hector McKinnon that Vernon McKenzie would be resigning within the year, and, providing he made a good show as associate editor, the editor's chair might well fall to him. Being editor of *Maclean's* – now, that had real appeal.

A glimpse into his thinking can be found in a lengthy memorandum he wrote for Tyrrell soon after joining the *Maclean's* staff. Tyrrell asked for his thoughts on the kinds of work he might want to do at *Maclean's*. His response showed him to be self-confident – almost to the point of being cocky – and assured of his talents. 'Briefly, I do not want to look forward to being tied down to what might be called "The Horse Work,"' he began,

by that I mean the desk work which any capable man can do with sufficient training. I recognize the value of routine desk work such as I have been doing since coming to Maclean's Magazine. It is fundamental and is extremely valuable experience of a somewhat different type to that which I have previously had, but such routine work too long continued would probably have a reaction on me of a type that I do not want; it has a tendency to deaden initiative and originality and that is exactly what I do not want. If conditions here are such that I could look ahead – say – 5 years and see myself still doing this type of work, I certainly would be far from satisfied and would begin to look elsewhere for something more attractive.

So much for what he did not want. What did he look forward to?

To that I might answer that I would be more or less willing to go in either one of two directions viz. toward a wider scope for writing on the one hand, or towards an editorial direction that would still keep me in close touch with the writing game on the other. If possible I should like to combine the two. In fact

I intend to keep some writing going no matter what happens. If it isn't for Maclean's it will be for someone else.

Either of these, or a combination of both, would enable me to move around and keep in touch with men who are doing things, and keep alive to what is going on generally – a newspaper man's curiosity I suppose. Much as I appreciate the satisfaction of doing any routine job well, I will never be satisfied with the type of work that keeps a man in an office day after day, and I am not very much attracted by the business end of newspaper work. Not that I am afraid of responsibility – I rather enjoy it – but my instincts have always been towards the actual producing of the written word, rather than towards looking after the shekels that may or may not accrue. Not that I don't appreciate the shekels, but more of that later. I think I have said enough to give you an adequate idea of where I stand.

In a private note attached to this memorandum, Irwin added a few more thoughts 'which I did not wish to mention through a stenographer' – his salary. 'Provided I am satisfied with the type of work I am doing and provided you are satisfied with my work, I think we should have some understanding in regard to salary,' he informed Tyrrell.

On my side I want to know what lies ahead in regard to finance in order that I may know how to deal with other propositions that may come from outside. I do not want to be fussing with this and that on a money basis, if the prospects here are what I think they should be. Cash is far from being the largest considerations with me, but, still, it has to be a consideration.

I am not looking for or asking for anything at the moment but by a year from the time I came in here – provided my work is satisfactory – I think I should be getting at least $15 or $20 a week more than I am at present. Two years from now I should expect to look forward to further increase – always provided I make good, of course.

You may be inclined to say, 'He doesn't want much' to this, but it is only fair to you, I think, that you should know what I do want.[3]

These were hardly the thoughts of a new employee fearful for his job. Here was a young man – not yet twenty-eight – informing his employer of his conditions for staying on, implicitly suggesting that his employers were on trial as much as he was. He would stay – provided the job matched up to his expectations. It is difficult to see in this memorandum an individual with long-term plans to make a career at *Maclean's*, let alone to stay on the staff for a quarter of a century.

'Today,' W.S. Wallace boasted in the second issue of the *Canadian Historical Review* in June 1920, 'he would be a bold man who would deny to Canada the existence of a distinctive national feeling – a national feeling not French-Canadian or British-Canadian, but all-Canadian.' The seeds of this national feeling had taken root by 1914, Wallace argued, but it was during the war that they blossomed in an outburst of nationalism: 'In the Great War the maple leaf badge came to be recognized as the symbol of a strong national spirit which never failed before any task with which it was confronted ...' The new national spirit, moreover, had unique attributes. 'Canadian nationalism differs from the nationalisms of the Old World in this, that while they draw their inspiration largely from the past, it draws its inspiration mainly from the future.' In addition, there was the Canadian fact – its duality – the mingling of two peoples, two languages, and, indeed, two nationalisms. Here was Canada's great opportunity, or destiny some would say: to set an example in tolerance and show other nations how different languages, religions, and peoples can live together in harmony.[4]

Wallace was not alone in sensing the growth of a Canadian national spirit. Indeed, Canadians in the 1920s witnessed an unprecedented outpouring of cultural nationalism and a flowering of artistic endeavours unmatched to that time in Canadian history. While most nations of the postwar world mourned the destruction of a civilization or bore witness to the rise of lost generations from the ashes of the war, Canadians were uniquely optimistic about their future. In the collective psyche of the true north, Canadian nationalism was born – not destroyed – in the mud of Flanders.

The evidence was there for all to see. The 1920s witnessed an outburst in Canadian art and literature, enrolment in Canadian universities jumped to unprecedented heights, and new students learned more about their history and literature than ever before. Art galleries, theatres, and concert halls were built, replacing the breezy town halls and hockey rinks of the past. New national cultural organizations were created, like the Canadian Authors Association, the Canadian Institute of International Affairs (CIIA), and the Canadian Historical Association. Across the country, meanwhile, clubs, associations and local cultural groups sprang up in every town and village.[5] All promoted 'Canadianism,' which could mean anything from serious research on national themes to crude chest-thumping patriotism.

It remained to be seen whether or not the Canadian public would flock to the cultural output of the new nationalism. At the same time that a home-grown Canadian culture seemed to blossom, Canadians were being inundated with the products of American mass culture. American magazines flooded the country and threatened to capture the Canadian market. Hollywood movies were wonderfully captivating and unrivalled by anything produced in Canada. American radio programs seemed to speak to Canadian families as easily as American. American culture was entertaining, magnetic, and inexpensive. And for many talented Canadians there were no outlets in their own country, and so began long years of emigration of artistic talent to the United States.

When a Canadian picked a magazine off the rack or pulled one out of the mailbox, it was most likely, by more than a two-to-one majority, to be an American one. 'We are merely being used as a dumping ground for surplus U.S. production,' one *Saturday Night* editorial growled in 1926. 'Slowly but surely Canadian publications are being crowded to the wall, and each day the position becomes worse.' American periodicals had an unfair price advantage vis-à-vis Canadian ones, it was argued, and some drastic governmental action was imperative. 'However, as I said before, nothing will be done, and in a generation simon pure Canadian publications, with very few exceptions, will be scarce as the dodo. They simply cannot survive under such conditions.'[6]

Canadian magazine publishers began to fight back against what they considered to be this unfair competition from American periodicals. The main focus of their attack was the tariff. American magazines entered Canada almost duty-free and, given the disparity in market size, the Canadian market was easily provided for with an increased American production. Overhead costs were raised only slightly as a result. Canadian magazines, in contrast, were burdened with a small market and high overhead costs, and, to make matters worse, had to pay high duties on some of the essential materials for their magazines. The situation was patently unfair according to magazine organizations, and appeals were made to the government to slap a tariff on American magazines.[7]

In the forefront of this assault on the Canadian tariff was Colonel J.B. Maclean. John Bayne Maclean was born in 1862 in the small village of Crieff, near Guelph, in what was then Canada West. A son of a Presbyterian minister, Maclean left home to seek his fortune in

Toronto at the age of twenty. He got his first job as a reporter for the Toronto *World,* and moved on to other papers, including the Conservative Toronto *Mail.* He acted briefly as commercial editor for the *Empire* before resigning to publish his own weekly trade paper, *The Canadian Grocer,* in 1887. He followed his initial success with a series of other industrial and commercial newspapers, bearing titles such as *The Dry Goods Review, The Sanitary Engineer, Men's Wear Review,* and *Canadian Foundryman.*

In 1905 Maclean founded two new periodicals. The first, *Canadian Machinery and Manufacturing News,* was aimed at manufacturers and machinists, and it served up, in monthly instalments, news and information concerning the machinery industry. The second new project – a general magazine with 'mass appeal' – was far more adventurous. Maclean purchased a small Toronto magazine called *Business: The Business Man's Magazine* from a local advertising agency, and in October 1905 published his first issue under a new shortened title: *The Business Magazine.* Closer in size and shape to a modern paperback than a magazine, *The Business Magazine* offered little more than reprints of articles taken from other periodicals in the English-speaking world; the thought was that, although businessmen had wide and varying interests, they did not have the time to sift through dozens of magazines each month. *The Business Magazine* would do it for them, and pay nothing along the way to the original periodical for the rights to reprint or condense its material.

The new venture experienced immediate success and soon began commissioning original articles of specific interest to its readers: profiles and interviews with local businessmen and politicians, stories on the rise of successful commercial enterprises, and so on. The name of the magazine was amended to *The Busy Man's Magazine* on the publication of its third issue, suggesting, of course, that its readers should be not only businessmen but also all busy men. By the end of the first decade of this century it was clear to Maclean that a general magazine, geared to a Canadian audience, was a viable and potentially lucrative venture. In 1911 the magazine underwent a final name change, reflecting the broadening scope of its readership, it was christened *Maclean's Magazine. Maclean's* quickly came to rival the few other Canadian general publications, like *Saturday Night* and *The Canadian Magazine,* carving out for itself a secure niche of the Canadian reading public.

By the 1920s, Colonel Maclean had earned a wide reputation in Canada and was seen, depending on the perspective of the viewer, as anything from a strong-willed individualist and successful man of business, to a slightly eccentric millionaire, to a humourless and gruff old man. There was no disputing his success as a publisher, however. The Maclean publishing empire flourished, thanks to the success of the trade and technical papers, *Maclean's*, and the other Maclean periodicals, in particular *The Financial Post*, founded in 1907.

When Irwin walked into the colonel's office for the first time he met a man whose hair had thinned and gone white. His thick eyebrows and erratic moustache had also acquired a bleached look, but they still bounced and rippled as the colonel spoke. Irwin found his old-Tory imperialism and paternalistic approach to his employees a little unnerving, and he soon came to know some of the colonel's other rather peculiar characteristics. Maclean extolled the virtues of thrift, and raised the habit of frugality into an art form. Used envelopes were preserved along with old desk calendars to be used for memo paper. Signs posted around the building warned not to waste paper, others reminded staffers to turn out the lights. Just to be sure, every night after work the colonel made the rounds of the offices to ensure that all the lights had been put out.[8]

While he could be patronizing to those below him – he often referred to his staff as 'my children' – he acted quite the opposite in the presence of royalty. Depicted in *Time* magazine in 1932 as a man who 'looks like a Lord and generally feels like one,'[9] the colonel thrived on mixing in the society of the rich and powerful. Irwin later noted with reference to Colonel Maclean: 'He liked to give [the children of employees] a 25 cent present and a Christmas tree at the Royal York convention hall at Christmas. At the same time [he] cut their fathers' salaries by 10%.'[10] As he got older, the colonel began spending up to five months of the year away from the office, either hobnobbing with the upper classes in the grand hotels of Europe, or relaxing in the sun in Palm Beach. During his long absences the daily running of the company fell on the shoulders of two men, Horace T. Hunter and H.V. Tyrrell.

Horace Hunter was born in Meadowvale, Ontario, in 1881, and, after graduating from the University of Toronto, he joined the Maclean Publishing Company in 1903. His first job was as an advertising salesman for one of the trade papers, *Hardware & Metal*. His rise up the corporate ladder was meteoric. Within a year he was the manager of *Hardware & Metal;* by 1911 he had become general manager for the whole company. In 1916 he was appointed vice-president. With the vice-presidency came responsibility for *The Financial Post* and overall supervision of the trade papers. He had made himself indispensible to the colonel, and, in 1919 when the company was reorganized, Hunter purchased a large block of company stock.

Horace Hunter was remembered by one close associate as possessing 'a shrewd combination of two seemingly opposite qualities – an almost excessive prudence in making a decision, and unbridled boldness in carrying it out, once made.'[11] He struck Irwin as a rather prim and austere man – something of a cold fish – but he always admired Hunter for the conviction, courage, and tenacity he displayed in defence of any cause he believed to be right. When Irwin joined the staff in 1925 it was evident that control of the growing Maclean publishing empire was slipping into the hands of Horace Hunter.

Victor Tyrrell joined the company in 1898 and followed Hunter as general manager when the latter assumed the vice-presidency. Part of his duties included the responsibility for *Maclean's* and the technical papers. Hunter and Tyrrell lorded it over their respective divisions, and it was clear that Colonel Maclean hoped to play the one off against the other. Healthy competition, he would have called it, but it was no contest. Hunter was far the superior in vision and business acumen. While he grasped the larger issues of running a large, variegated company, Tyrrell mired himself in detail and minutiae. As one colleague wrote years later, Tyrrell 'had been drowning in self-inflicted paperwork.'[12]

The other emerging personality in the Maclean Publishing Company was Floyd S. Chalmers, who, like Irwin, was a relative newcomer. Chalmers was born in Chicago in September 1898 but grew up in Orillia and Toronto. After high school he served overseas in the Canadian forces, before joining the staff of the Toronto *World* as a reporter. In 1919 he started with *The Financial Post*, covering the insurance beat. In 1923 he was promoted the *Post's* Montreal editor, and, in 1925, editor. A man of enormous ability, insight, shrewd judgment, and, above all, ambition, Chalmers knew what he wanted from the beginning and spent his career climbing his way up to the very top of the Maclean corporate ladder.

In the early years of *The Busy Man's Magazine*, the colonel acted as *de facto* editor, with the help of Arnot Craick, a journalistic jack-of-all-trades who served as his editorial assistant. In 1914, after the name change to *Maclean's* and as the magazine increasingly came to rely on original articles rather than reprints, the colonel hired Thomas Bertram Costain, a Brantford, Ontario, native who had joined the company in 1912, as a full-time editor. Under the leadership of Costain and the watchful eye of the colonel *Maclean's* came into its own as a general-audience Canadian magazine in the years before and after the First World War.

Changes that had been introduced to the magazine were continued under Costain: page size was increasing, as were the number and quality of illustrations; advertising was spread throughout the magazine, rather than lumped together at the back as had been customary in the past. Most important, the colonel had landed on a formula for success – Canadianism. 'The two features that should distinguish *Maclean's* from others,' the colonel wrote in a memo to his new editor, 'is the Canadianism of the original matter and the educational and informing character of the review section. Nearly all letters received from readers show the Canadianism of *Maclean's Magazine* appeals to them. This is the strongest feature in the magazine. Make it the guiding principle of your work.'[13]

Costain left *Maclean's* in 1920 for a senior editorial position with the *Saturday Evening Post*, and went on later in life to write a shelfful of books: historical romances, adventure novels, and popular histories. His place as editor was assumed by J. Vernon McKenzie, who had been serving as his assistant for several years. McKenzie was a capable editor but lacked Costain's intensity and originality. Moreover, Maclean and his new editor did not see eye-to-eye on a number of issues, including the colonel's personal intervention to prevent the complete publication of a serialized version of Gordon Hill Grahame's novel *The Bond Triumphant*.[14] Relations soured between the two men, and McKenzie began to seek other positions. His associate editor, Joseph Lister Rutledge, who might have benefited from McKenzie's disenchantment had he stayed on, resigned his position in the summer of 1925, and eventually became editor of one of the country's oldest magazines, *The Canadian Magazine*. His resignation created the vacancy in the associate editor's position that was filled by Arthur Irwin.

◆

The day Irwin joined *Maclean's Magazine* it was already the leading national magazine in the country. He walked down University Avenue that chilly November morning to the Maclean offices on the corner of University and Edward Street. City planners had fashioned University into a wide and elegant boulevard in the grand style, with a distinct European flavour, stretching from Front Street in the south to College Street in the north. But this was Toronto the Good; rather than the shops, cafés, and bohemian artists that one might expect in a Parisian counterpart, University Avenue was lined with hospitals and insurance companies, and was dominated from the north by Queen's Park, the imposing seat of the provincial capital. Irwin entered through the large black doors of the Maclean building, and, rather than waiting for the elevator, walked up the stairs to the editorial office.

The *Maclean's* editorial office consisted of three small rooms connected by a single passageway. The two largest rooms were divided by a stained oak partition with small opaque glass windows and one small opening on which sat one of the office's two telephones. It was not an impressive sight. But Irwin could see the bright side; because there were only three full-time employees on staff he was sure to get his own office. The largest was occupied by McKenzie, and the adjacent office, across from the telephone, was reserved for Irwin. In the smallest room, which was little more than an entrance hall, sat the secretary.

Where should he start? Flipping through the pages of the most recent issue of *Maclean's* (the 1 November 1925 issue) he found a variety of articles and short stories, ranging from short character descriptions of famous Canadians who had left for Great Britain and success, to the article 'The Canada I Knew,' the first of a four-part serial by Jane Seymour, an eighty-seven-year-old woman. Advertisements were in full display on most pages, ads for Wrigley Juicy Fruit Gum, Fuller Brushes, Swift's Premium Hams and Bacon, Old Chum Smoking Tobacco, and Vapo-cresolene, the self-professed remedy for whooping cough. The fiction, a short novelette by Norman Reilly Raine entitled 'Mutiny,' grabbed his attention. 'What would you have done,' the story began, 'had you been master, in mid-Pacific, of a tramp ship with eighteen murderous Chinese lepers at one end, a mutinous crew at the other, and a tropic gale blowing up!' Perhaps the most interesting piece was 'What the Censor Saves Us From,' by R. Laird Briscoe. Sex and violence, of course, but Briscoe's main concern was the overt 'Americanisms' and 'propaganda' that Canadians saw in their theatres. There also was a certain moral laxity in American films from which the Canadian public had to be defended, as a 'measure of self-protection.'

Irwin's major concern that first day was less with the content of the magazine than it was to learn the office routine. 'I literally had to start from scratch and learn from experience,' Irwin later wrote. He was given no direction from McKenzie, but he understood the essential element of his job: the editor was in charge of producing a magazine; the associate editor did whatever the editor did not do. On his desk he found a stack of manuscripts – unsolicited articles sent in from across the country, all of which had to be read. Wading through the 'slush pile,' as it was called, was tedious at the best of times. Many of the articles were farmed to outside readers for their opinions, but even so he had to supervise personally the long process of producing a magazine. 'I quickly found myself functioning not only as Associate Editor,' Irwin explained, 'but as Articles Editor, Fiction Editor, Copy Editor, Art Editor and Production Editor.'

Surprisingly, he found time to research and write a few original features. His first piece appeared in the 15 December issue. Entitled 'Clever Farmer Reaps Unique Success,' it was a short and unspectacular article on a family of Saskatchewan farmers who won a number of prizes at various fairs for their seed grain and sheep. A second piece followed on 1 February 1926. Entitled 'A Black Eye for Sectionalism,' Irwin later described it as 'a rather sophomoric article on the election of S.B. Gundy to the Presidency of the Toronto Board of Trade ...'[15] A third, more substantial article – 'Shall We Deepen the St Lawrence?' – appeared in the next issue, 15 February. Here was a topic more to his liking; he collected mounds of background material, interviewed the investigating engineers, and spent time snooping in their offices. Then he sat down and wrote a detailed piece on the St Lawrence, discussing the effects development might have on river navigation and weighing the pros and cons of hydroelectric development.

Irwin found McKenzie to be an easy-going and gregarious boss, but the two editors did not discuss the one thing uppermost in Irwin's mind: who would succeed McKenzie when he moved on to *Cosmopolitan.* McKenzie's imminent departure was meant to be a secret (Irwin, after all, had learned from Hector McKinnon, not McKenzie); hence, there was no discussion of a successor. Nevertheless, Irwin considered himself a candidate. And the best way to get the job was to earn it – by proving that he could run a magazine.

He certainly got his opportunity. At first the work was new and the burden bearable, but gradually he found more and more of the responsibility resting on his shoulders. Soon he was doing almost everything, to the point where the workload verged on the impossible. McKenzie 'was spending less and less time in the office,' Irwin remembered. 'Some days he would put in an appearance and then quickly leave. Other days he wouldn't show up at all. I soon found myself struggling desperately just to keep the apparatus going. Frequently I would find myself working at home until 3 or 4 o'clock in the morning. McKenzie offered no explanation and I dug in my heels and did the best I could.'[16]

Was McKenzie testing him, preparing him to assume the editorship? Irwin hoped so and toiled away, his confidence rising with every issue. Then the unexpected happened. A rumour circulated that the job was to go to a newspaperman from Montreal, someone named Napier Moore. Irwin rushed into McKenzie's office. McKenzie had given no indication of dissatisfaction with his work; indeed, everything he had heard convinced him that the opposite was true. If McKenzie did not think he could handle the job, all he had to do was say so and he would find other employment. McKenzie assured Irwin that he was confident he could do the job. But, it was not his decision, he protested; it was up to Tyrrell and the colonel, and *they* believed him to be too young and too inexperienced. An older person was needed, and that person was to be Napier Moore.

'What to do? Stay or get out?' Irwin explained his decision to stay: 'I had no idea whether I could work with him [Moore] but I liked what I had seen of the magazine business; in fact I found it fascinating. It was disappointing to be passed over for someone who had no more magazine experience than I had, in fact not as much since I was already on the job. But I was young and if I stayed I would be able to continue my education in a field which offered challenging opportunities. If things went wrong I could always go back to newspaper work – where I felt I would not have too much difficulty in getting a job.'[17] He would stay and work under the new editor, for the time being at least.

Irwin was disheartened by the decision of his superiors. He wanted the editor's job; he believed he could do it. And only a few months earlier Floyd Chalmers had been appointed editor of *The Financial Post*, and Chalmers was a full four months younger than he was. True, Chalmers had a few years' experience at the *Post*, but age apparently did not seem to matter in his case.

At any rate, the events leading to the appointment of Napier Moore as editor left a legacy of disappointment in Irwin's heart. He never stopped seeing Moore to some degree as the man who got the job he should have had. Moore's subsequent triumphs and disasters were measured against what he believed he could have accomplished himself. Over time, he came to appreciate Moore for his very real talents, but Moore's weaknesses seemed to vindicate Irwin's original feelings that he was the better person for the job. The circumstances of Moore's hiring never prevented the two men from working together, but as the years passed the legacy of these original and crucial events – never spoken but always present – inevitably coloured their whole relationship.

There are all kinds of 'what ifs' and 'might have beens' surrounding the appointment of the new editor at *Maclean's* early in 1926. Had Irwin been a little older or more experienced, had he made a more favourable impression on the colonel, had Vernon McKenzie had more influence with either the colonel or Tyrrell, and so on, he might have had the job for himself. In any event, thanks to chance and timing as much as anything else, the administrative ladder was firmly in place: one side running from Irwin through Moore to Tyrrell; the other running from Chalmers at *The Financial Post* to Hunter; and the two sides coming together at the top in the person of Colonel Maclean. This corporate structure remained essentially unchanged until the darkest days of the Second World War.

PART TWO

1926–1940

SIX

◆

'The Horse Work'

'Does the advent of a new editor mean a change in the policy of Maclean's Magazine?' Napier Moore asked rhetorically in his first 'Editor's Confidence' on 1 April, 1926. Surely not. 'The foundation on which Maclean's rests is Canadianism,' Moore explained. 'Expansion, of necessity, means structural development, but it will be on the same foundation. That is secure, permanent.' Moore went on to outline his magazine's objectives: to provide a forum for established writers and to seek out new Canadian talent; to 'smash down the inferiority complex' arising from the close relationship with the United States; to 'awaken a consciousness of what we possess': and, to 'show, not by complacent platitudes, but by revelation of facts, that in the battle with geography, in the wrestle with nature, in business, trade and commerce, in the sciences, in education, in the rearing of men and women, and in the development of a national consciousness, Canada already has a record of prodigious achievement, a record of which we are not sufficiently proud.' It was best summed up with one sentence: 'To live up to the sub-title of Maclean's – "Canada's National Magazine."'

Henry Napier Moore was an Englishman by birth and a Canadian by choice. Born in Newcastle-on-Tyne, Moore began his journalism career as a reporter for the Newcastle *Daily Journal.* He emigrated to Canada in 1912, and worked on several different papers in the west before taking a job in Montreal with the *Daily Mail* in 1915. He soon moved to the Montreal *Star* and from 1919 to 1923 served as the *Star*'s

New York correspondent. In 1923 he returned to Montreal to head the *Star*'s news bureau. In addition to newspaper work, Moore contributed articles and short stories to a variety of magazines, and several of his pieces appeared in *Maclean's*, which is likely how he came to the attention of Colonel Maclean.

When Moore arrived in Toronto he checked into the Waverley Hotel, on Spadina Crescent, a short walk from the Maclean offices. Soon after his arrival, Irwin stopped round at the hotel to introduce himself to his new boss. Entering Moore's room he met a clean-shaven, dark-haired, rather short man with a handsome face. Moore turned out to be pleasant, witty, and bright. A man with aspirations for the stage, he appeared more suited to the role of front man; comfortable in representing the image of the company and the magazine, but not a man bubbling with creative energy and ideas.

Of all the leading staff at the Maclean company, Moore is the most difficult to grasp. He seems to have left no shadow. Easygoing and affable, witty with friends and a first-class public speaker, he gave differing impressions to different people. To some, he was a good actor and talented editor who hid his real qualities behind a mask of manners and civility. To others, that mask of civility covered the fact that there was not much depth there to begin with.

Irwin was anxious to discover just what kind of person Moore was. He still was not convinced that they would be able to work together. 'I was a passionate nationalist and had a head full of ideas about the drama of Canada as a new world nation in the making and the role a national magazine could play as both interpreter of, and participants in, the creative process,' Irwin later wrote in his memoir notes. Would Moore share his views on the direction and potential of the magazine? He hoped to find out – one on one – in the Waverley. For three nights he sat in Moore's room discussing the future. Irwin later wrote that he

> tried to fill [Moore] full of the story of Canada as I saw it and felt it – the land; the people; the history; the struggle to possess half a continent; the triumphs, the failures; the strengths, the weaknesses, the doubts; the groping for something sensed but not known; the yearnings for self understanding, of fulfillment and a sense of direction; the sudden flashes of awareness; all the drama and turmoil of a nation struggling to be. Here was the life-stuff on which to build a vital national magazine. These were the readers who would respond to revelation of themselves to themselves. All we had to do was to tell

the Canadian story, to hold up a mirror in which Canadians could see themselves in action – their successes and their shortcomings, tragedies and triumphs, gropings and dreams; and if we had the wit, the skill, the guts to devise an honest and genuinely perceptive mirror, we would be on our way.[2]

Moore left no record of these meetings, and Irwin was unsure of his effect. 'I don't think I ever really knew or understood whether Moore in any fundamental sense either understood or accepted the thesis – his ingrained instincts were lower middle-class provincial English – but he was pragmatic enough to recognize the ingredients of an omelet when they were handed to him and this was the thesis which with extensions, aberrations, enlargement, fumbling and occasional glaring backsliding, became the basis of Maclean's editorial policy for the next 25 years.'[3]

But had anyone asked Napier Moore, he too likely would have said that he was a Canadian nationalist. Moore's brand of nationalism, however, accepted and praised Canada as a British nation: his nationalism heralded Canada's British connection – the shared cultural traditions, political systems, and common history – and emphasized how Canada differed from the United States, not what made it unique or different from Great Britain. Irwin was a member of a younger generation, a generation of Canadians who had fought in the war and had come to see Canada as a North American nation, not as a British nation in North America. On this point Moore and Irwin were fundamentally different. In Irwin's mind, Moore was and always would be an Englishman.

The two men never became real friends 'Both in the office and socially we maintained a surface show of friendship but the differences between us were much too deep to make real friendship possible,' Irwin wrote. They had their share of arguments; one time on a night train to New York City they debated some issue for several hours, becoming so loud at one point they were forced to carry on in the cramped vestibule between two cars. Never, over all the years, however, did they ever have 'an outright showdown. At times we almost seemed to achieve momentary empathy but the tension was always there; and I suppose it says something for both of us that we were able to co-exist for as long as we did.' Thus began what Irwin later came to describe as the 'long drawn out struggle for control of the magazine's editorial policy.'[4]

The history of *Maclean's Magazine* is not unique. The industrialization and urbanization of North America in the late nineteenth and early twentieth centuries produced a new, larger, and better-educated audience with more disposable income to purchase consumer goods and more leisure time to read magazines. At the same time, the spectacular rise in mass-produced consumer goods, often sold through nation-wide chain stores, sparked an increase in advertising and a growing awareness of the commercial value of magazines as a vehicle to reach consumers. Advertising was an obvious way to bring together the standardized products of the new industrialization and the growing and literate population with more free time and money to spend.

By the 1920s a close and mutually beneficial relationship had developed between advertisers and the magazine industry. Advertisers wanted the audience that a magazine could supply and publishers quickly learned that more profit could be realized by selling advertising space in their magazines than by selling the magazines themselves. Inevitably, circulation figures rather than editorial content guaranteed the success or failure of a general-audience magazine, and efforts were made to increase circulation by any means, including reducing cover prices and subscription rates, and by producing editorial content that would appeal to the largest numbers of potential readers.[5] The result was cheaper and more standardized magazines with huge circulations, geared to a vast middle-class audience; at the lowest level, the subscribers were no longer viewed as readers but, rather, as consumers.

In the United States, the general-audience magazine industry was flourishing in the 1920s. The 'new journalism,' one historian has noted, 'with its pressure for huge circulations, its pitching of content to mass audiences, its scramble for the advertising dollar, was well on its way.'[6] Magazines such as *Saturday Evening Post* (1821), *McCall's* (1870), *Collier's Weekly* (1888), *Red Book* (1903), and others had expanded into low-price, mass-circulation, middle-class magazines and were bringing the product advertisements of their 'silent partners' into millions of American homes. Indeed, by mid-decade there were over twenty-five American magazines with a circulation of over one million, and, in 1926, advertisers spent over U.S. $126 million in general magazines alone.[7]

Magazines in Canada have an equally long history, dating back to the late eighteenth century, and since that time all Canadian magazines have shared one problem – surviving in a small market in a world dominated by larger, more powerful, American competitors.[8] By the late nineteenth and early twentieth century Canadian demand for magazines was being filled by U.S. imports and a host of domestically produced literary, trade and business, regional, women's, and general magazines. Most Canadian publishers turned to the United Kingdom and, increasingly, to the United States for their models in design, format, and even title. Many were blatant copies of foreign publications; others were influenced in more subtle ways.[9]

Canadian magazines were different from American ones in size and content more than economic structure or design. In style and format, for example, *Maclean's* in the mid-1920s resembled, quite consciously, the *Saturday Evening Post,* one of the most popular American magazines (in Canada as well as the United States) *Maclean's* was a semi-monthly, general interest magazine, using 11 1/2 by 14 inch paper, and costing ten cents per issue or two dollars for a year's subscription. The price was decreased from fifteen cents and three dollars, respectively, as of 1 January 1926. An average issue consisted of anywhere from eighty-four to ninety-six pages, and the average circulation for the last six months of 1926 was 82,013 (far behind the *Saturday Evening Post). Maclean's* aimed at a wide, middle-of-the-road audience, offering a selection of short stories and non-fiction articles for literate Canadian men and women.

Apart from the three full-time staff, *Maclean's* employed a handful of part-time outside contributors. Charles Jenkins, an old colleague from Irwin's *Globe* days, put together a 'Review of Reviews' section, an assortment of short articles and news items, usually clipped from other newspapers and periodicals, such as the *Sunday Times* and *Round Table.* A.W. Blue contributed a regular 'Business and Investments' column, and a letters-to-the-editor section was included under the title, 'Brickbats and Bouquets.' Each issue (beginning 1 April 1927) included a short popular science column entitled 'Science Chats,' by the anonymous 'Don,' sporting titles such as 'The Ubiquitous Electron' and 'Radium: An Answer to the Alchemist's Dream.'[10] On the lighter side, there was 'Wit, Wisdom and Whimsicality,' which comprised short jokes and anecdotes culled from national and international publications. For women readers there was a regular section 'Women and their Work,' which consisted of a variety of articles on 'women's' issues by different authors: recipes ('Dried fruit Delicacies'), home decorating ('The Home Beautiful'), and so on. Close to the back of the magazine was 'In the Editor's Confidence,' a regular column that, as the title suggests, permitted Moore (and Irwin on occasion) to opine on any subject he wished.

In addition, a handful of outside readers and part-time staff were used regularly for first screening of potential manuscripts. The magazine staff also relied on other departments within the Maclean Publishing Company to produce each issue of *Maclean's*, including the accounting, advertising, and circulation departments, and, of course, the operating plant. All the other tasks – structural, copy, and production editing and art direction – were handled by Irwin and Moore.

As with virtually all general magazines, the planning for an issue of *Maclean's* began in the advertising department. The bottom line for the magazine was sales and advertising, and each issue would have so much space set aside in advance for advertising, which, in turn, determined the space devoted to editorial content. Irwin ran a constant battle with the advertising department over space allotments, and articles regularly were trimmed or expanded depending on the amount of advertising in each particular issue. Advertising went through an annual cycle, with highs in April-May and again in the two months before Christmas, and low periods in January and February and again in late summer. The time of the year, therefore, had a direct bearing on the size of each issue.

The average monthly budget (two issues) increased steadily between 1925 and 1930 from $4500 to $7500. From this amount came salaries, editorial costs, art work, correspondence, and miscellaneous expenses. The budget was tight and actual costs regularly ran over budget, although not in any catastrophic way. In 1927, for example, the monthly budget was $5500 per month; actual costs for the year came to $3024 per issue (or $6048 per month). The total cost for the year came to $72,592, or roughly $6500 over the annual budget of $66,000.[11] One of the largest costs was salaries. In 1928, Irwin's salary was $80 a week ($4160 a year) while Moore's was $112.50 per week. Editors in the Maclean company received an annual bonus, depending on the performance of the magazine, and in 1928 Moore received a bonus of $4508, bringing his total salary for the year up to $10,350.[12]

Contents sheets for each issue were drawn up based on the space allotted from the advertising department. The time between final editorial changes and publication date was two weeks, and three issues of *Maclean's* were regularly under preparation simultaneously, at different stages of development. Such planning was never carved in stone; many ideas circulated for months in advance and Moore and Irwin were constantly buying good material long before they had a specific issue to place it in. Conversely, at odd times, circumstances changed unexpectedly and a replacement article had to be substituted at the last minute.

Like most other North American general interest magazines, each issue consisted of up to a dozen feature articles, human interest stories, personal profiles, and fiction pieces, ranging from one to ten thousand words (longer articles or fiction works might be serialized over a few issues), not including the regular columns and Editor's Confidence. The magazine was especially reliant on fiction, either short stories or serialized dramas, and, during the summer months, it was not unusual for one whole issue to be devoted entirely to fiction. There also was an annual travel issue. In the 1920s, most of the non-fiction articles and up to 75 per cent of *Maclean's* fiction was Canadian in origin, the rest being made up primarily from British and American authors.

The editors had several writers on call, to whom they would assign articles, and it was not unusual for either Irwin or Moore to approach a specific individual with a story proposal. In this way they expanded the pool of authors and broadened the scope of issues discussed in the magazine. And there always was the overflowing slush pile. Occasionally a nugget was discovered in it, but most often the unsolicited manuscripts were read and returned with a polite letter of rejection. In any event, Irwin spent many of his evenings lying in bed, reading through a stack of manuscripts. At one stage he estimated that he read 'intensively,' on average, fifty to sixty thousand words per week.

All the articles were edited; many were completely rewritten. Early in 1928, Irwin reflected on the amount of rewriting he had done in the previous months, indicating not only the quantity but the variety of topics he handled. 'I can recall making extensive revisions to Mr. MacDowell on railway crossing accidents, to Mr. Fenwick on Oriental penetration of British Columbia, to Mr. Hood on the man who refused a million, to Mr. Woolacott on the future of Vancouver, to Mr. Raine on the department of labour and to Mr. Blue on the United States Chamber of Commerce.'[13]

Some original manuscripts were virtually unrecognizable by the time they appeared in the magazine. One example was an article on Canadian hens, submitted by E.A. Lloyd of the University of British Columbia. The original title was 'The Romance of the 300-Eggers,' and each page of the manuscript was darkened by the scrawl of Irwin's pencil: words changed, tenses changed, word positioning changed. Page after page of manuscript were crossed out, whole paragraphs deleted or completely rewritten. The article appeared in print (under Lloyd's name, of course) in the 1 April 1931 issue, sporting the new title: 'Something to Cackle About.'[14]

Even when the manuscript arrived in relatively good form, there was some editing to do; titles were often changed and the accompanying 'blurbs' had to be invented. Blurbing was essential and always tricky, because, as Irwin explained, 'the dress of an article or story pretty well determines whether or not it will attract the attention of the reader. The article may be a world-beater but if the heading, blurbing and lining are done indifferently, the chances of its attracting the reader's attention are poor. Very often the writing of a one-line blurb involves more thought and real writing than would columns of straight-away stuff. It takes a very definite kind of skill.'[15]

The treatment of fiction pieces was quite different. When Irwin arrived in 1925, *Maclean's* had a running agreement with *Cosmopolitan* for first choice on their fiction. *Maclean's* paid one dollar for galley proofs of all *Cosmopolitan* fiction, and if they decided to reprint a story in *Maclean's* they could buy second serial rights for Canada for one hundred dollars. Along with the fiction pieces came the use of the original *Cosmopolitan* illustration plates. Irwin disliked this style of operation, and as soon as he could he put an end to it and relied on finding his own Canadian authors.

Maclean's would not change a piece of fiction in any major way without the author's permission, and then it would be left to the author to make the revisions. The touch of the editor was more keenly felt on the *kind* of story chosen for the magazine. *Maclean's* looked for a particular style of fiction, what Irwin called 'formula plus.' *Maclean's* did not want 'puppet stories, nor type characters. Write about real people. Don't rely too much on the drama of external catastrophe. Wreck and rescue. Treasure Hunt. Fire. Blizzard. Flood.' Early in 1931, in a speech to the Women's Press Club, he explained what *Maclean's* was looking for: 'External action versus subjective treatment,' he jotted down in his speech notes. 'The psychological story not wanted yet want sound psychology with adequate characterization. Three elements – external action, adequate plot and adequate characterization. Variation toward two extremes. Not interested in so-called highbrow or "Literary" story yet our stories must have literary quality.'

As for the specific type of story the magazine purchased, Irwin and *Maclean's* reflected the prevailing standards of the day. There was a wide variety of fiction, ranging from straight love stories to historical or costume romances; action adventures on land, sea, or in the air; war stories 'only when exceptional quality'; regional pieces (with a western or French Canadian flavour, for example); collegiate and flapper stories 'with reservation'; and murder mysteries and detective stories (although not all crime stories were acceptable). What was forbidden? 'Heavy sex. Our requirements simply a reflection of demand of our market. The middle of the road again. We're not catering to W.C.T.U. mentality nor to clientele of Snappy Stories, or True Stories. Haven't yet reached the point where we can have our heroines living in sin. But tend towards a greater frankness.'

Irwin applied the same standards to fiction that he did for feature articles, and, indeed, the same that he applied to his own writing. Be careful with your facts, know your subject inside out, and avoid inconsistencies. 'Clearness, simplicity' were two essentials. 'Avoid big words, excessive quotation, (scalping) the hackneyed way of saying things. Cliche's. Use superlatives sparingly. Trim your adjectives. Economize your reader's effort.' Above all, make the words ring true. 'A plague on cutey-cuteyism, the pretty-pretty,' he continued. There was nothing worse than someone trying to write. 'fine English.' 'Too often the "master of magic prose" is master of nothing but the art of making an ass of himself.' Finally, find your own voice, your own style. 'Don't imitate. Learn the rules and then break 'em if you can get away with it. Technique should be a tool not a strangling of individuality.'[16]

After the articles for an issue were in relatively final form, Irwin donned his hat as *Maclean's* art editor. If a photograph or illustration were needed he would write or call someone involved with the story to see if they could help. If the subject was in the Toronto area he would go there personally. 'We have to illustrate an article on halibut fishing at Prince Rupert, for instance,' he wrote in 1928. 'As things are at present, we have to make the best of what photographs we can get by correspondence with Prince Rupert, without sending a trained news photographer to get what we really want and really need. Prince Rupert is mentioned only by way of example. It might be Hereschal [*sic*] Island or Grand Falls, Labrador.'[17] Not long after he arrived at *Maclean's*, Irwin's burden was eased considerably when an assistant art editor was hired.

Once the illustrations arrived, Irwin personally supervised the layout of the articles. Each feature article was prominently introduced and illustrated in the display pages of the issue, with the turnover carried over to the narrow columns in the latter half of the book, usually squeezed in between advertisements. In the 1920s the masthead article was brought closer to the front of the magazine, displacing a few pages of advertisements (although ads still dominated the pages at the front). It was stimulating work, but it was also very time consuming, especially for someone whose strengths were on the writing and editing side.

Irwin had a less obvious but more profound influence on the direction of the magazine's content, and it was in the types of articles he selected for the magazine that he had his greatest impact in the early years. In the late 1920s, when he began his career, *Maclean's* was quite similar to *The Canadian Magazine*, run by Hugh MacLean (Colonel Maclean's brother) and his editor J.L. Rutledge, Irwin's predecessor at *Maclean's*. *The Canadian* offered middle-class readers a selection of fiction and non-fiction articles: personal profiles, women's articles and recipes, and stories of adventure, drama, and triumph. The two magazines shared many of the same authors as well as a basic commitment to 'Canadianism.' 'More than ever,' Maclean pronounced in January 1928, 'The Canadian Magazine will strive to justify the name. It will be our policy to represent the Canadian spirit, and to foster and encourage a wholesome belief in ourselves ... It will, in a word, endeavour to give a full and truthful picture of Canadian life.' Similar words could have been found in any issue of *Maclean's*.

What Irwin brought to *Maclean's* was his own keen interest in contemporary politics, international affairs, and a personal love of science. After his arrival, he gradually shifted emphasis towards public affairs and current events, with more coverage of political events, such as elections, international affairs from a Canadian angle, more profiles of local and national politicians, and in-depth articles on national questions (several of which he wrote himself). 'Canadianism' remained at the heart of *Maclean's*, but under Irwin the viewpoint was evolving. The tone of the articles became slightly more contemporary and investigative in approach. More important, Moore (like the colonel and Costain before him) leaned towards the old country – articles from a British perspective and on imperial affairs, profiles of 'empire' personalities, – Irwin was rooted in a Canadian perspective, and the changing look of the magazine after 1926 is evidence of his influence.

He became a frequent visitor to Ottawa, rekindling old friendships and establishing new contacts, interviewing politicians and members of the burgeoning civil service, and sniffing for gossip and scuttlebutt – anything that might prove to be of interest to a growing readership. He could call on his ever-increasing pool of contacts in journalism, politics, and the arts. Grattan O'Leary was already a regular contributor to *Maclean's* and he, along with Grant Dexter, contributed a steady steam of political profiles and articles. Bruce Hutchison became a regular contributor. Irwin invited others to contribute and his bias can be seen as early as the 15 April 1926 issue, which included an article on George Graham (a former government minister) by Charlie Bishop, an old press gallery friend. A second article examined the 1926 customs scandal which rocked the already weakened and reeling King government. Irwin approached Gilbert Jackson, one of his old lecturers from the University of Toronto, to write a piece called 'An Economist Looks at Ottawa.' Leading up to the 1926 federal election, space was opened for articles by the leaders of the two major parties under the heading 'The Issues as I See Them.' Early in 1927, articles appeared on such diverse political topics as the tariff (a topic close to Irwin's heart!), on the Duncan Royal Commission, called to investigate the economic troubles of the Maritimes, and a profile of Vincent Massey, recently posted to Washington as Canada's first minister to the United States. The first issue of 1928 sported a piece by O'Leary on Senate reform.

On the fiction side, Irwin wanted to emphasize Canadian urban life more than in the past, with an edge towards realism. He actively sought out new writers like Morley Callaghan, who he felt was a 'comer.' He took a story from Lloyd Roberts, another friend from his Ottawa days. But working with a strictly limited budget, Moore and Irwin had to take economy measures, and the amount paid to authors was consistently lower than that paid by their American competitors. *Cosmopolitan*, for example, could afford to pay over $2500 for a story (and even more for a serial).[18] How could *Maclean's* compete with that? The result was that, in its search for material it could afford, *Maclean's* sometimes found itself dealing with talented but unpredictable and unstable people. Nevertheless, a partial list of the authors appearing in the magazine in the late 1920s reads like a Canadian literary *Who's Who*, including: Hopkins Moorhouse, Laura Goodman Salverson, Bertrand Sinclair, Frederick Philip Grove, Arthur Stringer, Frank L. Packard, Alan Sullivan, W.G. Hardy, Raymond Knister, Isabel Ecclestone Mackay, and Thomas H. Raddall.

Irwin also resurrected the annual *Maclean's* short story competition for 'distinctively Canadian' stories, in an effort to attract new writers. Offering prizes up to $500 did the trick, and hundreds of entries were received each year (935 for the 1927 contest, for example). Judges were selected from outside the magazine, and the stories were assessed anonymously to prevent favouritism. It was a great success. The 1927 winner was 'Five Cents for Luck,' by Lillian Beyon Thomas from Winnipeg. The story appeared in the 1 September issue and was sold simultaneously to an American magazine (a reversal of the usual practice).[19]

On the art side, Irwin was adamant about using Canadian illustrators, and he began a conscious program to attract good Canadian artists to *Maclean's*. Arthur Heming's cover illustrations were already a regular feature of *Maclean's,* and after 1926 illustrations by artists such as Rex Woods and Group of Seven members A.J. Casson and Franz Johnston were not uncommon. One of Johnston's earliest assignments was to do the illustrations for the serialized version of Robert Stead's prairie novel *Grain*. In addition, A.G. Racey, one of the country's leading cartoonists, was invited to contribute to the magazine, as was E.J. Dinsmore, who later won an award for his work in *Maclean's* from the Canadian Society of Graphic Art.

When Moore was away from the office, Irwin assumed responsibility for the Editor's Confidence column, which gave him a chance to expound on his favourite themes. In October 1927, for example, he wrote of an 'Englishman' who had recently completed a whirlwind campaign through Canada, and left saying that 'the Canadian people talk too much about their country and themselves.' Irwin could not disagree more, and he said so. '[E]ven at the risk of boring visitors,' he noted, 'we can't talk too much about Canada. There is a vast ignorance in Canada about things Canadian. That has been one of our weaknesses. Canadians do not know their own country, and if they do not talk about Canada, no outsider will – and they'll never know – unless they read Maclean's.' He could hear his Englishman moaning, as he sailed away: 'They're at it again.'[20]

◆

Despite the growing demands of the associate editorship, Irwin still regarded himself as a writer first and an editor second, although the line between the two was gradually fading. Following the publication of his first rather sophomoric pieces in the magazine, he began to branch out into longer, more in-depth subjects of his own choosing.

One of the earliest was an article on the problem of wheat rust in the Canadian prairies. For research he travelled to Winnipeg to see firsthand the work of the Dominion Rust Research Laboratory and its efforts to develop a variety of wheat that was immune to rust attack. Rust damage to the Canadian wheat crop cost millions of dollars every year (1916 had been a particularly devastating epidemic, destroying some 3.6 million tons of wheat). Irwin was shocked to learn of the low priority that government (both federal and provincial) put on this research and of the low salaries paid to the scientists in the lab. He decided to write their story.

It was no easy task. 'In the first place,' he explained in a long letter to Tyrrell,

I ran head first into the ramifications of one of the most involved sciences that you could meet in a month of Sundays, plant pathology, genetics, and all the rest of it. My knowledge of the subject was only casual. Somewhere in that mess I had to find a story that would be a story to the reader in Halifax who didn't give a tinker's curse for genetics and had never seen rust and cared nothing about it. After finding it I had to get it across to him in simple readable English that he could understand and in a way that would make him interested in a subject in which he didn't know he could be interested. At the same time I had to get a story that the most scientific-minded of the technicians would regard as accurate. I may be wrong, but that's the kind of story that I think should go into a national magazine.

Irwin went on to describe what was involved in the task, and to describe the essence of writing a good magazine article – a technique that a later generation of Canadian writers at *Maclean's* came to know so well. To really learn his subject, 'I had to go out to the lab and *see* what was going on and *see* it in relation to this story that I had in mind, *see* the story that nobody else could see. Then I had to study the subject until I really understood what was involved, not accepting parrot-fashion what some scientist had written in a pamphlet, but studying it until I *knew* it, knew it so well that I could toss sound ideas about it around as I pleased in order to get the effects I wanted and still retain clarity and accuracy.'[21]

While in the west working on the rust articles, Irwin began preliminary research on a larger project, the history of the western wheat pools: 'the world's largest farm, the world's largest shipper of wheat, the biggest big business in Canada and the world's largest commercial enterprise of the kind.' Wheat pools were formed in each of the Prairie provinces in the 1920s, largely the product of the downturn in wheat prices following the First World War, and the widespread discontent of western farmers from years of dependence on outsiders (and easterners at that) for their banks, marketing, grain elevators, and transportation.

Irwin's wheat pool story ran in three parts, and the articles were so well received that they were reprinted in pamphlet form and thousands of copies were sold to the wheat pools for distribution. Irwin was gratified, of course, but also a bit angry that the Maclean company made a substantial profit from his work but never considered sharing any of those profits with the author. All in a day's work, he surmised, but when an offer came from the west to leave the magazine and write a full-length study of the wheat pools ('a popularized fact romance' is how he described it) he seriously considered it and even went for an interview. The greatest attraction was that it would give him an opportunity to write, which was what he really wanted to do. 'If I succeed [in writing the wheat pools book], I hope that my reputation as a writer will be sufficiently established to make it possible for me to make a living out of writing,' he wrote his prospective employer. 'Only those in the game in Canada now know just how long a chance the latter is but I'm willing to risk it.' On the opposite side, he would have to 'deliberately step out from the direct line of succession to the highest paid magazine editorship in Canada, and by the same token, one of the most influential editorships in Canada.'[22] In the end the project collapsed, and Irwin never had to face the final decision to leave the magazine.

Irwin's most enduring work from his early years at *Maclean's* was his series of articles on Canadian emigration to the United States – an early indictment of the 'brain drain,' a serious problem facing Canadians in the 1920s and later. Irwin's interest was not surprising; for a growing number of young Canadian nationalists like Irwin, the presence of the United States and its growing economic and cultural influence on Canada was becoming a serious concern. It was difficult to be a young university student or graduate in Canada in the 1920s and not be aware of those classmates who left Canada for greener pastures in the United States. The opportunities were there, and for anyone interested in graduate studies, industrial research, private medical practice, or in climbing the corporate ladder, the United States offered far more potential for young Canadians. Irwin knew all too well, and later acknowledged that he too had for a time considered looking to the United States for work. As a magazine editor it struck him as odd that a country could celebrate the success of its immigration policy while virtually ignoring its very serious emigration problem. It was a first-rate story waiting to be told.

After some preliminary research in the field, Irwin obtained the alumni lists from eight Canadian universities. From these lists he plucked some 1000 names of Canadians who had moved to the United States, and to each he sent a questionnaire: Why had they gone to the United States? Economic advantage? Job opportunities? Because of the weather? What kind of experience did they have? To give his questionnaire a more important look, he had Moore, the editor, sign the covering letter.

The response to the questionnaire surpassed expectations as more than 200 replies flooded in, some including ten-page letters retelling the emigrant's life story. It made fascinating reading, but at first office politics intervened to keep Irwin from seeing the letters. By this time (mid-1927), the offices of the *Maclean's* staff (Moore, Irwin, and the secretary) had moved to the front on the third floor on the University Avenue side of the building. Moore and the secretary had the corner rooms, while Irwin was across the hall beside the elevator. Each day additional questionnaire responses arrived (addressed to Napier Moore) and the secretary promptly directed them to the editor's office.

From time to time Moore stuck his head into Irwin's office. 'I'm getting some wonderful replies to that University graduate letter,' he said, making no offer to share them. Irwin was outraged ('since the whole operation was my idea and I had done the initial research, not unnaturally I was upset').This same incident occurred several more times, with Moore appearing, muttering 'wonderful stuff, wonderful stuff,' and then disappearing back into his office. At last he arrived with some handwritten notes, ready to talk. He began by reading one or two selections.

'What does it mean?' Irwin asked, referring to the mass of material.

'I'm telling you what it means,' Moore replied, waving the letter in the air.

Irwin later recalled how his temper rose to the explosive point. 'No,' he said. What did the totality of the material mean? Why did all these people go to the United States? Here was a unique mass of primary material, the raw ingredients for a first-rate article on a significant and timely issue. Why not take the letters and integrate them into a larger study of the emigration phenomena, add more comparative material on non–university-educated emigration, and look for patterns.

Was the problem in the Canadian educational system? Or, was Canadian business at fault? And, in the end, perhaps they could provide some answers to the dilemma.

'Here, *you* take it!' Moore blurted, his hands flying up, conceding defeat. Moments later a box of dog-eared letters was dumped on Irwin's desk. It was his story again.[23]

Irwin's series on the Canadian brain drain ran in four monthly instalments in the late spring and summer of 1927. Entitled 'Can We Stem the Exodus?' a caption on the first page set out the problem: 'In six years, 1921 to 1926, the Federal Government alone spent $13,002,067 to bring Canada 667,349 immigrants. And in the same period, 524,000 Canadians went to the United States. WHY?' He began with statistics – national figures and ones drawn from his survey – and then moved to the general and theoretical levels. Not surprisingly, over 75 per cent of those who responded left Canada for economic reasons: a better, higher paying job, more opportunity for advancement, for specialization in a particular field not available in Canada, and so on. 'After graduating from the University of Toronto in chemistry,' wrote one expatriate from Connecticut, 'I endeavoured to find a place in a Canadian industry. Everywhere I applied, not only did I not get the job, but I was looked upon as being somewhat crazy to think that a chemist had any place in the industry at that time. I then turned to the United States and my first application was promptly accepted by the company I am now with.'[24]

Irwin argued that American employers placed a far higher value on the university graduate than did their Canadian counterparts, both in terms of hiring opportunities and payscale. Likewise, he attacked government for not pursuing and developing greater research facilities in Canada. With no opportunities for research in Canada, no wonder young Canadian scientists drifted across the border. Only the federal government was capable of undertaking the enormous task of solving the problem of emigration. Irwin ended with a call for action: it was essential that the country develop a comprehensive policy for scientific research and its application to modern Canadian society.

Canada's history is the thrilling story of the struggling upward of a pioneer people. For generations, Canadians have been on the march, enduring untold hardships and conquering immense obstacles in extending their country's physical frontiers. Geographically, we are ten times greater than we were at Confederation. We have pioneered in the realm of statecraft; the story of our pioneer railway builders is an epic; today the farmers of the West are pioneers extraordinary in the realm of economics. But there is one frontier that we have not manned, one frontier that we are not extending as we might extend it, and that is the frontier beyond which lies knowledge that would enable us to possess fully our national heritage.

Says Lord Burnham: 'The future of the British Empire is in the hands of science.' So also lies the future of Canada and with science and scientific method we can make that future what we will.[25]

Of all his pieces in *Maclean's* Irwin probably took the greatest pride from the one on emigration, and for the rest of his life he found great satisfaction in seeing his work quoted and discussed by others.[26]

◆

While Irwin's series on emigration ran in the magazine, his wife Jean was at home, pregnant with their first child. A girl, Patricia Jean, was born that September. Within five years there were two more babies: another girl, Sheila Ann, in August 1930, and a boy, Neal Alexander, in January 1932. Jean gave up her job at the hospital to devote her time to raising the children. A home was a necessity now, and on 28 April 1928 the family moved to 111 Eastbourne Avenue, in the north side of town, not far from Eglinton Park.

The proud father went into town soon after the birth of his first child in order to complete her birth registration form. He ran into trouble when he entered 'Canadian' on the form and discovered, to his great surprise, that he was expected to include 'racial origin,' not nationality. 'I explained that she was a mixture of English, Irish, Scotch, French and Dutch and that she couldn't be anything but a Canadian,' Irwin later explained. 'Furthermore, in the direct male line, her great-great-grandfather, who had come to Canada from Ireland was not Irish because his ancestors had emigrated to Ireland from Scotland a couple of centuries earlier. How far back did they want to go?'[27] He adamantly refused to budge from his position and, despite the bureaucratic protests from the registry office, Patsy remained listed as a Canadian.

His battle with officialdom led to further investigation and a comment in the Editor's Confidence: 'Canadians from Canso to Comox and from Pelee to the Pole are taking an increasingly active interest in the fact that they are Canadians. Most of them are proud of it; in fact, would rather be Canadians than anything else. And yet, when it comes to submitting themselves to the coldly inquiring eye of the census enumerator or vital statistics clerk – also Canadian – they find they are anything else but.' 'When is a Canadian not a Canadian?' the question was asked. 'Answer: – When he is born, lives, marries or dies in Canada'[28]

Soon after joining the *Maclean's* staff Irwin was sponsored for membership in the Arts and Letters Club by Vernon McKenzie. The Arts and Letters Club was an association of musicians, writers, architects, and artists, founded in Toronto in 1908. Napier Moore joined shortly after Irwin, and he quickly became a prominent club member and producer of the annual spring show, which included the best acts of the previous year. Moore often starred in the revues, while Irwin usually served as a stage-hand. On occasion he took to the stage himself, one time his dedication was so great that he shaved off his treasured moustache to play a particular female role. Legend has it that Moore dominated the shows from start to finish, and could be a tough taskmaster. Once, during a difficult and noisy rehearsal, he was heard to shout: 'How many sons of bitches are directing this show?' In the silent moment that followed, a lone voice replied: 'Only one, Napier.'[29]

Over time Irwin became disappointed with the Arts and Letters Club of that day. For one thing, he was put off by the 'Englishness' of the place and the people in it. While he enjoyed the company of many individual members, he found the club as a whole dominated by artists and musicians. At the same time, he believed that the 'letters' section (which he categorized as 'right-wing old establishment') was weak. More irritating was the presence of Napier Moore. 'By birth, early training, and mental set, Moore, despite his exposure to the Canadian scene, was indelibly English and he took to the place like a duck to water,' Irwin later wrote with a degree of irritation. It was too much to ask to work with Moore at the office and to be in his shadow at the club. 'Co-existence in the office, was one thing, however; co-existence in the halls where the ghost of St. George stalked at nights and Napier strutted by day was another.'[30]

To get away from Moore and the atmosphere of the Arts and Letters Club, Irwin joined the fledgling Toronto Writers Club, whose membership and atmosphere he found much more congenial. Founded in 1923, there were close to one hundred members in the Writers Club by the early 1930s. An all-male club, its membership included writers and those involved with writing: editors like Irwin, novelists like

Charles G.D. Roberts, critics like William Arthur Deacon, journalists like Gordon Sinclair, and poets like E.J. 'Ned' Pratt and Ron Everson. Essentially a luncheon club, the Writers Club had regular luncheon meetings (or 'drinking meetings' one ex-member recalled) and a dinner meeting once or twice a month. It was a place for writers to meet other writers and to talk about writing.

Interesting people were invited to the club, as were international authors and the occasional politician – J.S. Woodsworth was one luncheon guest, for example. Visitors as well as members were asked to give speeches; Gordon Sinclair was a favourite, usually having just returned from some exotic foreign trip. He would speak on his adventures abroad, using the material that the *Star* couldn't print. On another occasion, famous stage actor Maurice Evans visited the club and gave a marvellous speech on the difficulties of keeping toast hot, and how toasting habits differed in Canada, the United States, and Great Britain.[31]

Irwin revelled in the atmosphere of the Writers Club and it gave him a chance to meet many of those writers whose work he published in *Maclean's* as well as new writers. He became deeply involved in the administration of the club, serving as secretary and then as president from 1929 to 1931. Involvement in the club also brought him into close contact with the established writer, journalist, and critic, William Arthur Deacon, who served as vice-president under Irwin. When the two men met, Deacon was book review editor at *Saturday Night,* and in 1928 he became literary editor at the *Mail and Empire,* a post he maintained (at the *Globe and Mail* after 1936) for more than thirty years.

The similarities between Deacon and Irwin were intriguing. Both were Ontario-born but lived for a short while in Winnipeg; both grew up in strongly Methodist households (and attended Victoria College); and both rebelled against their upbringing, turning to Canadian nationalism as a kind of secular faith. Both retained the moral underpinnings of their Methodist upbringing and devoted their careers to writing and editing in Canada, working with self-discipline and intensity and ending up with ulcers in mid-life. Both were staunch North Americans, never at ease with the 'Englishness' they found in Canadian society. 'I appeal to you, as a Canadian,' Deacon lightly scolded Irwin, 'not to continue the ridiculous Englishism of saying Continent, when you mean Europe. If "the" Continent, coming from you, means any geographical division of the earth, it should mean North America. Why in hell must you look at world situations through

English, i.e. foreign eyes, so that your casual idiom is imitation-English?'[32]

Nevertheless, Irwin did not particularly like Deacon, and, at times, saw him more as a booster than a critic, as a man who gushed with enthusiasm for virtually everything he read, providing it was Canadian. And Irwin's bluntness made it difficult to keep his feelings a secret. 'I am afraid that you misunderstand me, and I am sorry that you should,' Deacon wrote. 'Where you got the idea of me as a person [who?] combines ignorance and scorn I do not know. I am glad to think it was not an impression gained from reading my work, as you once told me you never did that.'

Irwin's feelings did not prevent Deacon from boosting and encouraging Irwin in his work. 'You seem to be very sensitive and needlessly so. You are expecting a critic to scorn you; but this one does not. When you look back over the years, as I am better able to do, being somewhat older, the improvement in Canadian magazines is most gratifying. If you do not realize that I am proud of Maclean's and your work there, that can only be because you do not know much of me. And if you haven't quite a degree of pride in your work you must have less intelligence than I have always credited you with.'[33]

A degree of personal incompatibility did not prevent the two men from collaborating on the production of a writer's market survey in 1930. At the time there was no single source of information on potential markets – either in Canada or abroad – for Canadian writers. There might be dozens of magazines, for example, that would purchase material on Canadian themes, but if few Canadian writers knew of them they could not take advantage of them. There was talk in the Writers Club that something should be done to fill this serious gap, and a small committee was formed to oversee the project. From this committee sprang an editorial board, – consisting of J.H. McCulloch in the chair, Irwin, Deacon, and Wellington Jeffers – to actually prepare the manuscript.

What began as a small-scale project for members' use only, gradually expanded into a book-length project, as the editorial board canvased magazine and periodical editors in Canada, the United States, Great Britain, and Australia, asking two questions: Do you use fact articles dealing with Canadian subjects? Do you use fiction with a Canadian setting? Members of the board also added short chapters on various subjects of interest to the Canadian writing community, topics dealing with copyright, agents, the radio and motion picture industries, and so on. Irwin contributed a short piece on how to prepare a manuscript for submission to a magazine ('A removable paper clip is sufficient binding ...' 'Always enclose sufficient postage ...,' 'Don't forget to punctuate carefully ...').[34] The *Canadian Writer's Market Survey* was published early in 1931 by Ottawa's Graphic Press. One thousand copies were printed and divided equally between the press and the club, which in turn sold them at $2 a copy.

Not long after the publication of the market survey Irwin was approached by Deacon and Wilfred Reeves, another club member, to contribute a short piece to a book of essays. The plan was to collect twenty or so articles by club members; the field was wide open, and each author was left to express his ideas and opinions freely. Irwin did not have much faith in the editors or their project (later describing the result as 'a hodge-podge of punditry, some of it with style and point, but some of it so badly written and sophomoric as to be embarrassing').[35] Rather than writing a new piece, he submitted an article on the history of the Welland Canal which earlier had appeared in *Maclean's*. The editors had to bend over backwards to explain how a piece on the Welland Canal fit into a book of ideas and opinion. In any event the book *Open House* appeared in 1931, including Irwin's piece. 'I shall scrutinise with object of deleting a *few* of the statistics,' Deacon wrote shortly before publication. 'Thanks very much for the piece. It "belongs" all right; and could not have been better chosen.'[36]

◆

After five years, Irwin and Moore could look back with satisfaction over their accomplishments. 'I think it will be generally admitted that the past five years have seen a remarkable change for the better in the magazine's prestige with the public,' Irwin wrote to Moore early in 1931.[37] Circulation had doubled from around 80,000 per issue in November 1925 to 160,000 by the end of 1929.[38] In that same year, *Maclean's* had the largest circulation of any magazine in Canada, surpassing even the circulation of its American competitors. In December 1928, for example, *Maclean's* sold 148,000 issues, compared to 126,000 for the *Saturday Evening Post*, 124,000 for *Ladies Home Journal*, 44,000 for *Collier's*, and 57,000 for *Cosmopolitan*.[39]

Still there were injustices, at least so Irwin believed. Moore was spending more and more time away from the Maclean offices – he spent five weeks touring the west in the summer of 1926 and was away almost two months in the United Kingdom during the summer of 1927 – and in his absence, all the 'horse work' fell on Irwin's shoulders. In addition, Moore continued to receive his annual editor's bonus (1929 was a particularly good year, and Moore received a $8566 bonus), while Irwin received nothing although he believed that he was partially responsible for the success of the magazine. He believed he was not getting the recognition he deserved. 'You, of course, as editor,' he wrote to Moore, 'are responsible to the company for that success, and naturally, reap the major share of the rewards, both tangible and intangible; it would be false modesty on my part, however, were I to say that I did not feel that I have had a share in making it possible.'[40]

Irwin reflected on his understanding of his job, and on the need for two competent persons, both capable of handling the production of the magazine independently. But Moore was not fulfilling his side of the bargain. He had taken on other responsibilities and duties outside the magazine, and he was spending much of his time giving speeches – 'becoming what might be called the company's public relations counsel.'

'This is as it should be, and more power to your elbow,' Irwin added. But, as a result, 'you are able to devote less and less time to the immediate supervision of the editorial work on Maclean's. This means that much of the technical direction of the work of getting out the magazine from week to week falls on the shoulders of your associate. Which is again as it should be.' Irwin's resentment can be felt, bubbling under the surface over 'what may be termed your extra-mural activities.'

Irwin was skimming an issue that was never completely resolved in all his years as associate editor. He was second in command, and consequently, while the workload would be heavy, the public recognition – the 'kudos' – all fell to Moore. This situation rankled him a little, but his Methodist upbringing taught him that good work was its own reward, and so be it. But he felt it essential that he at least be recognized within the company for the work he *was* performing. Surely Tyrrell, Hunter, and the colonel could see the job he was doing. He took small comfort from the fact that he managed to keep his job, and run the whole show in Moore's frequent absence, proving at least that the administration felt he was doing good work. Yet, on occasion, a memo would descend from the upper echelons suggesting that he take on a new duty – as if he had the time! Why not give young Irwin responsibility for the financial writing at *Maclean's,* Tyrrell once minuted. He already spent three or four nights a week reading at home; research for his own articles he undertook on his spare time; how could he squeeze a new task in? Just to have it suggested indicated to him that his work was going unnoticed.

As a result, Irwin periodically fumed about his situation at work, contemplated the wrongs of the world, and considered looking elsewhere for another job. In the end he wrote long letters to Moore or Tyrrell asking for a raise. 'At times it's been pretty stiff,' he wrote, concerning his workload, 'so stiff that my medical friends in observing the results have called me a damn fool. I don't want you to think that I'm trying to give the impression that I've been killing myself because I'm still a pretty healthy specimen, and I'm not grousing about the work. The point is when I examine my personal finances at the end of five years I see a great big question mark. I can't help but begin to wonder whether or not this way of going at things is sound economics from my personal point of view.'[41]

What became crystal clear was that if *Maclean's* was to become a truly national magazine, more quality people would be needed. This meant more staff: an art editor, a photographer, and a feature writer, for a start. And they would have to pay competitive rates to attract those people who could write well. 'Here's the way I look at it,' he wrote Tyrrell. '*Maclean's* aspires to be and is becoming Canada's national magazine in a very real sense. In view of that fact, our aim should be to give our readers material written in a manner worthy of a national magazine. In a word, on any given subject we should have the best written, the most accurate, the most readable, and the most authoritative story it is possible to get. As things are at present, we do not pay sufficient to have much of our material written by the best talent available [the average rate at *Maclean's* was $85 to $100 per article]. As a result we have to do the best possible with the means at our disposal.'[42] Irwin longed to take *Maclean's* away from the three-person operation, expand it in terms of staff and content, and shape it into a major force in Canadian society. As associate editor, however, there was not much he could do about it on his own.

In addition, he felt that the magazine was too much dominated by a central Canadian viewpoint. 'We are a national sheet and we boast that Maclean's mirrors Canada,' he argued. But *Maclean's* had no staff writers from the Prairies, or the West Coast or the Maritimes – it was edited and largely written from a Toronto perspective. 'It seems to me,' he continued, 'that we as individuals concerned in the editorial department of that mirror have relied a little too much on secondhand images.' The time had come for the recruitment of at least one staff writer – a contributing editor – to at least share responsibilities with the associate editor, which was more than a full-time position. At the very least, the editors should be encouraged to get out of their Toronto office to tour the country and see a little more of what average Canadians were thinking and doing from coast to coast.

'I do feel that under our present system we are not making the most of the material available in certain directions, and therefore not making the most of our opportunities to strengthen and extend our hold on the reading public. And I do feel that this disability would be overcome in a measure at least by the magazine's utilization of the services of at least one competent staff feature writer.'[43] Who did he have in mind? Himself.

Irwin was still far from realizing his goal at *Maclean's*. It would be years before he would be able to expand the staff, pick and choose the right people to run a first-class operation and then it would be done only gradually. It was not that he felt the magazine was weak – on the contrary, he thought it had made great gains – it was just that he believed it could be much more. As for his salary, it too would take years to expand. Indeed, as Canada teetered on the brink of the most devastating depression in its history, Irwin unknowingly faced years of retrenchment and pay cuts. Only after a decade of depression and the start of another world war would he again reach the salary level of 1929.

SEVEN

Getting Down to Brass Tacks

Looking forward to a new year and a new decade, Napier Moore felt optimistic as he wrote his first Editor's Confidence in January 1930. He took the reader on a coast-to-coast tour showing how, despite the minor economic and financial problems of the past few months, the country was indeed booming. 'Base your judgments, your faiths, on facts, not on rumours,' he wrote. 'Half the yarns you hear about large business concerns are not true and the other half are stretched.' Ignore the warnings of the melancholy pessimists, cynics, and worrywarts, he advised; the country was strong, the economy was on the upswing, and the future was bright. 'Most people who lost their money in the stock market crash never had it to lose. They only thought they had it. Their buying power was a false buying power. And for every person who gambled and lost, there were hundreds who didn't gamble at all. Regular salaries are still coming in. Sound buying is out of those salaries.' Indeed, he concluded, the 'stock market flop was a good thing. It got things down to brass tacks. The year 1930 will be exactly what sound thinking makes it.'

Moore was forced to eat his words within a few months' time, of course, as things did not improve and the country slid deeper into the morass of depression. Even the most optimistic realized that this was no ordinary 'downswing' in the economy and that recovery was not 'just around the corner.' Everything fell: gross national product, national income, imports and exports, primary production, small businesses, banks, and employment. Everything fell except for rain. On the Prairies, economic disaster was coupled with a drought which turned the Canadian west into a dustbowl, where prairie farmers watched helplessly as their farms blew away with the wind. There seemed to be no end in sight, governments appeared impotent, and radical causes on the left and the right attracted thousands into their ranks. Most Canadians muddled through, but many believed that the new conditions would become permanent. Suddenly the 1920s – the excess and unfairness – took on a nostalgic air, and Canadians began longing for the 'good old days.'

As the depression deepened it began to take its toll on *Maclean's*. Moore's recurring dream of turning *Maclean's* into a weekly magazine became, first, a fantasy and then a bad joke. Plans for expansion were scrapped; schemes for hiring new staff trimmed; forecasts for circulation increases dispensed to the wastebasket. Dropping revenues led to two across-the-board 10 per cent salary reductions by October 1932, shattering any hopes Irwin may have had for financial advancement. 'I hope you will understand how badly I feel about it,' Moore wrote. 'Personally I can do nothing, but if talking things over will help any, I'll be only too glad to see you.'[1]

To earn some extra money, Irwin took on a couple of outside writing jobs – preparing two briefs (for the Toronto Transportation Commission and Gray Coach Lines, and for the Canadian Electric Railway Association) for the Royal Commission on Railways and Transportation early in 1932.[2] Both tasks required weeks of gruelling all-night writing sessions – following a normal day's work at the office – and the strain began to show in headaches and stomach problems. Still, Irwin was one of the lucky ones: he kept his job throughout the decade.

At the very top of the Maclean Publishing Company there were a few minor changes to the corporate structure. The colonel, now in his seventies, was finding it impossible to keep his hands on the running of the company, and he gave up the presidency to assume the chair of the board of directors. Although remaining titular head of the company the real power shifted to Horace Hunter, who assumed the presidency. With the movement of Hunter and the end of his rivalry with Victor Tyrrell who was gradually being pushed aside, a new rivalry emerged between two of the editors: Napier Moore and Floyd Chalmers. In terms of ability and business sense it was no contest; Chalmers rapidly established himself as the rising star in the Maclean company.

As advertising revenue fell so did the size of *Maclean's* dropping to an average of fifty-six pages by mid-1932. A smaller magazine and fewer subscribers contributed to a drop in price (from ten to five cents per issue) with the 1 October 1934 issue. Moore and Irwin were forced to take other drastic economy measures. Annual events, like the short story contest, were cut back or dropped altogether. The Review of Reviews section was dropped from the magazine temporarily; its format of brief notes and article reprints, and the fact that it had always been used to fill space depending on the amount of advertisements, made it an easy target. The Brickbats and Bouquets (letters to the editor) and business sections also were dropped occasionally. An all-time low was hit by the end of 1933, as the magazine bottomed out at forty pages. None of the above sections was included and the number of original articles was down to four features and five short stories. The size of the magazine languished around the forty to fifty-six page mark for several years. Not until 1937 did the average number of pages gradually rise to a level of over seventy pages.

Maclean's articles of the early 1930s, reflecting the mood of the country, took on a dry, ineffectual air; the optimism and buoyancy of the 1920s was replaced with pessimism, anxiety, and gloom. Not surprisingly, Irwin and Moore selected many articles focusing on the depression and potential remedies for it. Titles such as 'A Remedy for Unemployment,' 'Are the Banks Refusing Farmers Loans?' and 'Idleness Relief' became commonplace. Others debated novel solutions: 'I'd Unite the Prairie Provinces' sparked a rejoinder the following month, 'Why Not Unite all 9 Provinces?' Grattan O'Leary complained 'Our Cabinet Ministers are Underpaid,' while Grant Dexter wrote articles on 'The Constitutional Impasse,' and, perhaps the gloomiest of them all, 'Do We Kill our Finance Minister?'

In addition to the 'depression pieces,' *Maclean's* contained its usual assortment of short stories and feature articles. Escapist fiction, love and adventure stories, remained as the mainstay on the fiction side. In 1930, for example, *Maclean's* boasted the new serial of Robert Stead's *The Copper Disc.* Grattan O'Leary continued his semi-regular series of cabinet portraits, and many issues sported sketches of the huge megaprojects of the day: hydroelectric developments, Irwin's piece on the Welland Canal, and so on. Other articles examined the burgeoning movie industry, and, while the admiration for Hollywood movies was clear, there was growing anxiety over the state of the Canadian film industry faced with enormous American competition.

A number of new regular features appeared in these years, and two of them in particular reveal the different perspectives of Irwin and Moore: one was national and political in scope the other British and gossipy, and both were immediate and enduring successes. The first began with Grattan O'Leary's 1930 article, 'An Election in July?' signed by 'A Politician with a Notebook,' and it evolved into a regular feature, ultimately under the title 'Backstage at Ottawa.' Backstage offered a behind-the-scenes look at the comings and goings in the national capital and provided thousands of Canadians with the 'news behind the news.' By 1931 Backstage had established itself as an important semi-regular column, thanks to O'Leary's skill and extensive government contacts.

The second began in September 1934, when Moore introduced *Maclean's* readers to Beverly Baxter. Described as 'the Toronto boy chorister who rose to be a power in Fleet Street,' Baxter was one of several expatriate Canadians who had made his name and fortune in British journalism.[3] Born in Toronto in 1891, Baxter was lured to London after the war by an appointment to Lord Beaverbrook's *Daily Express*, and in 1935 he was elected to the British House of Commons as a Conservative. Moore arranged to publish Baxter's reminiscences in *Maclean's*, and his initial success led to his becoming a regular contributor – *Maclean's* British correspondent – with a 'London Letter' column, beginning in February 1936. Irwin did not oppose the introduction of Baxter's column (and became good friends with Baxter over the years), but his interests were not in the profiles of British leaders and the mixture of news and gossip that Baxter provided. But the British connection still had its appeal, and Moore, the colonel, and others knew it; Baxter's subsequent inside scoops on the abdication crisis solidified his reputation and the success of the London Letter.

In the Toronto office, two new staff members were hired. The first, Harold Eldridge, was, in Irwin's words, 'a Yorkshireman with an accent as thick as porridge'; a brilliant illustrator 'with a flair for the comic ... his drawings had both wit and verve, and he was adept at giving a visual form to an idea.'[4] Eldridge took over as art editor, with responsibility for layouts, photos, and art work for each issue. Secondly, in 1935 Norval Bonisteel was hired by Moore as Eldridge's assistant. When Eldridge resigned a few years later, Bonisteel assumed his position, and before finishing his career at *Maclean's* served briefly as fiction editor, photo editor, and finally production editor.

Irwin struck Bonisteel as an honest, 'tough-minded man.' He was not an easy man to get close to, but, in contrast to Moore, you always knew where you stood with him. He was aware of the tension between Irwin and Moore and sympathized with Irwin's difficulties as the number two person in the office. 'Art Irwin was the first man,' Bonisteel later noted, 'who inspired a feeling of nationalism and what it meant to be a Canadian in me.'[5]

By 1934, the Editor's Confidence column was moved to page two. Ads still dominated the inside cover, pages one, three, and four, and articles began on page five. Beginning in April a mid-magazine editorial was included as a regular feature and institutionalized under 'Special Departments' in the table of contents. The editorials, which tended to deal with national political and social questions, were Moore's idea; Irwin opposed their inclusion in the magazine. Irwin later explained his reasons for resisting such a move: first, he believed that the source for ideas and opinion was in the articles, not from the pen of the editor. Secondly, he was concerned about the kinds of editorials Moore would write. 'I had little respect for Moore's ability as an editorial writer,' he confessed, 'and was afraid that the stuff he would write would label us as a reactionary Magazine.'[6] This was one battle Irwin lost; the editorial section remained.

Irwin occasionally wrote original articles for the magazine, but as the decade progressed his time was more and more taken up with the editor's task; he had little time to research stories like the wheat pools of the 1920s. The one exception was a series on 'The Railway Problem,' which examined the troubles the two large railway companies were experiencing because of the depression.

Maclean's found another semi-regular contributor in the person of Lieutenant-Colonel George Drew. A native of Guelph, Ontario, and a war veteran, Drew developed a thriving law practice after the war. His political life began at the municipal level, first as an alderman and then as mayor of Guelph in 1924. Between 1931 and 1934 he chaired the Ontario Securities Commission. Drew began another career – as a writer – in the 1920s, with the publication of 'The Truth about the War,' which appeared in *Maclean's* on 1 July 1928. Drew heralded the titanic efforts of the British empire in the First World War, particularly against some American authors who, he believed, had unduly inflated the American role in that conflict.[7] The piece struck a responsive chord and was subsequently published in pamphlet form.

Typically, Irwin suggested getting Drew to write a piece specifically focused on *Canada's* war effort. As Irwin explained later, 'I was all for getting the Empire's record straight, but I also felt strongly that Canada's part in the war had been downplayed by both Britain and the United States and that something ought to be done about that.'[8]

Drew responded with a two-part article entitled 'Canada and the Great War,' which appeared in 1928. Drew's next project was even more ambitious: an eighteen-part series entitled 'Canada's Flying Airmen,' published in 1929–30. These articles were subsequently published in book form, topping the best seller list in 1930.

During the later 1930s Drew's attention shifted away from the magnificent exploits and bravery of young Canadians in the First World War to the malevolent and money-seeking exploits of arms manufacturers; one of his *Maclean's* articles appearing with the Irwin-inspired title: 'Salesmen of Death.' He continued through the decade with many more articles on defence-related issues. He grew increasingly combative with each passing year the more the international situation deteriorated and the longer Mackenzie King and the Liberals remained in office in Ottawa.

◆

Irwin was not a party to the close personal relationship that developed between Napier Moore, Colonel Maclean, and George Drew, and if invited he probably would have declined to join them, because on fundamental political issues he was on the opposite side of the fence. Outside the office he rarely if ever socialized with the others in the Maclean company hierarchy. There were a few occasions he could not ignore: the annual summer picnic on Centre Island, the company dances and, most important, the Maclean Christmas party. ('I hated it,' Irwin later recalled. 'I just loathed it.') He far preferred to meet with a new prospective author or to lunch with friends at the Writers Club where he felt more comfortable.

Irwin took pride in being a father and devoted as much time to the children as he could, but it was Jean Irwin who raised them. She was a lively individual, bright, warm, and responsive. She had been a natural athlete during her college days but the burden of child-raising and a gradually worsening asthma condition slowly decreased her participation in strenuous activities.

Their marriage was basically a successful and happy one, but there were some tensions. Arthur was occasionally preoccupied and distant at home, especially during stressful periods at work, and at times seemed to take his wife for granted; Jean, conversely, grew restive as her life became increasingly focused on the home. Jean was very close to her sister Dora, but Arthur had little time for any of his wife's relatives. He had his activities such as the Writers Club and outdoor activities; she had her interests too, most but not all of which revolved around the home and school.⁹ In some ways the couple developed elements of separate lives.

One love that Jean maintained and shared with Arthur was skating, and in the 1930s the Irwins became prominent members of the Toronto Skating Club. The club boasted full-time professional skating instructors and Arthur took figure-skating lessons.¹⁰ The highlight on the skating club's calendar was the annual carnival, which it had been staging for close to thirty years. The event had evolved into quite a spectacle, with hundreds of skaters performing before thousands of spectators crammed into Maple Leaf Gardens for four or five nights each year. In 1938 Irwin was put in charge of the program and this gave him an opportunity to put into action an idea – for a 'modernistic ice ballet' – that had been bouncing around in his head for some time.

His plan was to stage a short ice ballet in three scenes depicting the rise of the machine in modern society. The first scene consisted of 'toilers' working and moving to the rhythms of the earth; scene two has the Man with the Idea invent and then introduce his machine which gradually replaces the toilers, freeing them from their daily grind. In the third scene the machine grows to immense proportions and one after another the Soldier, the Cop, the Man of Business, and the Man in the Top Hat are unable to control it: 'The workers now are seen coming on the ice from the opposing end. Another day. But what a day! They sense the menace of the machine, which has grown to such magnitude. They are startled, afraid, terror-stricken. They move out toward centre ice only to retreat before the menace.' In the end, the machine dominates and engulfs all those who come before it.¹¹

Irwin wrote the story and he approached Hal Eldridge, his colleague at *Maclean's*, to develop it graphically. Together they produced a short book, consisting of the story-line and sketches developing possible choreographical patterns and costumes. Next, the American composer, Walingford Riegger, was commissioned to write the music.

The Machine ballet created some controversy in skating circles, and even within the club itself. 'Arthur Irwin's brainchild,' one columnist noted 'is giving the committee et al the jitters ... they fear unsympathetic spectators may accuse them of communistic tendencies ... yet the ballet motif is, as far as we can see, entirely lacking in subversive influence ...'¹² Some members resisted making any changes to the proven formula; others questioned the theme of the ballet – surely a ballet on the relationship between man and the machine was too unconventional for the annual carnival. Opposition in the club rose to such heights that hecklers were sent to disturb rehearsals and petitions were circulated to have the teenagers in the cast withdrawn from the show. Nevertheless, despite the internal bickering and logistical hurdles, 'The Machine' (with its cast of eighty-eight skaters) played as part of the 1938 annual Skating Club Carnival before close to 50,000 people in Toronto.[13]

Irwin's interest in society and politics found an outlet in other areas as well. In 1936 he joined the Toronto branch of the Canadian Institute of International Affairs (CIIA). The CIIA was founded in 1928 by a handful of prominent Canadians (including former Prime Minister Sir Robert Borden and John Dafoe, the ageless editor of the *Winnipeg Free Press*), and branches were organized in several major cities. Irwin was a great admirer of Dafoe, and he had tried (unsuccessfully) to get the Manitoban to contribute to *Maclean's*. In any event, it was the calibre of individuals like Dafoe in Winnipeg and G.P. de T. Glazebrook of the University of Toronto which attracted Irwin to the CIIA.

A good deal has been written of this loose knit group of educated, literate, and middle-class Canadians that emerged in the decades between the wars.[14] Despite their various backgrounds in business, politics, and journalism, the members of this informal network shared a common sense of Canadian nationalism: a nationalism that advocated a more autonomous Canada within the empire-commonwealth and a greater independent role for Canada on the world stage. Scarred by war and weaned during the long struggle to achieve dominion status, these men (and they were virtually all male) were determined to prevent a repetition of the mistakes of the past. 'I came out of the first war with the feeling a lot of us had,' Irwin later explained, 'that not only were we wanting to become independent of Great Britain, but we didn't want to be dragged into these damned European wars.'[15] Domestically, they were federalists and centralizers, individuals who increasingly looked to the federal government for solutions to the massive problems facing the country. In an era of squabbling and impotent provincial governments that appeared unable to cooperate on even the most basic levels – let alone solve the enormous and intransigent problems of unemployment – a greater role for the federal government was essential. Many of these persons turned to Ottawa for the answers.

Irwin fit into this group – philosophically and socially – with ease. His personal network was already incredibly widespread. As associate editor of *Maclean's* and, to a lesser degree, as a member of the Writers Club, he was introduced to a wide range of writers, poets, critics, and journalists. His years spent in the newspaper business and in the Parliamentary Press Gallery established contacts in journalism, the bureaucracy, and political arena. Even his army experience produced a few contacts – with individuals like Brooke Claxton, who was soon to enter the King government – and enabled Irwin to move freely in the company of other veterans who maintained an interest in national affairs.

Through his participation in the Toronto CIIA group, moreover, Irwin became associated with a small but capable group of young Canadians who later made a mark in government and diplomacy. Others in the Toronto group or the national organization, for example, included: Escott Reid, whom Irwin approached for articles for *Maclean's* and who later went on to serve in the Department of External Affairs and diplomatic corps; John Baldwin, who acted briefly as national secretary, before serving in the Privy Council Office, Air Transport Board, the Department of Transport, and ultimately as president of Air Canada; and John Holmes, also a national secretary, who went on to have a distinguished career in External Affairs.

Irwin acted as chair of the Toronto branch for two years (1938–40), and participated in the National Council and Research Committee. As a member of these national bodies he became closely involved with the CIIA's research endeavours and speakers' program. John Holmes later categorized him as a first-class chair; pragmatic, energetic, and conscientious, he would introduce a speaker nicely – and quickly. Although Irwin was not outwardly enthusiastic or animated in conversation, Holmes recalled 'a little smile always played around his mouth.'[16]

Irwin's involvement in the CIIA and his association with Glazebrook led him to contribute an article on Canadian defence problems to the June 1937 issue of *The Round Table,* a British-based periodical of commonwealth affairs. Entitled 'The Canadian Defence Dilemma,' the article gave him an opportunity to air many of his growing concerns over the lack of defence preparedness in Canada. 'One of the by-products of world rearmament,' Irwin began, 'has been the discovery by eleven million Canadians that their country has not yet evolved a foreign policy on which it can base a rationally planned defence programme capable of commanding the united support of its citizens.'

How would Canadians react if war were declared tomorrow? Some would automatically line up behind the mother country – 'ready aye ready' – but there were other Canadians who questioned the benefits of submerging Canada in a common imperial foreign policy. Canada had no colonies and no territorial ambitions; Canadian interests were not always aligned with the other members of the commonwealth. Canada also had a special relationship with the United States, and in some instances this relationship must take precedence over ties of blood and history.

Irwin continued with an explanation of the differences between nationalism and imperialism in Canada. Ostensibly non-partisan, it was a thinly veiled defence for his brand of nationalism. 'Subconsciously,' he explained, the Canadian 'is aware that his geographical position is his strongest protection. One North Pole, two oceans and a friendly State, which has announced its intention to protect its neighbourhood against aggression, are comforting neighbours in the pre-war world of 1937.' In addition, he added, in a rather romantic and idealistic tone,

the Canadian, whether French or English-speaking, knows nothing of the population pressures, the racial hatreds, the deep-seated economic stresses of the European's existence. He knows something of the conflict of man against Nature, not of people against people. Such a man finds it difficult to understand the armed rivalries of Europe, and it is not unnatural that he should tend to isolate himself from that which he does not understand.

On a more positive note, Irwin sensed the 'growth of an emotional, as distinct from an economic, Canadianism.' He certainly felt it in himself. 'In its most rudimentary expression this attitude is simply a reflection of a passionate attachment to the native soil, a love of the homeland, and a willingness to sacrifice self to preserve the homeland's integrity.' All of which could be comforting to any concerned Briton reading between the lines: 'The British Columbian will defend the soil of Nova Scotia, not because of his British-ness, but because he is a Canadian. This, as a matter of fact, is the one point on which the defence views of imperialist and nationalist converge. At the moment it is the one premise on which it is possible to base a defence programme that will not strain national unity.'

Irwin took the defence debate to the pages of *Maclean's*, publishing articles on appeasement and the deteriorating international situation, and through a two-part series on 'The Defense Problem,' which argued for and against the need for greater defence preparedness in

Canada. On the pro side was Howard Ferguson, former premier of Ontario and former high commissioner in Great Britain. 'Entirely apart from sentimental attachment to the motherland,' Ferguson began, 'Canada's participation in a general plan of Empire defense is plain common sense, just ordinary good business.' Ferguson reviewed the alternatives – exit from the empire, neutrality, and reliance on the United States for defence – and dismissed them. Canada had much to lose in a war, he argued, and *must* do its share.[17]

For the opposing side Irwin commissioned Professor Frank Underhill of the University of Toronto's history department. Underhill did not share Ferguson's view: 'It is too late now,' he wrote, 'to pretend to believe that, by promising our military support to the League of Nations or to Great Britain, we help to assure peace in Europe. All that we help assure is the burying of 60,000 more Canadians somewhere across the ocean.' 'I believe,' he continued, 'that we in Canada should emulate Ulysses and his companions, and sail past the European sirens our ears stuffed with the tax-bills of the last war.' Canada's security was not dependent on the empire, but, rather, on its 'geographical position. As the Russians used to depend upon their famous Generals January and February, so we are guarded by Generals Atlantic and Pacific.'

Underhill went on to underline his concerns for national unity should Canada be dragged into another war. The problems of Europe were no longer our problems he stated; we should look after our own needs first. Then he added a paragraph which Irwin could have written himself:

There still survives in Canada a dwindling body of belated colonials who treat any frank discussion of our relations with Great Britain as high treason, and who regard it as our duty to spring to arms whenever the summons comes from Westminster. It is useless to argue with such people. But there are not many of them left, and there are no more of them being born. They have an undue share of the more dignified posts in church and state, and this makes them a more important section of our community than they are. The rest of the community, and especially the younger members of it, are now for the most part able to discuss the question of our British relations from a purely Canadian point of view.[18]

The defence of Canada was emerging as a serious issue among a relatively small (but growing) segment of the population in the late

1930s. Like most Canadians, Irwin heard, with each newscast, the shrill and incomprehensible voice of Adolph Hitler blaring from his radio and, even if he could not understand the words, they left him feeling cold, with memories of 1918 swirling in his chest. And his *Round Table* article was aptly titled. By the time most Canadians began to think about 'defence,' the word was already inexorably linked to its partner 'dilemma.'

◆

The depression has been called the lost years by more than one Canadian writing about a time that scarred a generation of Canadians who lived through it. No one could escape its effects, not even someone like Arthur Irwin, who, on any scale, had a relatively easy time of it. His family had grown around him, his home and his job were secure; there was even a little money left over for summer holidays and movies.

Nevertheless, his hopes for *Maclean's* had not been fully realized. On the positive side, the magazine had survived – indeed, prospered – while many others failed. The demise of *The Canadian Magazine* served only to underline the precarious nature of the magazine business in Canada in the late 1930s. Increases in circulation, which in the 1920s seemed to be growing beyond expectation, began to slow (although in 1938 circulation remained 68 per cent above the level of 1929).[19]

As for his salary, in 1937 he still had not caught up to the levels of the 1920s. 'I would like to point out,' he growled in a draft letter for Moore, 'that I have served the magazine for a period of eleven years. At the end of that period I find myself earning substantially less than I was earning at its mid-point. In the meantime the magazine has made substantial progress editorially and my own responsibilities in relation thereto have increased.'[20]

More important to Irwin was the need to increase the size and quality of the staff; it was here that he was convinced that the future lay. Similarly, he argued that *Maclean's* should be made more responsive to the different regions of the country. 'Scratching around trying to bolster up a lean inventory,' he lamented to Tyrrell in May 1937, 'has forcibly reminded me of what I have always felt was a weakness in our editorial set-up. This is the lack of continuous contact with our constituency, meaning by that the several provinces of the Dominion.' There were articles and correspondence from all over the country, but what he had in mind was a regular contribution of immediate material, something akin to a backstage section for the different Canadian regions.

'There is very little in the stream as it now runs which gives us a general picture of what's going on in the various sections of the country, week by week. I'd suggest it might be a good idea if we were to consider the possibility of having confidential news letters written for us in the several provinces every two weeks. The purpose of these would be to indicate to us the background news for the two weeks in politics, industry, finance, labour, sport and any other news-worthy issues which may be agitating the particular community at a given time.'[21]

More changes were in store for Irwin and the magazine. Some were anticipated and hoped for. Others, especially on the international scene, were ones that he dreaded but somberly expected. In 1937 he looked forward to a second decade at the magazine, confident that he had made a significant contribution to its success, but unaware of the turn his professional life would take in only a few months time.

EIGHT

The Bren Gun Scandal

The last few months of peace were eventful ones in Irwin's life. Like most Canadians he viewed developments in Europe with an increasingly pessimistic eye, his hopes and fears for the future rising and falling with each day's headlines. With the Munich agreement in September 1938 many Canadians breathed a sigh of relief that war had been averted; at the same time they realized that war – at some time in the future – was almost inescapable. Canadians were forced by circumstance to evaluate their defence needs and to examine their defence capabilities. Irwin did not realize, in that long summer of 1938, just how involved he would become in that examination. It all began with an article in *Maclean's*.

◆

Defence production was not often a topic of discussion in Canadian social circles in the 1930s. Indeed, Canada had virtually no industrial defence capability between the wars, and no one seemed to mind. There were other, more important considerations, especially in the 1930s, when the devastation of the depression precluded the expenditure of vast sums on weapons. The beginnings of a rearmament program in Great Britain in 1935 raised a few hopes in Canadian military and business circles that some British orders might be placed in Canada, or, even better, that the Canadian government might follow suit and initiate its own program. At the same time, there were growing concerns over the security of supply for the Canadian forces. Could the Canadian forces still rely on British sources of supply in the future, as they had in the past? Such a likelihood was not at all a certainty.

The pleas of military leaders fell on deaf ears in Ottawa, where the government was committed to retrenchment and not philosophically sympathetic to military expenditures of any kind. Prime Minister King was especially hesitant to lead his government towards rearmament. For one thing, he found peacetime military production distasteful and was outraged at the requests from business leaders for munitions and armament contracts. For another, his reading of public opinion told him that Canadians did not want government funds wasted on armaments while thousands of Canadians lingered in unemployment lines.

As the prospects of maintaining the peace deteriorated in 1937–38, the government considered a modest rearmament program. One of King's greatest concerns was to control undue profits and prevent abuse by unscrupulous industrialists. The last thing he wanted was any whiff of scandal rising from one of his government's contracts. To prevent such an occurrence, an advisory interdepartmental committee was established, with representatives from the departments of National Defence, National Revenue, Labour, and Trade and Commerce, to 'advise on the letting of government defence contracts.'[1] In the chair of the new committee sat Colonel L.R. LaFlèche, the deputy minister of national defence. After serving in the Canadian Expeditionary Force (CEF) during the First World War he joined the Department of National Defence (DND), and in 1932 became deputy minister. In this capacity, and as chair of the interdepartmental committee, LaFlèche came to play a prominent role in the most significant prewar defence contract: the manufacture of the Bren light machine-gun.

Enter Major James Hahn, president of the John Inglis Company and would-be arms manufacturer. American-born of Canadian parents, Hahn served overseas with the CEF, where he was wounded three times and was awarded the Military Cross. After the war he launched the De Forest Radio Corporation which manufactured radios, clocks, washing machines, and other electric appliances. In 1936, Hahn acquired control of the John Inglis plant in Toronto which had closed shortly before and was in the hands of receivers. The John Inglis Company had for many years been a leader in the production of precision steel tools and machinery. Under Hahn's direction a wholly new company was organized, although the John Inglis name was preserved. All he needed now was something to manufacture.

Major Hahn appeared in Ottawa one afternoon in the summer of

1936 with a scheme to turn over his idle Inglis factory to the production of the Bren gun, which he hoped would fill both Canadian and British needs. The Bren gun was a light machine-gun, invented in Czechoslovakia and modified for British use in the early 1930s. The DND was interested in the weapon and had acquired two prototypes in 1936. After careful examination, the DND estimated the needs of the Canadian militia at 7000. Hahn also travelled to Britain – carrying a letter of introduction from Ian Mackenzie, the minister of national defence – where he met with a number of British officials and found considerable interest in having Bren guns manufactured in Canada.

Following months of informal discussion, a contract with Hahn was signed on 31 March 1938. Briefly, it called for the manufacture of 7000 Bren guns on a cost plus 10 per cent basis, with delivery dates beginning in March 1940 and spread out until the end of July 1943. The government agreed to supply the John Inglis Company with the remaining tools and machinery from the Ross Rifle factory which had been idle for almost twenty years, and, in addition promised to purchase (and maintain ownership of) the necessary equipment. The costs of the project were run through LaFlèche's interdepartmental committee and it was estimated that the unit cost for each gun would be approximately $411.91 (or $2,883,370 for 7000 units).[2] An identical contract was signed with the British government, calling for the manufacture of 5,000 Bren guns. Tenders were not requested, nor were any other companies considered for the contract.

Information on the contract was not released to the public until May, and some of the details were published in *The Financial Post* on 14 May. Questions were raised almost immediately, especially concerning the government's decision not to seek tenders for the contract. One government critic who had a few questions of his own was George Drew. Only days before the signing of the Bren gun contract Drew published an article in *The Financial Post*, entitled 'Canada's Defense Farce,' in which he condemned the government for inaction and incompetence with respect to supplying its forces with the necessary arms and equipment.[3] The negotiation of a defence contract on the scale of the Bren gun naturally interested Drew; his inability to learn much about it infuriated him. Questions were also asked in the House of Commons concerning the terms of the contract and why it had not been released to the public. Irwin became involved, using his contact with J.S. Woodsworth to have a question raised in the Commons. Persistent challenging paid off: near the end of June Ian Mackenzie made the contract public by tabling it in the House, and, a few days later, a plain envelope containing a copy arrived on Irwin's desk.

There were apparent discrepancies between what Irwin read in the contract and what Mackenzie had said in the House of Commons. Mackenzie claimed never to have met with Hahn, and stated that no collaboration with the British government had occurred. Was this really the case? The contract made reference to the government's paying some of Hahn's earlier expenses. Why would this be done if there were no preliminary discussions or collaboration? Mackenzie had boasted that it was an excellent contract, one that would serve as the model for future defence contracts. Did that mean that in future there would be no competitive bidding? These were nagging questions, and Irwin believed there might be a story in the answers.

Moore was out of town when the contract arrived so Irwin took his idea straight to Horace Hunter. At first Hunter had to be prodded to read the contract, and in fact he agreed to commissioning an article before he actually read it.[4] Hunter at first suggested moving the story to *The Financial Post*, but accepted Irwin's point that using *Maclean's* as the vehicle, although less immediate, would attract a larger audience. Hunter was firmer on who should write the article. Drew was the logical choice.

Irwin did not believe that Drew was the one for the job. A known Conservative, Drew's byline would inevitably invite charges of partisanship in any article attacking a contract negotiated by a Liberal government. The arguments in favour of Drew, however, far outweighed these concerns. Drew was a national figure, with a wide audience from his earlier works in *Maclean's*. He was a war hero and an acknowledged authority on the DND. He was also a close friend of Colonel Maclean and Moore, and they knew Drew as a man of sympathetic Tory-imperialist views, who could be relied on for a hard-hitting expose. Drew's good qualities were self-evident; uncompromising and charismatic, he was a man who never backed down from a fight, especially when there was an opportunity to bloody Liberal noses.

Irwin called Drew in to discuss his proposal for an article on the Bren gun contract. Drew took the contract, tucked it under his arm, and disappeared. As the deadline approached Irwin tracked him down on an island in Georgian Bay. Drew reported that he had unearthed a connection between Hahn and a Liberal MP, and he asked for an extension to flesh out the details. Irwin agreed, reluctantly, and gave

Drew two more weeks, pushing publication date back to the 1 September issue.

The article arrived at last, and was promptly put into production. Every paragraph, every assertion, every fact was scrutinised by Irwin and Moore. Any error, however insignificant, could seriously detract from the article's impact and potentially overshadow the very real points to be made. In Drew's original draft, for example, he referred to a sitting member of parliament as being a member of the law firm behind Hahn's company, which was, in fact, no longer the case. Irwin spotted the point and forced Drew to check his facts. Drew subsequently discovered his error and changed the text, thereby preventing a potential law suit.

Drew's article – entitled 'Canada's Armament Mystery' – began with an historical overview of the negotiation of the Bren gun contract, and he commented on the government's apparent secrecy and unwillingness to reveal its details.[5] The public statements of Ian Mackenzie were rehashed in an unflattering way, suggesting that Mackenzie was acting, if not in a dishonest way, at least in a disingenuous one when he claimed that there was no cooperation between the Canadian and British authorities. Why, then, did the Canadian government agree to pay for the company's 'preliminary investigation,' which undoubtedly included Hahn's travel expenses while in Britain?

Drew's most scathing criticisms were reserved for the financial arrangements. 'Agreements providing for production on a "cost plus" basis are not at all unusual,' Drew noted. 'But many of the items on which the ten per cent profit is allowed in this contract are extremely unusual'; including, for example, travel expenses and salaries for the company executives. In addition to the outrageous profits, Drew sniffed the scent of a stock-profiteering boondoggle. Drew pointed to the fact that Hahn was the major shareholder in the John Inglis Company, with a second large block of shares being held by Investment Reserves Limited, a mysterious firm whose directors were all employees of Plaxton and Company, the Toronto legal firm that had acted as Hahn's solicitors. Investment Reserves Limited had been incorporated only a few weeks before the signing of the contract and Drew noted that Hugh Plaxton, a Liberal backbencher, had been a member of the firm until very recently and still maintained an office in the firm. There seemed to be too many connections, between Hugh Plaxton, MP, his previous law firm, and its share of Investment Reserves Limited, and the fact that it was incorporated and acquired shares in John

Inglis only a short while before the signing of the contract which, in turn, would greatly increase the value of the shares. 'Was it known,' Drew asked rhetorically, 'that the contract with Hahn's company was soon to be signed?'

Drew examined every aspect of the contract, questioned all the details, and squeezed out every ounce of innuendo that he could. No specific charges of wrongdoing were made, but the implications were that some persons had benefited, above and beyond the norm, at government expense. The finger of guilt was not pointed directly at anyone, but it was equally clear whom Drew held responsible: Hahn, Plaxton, and, ultimately, Ian Mackenzie, the minister.

The 1 September issue hit the stands on 25 August and created an immediate sensation. The people at Maclean Publishing Company had already had a hint of what was in store. As soon as the article was completed – almost two weeks before publication date – Moore circulated tear sheets to a few interested parties, and by publication date Hahn himself had heard rumours that a potentially damaging article would soon appear in *Maclean's*. Hahn telephoned Hunter to warn him that he would take legal action against the Maclean company if the anticipated article in any way stepped outside the bounds of the law. Hunter replied that it was too late to back out, assuring Hahn that his editors had 'no axe to grind' and that they would never publish unsubstantiated material. Hahn agreed, but, according to the memo of the telephone conversation, threatened legal action at least three times.[6]

Hahn was as good as his word, and soon after publication the Maclean company was served notice of libel action from three sources: the John Inglis Company, Hugh Plaxton, the Liberal MP mentioned in the article, and Hahn personally. These were only preliminary notices, however, and Hunter was confident that none of the three would proceed. 'I don't think we are in any danger of damages,' he wrote Colonel Maclean, 'and I do not think they will proceed with them at all.' Indeed, there was a positive side in being singled out for libel action. 'The notices,' he continued, 'will serve to give the Magazine some good publicity, and will emphasize in the minds of the public that we initiated and took the responsibility in publishing this article.'[7]

Publicity was the one thing Mackenzie King did not want. It was a messy business, and once again King felt the hot breath of scandal caressing the back of his neck. He had been prudent, he had acted cautiously in introducing a modest rearmament program, and he had taken great pains to keep at arm's length from the British throughout the whole affair. Now it appeared that his one major venture into arms production could degenerate into a political mud-slinging match. All speculation must cease; all rumours must be stamped out before they had a chance to circulate. On 30 August the cabinet discussed the charges raised in the article, and it was agreed that a royal commission should be established to look into the charges. 'I took the position very strongly that a judicial inquiry should be had, and had immediately,' King wrote in his diary the following day. 'It is not the enemy we need to fear,' he concluded, 'but selfish interests within our own party, and a desire of Ministers to meet the wishes of political friends.'[8]

◆

The Royal Commission on the Bren Machine Gun Contract held its first session on the morning of 19 September 1938 and concluded on 24 November. In the commissioner's chair sat Justice Henry Hague Davis, a member of the Supreme Court. The commission examined the activities of Hahn and Plaxton from 1936 to the signing of the contract, reviewing how Plaxton had introduced Hahn to LaFlèche, followed by Hahn's meeting with Ian Mackenzie. The infamous letter of introduction was read into the record, and questions were asked concerning Hahn's overseas trip. The financial background of Hahn's company was explored, as was the workings of LaFlèche's interdepartmental committee set up to control excess profits. In the end, Davis found no hint of corruption and no evidence of wrongdoing on the part of the government, its officials, Hahn, or his company.

Still, the general thrust of the proceedings did not reflect well on those concerned. LaFlèche's role had not been exemplary; he had backed Hahn for the contract but claimed on the witness-stand that he had no idea who his partners were. Plaxton, thanks to his efforts to secure a factory for his riding, was seen to be treading dangerously close to that line of impropriety, but there was no evidence that he had crossed it. Ian Mackenzie looked even worse. On the stand he claimed to support government ownership of defence industries, and, failing that, advocated public competition for government defence contracts. But in this case he had taken neither route. He seemed out of touch with his department and totally reliant on his subordinates.[9]

Davis made one concrete recommendation: the creation of a defence purchasing board, responsible either to the prime minister or minister of finance. The present system did not work well because the

DND, while capable of deciding on military requirements, could not be relied on for its business sense or ability to negotiate the best contract with private industry. This role should be removed from the DND and placed in the proposed board – 'an expert advisory group of competent businessmen.' Davis added that this suggestion was not to reflect badly on those already doing the work, but clearly he believed that the DND and LaFlèche's interdepartmental committee could not do the job adequately.

Mackenzie King breathed a large sigh of relief when he read through the Davis report, especially as it was free of criticism of any individuals, including himself. As expected, the DND's methods, not the people in charge, bore the brunt of the criticism. The report was tabled in the House of Commons early in the new year. A few days later, in the Throne Speech, the government announced that it would be establishing a Defence Purchasing Board to oversee the letting of government defence contracts. It was hoped that the new board would prevent any future charges of patronage or corruption, and presumably prevent any possible profiteering.

Ian Mackenzie returned from a Florida holiday to face a storm of criticism in the House for his role in the whole affair. His previous statements were dug out of Hansard and repeated in light of the Royal Commission Report. Did he still deny knowing Hahn prior to the signing of the contact? Did he still deny that Hahn was working as an agent of the Canadian government in his trips to the United Kingdom? And there was no end in sight; the Bren gun contract had been referred to the Public Accounts Committee and there would be more questioning there. In the process, moreover, Prime Minister King's faith in his minister of national defence, already slipping, was shaken badly.[10]

In the offices of the Maclean Publishing Company the mood was radically different. Irwin derived great satisfaction from the important role he had played. He had not written the article but he had sniffed a good story and had the wherewithal to see that it made it into print. Perhaps most gratifying was knowing that not a single point in the article had been shown to be incorrect; every aspect had withstood the rigours of cross-examination. Drew had found himself in hot water over statements he had made during the inquiry, but the original article – the article Irwin had watched over as editor – remained unsullied.

Collectively, there was tremendous satisfaction over a job well done, especially with the government announcement of its plans to establish the Defence Purchasing Board. The board was 'the main achievement, so far, of the article,' Moore noted in a staff conference on 21 January. At the same time, there were several unsettling aspects, and a nagging sense that the company had not received its due. Publicly, the government claimed victory; it had been exonerated of corruption and graft. Ian Mackenzie had not been forced to resign, and it appeared, on the surface, that it would be business as usual. In contrast, *Maclean's* was seen in some quarters as having 'lost' because no smoking gun was found. Such a view was totally unacceptable to Hunter, Moore, and Irwin. 'At no place in the article,' Moore complained, 'and at no time subsequent to the publication of the article, was it ever suggested that there was corruption; and the hullabaloo that is being raised about "no corruption" being found is a smoke screen.'[11] *Maclean's* had not charged corruption, it had charged incompetence, and Davis had not responded to these charges; in every case involving an individual he had thrown it back to the government to decide.

The Bren gun article in *Maclean's* turned out to be only the first round in the company's assault on the government's system of defence contracting. The suspicion aroused by the article had not been removed. The company would continue attacking until the issue of incompetence was satisfactorily addressed. 'The Bren Gun matter is not ended by any means,' Moore fumed. 'It is just beginning.'

◆

'Reading the reports of the debate in the House during the past two days,' Napier Moore reported to Hunter on 9 February 1939, 'you will notice that more recent speakers are bringing out the more salient points which formed the basis of our attack on the contract. At the same time, the public still has a confused idea as to what it's all about.'[12] Indeed, the focus of attention was shifting from what was actually alleged in the article towards its general effect on public opinion.

Questions were also being raised concerning the motives of those responsible. One Liberal backbencher slammed *Maclean's* as a 'slander sheet' in its futile effort to embarrass the government and minister of national defence. 'From the moment Colonel George Drew's magazine article appeared,' he charged, 'suspicion was created in the mind of the public that graft and corruption were rampant in connection with the awarding of government contracts. Frankly I think irreparable damage has been done by that article. I am sure that if this contract were suddenly to sprout wings, some people would not admit it past the portals of heaven.'[13] The prime minister joined the debate too. On 1 March he launched an attack on 'certain' journals and journalists who had succumbed to bad influences and swayed from the path of true journalism. No names were mentioned, but in the next breath he was referring to 'that scurrilous article' in *Maclean's*. 'But when day after day the administration's point of view is misrepresented in news or editorial columns,' King warned ominously, 'the public very soon judge for themselves as to whether or not the purpose underlying it is that of fair comment, or whether there is some other objective in view.'[14]

Others spoke in a similar vein and attacked the magazine for doing a disservice to the nation. But the real venom was reserved for George Drew, not *Maclean's Magazine* or its proprietors. As Irwin and Chalmers had feared, Drew's connections with the Conservative party (he was now leader of the party in Ontario) sparked accusations that he was merely seeking publicity and serving his own political ends. During the Davis inquiry he had lost his temper and blurted out that the Bren gun contract was 'conceived in sin, born in iniquity and cloaked in fraud.' The company's critics focused on this comment, despite the efforts of Maclean company to distance itself from Drew's personal statements.

In the Maclean offices there was ambivalence over these developments. On one level there was little desire to bear the brunt of public attack and criticism, but on another there was a wish to secure for the company and magazine the recognition they deserved for their role in the affair. Hunter in particular was incensed that Drew – rather than *Maclean's* or the company – had been tagged as the prime mover in the attack on the defence department. *Maclean's* was not Drew's personal sounding board; he could not print anything he wanted in the magazine. Just the opposite: the company had approached Drew with the idea; now he was getting all the attention.

The public criticism began to have an effect on the company, forcing it to pull back and reassess its position. With attention increasingly directed at the messengers rather than the message, and with questions being raised concerning their motives, it seemed as if the original purpose of the article had been lost. What was the company trying to do? It was clear from the debate in the House that the government was not prepared to take any further action. King and the others patted themselves on the back for having instituted the inquiry, were relieved that no wrongdoing was proven, and appeared content to debate the findings and after, when the storm passed, let the whole matter drop. Should the company step in and ensure that the matter was not forgotten? And would it be worth the cost?

Some of these questions were addressed at an editorial conference held in the Maclean offices on 25 March. What were the company's objectives? Irwin believed there were three: (1) to have the Bren gun contract cancelled, or at least changed significantly, (2) to reform the method of letting defence contracts, and (3) a top-to-bottom overhaul of the Department of National Defence, including the dismissal of Ian Mackenzie. One alternative was to step up the attacks with a view to 'scaring' the government into action; the other was far more audacious. 'I think it is at least reasonable to suggest that to achieve cancellation of the contract or dismissal of the minister now,' Irwin postulated, 'we might have to bring about the defeat of the Government. That may be debatable, but I think it is at least arguable. Do we want to go to that length?'[15]

No one was willing seriously to consider such a proposal, but neither was anyone willing to back down. Hunter especially had dug in his heels and was bracing for a fight. 'The Davis Commission did not settle the matter and did not attempt to settle it,' he explained. 'They handed it over to the Government for action.' The forces against the company had put out its propaganda and had become more organized: 'We must answer that propaganda or sacrifice absolutely the whole position we have taken. I cannot see any other alternative.' No overall plan was reached at this meeting, but what had started as an attack on the government had been transformed into a campaign. Ian Mackenzie and Colonel LaFlèche were the villains; patronage and corruption their crimes.

The first skirmish in the campaign was staged in the Public Accounts Committee, which began investigating the Bren gun contract in March 1939. No new information was uncovered and for weeks it appeared that the committee would meet a few times, reach no startling conclusions, and promptly adjourn to the golf course. The state of calm was disturbed only when Colonel LaFlèche exploded and let loose a torrent of invective against Drew, his article, the magazine, and the company. The significant testimony follows:

LaFlèche: Had it not been for the hampering effect of the Bren gun inquiry, had the department not been hounded – and the department being hounded the war office is humiliated and hounded, equally because we acted very much on their advice; we followed very much their example; we did not act until they were satisfied – I am making this statement, that Canada's rearmament would be very much more advanced than it is to-day. The inquiry started last September and is still continuing eight or nine months after. The adverse effect upon the rearmament of Canada and, therefore, the weakening of our defences of Canada and of the Empire and whatever any individual holds dear in that connection, has been severe; I say rearmament has been dangerously hampered and impeded. I say further that Canadian workmen who have a right to expect employment have been robbed, denied honest employment to the extent of millions and millions of dollars by the people who started this dastardly, traitorous attack on the Department of National Defence and the war office in this respect.

Mr. MacNeil: Mr. Chairman –

An Hon. Member: Sit down.

LaFlèche: It is the absolute truth.

Mr. MacNeil: The witness is making an unusual statement.

LaFlèche: I am not. It is time that somebody did speak out in defence of the people of this country.

An Hon. Member: Hear, hear.

LaFlèche: In the defence of this country and of the war office officials who have been insulted, humiliated, by many, many people. I am saying this personally. I am not speaking for myself. I cannot. A public servant is a target for any public man who wants to attack him; but a public servant still has the right to stand up for people who have been the nation's friends, and that is what I am doing. I am defying – I am throwing that in the teeth of all the liars who have gone after the war office officials in this respect. I am not doing it in respect of myself. I cannot. It is a dastardly betrayal of Canada.

Mr. MacNeil: Mr. Chairman, the witness is a prominent civil servant appearing before a parliamentary committee.

LaFlèche: I am an old soldier and it is my duty to look after the rearmament of this county; and I am stating that my work in respect to the defence of Canada has been seriously impeded by men who have sold Canada, who have sold out Canada's defences and the defence of the Empire.[16]

'Liars'? 'dastardly, traitorous attack'? "betrayal'? 'sold out Canada's defences'? 'insults and humiliation'? Was the company responsible for such things? Hunter, Irwin, and the others exploded when they read the testimony. Drew exploded too. Angry letters were sent off to Ottawa immediately, demanding the right of the company to be heard, demanding the right to respond to these outrageous and slanderous allegations. Near the end of May, permission was granted.[17]

Moore was out of town when the invitation arrived. He had studied the proceedings of the Davis Commission the previous autumn, and would likely have accompanied Hunter to Ottawa now, but his absence meant that responsibility fell to Irwin. He immediately set to work preparing Hunter's statement, to which Floyd Chalmers added a brief historical summary of Canada's experience in munitions production in the First World War.

Irwin travelled to Ottawa with Hunter, and the two men spent the duration of their train trip huddled in conference, charting their game plan for the committee. Arriving at the Chateau Laurier, Irwin discovered that there was no room reserved for him, and rather than have him stay at another hotel, Hunter insisted he stay in his room where they could work. Irwin was a bit put off at first; he did not know Hunter well – his allegiances were always to the magazine, Hunter's were to the company, a basic difference between the two men – but agreed with the wisdom of Hunter's suggestion.

Hunter began his remarks before the Public Accounts Committee with a lengthy prepared statement which outlined the genesis of the *Maclean's* article (and Hunter made sure that it was clear that the magazine approached Drew and not vice versa). He went on to refute all the charges made by LaFlèche, reiterating what he felt to be the central point – after months of investigation not one point raised in the original article had been proven incorrect, and thus the original suspicions must still remain. How can the truth lie, betray, or sell out Canada's defences? Indeed, it was the company that had the interests of the Canadian people in mind when it published that article.[18]

At night, Hunter, Drew, and Irwin regrouped to review the day's testimony and prepare themselves for the next day's questions. Hunter found the ordeal strenuous. 'They work on three shifts down there [in Ottawa], morning, afternoon and evening,' Hunter explained, 'and every night we had a conference after eleven o'clock to discuss the evidence of the day and the plans for the following day.'[19] For Irwin the experience was exhilarating: days spent in the committee room sitting at Hunter's side, offering information and advice like legal counsel; nights spent in the Chateau Laurier planning strategy and tactics as if preparing for an elaborate chess match.

Hunter's main antagonist on the Public Accounts Committee was Gerald McGeer, a Liberal MP and former mayor of Vancouver who was first elected to the House in 1935. A lawyer by profession, McGeer set out to expose Hunter as a self-serving fraud who sought public controversy and hoped to smear the defence department. 'I am going to show you before you leave this room,' he stated, glaring across at Hunter and Irwin, 'that this article is based on a tissue of lies.' McGeer proceeded to accuse Hunter of pandering to those Canadians who did not support the government's modest rearmament program, or believed that Canada should not automatically go to Britain's aid in an emergency. These people opposed all rearmament, McGeer claimed, and *Maclean's* had helped their cause and, in turn, weakened Canada's ties to the empire. *Maclean's* was out to destroy the reputation of Major Hahn. Why had the magazine not mentioned that he was a war hero and had been decorated? Because they wanted to slander him – is that not the way it is done in magazines? Why had the magazine included such an unflattering picture of the Inglis factory – taken from the back rather than from the front – unless it wanted to spread malicious propaganda about it? Finally, he asked: 'Are you aware that substantial extracts from this article have been published with approval in the Hitler controlled press of Germany?'[20]

Hunter brushed aside McGeer's allegation, his voice never rising, but his determination bubbling over. Drew, who appeared second, did the same. (Drew began by saying that he had no prepared opening statement and then proceeded to talk non-stop for nearly two hours.) 'It is a most amazing fact,' Hunter later boasted, that after a Royal Commission, all the newspaper coverage, debate in the House, and a grilling by McGeer and his committee, the article still stood. 'We were told continually: "Before you get through with the inquiry we will show you that it is made up of a tissue of lies." But they never showed it.'[21]

Irwin and Hunter returned to Toronto, with the latter in particular ready for a fight. Hunter immediately called together a meeting of his editorial staff to discuss the company's next step. 'Some opposition has developed to aggressive policy we have been following,' he explained in an office memo. 'This was, of course to be expected. We have done a big job. We have still certain objectives definitely before us.'[22] First, a full-scale counter-attack was necessary to combat the spurious 'propaganda' spread by LaFlèche, Mackenzie, and others, suggesting that the Maclean company was full of traitors, hell-bent on damaging the DND's efforts to rearm the Canadian forces. Second, the campaign against Mackenzie and LaFlèche (not the DND – for Hunter it was becoming personal) would be continued and broadened to include all defence contracts negotiated by the government over the preceding years.

There is also a sense, unspoken but clear in the minutes, that the company was beginning to distance itself from Drew. Drew continued to make public statements (referring to Bren guns as 'killing arms,' for example) not in accord with Maclean policy and his political ties to the Conservative party inevitably brought everything he said into question. There was no desire publicly to disagree with him; it would be better just not to refer to him at all.[23]

With respect to tactics, it was agreed that *The Financial Post* was the best medium for the campaign. The weekly format was far more suitable for breaking a news story or for responding to government pronouncements and outrageous editorial comments. The time-lag at *Maclean's* was too great to make it an effective vehicle. What was also needed was one person to undertake the investigation of the defence contracts ('to devote his full time to investigation of this matter and any other matters that are relevant to it,' Hunter suggested). At one point Moore might have been chosen, but he had missed his opportunity. After the experiences in Ottawa before the Public Accounts Committee there was only one suitable choice. That person would be Arthur Irwin.

NINE

The Campaign

For the prime minister the most important event of the spring of 1939 was the royal visit. The pages of Mackenzie King's private diary from mid-May through most of June were filled with endless descriptions of royal sightseeing trips, gushing accounts of royal enthusiasms, and bursts of anger over petty humiliations and slights when things did not go quite right. Protocol was a constant headache and great concern was shown over every detail; King had earlier flown into a rage when he discovered that the flowers for a Quebec reception were to be blue rather than red – was this some kind of a Tory plot?[1]

As Mackenzie King dined at state dinners with the king and queen, and relaxed over a picnic lunch with the American president at Hyde Park, the Maclean company was busily laying the groundwork for its campaign against the DND. A small informal committee was created, with Horace Hunter in the chair and the principal players being Tyrrell, Moore, Chalmers, and Irwin.

The first step must be investigative – to gather sufficient incriminating evidence to mount a successful campaign. An immediate opportunity arose during the annual convention of the Canadian Manufacturers' Association (CMA) held at Bigwin Inn north of Toronto, at which Ian Mackenzie was scheduled to speak. It was agreed that Chalmers would be the company's official representative, while Irwin would 'keep under cover' and 'listen in.'[2]

Irwin quickly made an important contact with General A.G.L. McNaughton. McNaughton had watched recent developments in the DND with increasing alarm, and sympathized with the efforts of the Maclean company. McNaughton was especially critical of LaFlèche and Mackenzie; the former he referred to as 'that man,' the latter as 'that lazy rascal.' He slammed LaFlèche as a power-hungry bureaucrat with widespread tentacles throughout the defence establishment and among the French Canadian MPs. He suggested that his military credentials were gained through questionable means and certainly not deserved. Mackenzie was even worse in McNaughton's opinion – a stupid man who could not even grasp that he had lost control of his department. McNaughton continued with a venomous allegation that the defence minister had been removed from his unit in the First World War for cowardice. He could offer no proof for his allegation but told Irwin: 'If I were in that position I'd commit suicide.'[3] Only the removal of these two individuals would rectify the patronage problem in the DND.

Irwin and Chalmers reported their findings at two editorial conferences held in late June and early July. McNaughton's accusations served only to reinforce the general agreement that LaFlèche and Mackenzie had to go. More concretely, from his informal conversations with the general and others at the CMA convention, Irwin had picked up several leads on 'shady' government defence contracts. It was agreed that he should follow up on them. 'I was taken off the magazine,' Irwin explained later, 'given an expense account, and had no instructions other than to get rid of Mackenzie and go anywhere I wanted to in the country.'[4]

Irwin's first stop was Ottawa. 'Acting on the suggestion of a certain member of Parliament,' he visited the Sessional Papers office in the House of Commons 'to look at a file called 102 – 1939, which was a file of contracts made by the defence department and tabled in the House of Commons in response to an order for return made by Mr. Bennett on the fourteenth of February, 1938.' When he got there he discovered a second file, 'about which I knew nothing.' Together, he reported, the two files contained 'something like eight thousand pages of contracts, tenders, specifications, maps, correspondence all thrown in helter-skelter. There is no index, no order, either chronological or by subject, except that on each bundle in each subdivision there is a typewritten list which gives a clue to the contents of the bundle. An index could be made from that.'[5]

Looking through the bundles of documents scattered around him, Irwin quickly realized that he had a gold mine of information in his hands. He found dozens of defence contracts, big and small, many of them with a familiar ring. A good half dozen were 'of the same general form as the Bren gun contract with the exception that in so far as I have read (and I have not read them all) there are no limitations on profit. It is a straight cost plus ten per cent.' No limitation on profits meant that there might be no limits on inflated costs. For this reason alone these contracts warranted closer investigation.

For the next week Irwin was buried in the Sessional Papers office, his excitement building with each new discovery. 'I got in there and worked away, and it was very interesting,' he noted, 'because you had contracts over a period of years, with the names, and you could see a pattern, a web, being structured, that went all the way from Halifax to Victoria; of individuals, entrepreneurs of one kind or other, farmers and so on, who were interlocked with an idea of getting arms contracts when the war came.' This information would form the basis for all his subsequent investigations.

The campaign was beginning to take shape. Irwin found a number of solid leads in the Sessional Papers office: information on aircraft manufacturing contracts in Vancouver and Montreal, information on a mysterious company that had won a contract to manufacture practice bombs for the RCAF by undercutting the lowest tender by one cent per bomb. He also had his leads from General McNaughton, and he received more information from the others in the Toronto office. One tip, for example, was the name of an individual, a close friend of the minister of national defence, who had received several defence contracts. He was 'always involved in government dealings,' Chalmers informed. 'If dry docks happen to be the vogue of the moment, he is in the dry dock business. If dredges are being built, he is in the dredging business. Now that airplanes are the thing, he is in the airplane business.'[6]

Irwin embarked on an exhaustive fact-finding mission that zigzagged the country for the better part of eight months. In Montreal he interviewed one aircraft manufacturer to see if his company had delivered on its airplane contract. 'You've no idea of the harm you have been doing,' he told Irwin, referring to the effect of the Bren gun scandal on the business community.[7] In Ottawa he arranged an interview with R.C. Vaughan, the new chair of the Defence Purchasing Board, with hopes of uncovering new information. 'You haven't got another Bren gun up your sleeve, I hope,' Vaughan remarked.[8] In a Vancouver hotel room, he had a conversation with an MP who despised Ian Mackenzie and had more to add to the rumours about his military career. Irwin talked to dozens of others, cornering businessmen and politicians in their offices, political organizers and bagmen in hotel lobbies and dining cars, on the telephone with his old friends and contacts in Ottawa. All new leads were investigated; every source checked. It was engrossing and exhausting work.

An unexpected source was found in Ian Mackenzie's office. Early in August, Irwin was introduced to a member of Mackenzie's staff who had earlier worked for and been fired by General LaFlèche. He had access to the files on DND defence contracts and offered to act as a mole for Irwin in his investigation of the department. His reasons for doing so, at least so Irwin believed, sprang from a genuine desire to improve the DND system of defence contracting and to help initiate a clean up of the department. He came to Irwin with two conditions: his identity was to be known only to Irwin and Hunter, and the information he supplied would be used only in the 'public interest.'

Irwin dubbed his new informant 'X' and General McNaughton believed the man to be reliable (Irwin later disclosed that McNaughton was 'involved' in his original contact with X). Irwin's personal 'deep throat' added a touch of the cloak and dagger to the investigation, with the two men meeting occasionally in the Chateau Laurier, but more often on the outskirts of Ottawa, or over the telephone. X proved to be an excellent source, not for exposing major scandals or hidden secrets, but for adding crucial bits of information or a specific name that helped clarify confusing masses of data.

From X, Irwin learned firsthand of the activities of Ian Mackenzie and his office, including that the minister was seriously considering hiring a private investigator to tail Irwin as he snooped around the country! X reported that LaFlèche and Mackenzie had fallen out over the Bren gun scandal, and that Mackenzie was outraged over LaFlèche's outburst in the Public Accounts Committee. Up until that moment, Mackenzie believed that the whole affair would blow over. X also claimed that Mackenzie admitted to not having read the contract before signing it. Such allegations were not accompanied by any evidence, and, although they confirmed many suspicions, Irwin was the first to admit that nothing X said should be accepted without outside verification.[9]

By the middle of August, Irwin had a briefcase full of material on dozens of defence contracts. He had been reporting back to Toronto, returning for regular editorial conferences in the Maclean offices. At the 18 August meeting, he arrived armed with a memo listing twenty-one subjects at various stages of examination. These subjects included such items as the purchase of buildings and properties by the DND, the activities of friends of the minister who had received defence contracts, and a survey of aircraft deliveries compared to specified completion dates. Each subject was set out neatly, accompanied by lists of information in hand and what was left to be done. Some were at the preliminary stages, others were ready to be written as articles.[10]

At this meeting it was agreed that the time had come to get some of these stories in print. Irwin would continue the investigation and put the facts down on paper. Floyd Chalmers would then take Irwin's material and add some editorial comment for publication in *The Financial Post*, beginning the following week. The articles would continue each week as part of a series and would be unsigned, representing the opinion not of one person, but of the paper as a whole. Only the outbreak of war could derail things now. Should that happen, Irwin wrote, 'the basic policy would have to be reconsidered.'[11]

The first article appeared in the 26 August issue. Entitled 'Canada's Defense Crisis,' the Irwin influence was apparent in the sub-title: 'What Have We to Show for the Millions We Have Spent? – Mr. Mackenzie's Statements Versus the Real Facts.' Wasting no time, the attack was launched:

The world is in the throes of another crisis. The issue of peace and war trembles in the balance. Today no more vitally important question confronts the Canadian people than the state of the nation's defenses.

In this hour of grave peril, in which no one can forecast from day to day what the morrow may bring forth, Canadians must consider anxiously the manner in which this country is to be defended against attack.

Canadians are asking themselves if the defenses of the country are in the hands of a minister in whom they can have confidence. They are asking themselves if that minister has spent our defense millions wisely and effectively.

Irwin's survey of the aircraft industry and of all aircraft contracts revealed surprising differences between what the minister was stating publicly and what was actually the truth. Mackenzie's claims concerning the number of existing airplanes and the rate of delivery of new aircraft were far from the mark. 'It is evident,' the *Post* charged, 'that at April 1, 1939, after three full years in office, during which he was voted $26,282.444 for the Air Force, Mr. Mackenzie had succeeded in building up a first line air fleet of only 14 modern service type planes, as against his own stated "minimum" requirements for this category of

312 planes.'[12] The RCAF had only a handful of airplanes to defend the country, and the responsibility for this national tragedy fell squarely on Mackenzie's shoulders.

The attack continued the following week, with a listing of the 'unhappy truths' concerning Canada's defences. '1. Incompetence, political favouritism and dilatoriness have ruled in the expenditure of Canada's defense millions. 2. Canada this week was brought face to face with war, with the administration of our national defense under the very minister who has bungled it so badly.' The article appeared the day before war was declared. Should the *Post* back off, as some had suggested, for fear of 'advertising' Canada's weakness? The answer was no.[13]

As the country edged towards war, the *Post's* attack became more focused. No longer was the purpose of the articles merely to rid the government of patronage for its own sake, now the campaign had a clear goal: efficiency in the DND to help win the war. The British government immediately introduced significant cabinet changes; Canada should as well. Throw out the dead wood, bring in a complement of strong, new leaders. 'Let us not in a time of crisis mince our words or fail to speak plainly where plain speaking is necessary. The biggest hole in Canada's front line is the direction of the Department of National Defense. That hole should be plugged without delay.' For those who did not get the point, it was added: 'Mr. Mackenzie should at once be replaced by a stronger, more experienced, more efficient administrator.'[14]

Prime Minister King and his government had been anything but inactive. Since the outbreak of hostilities, King had been considering moving Mackenzie out of the DND, perhaps even out of the government. His faith in his minister had not been restored by the wartime crisis,[15] and on 19 September Mackenzie was moved to the Pensions and National Health portfolio and Norman Rogers was transferred to the DND from the Department of Labour. Moreover, the Defence Purchasing Board was transformed into the War Supply Board, which, like its predecessor, was responsible at first to the minister of finance.[16] As for LaFlèche, he was replaced as deputy minister and appointed Canadian military attaché to France.

With the removal of Mackenzie and LaFlèche, *The Financial Post* claimed victory. But the job was not finished. Norman Rogers, the new minister, would discover a department 'riddled with political favouritism and patronage. He will find it divided between overzealous propagandists for the former minister and men who have been thoroughly unhappy under that minister's direction. He will need all the courage and independence possible to restore unity in its work.' The *Post* would be watching to make sure he did. More changes to the cabinet were also required. What the prime minister had accomplished was little more than window-dressing, a reshuffling of the talent he already had. 'The Post stands for equality of sacrifice,' one article concluded. 'It stands, too, for efficient conduct of the war. To achieve the final victory we need to utilize every ounce of strength in the nation's material and spiritual resources. This can be had only under a strong cabinet of businesslike men.'[17]

Nevertheless, the outbreak of war forced the company, as Irwin had earlier warned, to reassess its position. On 15 September, as the prime minister was making up his mind with respect to Ian Mackenzie, the editorial leaders at the Maclean company were huddled in Horace Hunter's office. Among those present were Hunter, Tyrrell, Moore, Chalmers, and Irwin. For the most part there was general agreement to continue the campaign in the *Post*, not only against Mackenzie but also against waste and inefficiency in the DND.[18]

Hunter in particular 'felt very strongly' that Irwin continue his investigation. Hunter added that it 'was a very important piece of national service work that we could do during these very critical times. It would cost us considerable money; we would get very little, if any, increased revenue from it; in fact, we might make some enemies and it might cost us both advertising and subscription revenue. The interests of the publisher were 'secondary,' he continued in a slightly self-serving manner, 'we were not publishing this information because it would be popular or sensational, but because it would be helpful in winning the war.'[19] (Hunter need not have worried about the effect on advertising and subscription revenue. Reports had been coming in from dealers in the Toronto area that the *Post* was selling out at the newsstands regularly. Sales were rising steadily, and the 30 September issue was the best selling issue in two years.[20])

The removal of Ian Mackenzie had changed nothing, and the campaign continued, in weekly instalments, in *The Financial Post*. On 7 October the government was slammed for entering into a ten-year rental agreement for a building in Montreal. Irwin had discovered that the building was bought by a Montreal man for $62,500 only two months before he rented it to the government for a total of $237,000 over ten years. In addition, the owner negotiated a $90,000 mortgage loan on the building the day the lease was signed. Was this an example of efficiency on the government's part? On 14 October the focus switched to a West Coast land purchase near an airbase for use as an officers' mess. There was undeveloped land available near the airbase, but the DND chose instead to purchase the estate of a 'close friend' of Ian Mackenzie's. Moreover, the land in question was assessed at $49,150, but the government ended up paying $94,000 for it. Was this another example of government efficiency? 'Mr. Mackenzie,' the *Post* reminded its readers, 'has been rewarded by the Prime Minister for his blundering and inefficiency, and for Canada's war shortages and lack of preparedness, by being left in the Cabinet as the responsible minister of a department expending $57 millions a year, and where he himself draws a salary of $10,000 a year.'

Again and again the *Post* hammered away at Mackenzie and his previous activities. Irwin had uncovered numerous cases where cost-plus contracts were awarded without competition, with no ceiling on costs, and often to known friends and associates of the minister. Other examples of inefficiency were cited: contracts being awarded to companies that had no factory or plant; large payments being made to contractors without any guarantees and before deliveries of any kind were made; numerous contracts given to a single individual under the guise of several 'independent' companies.

As the campaign continued, the number of voices in opposition increased. While the Maclean company hoped to project the image of trying to aid the war effort, its critics had a clear message too – any criticism of the government during wartime was unpatriotic. Now that the war had begun, it seemed reasonable to expect that everyone would get onside, to see it through. Criticism that might have been unpleasant but at least tolerated during peacetime, was now nothing short of sabotage. In the Maclean offices there was concern. Perhaps the company was being misunderstood; perhaps the campaign was not being seen as a drive to improve government efficiency, but rather as a harping anti-government attack, a campaign that was not only vindictive but was also damaging the Canadian war effort. The latter in particular was a serious charge, and one to which the company was especially sensitive.

There were real worries among the members of the editorial committee that the force of the government would fall upon the Maclean offices. At any moment it was expected that the RCMP would burst into the offices and sweep away all the accumulated files, destroying months of Irwin's work and exposing the names of dozens of his sources. To prevent the latter, at least, office secretaries were equipped with razor blades and sent through Irwin's files, cutting away all names and other 'incriminating' evidence. In their wake was left a mass of documents dotted with little rectangular holes.

As editor of the *Post*, Floyd Chalmers received the brunt of the criticism. Early in October he reported to Hunter a recent conversation with a business friend who believed that the *Post* had gone too far. 'If one of our best friends and strongest supporters feels we are carrying on a fight after the victory has been won,' Chalmers wrote, 'then it is worth while considering whether or not we shall in the long run gain the most from resting on our laurels for a while and not giving page one display to further exposures of the period of Mackenzie's rule in the department.'[21] Mackenzie was a defeated man; did it make sense to carry on the attack? Criticism of another sort came from Walter S. Thompson, the government's chief censor. Late in October he telephoned Chalmers to express his concern over the continuing attack in the *Post*. Thompson suggested that perhaps the Maclean company was 'overlooking a large responsibility – namely that of winning the war.' The campaign had a 'snowballing' effect; at first it was doing a service to the country, but now it had begun to have negative effects.[22]

Irwin was receiving conflicting signals. His old friend, Bruce Hutchison, sent congratulations from Victoria on his 'magnificent success' – as if the campaign was finished. 'Surely you must have cleaned up the contract mess pretty well, now,' he continued. 'You caused, single-handed, a shuffle in the cabinet, a new purchasing system, and I think you have created such an atmosphere that no government will dare to be very rough in awarding future contracts.'[23] General McNaughton was equally positive and more encouraging. Irwin met the general in his office, as the latter sat anxiously awaiting a call from the prime minister concerning the command of the first Canadian Division. 'I've been convinced all along that Mr. Hunter and the rest of you were absolutely straight about this whole thing,' he told Irwin.[24]

In stark contrast, Irwin received a chilly reception from the new defence minister and his private secretary, on 8 November. Rogers repeatedly accused *The Financial Post* of not checking with the DND to get its side of the story. Thus, although the *Post* was printing the facts, it was presenting them in such a one-sided way as to create 'distrust' in the public's mind. Rogers's secretary interjected that not one word of praise for the Canadian fighting services could be found in the *Post;* indeed, there was nothing but 'a blast every week which was nothing more nor less than a direct act of sabotage.'[25]

Irwin was deeply concerned over the impact of the campaign, and increasingly concerned over its direction. He had earlier warned that inevitably it would lead to a call for a change in the government. No longer could they focus on Mackenzie without appearing to be carrying on a personal vendetta against a broken man, which, in the present circumstances, would not be well received by the public. If they wanted to carry on the campaign the focus must shift to the government as a whole. If the government was too weak, then some ministers must be replaced. If Mackenzie King was not the one to lead the country during war, then he must be replaced. And, if that too failed, then the whole government must be replaced. He was not at all sure that he wanted to go that far.

But if Irwin had begun to have some doubts, Hunter and Colonel Maclean had none. The colonel had played only a small role in the campaign up to this point. He rarely, if ever, attended the editorial conferences, and of course wrote none of the articles. But he was following developments very closely, and, late in November, he intervened decisively for a continuation of the campaign. 'There may be some feeling that we are carrying on a vindictive campaign against Ian Mackenzie,' he wrote Hunter. 'Such impression may be sincere. Much may be due to counter-propaganda from political sources and party-heelers; from the little fellows expecting pickings all the way up to big profiteers and looters. These may be quite numerous. They will fight viciously, but they are cowards. They greatly fear exposure to public opinion.' Then he added:

We must keep persistently, and without fear, exposing malefactors with facts and without persecution. Let the public pursue and put the fear of God into the higherups.
We must never cease to bring out the responsibility for all the dishonesty, inefficiency and unprogressiveness, of the man at the top, the P.M. in this case.

There were those who wished the company to 'soft-pedal; to let up.' To do so would be to destroy the public's confidence and trust in the company. 'Finally,' the colonel concluded:

we must keep in mind that our great work is to promote clean, honest principles and policies based thereon. Mackenzie, or whoever may be the figure at the time, is merely an important example of the bad principles and policies which have prevailed, are prevailing and will continue to prevail so long as we have a Prime Minister and a little inner circle of supporters – but happily not all even in his Cabinet – may continue to ignore public opinion and the people's interests, and make threats and attempt punishment to those who have the courage to express public opinion.[26]

For Colonel Maclean and Horace Hunter, it was no longer a campaign to arouse public opinion against waste and inefficiency, nor was it simply a vengeful personal attack on Ian Mackenzie, the former minister; it was an attack on the government's ability to lead the country in war. There was a growing sense that King was not the person who should be in charge. He had not demonstrated leadership in a time of crisis; his inactivity of the prewar years was unchanged. The campaign would continue, regardless of Irwin's growing concerns.

Tactics, however, were another matter. The atmosphere had changed because of the war (in December the first division of Canadian troops arrived in the United Kingdom), and to offset any future charges of disloyalty and negativism it might be best to inform Norman Rogers and his department before future attacks – to get the DND's side of things. Another avenue of approach might be through the House of Commons. A new session was scheduled to begin early in the new year, and perhaps Irwin or Chalmers could approach a few friendly opposition MP's in advance to discover their plans for the session or feed them information and questions to be raised in the House. Here was a way to shake the government out of its lethargy. Such tactics had worked in 1938, and they might again, in 1940.

By the end of the year, Irwin's defence-investigation check-list contained more than fifty subjects, including such diverse items as contracts for bacon, tent pegs, gas mask canisters, and army boots; plumbing, electrical, and building contracts; real estate deals for army hospitals, officers' quarters, and rifle ranges. Fifteen of his subjects had appeared in article form in *The Financial Post*. Many of his leads would result in dead ends, he realized this, and his prewar material was quickly losing its value. War cases would be the focus now.

◆

At the same time George Drew continued his personal campaign against Mackenzie King in the Ontario legislature. As opposition leader there was little concrete action for Drew to take, but he found an ally in his provincial rival Mitch Hepburn, the round-faced and feisty Ontario Liberal premier, who had been at loggerheads with Mackenzie King since the election of 1935 and had clashed since then on several political and personal issues. Hepburn was a harsh critic of King, and, in January 1940, his government, with the support of Drew's Conservatives, passed a resolution of censure condemning the federal government's war effort.[27] When Mackenzie King learned of the Hepburn-Drew resolution he huddled with a few senior ministers to determine an immediate response. On 25 January he called a snap election.

The election call again forced a rethinking of Maclean policy on its campaign against the government. The immediate problem was what to do with the material on hand – print the stories or withhold them until after the election? At an editorial conference held on 29 January, opinion was almost unanimous to continue publishing the material, election or not. 'Our motives, in publishing this material,' Hunter stated, 'should be stated very clearly. The material was not being published to damage a political party or to help a rival.' The lone voice in opposition was that of Victor Tyrrell, who feared that the company would be 'accused of playing politics.' Rather than go forward with the material, Tyrrell urged that publication cease until after the election. Meanwhile, Irwin should continue his investigative work, with plans for a renewed campaign in April.

Tyrrell was overruled by Chalmers and Moore. If publishing the material opened the company to charges of partisanship, surely withholding it until after the election would do likewise 'Why didn't you tell us about this before we voted?' the people would cry, according to Moore. 'By lying low,' he continued, 'we would be simply helping the very men whom we had been criticizing to be elected. Either we believed we were right or we didn't so believe. If we were right in the beginning we were still right and we should act on that premise.'[28] The 'logical conclusion' was to continue publication.

Either way, of course, the company would be playing politics, this was clear. All the rhetoric proclaiming high ideals, journalistic integrity, and public duty took on a rather sanctimonious air. Although officially neutral, the Maclean company opposed Mackenzie King's continued leadership and supported the reorganization of the government under a new leader, with new faces brought in from the business community or the Conservative party. The names of possible replacements for King were few: J.L. Ralston, the minister of finance, was regularly mentioned, and, in the Maclean offices, Justice Minister Ernest Lapointe was the favourite over the winter of 1939–40.

At the root of it, Hunter was furious with King for his lackluster war effort, and he fully supported the reasoning behind the Hepburn-Drew motion of censure. 'King was a nationalist with a leaning towards the United States,' Hunter exclaimed. 'He no doubt was banking on the belief that the country as a whole didn't really want too great participation in the war.' Hunter continued with two 'soundest criticisms' against King: first, his failure 'to provide real leadership,' and second, his 'failure to get the co-operation from other important political forces in the country.' Hunter argued that 'many Liberals were dissatisfied with King['s] leadership.' The best thing to do was to continue full blast with the campaign and urge a reorganization of the government – perhaps under Lapointe – after the election. These views were published in the next issue of the *Post*.[29]

True to its word, the *Post* followed the next week with more Irwin material on a Kingston construction company that, as of May 1939, had barely $10,000 in capital but had received at least seventeen government contracts worth well over $1 million. Questions were raised over the tendering procedures in a number of these contracts, and connections were found between the company executives and local Liberal associations and the DND. Another case involved a Trenton, Ontario, bridge company – with capital of only $603 – receiving large government contracts. Again links to the Liberal party were uncovered and revealed. A later article linked Norman Rogers's secretary – the man who had cornered Irwin outside the minister's office in Ottawa – to a company receiving government defence contracts. The method of attack was vintage Irwin. Here are the 'facts' according to the *Post*. No charges were made, only lingering unanswered questions: Can the government please explain? Is this the proper way for a competent government to act?

Ian Mackenzie was still an easy target. He had remained relatively out of view since his removal from the DND in September 1939, but the election campaign brought him back into the political arena and back within the sights of the *Post*.[30] In its 24 February issue, the *Post* devoted considerable space to permit Mackenzie to state his case. But the view of the *Post* was clear in the article's subtitle: 'Two Hour Defense of His Record Still Leaves Every Charge Made by The Financial Post and Maclean's Magazine Unrefuted.' In a kind of journalistic kangaroo court, each of the contracts was given a heading, followed by three sections: The Charge, Mr Mackenzie's Defense, Comment. All the segments ended with a variation of 'The Charge Stands Unchallenged.'

In its last issue before the election, the *Post* reviewed its case against the government and listed the various contracts that it had examined over the previous eight months. 'Numerous examples of political favouritism' had been exposed. 'It has revealed unbusinesslike methods, extravagance, delay and almost incredible bungling with vital matters of national defense.' There had been no satisfactory response from the government; parliament had not met since the declaration of war and the Canadian people had not been offered any explanation.

With only a few days to go in the election campaign, Irwin's investigation check-list contained almost sixty subjects that either should be dropped or required further investigation. It appeared that there were months of work ahead. The company had resolved to continue the campaign after the election, to expose new patronage and unbusinesslike practices, to reveal those responsible, and to actively support the replacement of the prime minister (presuming he won the election, of course) if the need arose.[31] Yet, the campaign was almost over. On 26 March Mackenzie King won a resounding victory at the polls, winning his largest majority ever (181 of 245 seats), while the Conservatives wallowed near the brink of extinction. The voters of Vancouver Centre had not heeded the advice of *The Financial Post* and had re-elected Ian Mackenzie. King's personal position as prime minister, moreover, was more secure than ever. Regardless of the wishes of the Maclean company and its publications, King would be prime minister and he could choose his cabinet as he saw fit.

The campaign also was showing signs of running out of steam. Irwin was finding it harder to unearth new 'unbusinesslike' contracts – thanks in part to the impact of the campaign – and it made little sense to rehash the old ones. How many times could the *Post* call for the ouster of Ian Mackenzie before it became boring? Especially after his re-election, a continued attack on Mackenzie would appear as little more than a vindictive witch-hunt. The question would be asked: was the attack in aid of the war effort or merely the settling of a personal grudge? The longer the campaign lasted, the more likely *Post* readers would believe the latter. And the announcement early in April of the establishment of the Department of Munitions and Supply effectively cleaned the slate by shifting the focus of defence contracting to C.D. Howe and his new department. Hunter, Irwin, Tyrrell, and the others had no quarrel with Howe, and the Maclean company could welcome the new department, pat itself on the back for playing a small role in its creation, and find an honourable way out of its campaign.

Finally, and perhaps most importantly, was the effect of the changing war situation. Within two weeks of the election, the 'Phoney War' ended in a sudden, dramatic moment, as Nazi troops thrust into Denmark and Norway. Within two months, France fell and the very survival of Great Britain appeared threatened. In the atmosphere of crisis in the spring of 1940, a campaign against unbusinesslike practices in the DND quickly became insignificant.

'We can't wait to worry over an extra ten thousand dollars; we've got to get ships to protect the St. Lawrence,' Irwin wrote. 'Putting [it] in its simplest form, we have been insisting that the primary consideration in placing defence contracts is efficient purchasing, conservation of the public money. Whether we say it or not, the implication is that other considerations are secondary. But conditions may arise and will arise in which military as opposed to economic considerations must be dominant. Price is not a factor when you need a machine gun to save your life.'[32] The charge of disloyalty and sabotage had always stung in the Maclean offices, but the campaign was continued because the cause was clear. In May and June 1940, however, that cause was anything but clear. Almost without discussion or debate, the campaign ended. It was time to get on with the war.

What had been accomplished? Irwin's investigative work had been responsible for some twenty-six feature articles in the *Post* and several others in *Maclean's*, and had sparked widespread editorial comment not only in Maclean publications but also in newspapers from one end of the country to the other. By the end of March 1940, a total of thirty-one defence contracts – worth over $11 million – had been examined in the *Post*. He had earned the praise of friends and colleagues for his months of tireless and exhaustive research. Unintentionally, he also had proved himself in the eyes of Hunter and the colonel as a man of initiative and resourcefulness. They would not forget.

On one level, the Maclean company was very successful: the Bren gun contract was amended and the article provoked the government into launching the Davis Royal Commission which, in turn, sparked the creation of the Defence Purchasing Board. The placing of defence contracting in the hands of this civilian agency was perceived as a tremendous victory for the company. Without doubt it was the greatest single achievement of the whole affair.

The campaign against Mackenzie and LaFlèche was less successful. Both men were removed from the centre of things, but neither was held publicly accountable for his deeds. Mackenzie, for one, was removed by King because he could not handle the job, not because *The Financial Post* demanded his resignation. But Irwin's investigation and the *Post* articles did help to expose his incompetence. In the end, however, the element of vindictiveness that ran throughout the campaign probably soured whatever sense of achievement there might have been for Irwin and the others.

Finally, the campaign against King and his government failed completely. The attack on King's leadership arose from a deeply rooted belief that the prime minister was less committed to the war effort than he should have been. Irwin had never fully supported the attack on King – it was essentially a personal one on behalf of Horace Hunter and Colonel Maclean – there was no real desire on his part to topple the government, or even to change governing parties, given the alternatives in the opposition. And, indeed, the implications of such an attack were never fully thought out. It was a campaign driven more by exasperation with the leader than by political design. What was revealed in the attempt, however, were the very real limits to the power of the Maclean company and all its publications.

The final act was played in January 1941 when the government announced that the original Bren gun contract had been replaced by two new ones (one covering capital expenditures for plant and equipment, the other for production of machine-guns). Under the terms of the new agreement, the Inglis factory would be run by the government, which would also own and operate all the necessary equipment. The present management of the company would be maintained to supervise the work and payment would no longer be on a cost-plus basis, but, rather, on a piece-rate basis, a small fee for each completed article. 'In other words,' the *Ottawa Journal* announced, 'this is not a case of extension of an old contract, or of revision or amendment of an old contract; it is a new deal entirely.'[33]

That the new contracts were retroactive to the signing of the original contract in 1938 was taken as an acknowledgment of victory in the Maclean offices. Horace Hunter felt vindicated. 'The general consensus of opinion,' he wrote Colonel Maclean, was 'that the important thing to leave in the minds of people was that we had attacked the contract itself and the way in which it was left. It had now been cancelled and to that extent we had won a complete victory.' Hunter then added humbly 'we felt we should state our case clearly and distinctly but not boastfully.'[34]

Less attention was paid to the fact that the contract had been revised because the experiment manufacturing Bren guns was a tremendous success. Throughout the months of controversy, work had continued in the Inglis factory, and by March 1940 finished Bren guns were rolling off the line. The government wanted to expand production and branch into the manufacture of other weapons; the cost was too high for the Inglis company, so the government intervened, renegotiated the contracts, and financed the expansion. The new expanded factory went on to produce more than 186,000 Bren guns by the end of the war.[35]

The signing of the new contracts officially signaled the end of the Bren gun 'scandal.' There was satisfaction on all sides, and all the participants claimed victory. After more than two years of controversy and debate, one reporter for the *Winnipeg Free Press* noted dryly, the original contract had 'been blotted out as if it had been written in water.'[36]

PART THREE

1940–1950

TEN

The War Years

On 8 September 1939, Irwin pulled from his wallet a small, faded white card with a pale green silhouette of the Parliament Buildings, which gave him temporary status as a member of the Parliamentary Press Gallery. Showing it to the guard standing on duty he passed into the House of Commons.[1] The atmosphere in the gallery was subdued and tense. Every seat was occupied and all eyes were on the floor of the House where the prime minister was speaking. War had broken out a few days earlier and everyone in the House that day knew what Canada was to do. All that was left were the formalities.

When Prime Minister King finished, J.S. Woodsworth, now an elderly white-haired man, rose to speak. As Irwin looked down from the hushed gallery he did not see the man who had been his father's friend and colleague from Wesley College, or the man with whom he had dealings over the past fifteen years. Rather, he saw a solitary figure, a single man standing bravely alone against the country, against the tide of history. Like the others in the gallery, Irwin sat in silence as Woodsworth explained his reasons for being unable to support Canadian participation in the war.

Irwin was much impressed by Woodsworth – by his courage and integrity and the strength of his commitment, maintained in the face of overwhelming opposition. But on the crucial question of the day – war or neutrality – Irwin and Woodsworth were on opposing sides. In the 1930s Irwin had toyed with the possibility of Canadian neutrality in a European war, but by 1939 these thoughts had vanished. It was not an easy decision; all the horrors of the first war rushed through his mind. Could we ask another generation of Canadians to sacrifice themselves because the British and the French could not handle their affairs properly? Surely some good had come out of the last war, or were we doomed to repeat the mistakes of the past?

But the rise of Hitler and the months of back-pedalling and appeasing of the dictators erased any question from his mind. By that September afternoon there were no longer any doubts. Like his friend E.J. Pratt, he agreed

> Appeasement is in its grave; it sleeps well.
> The mace had spiked the parchment seals
> And pulverized the hedging *ifs* and *wherefores,*
> The wheezy adverbs, the gutted modifiers.[2]

For most of the first year of the war, Irwin was detached from *Maclean's* to conduct his investigation into the government's defence contracts. It had been interesting work, work that he was suited for and found satisfying. But when the nations of Europe toppled like a row of dominoes in the spring of 1940 he was not unhappy that the campaign came to an end. As an offshoot of his work on the Bren gun investigation, Irwin knew the weakness of Canadian defences and how little the country had prepared for war. That was fine during the Phoney War but in the spring of 1940 Canada found itself in a rather precarious position.

Irwin's concern for the international situation found an outlet in the CIIA, where he chaired the Toronto branch and served on the national research and administrative bodies during the years before the war. It was a time of great anxiety, and the deteriorating European situation dominated the study groups in 1940. Before the war, several members – disillusioned by their own war experiences and with the antics of their European allies – felt strongly that Canada should maintain its neutrality at all costs. Others recognized, and emphasized, Canada's North American outlook, a view not to be confused with pro-Americanism. Irwin was not unsympathetic to such thinking. His anti-colonialism was evident; his distaste for 'Englishness' in his personal life and his politics was clear. But Irwin did not look at his country only in the negative light – what it was *not*; he had come to see Canada as an independent nation, a North American nation.

The fall of France and the wave of fear that followed forced a fundamental re-evaluation of Canada's defence. If Britain fell to the

Nazis – and many expected it to – then would the British government escape to Canada and establish a government in exile? Would Canada carry on the fight alone? Would Canada be next? And, would the Americans stand by and allow it to happen? These and other pressing questions brought the various branches of the CIIA together for study. Overnight the potential had arisen of North America becoming the front line of defence, and it was questionable whether the Canadian government had taken the necessary precautions to defend Canada.

During the last week of June and the first two weeks of July, the Toronto group met a half-dozen times to discuss the situation, and work began on a short memo on what should be done. The general consensus was that immediate action was necessary to clarify Canada's defence relations with the United States. The 'Toronto Memorandum' as it came to be called, reflected these concerns. 'All plans for Home Defence must be worked out in close collaboration with the United States,' one paragraph began. 'We cannot completely defend our own frontiers; and therefore, in addition to doing whatever is possible within Canada, we must explore the methods of joint defence. These relate both to the production of supplies and to co-operative military action.' But time was of the essence. 'In order to safe-guard our territorial sovereignty, it seems desirable to take the initiative without delay in regard to military co-operation. Staff talks should lead to a more or less formal pact for mutual assistance.'[3]

Other CIIA branches, in Ottawa, Montreal, and Winnipeg, were working in the same direction. 'I hear your Branch of the Institute is studying very seditious stuff,' Brooke Claxton, Irwin's ex-army friend and newly elected Liberal MP from Montreal, wrote from his office in the House of Commons. 'If you have an outline I wish you would send it to me as I got our Branch Executive stirred up along the same line.'

Claxton was helping to organize an informal meeting of concerned individuals in Ottawa, thinking 'it would be a good thing to get a group together from different parts of Canada to talk along this line.'[4] As one of the principal players in the Toronto group, Claxton hoped Irwin could make it to Ottawa to participate. 'I enclose a note and a draft agenda,' Claxton wrote four days later. 'Your presence is really essential.'[5]

Irwin did not make the trip. Shortly before he was scheduled to leave, he was diagnosed with cystitis, an inflammation of the bladder, and he and Jean left Toronto for a short holiday for rest and recuperation. Consequently Irwin was not present at the Ottawa meeting. In his place, W.T.G. Hackett and R.G. 'Nik' Cavell represented the Toronto group, and they carried with them the Toronto Memorandum.

The meetings were held in the Chateau Laurier, and, although the participants were all members of the CIIA, this Ottawa group acted as individuals, not as official representatives of the CIIA. In addition to Claxton, Hackett, and Cavell, the Ottawa meeting included seventeen others; a broad mixture of individuals from academic, business, and government circles. E.J. Tarr, an influential businessman from Winnipeg, was a prime mover in the group, as was the academic and poet, F.R. Scott. Two members of parliament were in attendance: Claxton and Paul Martin, a young Liberal first elected in 1935. Also present were J.R. Baldwin, who had already moved to his government position, R.B. Bryce of the Department of Finance, and J.W. Pickersgill, who had left a teaching position to enter the public service in 1937.

Irwin hated to miss the meeting, and he waited anxiously for any word of developments. Had their work been in vain? 'With due modesty,' Hackett reported, 'the Toronto Group can claim to have made, through [its] Memorandum, a very real contribution to the Ottawa meeting.' Hackett went on to explain. 'The Memorandum tended to focus and give point to discussions that were already in danger of becoming diffuse. It is very doubtful, in the opinion of the writer, whether the Ottawa discussions would have reached the point that they did, in the absence of the Toronto Memorandum, or some similar statement. It was particularly interesting to note how subsequent discussion made use of the basic concepts evolved in the Toronto Group meetings. Indeed the entire first session developed into a point by point discussion of the "Toronto Memorandum."'[6]

Hackett's letter undoubtedly contained a degree of hyperbole; he was, after all, a member of the Toronto group, and he was writing for an uncritical reader. Nevertheless, there was a good deal of truth in what he wrote. The final document, entitled 'A Programme of Immediate Action,' ran to more than a dozen pages and contained several of the ideas put forward by the Toronto members. It began with an overview of the grave situation Canadians found themselves in. 'Above all we are confronted with a startling new possibility: war on our own shores. This we have never seriously contemplated, and for it our defence strategy is woefully unprepared.' The new situation brought into question Canada's relations with the United States; up until this time those relations had been friendly but often taken for granted. Canada would have to cooperate with the United States on a program of continental defence, but – and this was the classic Canadian problem – it was essential that Canadian independence be maintained. 'Unless Canada faces the implications of this new continental plan she risks losing her national identity. Geography makes Canada an integral part of any North American defence system. Co-operation with Washington is going to be either voluntary on Canada's part, or else compulsory; in any event it is inevitable.'[7]

The original version, agreed to in the Chateau Laurier, was further distributed and discussed among a select group, before being sent on to Mackenzie King and his trusted adviser, O.D. Skelton, by Brooke Claxton. The ideas expressed in the paper were neither wholly new nor unique to the participants; others in and outside the government held similar views. Even the prime minister had been prompted into action on continental defence. 'It may be interesting to you to see that a number of other Canadians had independently arrived at the same position,' Claxton explained as he sent Mackenzie King a copy of the paper.[8] At almost precisely the same time, King travelled to Ogdensburg, New York, to discuss mutual defence problems with President Roosevelt. The result of their talks was the 18 August Ogdensburg Declaration which established the Permanent Joint Board on Defence (PJBD) 'for the consideration of the defence of the north half of the western hemisphere.' It was a turning point in Canadian-American relations.

It is difficult to assess the impact – if any – that the Chateau paper had on Mackenzie King or Skelton, or on the conduct of Canadian external relations. Despite the assertion by the former secretary to the Canadian Section of the PJBD, Hugh Keenleyside, in his memoirs that the paper was 'one of the most important documents produced in Canada during the war,'[9] chances are good that the Ogdensburg Declaration would have been born without it or the intervention of a small group of intellectuals and influential Canadians. At best, it perhaps gave King added encouragement at a crucial moment in time. As King wrote in reply to Claxton: 'As you have assumed, I was naturally not less pleased than interested in discovering the similarity of the views expressed with some entertained by myself and to which, fortunately, very practical expression has been given within the past few weeks.'[10]

It really did not matter. Irwin was relieved when he learned of King's and Roosevelt's actions, and he supported the thrust of the declaration while at the same time recognizing its potential future dangers (especially with the use of the word 'permanent'). He also was satisfied with the role he had played in helping to draft the Toronto Memorandum. But he never seriously believed that it influenced the prime minister in any specific way.

It was a very dark time in Canadian history, in any event. For a brief period Canadians were confronted – for the first time in more than a century – with the possibility of foreign invasion. The moment passed, of course. Britain did not fall and the eventualities envisioned in the summer of 1940 never came to pass. Life went on, and Irwin turned his attention to his personal war effort, directed from the offices of *Maclean's Magazine*.

◆

The war became the focal point for most mass-circulation magazines in North America, particularly after the fall of France in Canada, and after the Japanese attack on Pearl Harbor in the United States. South of the border *Life, Collier's,* the *Saturday Evening Post,* and a host of others, including the more literary magazines such as *Harper's* and *The Atlantic Monthly,* all turned their sights to the war and America's participation in it.

In Canada, one of *Maclean's* oldest competitors, *The Canadian Magazine,* went out of business in April 1939, but other Canadian magazines like *Saturday Night* took up the cause. *Saturday Night* differed from *Maclean's* in that it was more news-oriented and contained a business section, a literary segment entitled 'The Bookshelf,' and carried no fiction.[11] But like *Maclean's,* in the early 1940s it was filled with features on the war: profiles of generals and politicians, human interest stories with a military angle, you-are-there photo sections, and a host of articles looking ahead to the future (*Saturday Night* also had both a 'London Letter' and 'Washington Letter' section at various times during the war).

Saturday Night was also less overtly 'Canadian' than *Maclean's*. Between November 1944 and January 1945, for instance, *Saturday Night* featured Americans Eleanor Roosevelt, Edward Stettinius, Harold Ickes, Henry Wallace, James Byrnes, and Harry Truman on different covers, a descent into continentalism that Irwin would never have permitted. More important, *Maclean's* could not compete with the immediacy of the war coverage in the daily newspapers or even the weekly *Saturday Night,* and Irwin responded by seeking out better writers to supply war articles and by initiating special theme issues that covered specific topics in greater depth. The theme issues became the single most important development at *Maclean's* during the war.

As Maria Tippett writes in her book *Making Culture,* 'cultural producers' in wartime Canada sought 'to unify the nation through giving its people an understanding of Canada's role in the war,' and all of them 'operated on the assumption that the cultural producer ... was deeply involved in the business of teaching its members exactly what values the war was being fought to preserve.'[12] Irwin had always believed that his function at *Maclean's* was more than just to provide an entertaining magazine; he believed the magazine had a role to play in the national life of the country: to inform readers of national and international developments, to help mould opinion, and to provide a forum for debate – as well as to entertain. During the war his task appeared even clearer. At his editorial desk he felt part of a national war effort, and under his direction, the prime goal of *Maclean's* became to explain, interpret, and boost the Canadian war effort.

Irwin had for years been moving the content of *Maclean's* towards a more news-oriented and contemporary feel, and during the war fiction pieces were reduced and long serials became rare. In his mind the stuff of real life was far more alluring than fiction; moreover, reader surveys showed that non-fiction feature articles were more popular with *Maclean's* readers.[13] Still, short stories by Thomas Raddall and Morley Callaghan were not uncommon, and it was during the war that W.O. Mitchell made his first appearance in *Maclean's* with 'You Gotta Teeter.' This first piece was followed by several more 'Jake and the Kid' stories before the end of the war.

Beginning in January 1940 *Maclean's* introduced a multi-part series on 'Canada's Fighting Forces.' Written by various authors, the series dealt with a variety of topics on Canada's war effort, from coastal defence, to Canadians in the air, to the role of French Canada. In 1941 John Coulter, a Belfast-born writer and broadcaster, launched a series of articles on Winston Churchill. Thelma Le Cocq became a regular contributor with articles like 'Air Women' and numerous profiles on prominent Canadians such as Mitch Hepburn and John Grierson, the first film commissioner of the National Film Board and recent appointee to the Wartime Information Board.

The war articles themselves were essentially prewar style in military dress: the personal portraits, the human angle – informative and often up-beat – to bolster the reader in the common struggle. Wallace Reyburn, a former assistant editor of *Chatelaine* and correspondent for the Montreal *Standard,* who accompanied the Canadian troops ashore during the disastrous Dieppe Raid, wrote of his experiences in 'What We Learned at Dieppe.' George Drew added his own views in a piece entitled 'Beat Hitler at his Own Game.' Gordon Sinclair related a personal look at the war from the viewpoint of a member of a bomber crew with 'I Was the Wireless Operator.' C.E. Ross wrote a gripping three-part article on the fall of Hong Kong to Japanese invaders in 'Escape From Hong Kong,' while Morris Shumiatcher explained the ways of a foreign people to Canadian readers with 'Japan's Cult of Death.' Regular contributors played their part as well. Beverly Baxter's column, for instance, concentrated on British military and political topics and consistently ranked as the most-read column in the magazine.[14]

Other articles turned up the uglier side of Canadian life in wartime. Irwin approached two British Columbia MPs to respond to the question. 'Should We Send the Japs Back?' On the no side was Angus MacInnis of the CCF, who lamented: 'The taint of the superior race doctrine is not confined to Germany or to the Nazis; we find it on this continent. We find traces of it even in Canada.' On the yes side was Conservative MP Howard Green (later minister of external affairs in the Diefenbaker government), who played on the fears of a Japanese invasion of British Columbia. 'For nearly half a century,' Green began, 'those Canadians who face the Pacific – the people of British Columbia – have lived under a threat of eventual Japanese domination. They do not propose to do so any longer.'[15] The fact that the people in question were Canadian citizens did not seem to phase Green.[16]

The role of Canadian women was changing – at the front and in the factories – and *Maclean's* responded with articles on women's participation in the war effort. But as one historian has pointed out, most general magazines, including *Maclean's,* were written by middle-aged and middle-class men for middle-class readers, and rather than leading public opinion, they 'reflected the economic and social reality of the day, and by doing so reinforced and helped justify the status quo.'[17] Nowhere was this more clear than in the portrayal of women in mass magazines during the war. Irwin had very traditional views concerning the role of women in society, and articles in *Maclean's* did little to challenge those views. The focus of the wartime articles on women, for example, were more often concerned with the potential loss of femininity. In an article entitled 'They're still feminine!' Lotta Dempsey asked, 'What happens to Ma's old flair for making apple pies, when Ma gets busy building bombers?' Such questions were the subject of great debate, she added, and 'everybody has an opinion as to the lasting effect of khaki, Air Force and Navy blue, or well-worn denim and slacks on the softer side of Womanhood.' Not to worry, the article concluded: 'Clothes don't make the man and uniforms and overalls don't seem to be unmaking the female of the species.'[18]

Irwin had more success with his special theme issues. In the 15 May 1942 issue, for example, the focus was Canada's wartime industrial output. Articles examined the various aspects of defence production and the workings of the mammoth Department of Munitions and Supply, while other features, such as 'We Are the Workers,' looked at the daily lives of some Toronto munitions workers. A more ambitious theme issue examined the role of Canada in the development of international air travel. A new way of looking at the world was essential, and, to emphasize the point, Irwin commissioned a map of the world centred on Winnipeg, showing the reader how flight paths of the future would not follow the trade routes of the past. Accompanying the map was 'Canada: Main Street of the Air,' by geography professor Trevor Lloyd. 'Most maps cut off the northern 1,000 miles of the world and we never miss them,' Lloyd wrote, adding: 'We know that the world is round, yet almost every one of us pictures it as a rectangle.' Other articles included Grant Dexter's 'Whose Air?' and Leslie Roberts' 'Assets for an Air Age,' which painted a glowing portrait of Canada's aviation potential. 'Canada is sitting on the crossroads of world aviation,' Roberts proclaimed, and after the war 'Canada will become the hub for spokes reaching out from America to China, India, Russia and to almost everywhere in the world.'[19]

Irwin began planning for special theme issues months in advance; ideas were discussed and proposed articles matched with authors. The special navy issue is a good example. Scheduled for 15 March 1942, Irwin was hard at work on it the previous autumn. 'Suggest that basis of treatment be Navy in Action rather than the training or Making of a Navy,' Irwin wrote Moore in a long memo. 'Navy is the one service which is already in action in face of enemy on big scale. Why not make the central theme just that: Navy in Action in Face of Enemy?' What Irwin had in mind was 'selective rather than comprehensive detail,' in both story and photo, telling the story 'in a series of highlight flashes rather than by a multiplication of detail or the use of process sequences.' General themes were followed by questions: 'How is the

Navy Administered?' 'How Does the Navy Fight?' 'How is the Navy Equipped?' In addition, the human touch was essential. No issue was complete without character sketches of important naval people and descriptions of life on board a naval vessel. What was it like to be in battle on the open seas?[20]

From the original skeleton idea, articles were fleshed out in detail and assigned to specific authors and correspondents in Canada and abroad. Beverly Baxter, for example, was already interviewing key British naval authorities; he could shed some light on the limits of modern sea power. Irwin asked Grant Dexter to provide the character sketches of Angus Macdonald, the minister of national defence for naval services, and Vice-Admiral Percy Nelles, the chief of the naval staff.[21] Other articles in the navy issue included: Charles Rawlings's feature 'Fighting Ships,' which took the reader on board a RCN destroyer during a two-day battle with a German U-boat wolfpack; a short piece by Thomas Raddall entitled 'Navy Base'; Kenneth Wilson's 'This Is the Navy,' which answered many of those questions posed by Irwin the previous November; and a twelve-page photograph section on the RCN in action.

On the domestic front, a new series entitled 'Cross Country' began in 1942. Cross Country was essentially a review of important events in the nine provinces provided by regional correspondents. Irwin had suggested such a column – as a way of broadening the scope of *Maclean's* as a national magazine – years before. Another new feature fell under the category of 'You interest' articles; a variety of short pieces on personal topics. Titles included such things as 'How Long Will You Live?' 'The Weather – and You,' 'Are You Happy?' and 'Your Glands – and You.'

On the political side, Irwin and Bruce Hutchison devised a novel interview-article arrangement, in which the subject had no control over the questions asked and *Maclean's* waived any right to edit the replies. The first such interview was with M.J. Coldwell, the leader of the Cooperative Commonwealth Federation (CCF) ('What Does the CCF Stand For?' 1 September 1943). The immediate reaction was mixed (some readers complained that *Maclean's* should not act as a 'CCF propaganda organ'),[22] but the interview series continued for several years.

Bruce Hutchison also continued as one of *Maclean's* most frequent contributors with several war-related articles and others on Canadian-American relations. His coverage of American topics also included a series on the 1940 American election campaign. His relationship with

Maclean's and Irwin was not always clear sailing, however. On one occasion he complained – tongue in cheek – to his friend:

You are a perfectionist and hence doomed to constant and invariable disappointment; but beware how the cynicism of your evil life poisons and withers the tender blooms of young genius. I am no longer young and never was a genius. But if I were either your general attitude towards copy would have persuaded me to go in for plumbing or garbage collecting long ago. I have written despite you and a host of others like you and always been regarded by all such with contempt. This I have borne with a patient shrug, for sufferance is the badge of all our tribe. And the final irony will occur if one of us ever writes a good book and all the editors of Canada will burst forth and say: 'Why, of course, I trained him. I bought his first story.' In your case, I suppose, it will be true, which rather weakens my argument. Nevertheless, I warn you, in dealing with authors more tender than I am, that they can be shriveled at a word and probably are already if they've been talking to you.[23]

Occasional differences of opinion between author and editor did not damage their friendship. Early in the war, during Hutchison's cross-country tour researching his book on Canada (published in 1942 as *The Unknown Country*), Irwin took him on a sightseeing tour of the Niagara Peninsula, lumbering around the dusty highways of Niagara in Irwin's second-hand Studebaker. Irwin turned up in the book as the 'Man from Toronto' who 'said we must drive this time by the new highways. He was a kindly man, but with a hard tongue, logical brain, and a face of native flint, and he wanted to show me that the old turnpikes of Ontario had been made as broad and smooth as the superhighways of the United States. I saw that they were, but it didn't interest me.'[24]

◆

In August 1941 Irwin collapsed in the bathroom of his room in the Lord Elgin Hotel in Ottawa, suffering a duodenal haemorrhage that nearly cost him his life. After he left the hospital he took a month's convalescence at home, until his health had improved sufficiently to return to work. Even when his strength returned there would be changes; his diet, for instance, would have to be altered to suit his stomach.

Irwin never seriously considered leaving *Maclean's* at this time.[25]

Whatever the risks he still considered it the best job in the country and was not likely to throw it over without some direct evidence that it was damaging his health. He talked the situation over with Moore, who, according to Irwin's memo, suggested that 'if there was risk [of recurrence] I ought to go to Hunter, tell him that I couldn't carry on (with this particular job) and ask him what he had to offer.'[26] Irwin refused the advice and decided to stay on. It was a decision he never regretted.

The death of Victor Tyrrell in May 1942 left a vacancy in what was effectively the number three position in the company. A trio of contenders emerged in the ensuing scramble for the job: Napier Moore, a member of the board of directors since 1935 and with more than fifteen years experience as *Maclean's* editor. Tommy Howse, the company treasurer; and Floyd Chalmers, manager and editor of *The Financial Post*. In his memoirs Chalmers suggests that he was not an obvious choice for the position, but this assertion was false modesty at best. Chalmers had cultivated a close relationship with Colonel Maclean and was ambitious for the top spot in the Maclean hierarchy (even to the point where he acknowledged that Hunter suspected that the colonel would try to give Chalmers his position as president).[27]

Chalmers had far more talent and business sense than Moore (that was clear to Irwin at the time, and most likely to others as well), and his strong showing during the Bren gun investigation left no doubt that he was the coming person in the company hierarchy. In any event, in the company shake up that followed Tyrrell's death, Chalmers was appointed to the newly created position of executive vice-president. Two other vice presidents were appointed: Howse was given responsibility for finance, and B.G. Newton, who worked on the industrial papers, was handed the responsibility for the printing plant. Both were firmly under Chalmer's authority.

The shake up at the top inevitably affected Irwin and *Maclean's*. Moore must have known that he would rise no farther and that his advance to the top was effectively blocked by Chalmers. Indeed, his presence created something of a problem. Although well liked by the colonel and Hunter, Moore was unhappy with being passed over for the job.[28] Moreover, it had become apparent that Irwin was effectively running *Maclean's;* Moore's frequent absences had not gone unnoticed, and Irwin's brilliant display during the investigation of the defence contracts had left a favourable impression on Hunter and Chalmers. Chalmers appreciated Irwin's abilities, and his close association with Hunter, particularly during their three days of sharing a room in the

Chateau Laurier during Hunter's appearance before the Public Accounts Committee, solidified his position.

Soon after moving into Tyrrell's office, Chalmers instituted a reorganization within the Maclean company, part of which included the creation of a new position for Moore, that of editorial director. There was some justification for the new post: the Maclean company had expanded considerably since the late 1930s and a need for someone to act as a kind of liaison between the several magazine editors and Chalmers had developed. (Tyrrell used to handle this job himself, which bogged him down in the mundane daily running of the company.) Moore's new job was described by Hunter as 'a chairman of a company board of editors,' adding that the editorial director 'will provide a medium for bringing the various editors into closer contact with one another. It should add to the efficiency of each editor. It should strengthen our service to the public of Canada.'[29] Yet, the new post was created specifically for Moore as a way of gradually removing him from the editor's chair at *Maclean's*. As Chalmers wrote in his memoirs: 'I moved Napier [Moore] out of the picture by promoting him to editorial director. Besides, word had filtered through to me that the real power behind the success of *Maclean's* was the associate editor, Arthur Irwin. While Napier was an engaging front man, Irwin had all the best ideas and put the magazine together. Napier's promotion enabled me to make Irwin editor of *Maclean's*.'[30]

For the time being at least, Moore was to remain as titular editor of *Maclean's*, but his new responsibilities as editorial director meant that he would be able to devote even less time to the magazine. Irwin was given a new title – managing editor – and with it came control over production (supervision of art work and layout design, choice of covers, and so on) and editorial material in the magazine (accepting and rejecting articles, issue contents, without reference to the editor), budgeting, and supervising the staff (promotions, hiring, and firing, except for senior people). And, most important, at least for Irwin, the managing editor 'will be responsible for maintaining contacts with writers, agencies and artists; the assigning of writers to the writing of feature articles, consulting with the Editor when necessary; and for the expeditious handling of unsolicited material submitted to the magazine.'[31] 'I feel that there will be benefit all around in this reallocation of responsibilities,' Chalmers wrote in congratulations, 'and that it will provide you with increased opportunity for the exercise of your unchallenged genius in magazine editorial work.'[32]

The promotion to managing editor was a great plum, although in most ways it merely recognized officially what already existed – after all, he *had* been running things for some time. But with the new position came control over two key aspects which he did not have previously: budgeting and hiring. He had long advocated the recruitment of a solid staff, and the way to do that was to increase the budget and get more money to hire the best people. Not surprisingly, he never received as much money he thought necessary, but by the end of 1943 the monthly budget had risen to $11,850 and by mid-1944 had increased to $12,625.[33]

Working within the restrictions of a limited budget meant that Irwin could not hire indiscriminately. A few new faces could be added as sales and revenue increased, and as existing staff left the magazine they could be replaced by hand-picked Irwinites. He scoured local newspapers and national periodicals, looking for young writers with talent, and he took into consideration the need of the magazine to represent all of Canada's regions. It is what he had longed to do; it was still a plan that would take years to fully implement.

There had been a few staff changes that predated Irwin's promotion. Norval Bonisteel, for example, who had joined the staff in 1935, had been promoted assistant editor. One of the earliest wartime appointments was Jerry Anglin, a young, loquacious newspaperman who had received his early training at the Toronto *Star*. Responding to a job ad for an assistant editor on 'a national magazine' *(Maclean's* was not specifically mentioned), he was brought into the Maclean offices and interviewed by both Moore and Irwin.

Anglin found Moore to be 'genial and flamboyant,' a man who could be affable, entertain you with anecdotes and jokes, and inspire you to greater things. But afterwards, you would walk away muttering: 'He was terrific ... what did he say?' Irwin was exactly the opposite: a 'dry, stick of a man,' who had things to say about the country and its relations with the United States and Great Britain, and interesting insights into international affairs. Irwin asked a lot of questions, seeming 'a little more like a professor' with his analytical mind, and an obvious nationalist who was 'interested in what made the country tick.'[34]

Anglin left the *Maclean's* staff in 1942 to join the Air Force, but before resigning he came to know Irwin quite well. He lived in Toronto's Annex area, just north of Bloor Street, and Irwin often dropped him off on his way home. Following Tyrrell's death, Irwin would stop on Bloor, outside the Park Plaza Hotel, for upwards of fifteen minutes (there was considerably less traffic in 1942) to give Anglin a play-by-play description of the power struggle between Moore and Chalmers. Anglin remembered Irwin openly pulling for Chalmers, because he saw in him someone who had vision and ability, who, once in power, would hire the right people and not interfere. Chalmers also had 'big ideas' for the Maclean company, and Irwin rightly believed that the desire to expand the company would translate into more money for *Maclean's*.[35]

Once he had received his promotion to managing editor, Irwin needed someone to fill his old job, and he hired Harry C. Clarke from the *Star Weekly* as the new associate editor. Despite Clarke's talent and experience, Irwin soon regretted his decision, finding Clarke too 'timid' – unwilling to take a stand on a particular issue – and therefore lacking in those qualities Irwin felt necessary for the job. Clarke left *Maclean's* in December 1944. Another disappointment was Geoffrey Hewelcke, born in Russia to a British diplomat. Hewelcke emigrated to Canada in 1921 and worked on a variety of newspapers before being hired on at *Maclean's* as an assistant editor. He left soon after the end of the war.[36]

Clearly Irwin's most enduring wartime appointment was Blair Fraser. Fraser was born in Sydney, Nova Scotia, in 1909 and, after attending Acadia University, worked on several Montreal dailies, including finally the *Gazette*, as political correspondent and feature writer. He was a tall, thin man, with a large head and greying hair. By friends like Irwin, Fraser was remembered as warm and humorous, although prone to long, gloomy fits of depression. Fraser was liberal, but not radical in his political beliefs; he had been a staunch supporter of the Republican cause in Spain in the 1930s, and had worked to unionize Montreal's anglophone press.[37] Like Irwin he cherished individual liberty, usually sympathized with society's underdog, but did not challenge the basic fabric or institutions of Canadian life.

Irwin was well aware of the Conservative leanings of the *Gazette* (and assumed that at some point Fraser would leave), but his first attempt to lure him to *Maclean's* failed. Irwin bided his time, and, when rumours circulated that Fraser was unhappy at the paper, he renewed his offer. This time Fraser accepted, and in November 1943 he was given the post of *Maclean's* Ottawa correspondent.[38] It was arranged that Fraser would take over the regular Backstage at Ottawa column and also write a number of feature articles each year. His first article as Ottawa editor – an examination of the aluminum industry entitled 'Victory in Aluminum' – appeared in the 1 February 1944 issue. Very quickly Fraser developed into one of the most effective and popular *Maclean's* correspondents, and his extensive contacts in Ottawa made his backstage column essential reading for anyone interested in Canadian politics.

Of all those he appointed at *Maclean's* Irwin probably became closest to Blair Fraser, and over the years Irwin came to admire his ability and trust his judgment on important matters. The two men would exchange ideas frequently and discuss potential features; it was not uncommon for Irwin to get an idea, write it out as a memo to himself, and then, at the bottom of the page, add: 'Discuss with Blair Fraser.' Fraser, meanwhile, wrote a steady stream of reports of his Ottawa dealings which reveal the incredible extent of his inside information and still make fascinating reading for any historian of the period. A glimpse of the kind of feature articles Fraser wrote in the early years can be seen in an Irwin memo, written late in 1944, outlining Fraser's subject roster. The list included eighteen subjects, several already completed and crossed out:

1. xxxxxxxxxxxxxxxx
2. xxxxxxxxxxxxxxxx
3. xxxxxxxxxxxxxxxx
4. Recheck on Population.
5. Constitution Story. (Possible)
6. Crisis in the Maritimes. (If necessary, to be pushed off till later.)
7. xxxxxxxxxxxxxxxx
8. HOW DOES AN M.P. LIVE?.
9. Prostitution Racket. (Is it dead or not?)
10. How the M.P. Handles His Job. (For April, 1945).
11. Atherton Article. (Call Dana Doten)
12. Newfoundland.
13. Eldorado Mine Story. (Watch it.) U235
14. Graydon. His ideas on Education. Query him again. [crossed out but still legible]
15. Immigration.
16. xxxxxxxxxxxxxx
17. xxxxxxxxxxxxxx
18. French Canadians in New England. [handwritten at bottom of page][39]

In Irwin's mind, the other great need was for correspondents to cover the war itself, especially after the invasion of Sicily in 1943 and with the invasion of France anticipated. *Maclean's* had no official war correspondent and was forced to rely on what it could dig up from a variety of sources. Beginning in June 1943, Irwin tried to formalize the situation by making arrangements with specific correspondents to contribute exclusive reports for *Maclean's*.

One of his first targets was Matthew Halton, a CBC radio correspondent assigned overseas as a field reporter. Irwin and Halton met over lunch and agreed that Halton would contribute one story a month for six months (at $150 per story) once the Canadians went into action, and that during this time he would contribute to no other Canadian publication. Correspondents were in such demand – Halton had already agreed to write for the Chicago *Sun* – that Irwin felt this proviso necessary. Two days later Halton telephoned to inform Irwin that he had been offered $150 a week by the *Star Weekly* for war stories and that he could not honour the exclusive aspect of his agreement. Irwin backed away from his firm commitment as well, but said that Halton could still submit manuscripts to *Maclean's* which would be used if suitable.[40]

Irwin made similar arrangements with and accepted contributions from a number of other journalists, including Ross Munro of Canadian Press, Lionel Shapiro of the Montreal *Gazette*, Wallace Reyburn of the Montreal *Standard,* Peter Stursberg of the CBC, and Ralph Allen of the *Globe and Mail.* All these individuals were, of course, employees of other news organizations, and asking them to contribute to *Maclean's* raised the issue of conflict of interest.

'I have just received a letter from you,' Reyburn wrote Irwin from London, 'which unfortunately I have thrown away during a large-scale clean-up of my desk. But I have the essence of it in mind. There will be no harm in my suggesting feature articles for you from the field. My people will leave it to my discretion that I don't do for you something that they would particularly like to have. The Standard and Macleans dont really clash ... each calls for a different type of writing and treatment.'

Reyburn added: 'I feel bound to mention that there is criticism from certain quarters here about the fact that Macleans are getting war correspondents of the dailies and weeklies to write articles for them in the field. The argument is that the papers have maintained the men over here at considerable expense and then Macleans get the benefits of really "live" articles from the field without having had to outlay any expense in those long months of "training stories" and spadework that the correspondents have put in prior to the big show.' Then he added: 'I pass on the news of this criticism of Macleans (a) because I know you will be interested in hearing about it and (b) because I tend to share the opinion of those who feel that Macleans are in that way getting their coverage of the big show on the cheap.'[41]

Reyburn was perfectly right; *Maclean's* was getting its coverage 'on the cheap.' Irwin wanted an exclusive *Maclean's* war correspondent and was busily trying to get one (working both to find the right person and to get budget approval), but until such time he was willing to use this method despite the criticism. There certainly was nothing illegal about what he was doing; *Maclean's* paid for everything it used, and was usually supplied material that was unsuited to other kinds of publications. Reyburn, incidentally, continued to supply *Maclean's* with material; his proposed solution to the problem was to raise the amount *Maclean's* paid for a story from $150 to $200.[42]

To make coverage of the war even more difficult, when the invasion of Sicily began, the number of correspondents actually accompanying the Canadian troops was pared down to a bare minimum. The work of these reporters was then 'pooled' and distributed among the various news organizations. Such an arrangement ensured that, in the early going at least, *Maclean's* would not obtain exclusive material. Irwin made the best of a bad situation and cabled instructions through Canadian Military Headquarters in London to 'get in touch with any two of Ross Munro, Ralph Allen, Shapiro, and Reyburn [*sic*] and ask them to cable a 1,000 words each on what they consider to be the most dramatic highlight of the first week of the invasion of Sicily.'[43]

Despite these difficulties, *Maclean's* had considerable coverage of the Canadian forces as they fought their way across Sicily and throughout the Italian campaign. One 1943 memo on the invasion coverage gives some idea of the kinds of material *Maclean's* wanted:

Ralph Allen
 1. Supply and transport, ground, air, sea. How is an invasion organized and sustained
 2. Evacuation of wounded. Land, air, sea.

Matt Halton
 1. Personal adventure stories of fighting men, army, air and navy.
 2. Interviews with and personality sketches of key figures.

3. Stories based on his own personal experiences and observation ... how he broadcasts from the front.

Ross Munro
1. Action story on air borne troops.

Wallace Reyburn
1. A general story on the lessons of the initial attack [crossed out]
2. Tanks
3. Tank destroyers
4. Engineer bridge builders.[44]

Things were put on more formal footing with the appointment of Lionel Shapiro as *Maclean's* official European correspondent early in 1944. (Shapiro was never actually on the *Maclean's* staff; he always worked on a contract basis.) 'With a roving commission,' Moore wrote, explaining Shapiro's new position, 'he will go wherever the news is hottest; expects to be with our troops wherever their main blow is struck.'[45] Shapiro was a native Montrealer and a graduate of McGill who began his career in journalism at the sports desk of the Montreal *Gazette*. In the thirties he served as correspondent for a variety of newspapers, and after the war broke out he travelled to Europe and began his career as a war correspondent. Already a frequent contributor to *Maclean's*. Shapiro's first story as European correspondent appeared in the 1 February 1944 issue, under the title 'Armageddon's Zero Hour.' The epitome of the roving war correspondent, Shapiro followed the movement of Allied troops from North Africa to Sicily and northward up the Italian peninsula. In 1944, his focus shifted to the Normandy invasion and the sweep across Europe, and he was one of the first Allied journalists to arrive in Berlin.

Beginning in March 1944, *Maclean's* published an overseas edition – a smaller sized reproduction of the original issue, minus the advertisements, which was distributed (by the Department of National Defence) to Canadian service personnel in Europe free of charge.[46] Publication of the overseas edition continued for several months after the end of the war, and it was distributed to the Canadian troops stationed in Germany.

While his main focus was the war, Irwin had one eye on the future; the roving war correspondents would one day come home and some of them might make good writers for *Maclean's*. He began drawing up lists of potential staff members. John Clare, a former staffer with the Toronto *Telegram* who had become a war correspondent following a stretch with the RCAF, showed a good deal of promise. And there was Ralph Allen, a sports writer turned war correspondent, whose career Irwin had followed for some time. Allen would be no easy catch: one 1945 Irwin list included Allen's name at the very top, under 'Hard to Get.'[47]

Throughout the Italian and Normandy campaigns, Irwin sat behind his desk in the Maclean offices, directing efforts as best he could: arranging stories and assigning articles, writing memos to himself, talking long into the night on how best to organize the magazine's war coverage, meeting with correspondents on leave or reassigned back to Canada. The one thing he craved most was to be at the front to see for himself. But he was needed at home, and his stomach forbade such adventures. How could he expect the armed services to provide him with a special diet? But Chalmers had crossed over in 1940, and Moore made the trip two years later. Irwin hoped that he would get his chance.

ELEVEN

The 'Real Meaning' of Destruction

The Allied invasion of Europe in the summer of 1944 gave a glimmer of hope that the war might soon be over. Optimism returned, and the upswing in mood was reflected in the pages of *Maclean's*. What would have been impossible in 1940–1 – articles envisaging the postwar period – were put into production. At long last, it had become possible to speculate on the kind of world that would rise from the ashes of war.

Only a few weeks before the Normandy landing, Irwin turned forty-six. Outwardly he revealed the signs of age: the spread of wrinkles across his forehead, a receding hairline and thinning hair, the fleshy protrusion of a double chin. His dark horn-rimmed glasses were a regular feature now, and, combined with his rounding face, gave him rather owlish features. He had experienced a number of serious medical problems, and he fretted over his health to the point of hypochondria (which explained his penchant for having medical friends, one daughter remembered). But at the same time he remained remarkably fit. The pick-up shinny games of his childhood had given way to figure skating in his thirties and, although he may have lost a step or two, he retained his love for 'skating a ten-step with a good looking woman who can really skate,' as he wrote in 1945. A few years earlier he discovered the joys of skiing and it became an Irwin family ritual on winter weekends to head for the ski trails north of Toronto.

Irwin suffered from stomach troubles on and off for most of his life; his ulcer was only the most serious manifestation of a recurring problem. He gave up smoking and from being a light drinker became almost a teetotaler. He still loved certain foods: 'Lake Winnipeg goldeye; speckled trout pan-cooked the morning they're caught,' for example; but his diet had changed, and the food on the Irwin dinner table became rather ordinary if not actually bland.

'I like thick wing steak, medium rare;' he wrote in 1945, 'a chilled Northern spy apple in December; roast duck Chinese style stuffed with water chestnuts and garnished with green pea pods; Danish blue cheese; chilled celery and crisp lettuce (which I can't eat because my stomach doesn't like them).' Then he added: 'I don't like brussels sprouts and English cooking, English cooking and brussels sprouts.'[1]

At home, Irwin's children could feel the great stress under which he worked. They could sense that he was preoccupied, knew of his troubles with Moore, and heard him ranting over the social climbers around him at work. During the bad times he would come home, pale and tired, and flop on the couch for a half-hour or so and sleep. His son Neal recalled doing his best to remain quiet, and at times this meant sitting right next to the radio with an ear pinned against the speaker to hear 'The Lone Ranger,' 'Buck Rogers,' or one of the other popular radio shows. Most nights Irwin retired early, usually with a stack of articles or a new book tucked under his arm. He gave his children as much time as he could, but traditional attitudes and the demands of his job ensured that the burdens of housework and child-rearing fell to Jean. A warm and loving mother, Jean also was in charge of family discipline. Arthur was not a strict disciplinarian, rarely did he lose his temper. He was gentle, and remembered by his children as an excellent teacher.

Jean and Arthur did not have a large circle of friends, each continued to cultivate his or her own friends; Jean in the neighbourhood and in groups like the Home and School Association, Arthur at work or the CIIA. Jean also liked to write fiction, and joined with friends in a small writing group. Arthur was less than encouraging – and uncompromising in his estimation of his wife's writing skills – and his subsequent refusal to publish any of her stories in *Maclean's* was something of a sore point in their marriage.

When asked at the end of the war by the publicity department for things he liked, he wrote: 'making intelligible patterns out of a mess of data; playing the piano (very badly and not for public consumption); reading – or writing (almost never) – sentences that go off inside your head like a Roman candle; coming home to Canada up the St. Lawrence valley; the view from the citadel at Quebec; a soft voice in a woman; the feel of the earth gone fluid under your feet on a fast ski-run; ... talking with people who have something to say; the sight and smell of Vancouver harbour; the whippoorwill's call in the silent dusk; trying to make the obvious significant ...' As for his dislikes, he was decidedly blunt: 'I don't like afternoon teas; V2's; flying the Atlantic in a bomber; radio announcers whose voices drip with phoney unction; writers who don't do their homework; small talk – because I can't manage it, of course; false fronts in buildings or people.'[2]

His other interests were broad and consistent over many years. Irwin began saving his papers, and files for these years give an indication of his concerns. One file of clippings (significantly labelled 'fundamental issues'), for example, contains an assortment of clippings on a variety of topics collected from the early 1940s. His interests tended in the direction of the 'larger questions,' matters of war and peace and the defence of western civilization, and decidedly towards international issues rather than social ones. He was not insensitive to social problems, but few clippings dealt specifically with urban poverty, health care, or racism, and rather focused more on people (especially intellectuals) and ideas. Articles with titles such as 'The Eternal Concept of Peace,' 'What is Liberalism?' and 'What Chance for Free Enterprise After the War?' were common.

In the summers Irwin still loved to get out of the city and into the woods. Canoeing had always been a passion; 'paddling around a point I've never paddled around before' was still a thrill. Most years the family would rent a cottage for a month and Arthur drove up on weekends and for his vacation. In 1943, through the generosity of Jean's father, the Irwins acquired a cottage of their own on Belmont Lake, not far from Havelock, Ontario.[3]

For relaxation, Irwin tended to his garden or worked at the cottage (he even claimed to enjoy 'painting frame boathouses and chopping wood'). He was never a big 'joiner,' and was a bit of an enthusiast in his hobbies. He would pick up on something new – like kite flying – and throw himself into it intensively for a short period. His love for a good book did not fade with time, and his reading interests were wide. 'Occasionally I go on a whodunit binge,' he confessed. 'Other times I'll go for quality fiction, philosophy, science or Dagwood Bumstead.' Otherwise, there always was the family piano and plenty of music to listen to (his tastes ran to fairly conventional classical music).

Jean's asthma was always a concern, and as the years passed her ability to participate in family activities decreased. First to go were the long canoe trips with Arthur; by the beginning of the war she also gave up skiing. 'I don't know whether it was the air conditioning or just what, and I don't expect I ever will know,' Jean wrote from Ottawa after a long train trip, 'but something gave me an awful attack of coughing. It was like asthma. I felt suffocated and after that stopped my head filled up and I couldn't breathe. When I got off the train I recovered. Peculiar wasn't it?'[4]

◆

The mid-summer heat in the Maclean offices on University Avenue could be oppressive. There was no air conditioning in the building and barely a breeze blew through any of the few windows. It was standard for the staff to wear suits to work; once in the building, however, jackets were discarded, buttons loosened, and sleeves rolled up – anything to get some relief from the heat. Late in July 1944, Irwin was at his desk as usual. The news from Europe was encouraging; great Allied advances were being made, despite determined German resistance. Irwin paused, his fingers running along the edge of a letter. It was from his friend Nik Cavell, now the chair of the CIIA's national executive, asking him if he would consider being a CIIA delegate to the upcoming British Commonwealth Relations Conference to be held in London.[5] Irwin took the letter to Moore, who sent it on to Chalmers. Both men agreed that it was the chance of a lifetime (and exactly what Irwin had been hoping for months). The Maclean company agreed to pay his expenses, and, as Chalmers minuted, Irwin should 'arrange to be there long enough to make other contacts as well.'[6]

The British Commonwealth Relations Conference was scheduled to open in February 1945, in Chatham House, London, the home of the Royal Institute of International Affairs. The conference was the third in a series, the first having been held in Toronto in 1933 and the second in Australia in 1938. Members from all commonwealth nations with institutes of international affairs were invited and in 1945 this included the UK, Canada, Australia, New Zealand, South Africa, and India. Burma, Southern Rhodesia, and Newfoundland sent observers. The delegations were completely independent and unofficial; there were no government representatives included, thereby allowing a greater latitude and openness in discussion. It also meant that the conference had no direct power to influence governments; the best it could hope for was to sway public opinion.[7]

The proposed agenda was wide open. Here was an opportunity for influential persons from the various commonwealth nations to gather freely and discuss the future role of the commonwealth in the postwar world. Would the commonwealth remain as a major player on the world scene? Could it act as a suitable vehicle for international change and progress? Would it exist at all? And, how would it adapt in the new world – a world clamouring for democracy and bathed in the rhetoric of anticolonialism. No one dreamed that one conference would provide solutions to such intractable problems, but a start could be made.

The Canadian delegation sailed for Scotland on 26 January 1945. At the head of the delegation was Edgar Tarr, long-time CIIA member and president of the Monarch Life Insurance Company in Winnipeg. Among the other members of the delegation were: Roland Michener, a Toronto lawyer who would go on to become an MP and in 1967 governor general; F.A. Brewin, also a lawyer with a strong interest in civil liberties, who in 1962 was elected as a New Democratic Party (NDP) member to the House of Commons; B.K. Sandwell, the editor of *Saturday Night*; Queen's history professor R.G. Trotter; and Victor Sifton, publisher of the *Winnipeg Free Press*. It was a strong team with men of different backgrounds and varying experience, but all intelligent and able.

The voyage overseas was typical of wartime Atlantic crossings. The quarters were cramped (the twelve man delegation shared two cabins, six bunks in each), although the delegation members still had more comfortable surroundings than the approximately 7000 soldiers on board. The food was regular if unspectacular; Irwin wrote home that when he could find no milk he made do with cheese. In between the two daily meals he nibbled on biscuits. Nights were especially dark, thanks to security precautions, and Irwin bordered on seasickness for most of the voyage. Only one submarine scare occurred, erupting in an instant, followed by minutes of black confusion, as crew and passengers scurried on deck with their life-preservers. But, as in 1917, Irwin did not experience an actual submarine attack.

Home for the next two weeks was the Goring Hotel, not far from Buckingham Palace and an easy walk to Chatham House. By wartime standards it was comfortable – the rooms were heated and had private baths and running water. Irwin had his first experience with wartime rationing in Britain, and although he had no difficulty with his meals, he did have to scramble for a special ration ticket to obtain some milk.

The conference was held behind closed doors in the seclusion of the high-ceilinged Chatham House library, where the commonwealth delegates could talk undisturbed, with only the occasional V2 rocket rattling the windows.[8] There was also much socializing, of course, with lunches, dinners, receptions, and cocktail parties. At times it seemed that the main sessions were there only to provide the delegates with something to do between meals and parties. For Irwin, the most memorable evening of the conference was a dinner for the Canadian delegates at the Dorchester Hotel given by Vincent Massey, Canada's high commissioner in London. Also invited were two British newspaper editors and five members of the British cabinet. During the long evening of food, drink, and good company, all the participants made brief speeches.

Irwin was sitting directly across from Clement Attlee, the deputy prime minister who would soon be prime minister of the postwar Labour government. Remaining in his seat, and speaking directly to Attlee, Irwin launched into a discussion of one of his favorite themes: how Canada invented the commonwealth. 'When my turn came to speak,' Irwin later wrote,

I cut loose with the pitch that the Commonwealth had come into being as a result of Canadian initiatives arising out of the Canadian determination to become independent while at the same time retaining some kind of formal link with its root in Britain. I mentioned the various steps along the way, starting with the struggle for Responsible Government and ending with the Statute of Westminster and the concept of the divisible crown, finally winding up with the assertion that the new structure which had replaced the old Empire would not reach complete fulfillment until it had been extended to include the non-white peoples of the old Empire.[9]

When the conference ended in the first week of March Irwin embarked on the second stage of his trip: to make contacts in Britain and to get over to the front. He contacted Beverly Baxter, who took him on a tour of his London constituency to give him some idea of the effects of German bombing. Irwin was appalled by the devastation: whole city blocks blown to bits; other streets apparently untouched on the surface but little more than false fronts guarding buildings that were no longer there. But he was buoyed by the spirit of the people he met, men and women sweeping off the dust and getting on with things.

Irwin was fortunate to be accredited as a war correspondent on a temporary basis and was thus able to travel in uniform to the front as part of the Canadian forces. He crossed the Channel, thanks to an RAF pilot, and travelled first to Paris and then by jeep across Belgium and Holland, finally meeting up with the Canadian forces across the German border.

He spent several days with the 1st Canadian Army, meeting and talking with as many people as possible, soaking up the atmosphere, considering what the future would hold. He also contacted other Canadian war correspondents and *Maclean's* employees – present and future. He visited Jerry Anglin, who was overseas with the RCAF, and discussed his return to *Maclean's* once the war had ended. As Anglin explained, Irwin was overseas busily 'lining up staff.'[10] The one man he wanted most to meet was Ralph Allen – he wanted to offer him a postwar job – but he failed to find him. Irwin returned to England and after a few days wait, secured a seat in a Lancaster bomber bound for Canada.

Irwin contributed one article for *Maclean's* on his European trip. Going overseas in 1945 rather than in 1944 gave him a different perspective on the war. Rather than daring tales of heroism and adventure, he concentrated on the effects of destruction on the people and the cities of Europe, on the enormous task of reconstruction that lay ahead. 'Two months in Britain and on the fringe of liberated Europe,' he began, 'have convinced this reporter that the peace is going to be as hard to win as the war, if not harder.' Europe may have been liberated, but it was far from free. At first glance Paris seemed to have come through the fighting relatively unscathed, but scratch the surface, look beneath the brave faces, and one learned a different story: 'the simple brutal fact is that in the eighth month of liberation Paris has not enough to eat, to wear, to burn, or to operate its factories.'

Yet, to see the 'real meaning' of destruction, one had to go to Germany. He described Cologne, once 'a city about the size of Toronto. Now it looks as if a jagged-edged scythe had swept across the city, slicing off the tops of all its buildings so that their contents ran out as honey runs out of sliced honeycomb. All that's left is that gaunt and empty comb, mile after mile of it, with the cathedral still standing miraculously at its centre.' Still there was hope; he saw it in many faces in Britain, France, Holland, and Belgium. He felt it when he attended a soccer match in London's east end – an area that suffered some of the most devastating bombing raids. The home team – West Ham – was pressing the opposition and almost scored, save for the heroics of the visiting team's goalie, who managed at the last moment to deflect the ball. 'Then, like a drumfire of hail on taut canvas, sounds West Ham's salute to an opponent's prowess. No perfunctory handclaps these but whacking strong gorblimy handclaps, which start from the heart. Somehow or other I can't help but feel that the gentlemen from West Ham will be a stabilizing factor in the European scene.'[11]

Only a few weeks after his return to Toronto, the war in Europe ended. Word of the German surrender spread quickly through the Maclean offices and the celebrations began. Planning for an end-of-the-war issue was already underway, but now the green light was given and final preparations were initiated. Irwin picked Franklin Arbuckle to do the cover art, and E.J. Pratt was commissioned to write a poem commemorating the event. Both had finished their tasks before the fighting ceased.

The cover of the 15 June issue of *Maclean's* showed a single soldier – tired and expressionless – entering an open door with his rucksack slung over one shoulder, returning to his home ('only to find his wife living with another man,' Arbuckle later mused).[12] The simplicity of the moment – of the lonely soldier returning after six years of war – seemed more appropriate for the occasion than the bustle of victory celebrations or the gigantic mass demobilization of the Canadian forces. Pratt's poem, 'They Are Returning,' heralded the achievements of the Canadians overseas and what they looked forward to on their return.

> No dole or bread line must await
>   those hands
> That once clawed at the Ortona sands
> Or held that five-day bridgehead at
>   the Schelds...
>
> They shall come back to build in lofty
>   rhyme,
> Out of Laurentian rock and Norman lime,
> Memorial towers Canadian
> Across a continental span;
> To mix a mortar that shall never crumble
> Before the blasts of war or wear of time.

◆

In an unexpected moment, during one of the many cocktail parties during the London conference, Irwin heard a rumour of a top-secret research program launched by the American government. His source knew less than he did, and only introduced the subject hoping only to draw Irwin out.[13] Irwin could not oblige his British colleague – because he had few details to divulge – but like a good editor, he tucked the information into a dark corner of his mind where it would rest until a new lead jolted it back into his consciousness.

A few weeks later, after a conversation with a senior official in the Ontario Hydro-Electric Power Commission, Irwin wrote Moore of the 'large scale developments for the production of an explosive based on the manipulation of the atom about which there has been so much speculation recently is actually underway in both United States and Canada.' Irwin's source informed him that 'the material was still relatively unstable and that they had been having difficulties with it.'[14] Irwin had long been interested in physics, both as an intelligent amateur and as an editor looking for new stories, and he had some knowledge of the potential of atomic energy. But, like most Canadians, he was unprepared for the scope of the destruction of the atomic bomb.

It was a warm sunny August afternoon, the height of summer in southern Ontario, as Irwin drove home to Toronto from the cottage on Belmont Lake. What a strange place to hear news of such terrible devastation: the gently rolling hills of rich Ontario farmland, quiet and still in the August sun, stretching out to the horizon, a soft cool breeze slipping through the open car window, caressing his face. Forgotten music from the radio, lost in the moment and submerged in the grinding of engine and wheel; all broken suddenly by a news bulletin announcing the destruction of an unknown Japanese city on the other side of the world.

Irwin later remembered that moment, as he drove, listening to the bulletin:

I passed a shirt-sleeved farmer plowing the field adjacent to the road with a team of horses. Following the plowman was a bare-footed, bare-headed ten-year-old boy, I can still see him in a faded blue shirt and short pants, and I sensed the contented pleasure with which he buried his toes in the cool, fresh earth of the furrow as he followed his father. The contrast between the idyllic pastoral scene and the news from the air, struck me like a blow. I can remember thinking to myself: That's the past, the world will never be the same again.[15]

Irwin returned to the office with plans for a theme issue on the significance of atomic energy whirling in his head. He started in his usual way; he read everything he could find on the development of the atomic bomb, on nuclear physics, on the geopolitical implications of nuclear war, and on Canada's small but significant role. One of his first acquisitions was the famous Smyth Report, the study of atomic weapons prepared for the U.S. War Department by the respected Princeton professor, H.D. Smyth. Irwin devoured its contents and for weeks after stopped staff members in the hall, asking: 'What do you think of this Smyth Report?'[16] He also contacted Bruce Bliven, editor and publisher of *The New Republic* and widely published author of science-related articles, brought him to Toronto to discuss atomic energy, and commissioned him to write a piece for the special theme issue.

Other mass circulation magazines – like the *Saturday Evening Post* – were quick to feature articles on atomic energy in the months after the war, but few covered it in the same depth or as a special theme as the *Maclean's* 'atomic issue,' which appeared on 1 October 1945.[17] Bruce Bliven contributed two pieces, one entitled 'The Mighty Atom' which reviewed the historical development of the atomic bomb and explored the potential of atomic energy. The second – 'Atomic Dawn - What's it Mean?' – examined what 'may prove to be the most important single event in the whole history of mankind. Its possibilities for evil are tremendous, and its possibilities for good are equally great.' Blair Fraser contributed a piece on 'Canada's role in Atom Race,' which described the activities in the Chalk River plant not far from Ottawa, and the work of its team of scientists, most of whom came to Canada before or during the war.

But the most powerful article of the group was Max Werner's 'We Can't Risk War Now,' which struck directly at the haunting fears unleashed by the explosion of the atomic bomb. 'It is certain,' Werner wrote, 'that in comparison with the atomic bomb the most modern weapons of World War II are what the Stone Age club is compared with the machine gun.' Like millions of Canadians, he wondered if mankind could adjust to the new realities of war, and he concluded on a rather somber and gloomy note: 'Humanity probably has no more than a decade to prevent the explosion of the greatest evil and deadliest destruction in the world's history ... In this limited time the organized international community must take control over the new power of destruction or it may be engulfed by a catastrophe beyond imagination.'

The atomic issue was the last special wartime theme issue put together by *Maclean's*. Although published after the war, it effectively concluded the magazine's war coverage. Ironically, it can also be viewed as the first issue of the postwar era – *Maclean's* way of heralding the birth of the new atomic age, as the superpowers faced each other, with increasing suspicion, across the barbed wire and burned-out rubble of Berlin.

For the second time in his life, Arthur Irwin had seen the end of a world war. The first time, he returned to Canada as a confident young man who had seen a bit of the world and was ready to make his mark. Travelling up the St Lawrence he was overcome with a sense of new-found nationalism and a feeling of pride in being a Canadian. In 1945 his nationalism was unshaken, but he was older now – well into middle age – and it was harder to resurrect that optimism that filled him long ago. The waters of the Great Lakes still flowed into the St Lawrence and crashed across the rapids near Montreal on their way to the sea. But remembering the boy in that field, running his toes through the good Ontario dirt – only a few miles from the shores of Lake Ontario – he knew that his world would never be the same again.

TWELVE

The Man Who Made Maclean's

A few days before Christmas 1945, Irwin was asked by the Maclean company publicity department to define his job in fifteen words or less. He needed only ten: 'To edit the best edited and best read Canadian magazine.' Did he read other magazines for ideas – to help decide on *Maclean's* contents? No, 'the contents of Maclean's are not decided by somebody reading other magazines,' he responded sharply, and then crossed the words out. 'You've got to edit from life and not from what the other fellow is doing if you're going to get a dynamic and vital magazine. Some seventy magazines come to the office regularly. I look at a lot of them but read only a few regularly. Others I sample at intervals."[1]

Only a few weeks earlier, in the 1 November issue, the announcement of Irwin's assumption of the editor's chair was made. 'It is nigh on 20 years since the signature at the end of this column first met the eyes of Maclean's readers,' Napier Moore wrote in his last Editor's Confidence. 'This is the last appearance in that position.' Moore issued a few thank you's, using the editorial 'we': 'we leave the editorial bridge,' 'we transfer this chair,' 'we express appreciation,' concluding: 'Maclean's will continue to engage a share of our family interest, so to speak, but in regard to its editorship, this is H. Napier Moore signing off.' With that, Moore vacated the editor's chair, turning the remaining vestiges of office over to his managing editor. Moore's presence would be felt for several more years in the Maclean editorial offices but only on the periphery, infrequent and occasionally irritating, but never with a force that could not be bypassed or ignored.

For Irwin, the position he had hoped for and believed he was fully capable of handling in 1925 was now his – in 1945. There were certain satisfactions from seeing his name listed as editor in the magazine, but the promotion was really more a recognition of fact than a significant change in itself. For many years – as associate editor – he had been doing the lion's share of the work; for three years he had *de facto* control as managing editor and indeed had known that Moore's days as editor were numbered.

Still, it meant something to have the *fact* recognized in the magazine and by the company. Higher status in the halls of the Maclean company might give him a little more power to influence the direction of the magazine. He had the support and respect – if not the social standing – of Chalmers and Hunter, and he believed that they would allow him to operate his magazine within broadly based and loosely defined bounds.

The most important thing was that along with his promotion came the opportunity to implement fully the plans he had been brewing for several years, plans to expand the staff in a logical manner with talented newcomers from all parts of the country – young writers who could raise *Maclean's* onto a new plateau as Canada's 'national magazine.' The obstacles – Moore, financial restraints brought on by the depression, the war – had all been removed. Now it was time to act.

Irwin set out his basic plan in a lengthy memo reviewing the outlook for 1946, prepared for a year-end company meeting. Under the heading 'Pattern for 1946,' he began:

The year of transition – This is it.
Not a new program but an extension and enlargement of program we laid out year ago:
1. Staff. 2. Dress. 3. Fiction. Article Program.
What kind of year? Year One Atomic Age. Year of Decision.

The general introduction was followed by three sections, each representing a broad category. The first, 'Search for Peace – International,' listed the crises spots around the world, from Berlin to the Far East, from trading rivalries to the technological revolution in communications and aviation. The second two sections were more detailed and deserve fuller treatment:

2. Search for Peace – National Sphere
   a) *Reconfederation* – Product of new Canadianism stimulated by war

b) *More positive Canadianism.* Relation to outside world the country has grown up.
c) *Industrial and Agricultural Reconversion*
Scarcity consumers goods toward abundance – letter the dominant – Some shortages continue – Autos – Houses.
d) *Regional and local unemployment* – also labor shortages, e.g. housing. Trouble spot B.C. Later Maritimes.
e) *Labor* – management conflict – More strikes – Unlikely seriously retard –overall production.

3. Search for Peace – The Individual
   a) Reach for more things
   b) Retreat from realities outer world to realities within himself – Bored by Bomb – Go fishing or its equivalent.
   c) Reaction against authority – violence, crime wave – perhaps moral let-down
   d) Desire for self-expression through personalized achievement.
   e) On this continent a return to mobility. Travel. Want to see strange places. Revival tourist Business.
   f) When he isn't running away from it all gent is going to realize he lives in world in throes of one of great crises in human history and he'll want to know what score is and how it affects him personally.
   g) He'll be looking for a faith – something to believe in. A complicated, contradictory world in which one may expect unexpected and dizzy rate of change.

Our job not only to record events occurring in this world in such a way that they will have compelling interest for the Canadian reader but also to interpret these events in such a way that they make sense to Canadians who want a tolerable kind of life.[2]

After mapping out these broad categories, Irwin described how they should be implemented. With respect to feature articles, a 'broad approach' was necessary. There would be an emphasis on 'everything that happens inside man or external to man, and anything man may do with things.' A second approach he listed as 'positive and dynamic Canadianism against background of international world.' Under a further item he added: 'maintenance of the principle of the open forum. One most precious assets this magazine has its reputation for giving fair hearing to both all sides of a case.'

Such broad plans could not be implemented alone; the process of staff expansion already underway must be continued and improved. Only with the right people on staff could any of his plans be fully realized. 'Now we come to one of major projects for 1946.' he concluded:

The training of a corps of correspondents-writers within Canada who can be relied on to produce stories on Canadian subjects of a quality comparable to the best material now appearing in the book. All during the war the lack of first rate article writers in Canada has been one of our major problems. But now we shall have access progressively to more and more potential talent as demobilization concludes and the individual ex-service man shakes himself out of war's aftermath.

Steps had already been taken when he wrote those words at the end of 1945. The resignation of Hilton Hassel, who had followed Bonisteel as art editor, created a vacancy that was filled by D.M. Battersby. In addition, in March 1945, Adam Marshall, formerly of the Montreal *Gazette,* was hired as an assistant editor. Marshall was later promoted copy editor.

One of Irwin's first appointees was Arthur Mayse, a young fiction writer who had travelled east at the end of the war and joined one of the Maclean trade magazines. Mayse had already sold articles and stories to *Maclean's* and several American magazines which brought his work to Irwin's attention. Returning from lunch one day, Mayse was stopped in the hall of the Maclean building by a man he did not know or recognize. But he was struck by the stranger's 'ascetic face,' with its eyes 'like chips of ice.'

'You're Arthur Mayse,' the man said abruptly, without introducing himself. Mayse, bewildered, stared at him. 'Yes,' he replied.

'How'd you like to come to work for me?'

Mayse asked for time to think it over. Two days later, after they agreed that he could continue to freelance on the fiction side, Mayse joined the *Maclean's* staff as fiction editor.[3] His name appeared in the staff list for the first time in the 15 July 1945 issue, along with his article, 'Sissy Fish? No Sir!' a feature on Canadian fish hatcheries.

At first Mayse was not sure that he liked Irwin. He found his 'quick abrupt style' a little unnerving. There also was a difference in taste in fiction between the two men; Mayse recalled Irwin preferring literary fiction with darker themes and 'grim' undertones, while Mayse leaned towards the lighter side, straight-ahead popular material that would appeal to the average reader. It was, after all, the day of formula fiction (until television appeared and swept the field away).

Their differences of opinion led to frequent heated arguments. Mayse later recalled how he would head into Irwin's office with a choice collection of manuscripts tucked under his arm and his will 'braced for a real encounter.' Sometimes he included two or three terrible stories in the pile – stories he knew Irwin would have to reject – working on the theory that Irwin would 'get so desperate after he'd read two or three of these that the ones I wanted would begin to look good to him.' Only once did Mayse acquire what he felt to be the 'perfect story,' one he was so sure of that he submitted it to the editor on its own. Irwin kept the manuscript a rather long time and then called Mayse into his office. Irwin

sat holding the manuscript, not nipped by a corner, but lovingly in both hands.

'Not bad,' he pronounced. 'But on one point, the man's in error. He refers to the rung of a chair when he means the spindle.'

He inscribed the correction with a small, triumphant flourish, gave me one of his rare smiles, and passed over the story. He had found the hidden fault; our readers were preserved from loose writing, and all was well.[4]

The rest of the time Mayse was mired in a stack of mediocre fiction, only rarely finding one with promise. In 1946, *Maclean's* received 3429 stories or 285 per month (up from 2806 in 1945), he reported in a memo for Irwin.[5] Virtually all the stories were rejected, but they still had to be read and returned with a careful response attached. Most of the fiction used by *Maclean's* came to the magazine via a handful of agents who represented the established authors; rarely did *Maclean's* commission a fiction story. There was stiff competition for first-run stories, especially from American magazines which could afford to pay higher prices, and Irwin and his fiction editors waged a constant battle to increase pay scales for short stories.

Mayse grew to respect Irwin and his 'almost magical way of getting the best out of his people.' Irwin was never comfortable making small talk but he could ask searching questions, and his opinions mattered to his staff. He could be chilly, even distant, with those around him, but he always supported his staff in difficult situations. Years later, after leaving *Maclean's*, Mayse reflected that Irwin 'molded and guided us far more than we realized at the time.'[6]

Irwin made two other staff appointments near the end of the year. The first was Hal Masson, an Ontario-born writer who was hired as an assignments editor. Masson was introduced to *Maclean's* readers as a former 'RCMP constable, RCAF warrant officer, and, at the beginning of his career, a Maclean's subscription salesman in Ottawa.'[7] He began writing fiction while in the air force and joined the *Maclean's* staff in November 1945.

The second appointment was Scott Young, a young man – he was barely 27 – who had served in the RCN during the war (where, Irwin reported, he 'acquired a dislike for buzz-bombs and did channel convoy duty to France') and had worked as a correspondent in London for the Canadian Press.[8] He began contributing to *Maclean's* during the war with articles like 'It's Strictly Pusser,' a short piece on wartime slang. Young's name first appeared on the masthead on 1 December 1945 as *Maclean's* articles editor.

With the return of Jerry Anglin in January 1946, after three years in the services, Irwin had the foundations for a solid staff (Anglin 'has shown that he can both write and handle a desk job,' Irwin wrote late in 1946, and he was eventually appointed production editor). Blair Fraser continued his regular reports from Ottawa and had matured into one of the finest writers in the country. In London, Beverly Baxter hammered out consistently read columns on British political life. Lionel Shapiro, meanwhile, signed on for another year's worth of stories as European correspondent, although his writing career was showing signs of taking off, and it was clear that before too long he would be lured to Hollywood.

For the first time, an editorial routine had to be established. In the early years, communication was simple – a straight line from Irwin to Moore. Arrangements had become increasingly more complicated, however, with the expansion of the art department and the addition of several assistant editors. Irwin pulled out pen and paper and began sketching diagrams with boxes and arrows mapping out the office routine.

Assigned articles were to flow through the secretary's office to Scott Young and then to Irwin for approval before going to the art department for layout. Once the art department finished with the article, it returned it to Young: it then went back to Irwin for final approval, and then to the composing room, via the office checker. Unsolicited articles were to proceed from the office secretary to Masson for reading. Those he rejected were returned to the secretary; those he liked were sent up the line to Marshall for reading and then up to Irwin for approval. Once accepted, the article was moved to the art department for copy-editing and blurbing, back to Irwin for final approval, and then on to the composing room. Similar charts were prepared for all aspects of the office routine, including incoming fiction, all the art work (covers, photos, illustrations), and even the office mail.[9] Despite the disarray of Irwin's desk, which was usually covered with stacks of manuscripts and unanswered correspondence, every piece of paper, apparently, was accounted for.

There were still a few holes to fill; Irwin believed that a staff writer was required, and Geoffrey Hewelcke, who would soon resign 'on invitation' as Irwin put it, had to be replaced. The replacement for Hewelcke was found in the person of John Clare, one of the two war correspondents Irwin tried and failed to hire while overseas early in 1945. Clare was a Saskatchewan native who moved east during the depression after working for the Saskatoon *Star-Phoenix*. In Toronto he landed a job on the *Globe* in 1934. He worked briefly for the Toronto *Star* before joining the RCAF in 1941. After three years he rejoined the *Star* as a war correspondent and covered events in Germany until the end of the war. Following a brief rest in Canada he flew to the Far East and tramped around China, India, and the ruins of Hiroshima and Nagasaki. By 1946 he was back in Toronto, at his old desk at the *Star*, when Irwin called and offered him a job.

Irwin was impressed that Clare had been to Japan, and the interview was filled with questions on the effects of the dropping of the atomic bomb and the long-range implications of nuclear weapons. Clare knew his stuff (he had even read the Smyth Report) and Irwin was convinced that he had a future in the magazine business. 'Clare has shown definite ability as a writer both in the article and fiction fields,' Irwin wrote near the end of 1946, although, he added, 'I think it would require more time to estimate his potential.'[10]

Clare joined the staff in June 1946 as an assistant editor. A man of keen intellect and a sharp wit, Clare wrote both non-fiction and fiction (which he sold to other publications), and during his years at *Maclean's* served as fiction editor and managing editor. Not given to unnecessary praise, Clare had a sardonic and direct nature. Scott Young, who briefly shared an office with him, recalled an elderly visitor to the office saying to Clare that, as a writer, he probably rose each morning with a strong desire to get to work behind his typewriter. 'On the contrary, Madam,' Clare replied dryly, 'the most enthusiastic I ever get about writing is mild reluctance.'[11]

Irwin's most significant appointment of 1946 was Ralph Allen. Like Clare, Allen was a westerner: born in Winnipeg in 1913 and raised in Oxbow, Saskatchewan. After high school he returned to Winnipeg and a job as sports writer for the Winnipeg *Tribune*. In 1938 he moved east and joined the staff of the *Globe and Mail*, still as a sports writer, and in 1941 enlisted in the Royal Canadian Artillery. In 1943 he was discharged to become the *Globe and Mail's* war correspondent. Allen made a quick reputation for himself as a war correspondent, becoming, in Irwin's and others' minds, the best of a talented crew. At the same time, he was developing his skills as a novelist, and his first book, a war novel entitled *Home-Made Banners*, was published in 1946. Irwin followed Allen's career as a war correspondent and subsequently published excerpts from his novel in *Maclean's*. His first attempt to lure Allen away from the *Globe and Mail* failed. But, as he had with Blair Fraser, he waited patiently, and the second time he asked, Allen accepted.

Irwin was the first to acknowledge how different he and Ralph Allen were from each other. Irwin was a university-educated central Canadian, a cerebral intellectual with a probing and scientific mind; Allen was the gregarious westerner who was both blunt and direct, a man who knew what was right because he felt it. Irwin was a patient man with a private and cautious personality; Allen was outgoing and colourful, an earthy, grassroots man who was prone to fits of temper. Allen was a better creative writer and seemed able to write with an ease foreign to Irwin. He also was a hard drinker who was closer in age to the others on the staff and would participate in impromptu 'editorial meetings' at the opening of new downtown bars. Irwin never drank heavily, and even with a stronger stomach it is doubtful that he would have. He usually remained behind in the office, one time crying 'My whole staff is drunk!' as his editors stumbled in late one Friday afternoon.[12] (On another occasion Scott Young overheard Irwin saying to Blair Fraser over the telephone: 'You know, Blair, my whole staff just went out and got drunk and didn't come back until after 4 o'clock.' Then, following a long pause, he added: 'I don't know whether this is good or bad.')[13]

Both men had a sense of humour, but Allen's was far more accessible. Allen was a good storyteller who could easily joke with his colleagues; Irwin at times appeared stiff and humorless. Irwin once suggested to Allen and Scott Young that *Maclean's* commission an article on cross-border prostitution. He began his proposal with the words: 'I don't remember where I heard this story, but ...' when Young interjected, jokingly, 'probably from the Institute of International Affairs.'[14] Allen burst into laughter, while Irwin sat stone-faced, choosing not to see the humour in Young's play on words.

Still, beneath the surface differences, there were broad similarities between Irwin and Allen. Both had analytical minds, both loved the outdoors (although perhaps in different ways), and both were staunch nationalists who had turned their backs on organized religion. Both were innately 'good' individuals who took their responsibilities very seriously, and were ambitious for their work and for the magazine.

Irwin and Allen are usually remembered as the two main figures behind *Maclean's* golden years, with Allen building on the foundation laid by Irwin in the late 1940s.[15] But it is important to remember that in the early years Irwin was very much the boss. Allen was in his early thirties, and relatively new to the magazine business. Irwin was approaching fifty; he had the experience, and he had earned his position through two decades of 'apprenticeship' under Napier Moore. It was his magazine, to do with what he thought best.[16] Allen occasionally referred to Irwin as 'the boss,' but more often simply as 'the editor.' Even after Allen himself became editor he continued the practice. John Clare also referred to Irwin this way, and long afterward he would hear Allen say,' I've had a letter from the editor,' or 'I ran into the editor last night,' and he would know who he meant.

Irwin was impressed with his new recruit. At first he hoped that Allen would fill the role of feature writer, but soon realized that Allen had far more potential and might develop into a first-class editor. In his annual report Irwin wrote of Allen. 'He has developed a keen interest in overall planning and is now in charge of the article desk. He has a good, tough mind, good judgment and can write like nobody's business, both articles and fiction. I think we have here an able man whom we should develop.'[17] Irwin quickly gave Allen more responsibility, eventually naming him managing editor.

By the end of 1946 Irwin could boast: 'I now think we have the core of a good writing staff. Still to be achieved is the translation of key men into editors so that responsibility can be shifted down the line. We have made progress in this direction but I think it is too soon yet to make final decisions.' It was essential to continue these developments in the coming years. 'The next major step,' he added, 'is to develop writers in the several parts of Canada who can be depended upon to produce adequate magazine feature articles. As the magazine turns increasingly toward the Canadian scene this becomes more and more important.'[18]

The resignation of Hal Masson in mid-1947 created a vacancy in the staff that Irwin filled with Eva-Lis Wuorio, a Finnish-born writer who emigrated to Canada in 1931. After three years at the University of Toronto, Wuorio joined the staff of the Toronto *Evening Telegram*. In 1946 she left the *Telegram* for the *Globe and Mail* and at the same time began contributing articles to *Maclean's*. When she joined the staff in October as a staff writer, she became the first female member of the editorial staff.

Irwin's other need was a writer from the West Coast. Arthur Mayse had been consistently freelancing with the *Saturday Evening Post*, *Collier's*, and the other 'big slicks,' and he resigned from *Maclean's* to pursue a full-time writing career. With a new vacancy to fill, Irwin initiated a search for a suitable replacement. Bruce Hutchison had the right credentials; he had an established reputation as a writer and he lived in Victoria. But Hutchison was probably too old – Irwin wanted a younger staff – and he was not interested in any event. 'As to your question about a possible B.C. man on your staff. I know none of the men you mention,' he wrote Irwin from Winnipeg. 'As to writing some stuff for you myself, I cannot at present. I do not wish to take time to put down all my reasons here and they could not be presented in writing anyway; they are too subtle and insubstantial and could come out only in a frank talk between us. To this I look forward eagerly.'[19]

The two names topping Irwin's list of West Coast reporters were Jack Scott and Pierre Berton. Scott was a talented and successful reporter, already with an established reputation. Berton was a newcomer of energy and ability, and almost limitless potential. Berton was born in Whitehorse, went to high school in Victoria, and then to the University of British Columbia where his interest in journalism found an outlet in the *Ubyssey*, the undergraduate newspaper. Following graduation he became city editor of the Vancouver *News-Herald* and in 1942 enlisted in the army. He returned briefly to the *News-Herald* in 1945 before moving to the Vancouver *Sun*.

It was as a feature writer for the *Sun* that Berton came to Irwin's attention. The specific story was a series of yarns about the 'Headless Valley' in the Northwest Territories, a mysterious valley (reported to be a tropical paradise warmed by hot springs) that was given its name from the decapitated corpses discovered there. Berton was one of the first reporters to explore the valley and his series of reports was sold to an international audience. A milder treatment of the Headless Valley story served as his first *Maclean's* piece – 'Valley of Mystery.'

With the pending departure of Mayse, Irwin discussed Berton's potential with a number of contacts and dispatched Scott Young to Vancouver to meet with him and to talk to Jack Scott. Young met only with Berton. The specific events surrounding the hiring of Pierre Berton have become well known in subsequent years: the meeting between Berton and Young in the Hotel Vancouver; Berton's long speech on the beauties of life on the West Coast and his commitment to Vancouver; the job offer, followed by Berton's immediate acceptance; Young's admission that he could offer a salary of $4000 or, if necessary, go to $4500. 'I'll take the $4500,' Berton replied. He joined *Maclean's* on 1 June 1947.

Berton was a talented and dynamic newspaperman, still in his twenties but already with an impressive résumé. Like the others on the *Maclean's* staff, however, his background was in newspapers and he had little experience writing magazine features. (There was no conscious formula for writing magazine articles for *Maclean's*, Berton later explained, but there were a few rules which had to be learned and then broken. For example, it was best to start a profile in the middle to get the reader interested in the character, before going back to your subject's early life. When you meet someone interesting on the street, he added, you do not want to know where they were born you want to get to know them first.) Berton realized that his early months at *Maclean's* would be a kind of apprenticeship (in his memoirs he notes that he planned to stay for perhaps two years before trying his luck at one of the large American magazines).[20] But what better place to learn his trade? There were no schools or correspondence courses that taught anything about magazines; an aspiring writer had to go out and actually *do* it. And Berton knew that *Maclean's* was *the* place to do it.

Soon Berton's copy began returning back to him for revision, covered in Irwin's barely legible scrawl, with whole paragraphs circled for reorganization, and 'who he?' written in the margins beside unidentified names, or 'evidence?' next to an undocumented remark. He also soon learned Irwin's trademark, 'Have you done your homework?' and that it was next to impossible to sneak an article by him if you hadn't. It was not unusual to find him holding up a manuscript 'with the distaste he would show for a defunct rat,' one staffer later wrote. 'This man,' he would say, 'has not done his homework!'[21]

Walk into Irwin's office and he would more than likely have the pages of a manuscript spread out before him, either on his desk or on his office floor. And he practically always asked for a rewrite. John Clare met Ralph Allen outside Irwin's office one afternoon and Allen, astonished, reported that he had just had an article accepted *first try*! The two men stopped for a drink to celebrate the occasion.[22] To newcomers Irwin could appear chilly, his thoughts and feelings tucked away deep inside, rarely if ever surfacing. He was not given to effusive praise; he never told an employee he had done a good job if he hadn't. This made his rare compliments all the more valuable.

He also was a considerate man – this quality was consistently recalled by those who knew him well. In dozens of little ways he displayed a genuine concern for his staff – not in the paternalistic and patronizing way of the colonel, but more as an experienced friend and colleague. Late at night, after the office was closed, or Saturday mornings if something important had happened, or at any office meetings, he was readily accessible to his staff. Robert Allen, a long-time *Maclean's* contributor, later recalled the time he wrestled with the idea of leaving the magazine to freelance as a writer. He drove to Irwin's home and the two sat in his car going through all his financial papers to see if he could make a serious go of it. Most often it was just a case of Irwin's exchanging ideas with his staff, talking informally and *listening* to what they were saying.[23]

In the early years, the rules of conduct in the Maclean offices were fairly rigid. Staffers were expected to be punctual and to wear suits, and if their hair got too long they could expect to receive a brief memo. Drinking, of course, was forbidden (but such restrictions did not prevent many staffers from keeping a bottle in their desk drawers). More surprising, smoking was also forbidden, although employees were permitted to keep an ashtray for any smoking guests. When Jerry Anglin arrived for his first interview with Napier Moore he asked if he could smoke. Moore said, 'We don't smoke in here,' but then pulled out an ashtray and slid it across the table and motioned Anglin to go ahead. 'Well, you're not on staff yet.'[24]

Such stiff rules were gradually relaxed. They were impossible to police in any event, and were consistently ignored by the staff. Irwin was not concerned whether his staff smoked or wore suits or were punctual. His standards were strictly related to their magazine. If his editors did good work and met their deadlines he was satisfied.

Memos, however, were written relentlessly. Ideas, outlines for new articles, queries, complaints – everything was committed to paper. Names were reduced to initials, and it was not unusual for RA or PB to receive a summons from WAI to appear in Irwin's office. Memos could be lengthy deliberations on atomic energy or a reasoned discourse explaining why a particular staff member deserved a raise. Or they could be short and provocative; one of the most memorable WAI memos being simply: 'What is a lobster?'[25] As each new memo arrived, Arthur Mayse tucked them under his blotter, gradually building up a lump on his desk. When it became impossible to write over top, it was time to throw them out.

The highlight of the office routine was the weekly editorial conferences held in Irwin's office. All the staff editors were present and it was here that upcoming issues were scheduled and future articles discussed and assigned. Article selection fell within the general guidelines of audience and space, but otherwise the writers were free to develop their own ideas. Providing, of course, that they could pass the test of the editorial meetings. Scott Young recalled Pierre Berton's frequent interjections concerning article suggestions. 'We've *never* heard of that in B.C.!' Berton would announce, sparking, on one occasion, John Clare to reply: 'Nevertheless, Pierre, it exists.'[26]

The participants were colleagues and, indeed, close friends who socialized regularly outside the confines of the office. But friendship did not prevent these meetings from developing into wide-open, blunt, and sometimes vicious free-for-alls. 'This piece is *so* bad,' Berton remembered Ralph Allen once describing an article, 'I'll have to rewrite it before I throw it in the wastepaper basket!'[27]

The meetings were carefully orchestrated by Irwin who sat silently ('like Buddha' is how several participants later described him) leaving the others to do the talking. At some point during the meeting his secretary would enter the room and deposit in front of him a full glass of milk and a plate of arrowroot biscuits and quietly turn and leave the room, shutting the door behind her. The milk and biscuits were becoming his trademark – and the subject of some office jokes – and were as much a part of his *persona* as his bow ties, glasses, and suit. ('If the mood was right,' wrote Arthur Mayse later, 'the book well in hand and W.A. Irwin pleased with us, the biscuits might be passed. We were a bronco crew, not much given to biscuit-nibbling, but with that hawk gaze upon us, we ate the things as if we liked them.')[28]

The editors all got a turn to speak, to run through their article lists. Each issue could be described as something of a literary 'smorgasbord,' with an entree, a main dish, and dessert. It was important not to have two of the same kind of articles in the same issue. Irwin had a board in his office with such headings as 'profile,' 'you interest,' 'science,' or 'stinker' (an opinion piece included to arouse public discussion), in order to ensure a blend of article types.[29]

The discussion raged on, voices rising, tempers beginning to flare, before Irwin at last interrupted and settled the matter. 'This article needs more work,' he would say, or it needed a broader perspective, one that would be more palatable to a national audience. Other times his silence continued – at times it seemed forever – before he stopped the debate with a question. 'Somehow or other,' Mayse later mused, 'those questions of his always seemed to bring the thing into perspective.'[30]

Irwin looked at these meetings philosophically. He had purposely gone out and hired a staff – the best in the country he believed – that was ten to twenty years younger than himself. 'My theory,' he later wrote, 'was that any editorial operation to remain dynamic and vital over time had to have a constant infusion of young talent, otherwise it would ultimately lose touch with the upcoming generation and decline through ossification of its idea-generating capacity.' But a new generation brought with it new ideas and opinions which inevitably clashed with existing methods.

This clash of opinion was healthy, Irwin believed ('that was one reason that I had hired them' he wrote); indeed, it was essential for keeping the magazine fresh. But it brought its share of problems:

I used to play a sort of private game with them. Somebody would come up with an idea. I'd say to myself: We tried that 15 years ago and it was a bust. So I'd argue against it. In many cases that would end the matter; in others, I'd have to exercise the editor's veto. But in other instances, I'd say to myself: I think they're wrong but they've got a fresh point of view – I may be wrong and they may be right. Let's try it and see what happens. In some cases they did turn out to be right – and I learned; in others they turned out to be wrong – and they learned. I saw this part of my job as giving them wide enough freedom to enable them to learn from both failures and successes while at the same time making certain that they were not allowed to make mistakes which would seriously rock the boat. And although this method at times generated tension, it worked.[31]

It was a benevolent dictatorship: Irwin's opinions could be challenged and he was always willing to hear both sides, and, if the arguments were cogent and logical, he could be made to change his mind. But the final word was his.

◆

In an incredibly short period of time, Arthur Irwin assembled a solid staff of writers and editors, men and women who would go on to have distinguished and creative careers. In the process he transformed *Maclean's Magazine* from what was essentially a two-person operation into a solid team effort. He actively sought new talent and brought them to *Maclean's* and taught them what he knew of producing a magazine. And his greatest contribution may be found here – in his vision to see what was possible and his ability to secure the funds for expansion and to ensure his new staff worked in a creative environment with as much editorial freedom as possible.

Once the wheels of change were put in motion, however, he could never be sure which way they would lead. Some of the new 'broncos' on staff came up against the traditional ways of doing things and tried to change them. John Clare, for example, believed Irwin's selection of titles a little too mundane. Irwin liked his titles short, and he used the word 'big' far too often for Clare's liking. Clare recalled trying long and hard to loosen up both Irwin and his titles. The one article that stuck in his mind was a Mackenzie Porter piece on a Russian-born postal worker. It finally appeared under the title 'The Man with the Mail from Minsk.'

Others were critical of Irwin's florid writing style, his penchant for phrases like 'mind you' or 'mark you,' and his apparently uncritical acceptance of the views of those he respected, like Bruce Hutchison. As one of the country's most noteworthy authors and journalists, Hutchison made annual trips to Washington and New York and on his return to Canada regularly visited Irwin in Toronto. During each visit Irwin held a luncheon for Hutchison and his senior editors, allowing Hutchison to expound on international politics and 'the feeling on the Potomac.' Hutchison invariably painted a gloomy picture of the international scene. More than one participant recalled leaving these luncheons in a fit of depression.

'Bruce Hutchison was through, as you know,' Berton informed Irwin in 1950. 'I went to a tea his publisher gave – and where to my horror tea was actually served ... Later RA [Ralph Allen], JPC [John Clare] and I lunched with him. He is crying doom again but is good company. He is quite convinced that the nation and the world are headed for complete and utter ruin and he is probably right.'[32]

Stylistic matters and personal taste not unexpectedly caused a little friction. Jerry Anglin recalled an incident involving Irwin and Ralph Allen. Irwin was away from the office for a few days, leaving Allen in charge of the annual *Maclean's* all-star football team photo-article. Allen and D.M. Battersby, the art editor, worked on the layout together and had all the photos posted on a board in the Art Department. When Irwin returned to the office he saw the layout and immediately turned to Battersby, saying 'Dave, that picture ought to be bigger.' Battersby agreed to make the changes, muttering 'Everybody's an art director' under his breath. Later that day Allen reappeared, and, seeing the new photo arrangement barked: 'Who the hell changed this?' and insisted on the original photo. Battersby sighed and nodded his head, and as he walked by Anglin muttered again, 'Everybody's an art director.'[33]

The new staff had a far more significant impact on the magazine's content and direction. Annual reports that had fallen to Irwin in the past now became joint ventures, as he sought his editor's opinions and queried them for suggestions and comments. What did we do right last year; what was done wrong? he asked. What direction should the magazine take in the upcoming year? And Irwin found his new staff writers anything but reticent. If they saw something they did not like they said so and tried to change it.

'The current heavy use of reversed and surprinted heads, blurbs and cutlines is, in my humble opinion, wrecking some of our layouts,' one staffer complained in 1949. 'Our last two mastheads in a row (Mercenaries, U-Boats) have been given this treatment, and in Mercenaries we have succeeded in gumming up what wasn't a helluva a good picture to start with.' Others agreed. 'I think the white cutlines on the black background are passe and give the page a smudgy, old fashioned look. We should kill them,' Berton argued, adding: 'This has been brought up several times but nothing has yet been done about this. Can we please discuss again?'[34]

It would have been naive to think that individuals bursting with energy and talent – like Pierre Berton, Ralph Allen and others – would sit still while the world passed by. As they grew comfortable and confident in their jobs, they produced a steady stream of memos advocating change. Berton in particular suggested many innovations to the magazine's operation and he sent numerous memos to Irwin or to John Clare, usually with a 'Can we discuss this?' tagged on at the bottom of the page. 'It seems to me we should do something concrete about the state of our editorial page,' he suggested on one occasion. 'In my opinion, our editorials are not as good as they could be, the reason being, I think, that no one around the office really cares very much about them. They are almost invariably written at the last minute and, to me, they never seem to pack very much weight.'[35]

With each issue the strength of his team of staff writers became more apparent, and, not surprisingly, for Irwin the job became a little more routine. The role of the editor of North American mass-circulation magazines had been changing over the previous decades, as magazines became more standardized and produced to a given formula. As one historian has argued, this formula 'reduced the editor from a chef who created original masterpieces to a cook who simply gave his competent individual touch to standard recipes.'[35] These forces were at work on Irwin at *Maclean's* during the few years he spent as editor of the magazine: a daily editorial routine was put in place, articles were selected as various ingredients for the 'smorgasbord,' and, increasingly, they were being written by staff writers themselves.

During the war Irwin had been very much more on his own producing the magazine, trying out new ideas like the theme issues, scrambling for war correspondents and war news, squeezing more money from management. But following the war, and especially after his new staff was in place, his influence remained but his daily input gradually began to decrease. He never looked at himself as either a chef or a cook, but it was equally clear that a break with the past had been made, and that *Maclean's Magazine* – and his place in it – had changed forever.

THIRTEEN

'The Editor' and His Magazine

In March 1948 Irwin was invited by Louis St Laurent, the minister for external affairs, to join the Canadian delegation to the United Nations Conference on Freedom of Information, to be held in Geneva later that month. The delegation would be headed by Jean Désy, the Canadian minister in Italy, but the other delegates were all representatives of the Canadian media, and included Arthur Ford of the London *Free Press*, Lorenzo Paré of the Parliamentary Press Gallery, and Dan McArthur of the CBC News Service.[1] Among the advisers was Campbell Moodie, a staff member in the office of the Canadian high commissioner in London.

The Geneva conference lasted for a full month, and although the delegates had no authority to prepare an international convention, they were asked to discuss the meaning of freedom of information and report to the United Nations. The conference findings would then be considered for inclusion in a planned international declaration on human rights. For Irwin it was a stimulating and rewarding experience. Ironically, it was while he was out of the country – at a conference on freedom of information – that the single most serious management-editorial dispute during all his years at *Maclean's* erupted.

◆

Even in his earliest days at *Maclean's*, Irwin was part of a team. On one side, editorial content had to appeal to readers enough that they would buy the magazine. On the other, potential and existing advertisers had to believe that readers might be influenced to buy their products if they advertised in a particular magazine. Publishers had to be sensitive to the wishes of the advertisers, for without them they would not survive; editors, while aware of the central connection between advertising and the magazine industry, directed their efforts towards presenting editorial content that would be attractive to a potential audience. The two sides could never be totally separate, and, indeed, ultimately the editorial side would always be subservient to management. As Ralph Allen put it in a letter to Irwin, 'all of us who work here recognize that in almost every publication it is ownership and management rather than the editorial side, which will lay down the broad lines of editorial policy.'[2] Nevertheless, Irwin, like most editors, saw his subscribers more as readers than consumers, and he strove to maintain his editorial independence.

For most of his first two decades at *Maclean's* Irwin did not have to deal specifically with editorial-management relations. As associate editor he was primarily concerned with writing and editing the magazine, and the responsibility for dealing with management fell to Napier Moore. When Irwin and Moore met for the first time in Toronto's Waverley Hotel they made a verbal pact (like Irwin and Hector McKinnon had agreed to months earlier at the *Globe*) that if both disagreed with management on some major policy issue they would resign together.[3] Irwin was never asked to fulfil his part of the bargain; on most important matters Moore was a soulmate of Colonel Maclean and Horace Hunter, and disputes on editorial matters were rare.

After he became managing editor and then editor, Irwin had more direct dealings with management, usually with Hunter and, increasingly, with Floyd Chalmers. Articles were rarely, if ever, discussed with management before publication (the Bren gun article was a singular exception); any criticism or disputes, therefore, arose afterwards, and Irwin would be expected to defend his editorial judgment and decision. Irwin knew that he could be fired at any time if he went too far; conversely, he could always resign if he felt unduly pressured in any particular direction. He had done so in a previous job, and it is quite probable that he would not have hesitated in a real showdown.

But it never did come to a showdown. Irwin shared most of the values common to middle-class Canadians in mid-century: his politics were liberal not radical; his nationalism was positive and optimistic, not divisive; and his editorial opinions were determined and even unyielding, but hardly revolutionary. Irwin was unlikely to print material that management would find totally unacceptable. Had he done so he would have been fired; had he wanted to he would have quit. There were articles and stories that sparked controversy, but when disputes did erupt they tended to be over matters of tone, emphasis, and style, or in response to angry letters complaining about vulgar language, or concerns that some article had crossed the bounds of good taste.

Nevertheless, Irwin guarded his editorial preserve jealously. Pierre Berton later recalled overhearing Colonel Maclean during an office party saying to Irwin: 'I hear you hold regular editorial conferences. I'd like to sit in on one of those.' Irwin nodded yes, but a week later when the colonel approached the office door during a meeting Irwin barked: 'It's Colonel Maclean! Keep him out, keep him out!' The door was locked and the colonel's entrance barred.[4] The colonel may have owned the company, but Irwin was in charge of the magazine.

This incident in many ways typified the relations between Irwin and his staff and the administration of the Maclean company. The members of the editorial department had almost no contact with the colonel or Horace Hunter and only rarely saw Floyd Chalmers – with the exception of the obligatory Christmas parties. There were regular editorial-administration meetings which Irwin attended (along with a few senior staff editors), and it was here that policy matters were discussed. Otherwise management remained largely outside the world of the daily editing of the magazine.

Sometimes managerial interference could be avoided simply by ignoring it. For example, after 1945 when Napier Moore became editorial director, his impact on the magazine was almost nil, but occasionally he circulated a memo on guidelines for company policy, a short list of company objectives that he had been flaunting for years. His 'mission statement' was basically conservative and appealed to Hunter and the colonel. The Maclean company should strive to enhance individual liberty, defeat communism and socialism, and cut taxes. His memos on editorial policy were distributed to the senior editors, and Irwin, after discussing them with Blair Fraser and Ralph Allen, filed them away in a drawer and forgot about them. In the end little came of these attempts to establish company policies, at least in terms of the magazine, and if devising new schemes kept Moore busy, so much the better.

Floyd Chalmers, meanwhile, reserved for himself the right of consultation on editorial matters, but this is not to suggest that there was any significant interference in the magazine's editorials. After Moore vacated the editor's chair, the control of Editor's Confidence fell, with the job, to Irwin. Rather than adding his own name to the bottom of the column he signed simply 'The Editors,' and freely permitted other editors to contribute material for it. Irwin was even less enthusiastic with the editorial column, which he had opposed when it was first introduced, and, for the most part, he left the editorials to Blair Fraser. Occasionally Chalmers would write a memo to Irwin concerning recent editorials, indicating a mistake in fact or a questionable judgment. For example, one editorial on campaign funds and political donations attracted Chalmers's attention and he reacted to its apparent bias. 'The inference throughout' the editorial, he wrote Irwin, 'is that political donations are on the whole bad; that they should be exposed; that they pay for professional hucksters; political hangers-on, etc.' In Chalmers's view the opposite side, that parties had to be financed one way or the other, should be pointed out; he concluded: 'With the main point that there should be publicity for campaign fund donations I would agree, but with the general implications that campaign funds are pretty smelly things, I don't agree.'[5] Rarely was there a serious crisis over content in these editorials; management's past publication input in this one specific area was recognized and accepted on the editorial floor.

A far more serious concern was management interference in the kind of articles, their selection and content. Fortunately, such occasions were rare. And if they did arise, staff writers could count on Irwin to stand behind them on any controversial article and defend their freedom from the administration or any of the magazine's advertisers. John Clare later pointed out one key difference between Irwin and Moore: in any kind of a dispute Irwin always sided with his writers, Moore with the administration. Furthermore, management interference often produced the opposite to the desired effect. Pierre Berton recalled a confrontation with Napier Moore over one of his profiles of a well-known Canadian personality. When Moore learned of his research he appeared at Berton's desk, and suggested that he drop the article because his subject was known to be a 'pinko.' Berton, not surprisingly, became more determined than ever to complete the article.[6]

Even more ridiculous were the complaints of T.H. Howse, a company vice-president, who was offended by a Gordon Sinclair article entitled 'Beauty Contests Are the Bunk.' 'I think this article is definitely vulgar,' Howse complained. 'Sinclair seems to have gone out of his way to dig up slang; in fact, to my mind the whole thing is a lot of tripe, and certainly no credit to Maclean's Magazine. While it is probably true that most of these beauty contests are fakes, I think this manner of presentation will be offensive to quite a large section of our subscribers.'[7] Irwin dismissed Howse's charges in a polite but firm memo to the president.[8]

There is no evidence that Irwin ever suppressed an article because of pressure from the administration, but it is interesting to speculate how he would have reacted had he not been out of the country attending the 1948 Freedom of Information Conference when writer and activist Ted Allan submitted an article on Norman Bethune, the famous Canadian doctor who rose to prominence through his activities in the Spanish Civil War and revolutionary China. Knowing of Bethune's left-wing political views, Ralph Allen (who acted in Irwin's place while he was away) distributed the article to the other senior staffers for their comments. The verdict was unanimous – run the article. 'This is a medical-adventure story, not a political yarn,' Berton wrote. 'We don't worry about Dr. Best's politics. Why Bethune? As all his discoveries and work have been constructive his own beliefs are secondary, and I don't think they are relevant.'[9]

There was a good deal of concern over Bethune's politics in some quarters, however. Floyd Chalmers, in particular, was alarmed. 'I do not think we should run [the article] without further investigation,' he wrote Allen. 'Bethune is one of the great heroes of the Communist Party. The Communists in Canada have played him up continuously as a humanitarian.' Any article on communists or their sympathizers – especially if they were also humanitarians, like Bethune – would needlessly publicize their cause, he added. 'We cannot run this article in its present form without building up prestige for the Communists whom I regard, and I think the editorial staff of Maclean's Magazine should regard, as enemies of our nation and of our society.'[10]

Maclean's had already committed itself to the article and Ted Allan was paid for his work, but the article did not run. There was some bitterness, but in the end Ralph Allen acquiesced in the administration's wishes. Scott Young later confessed that part of his reason for leaving *Maclean's* in 1948 stemmed from his disappointment over the handling of the Norman Bethune article, which he strongly believed should have been published.[11] How Irwin would have responded is uncertain; he would have reacted sharply if he had felt pressured by the administration, but it is hard to conceive of him feeling so strongly on this particular question to have submitted his resignation. On his return he did not take up the issue; indeed, he chose to let the matter drop.

◆

The look of *Maclean's* had been changing over the years, and, although the size and length had not changed significantly from 1939, by the late 1940s the reader found larger, 'bolder' photographs, more colour, and the use of more Canadian artists and illustrators in each issue. Canadian competitors such as *Saturday Night* and *New Liberty* were watched for design developments, as were the American 'big slicks,' especially the *Saturday Evening Post*. Throughout the decade innovations from south of the border were adapted to the Canadian scene, and it was not unusual for Irwin to receive suggestions for design changes based on what one of his staff saw elsewhere. For instance, Pierre Berton wrote in April 1949 that in the offices of the *Saturday Evening Post* titles were prepared before the layout was made; 'in this way the layout is made to fit the title and not the title the layout. In my opinion this is far preferable to our way.' Couldn't this method be tried at *Maclean's*?[12]

But it had always been content rather than design that had differentiated *Maclean's* from the 'big slicks,' and this was a difference that Irwin continued to exploit during his years as editor. At home, moreover, he strove to maintain *Maclean's* in that middle area of Canadian magazines – less literary than *Saturday Night*, less 'progressive' than the *Canadian Forum*, but more oriented to news and politics than other general magazines, like *New Liberty* or *Reader's Digest*. Irwin's interest in international affairs and his passion for politics and personalities had combined into a successful format during the war, and he intended to maintain that blend in the postwar age.

The content of the magazine and the selection of writers were Irwin's prime concerns in these years. He had long advocated the building of a strong team of writers, and, now that he had what many considered to be the best staff in the country, more and more of the responsibility for producing articles fell on their shoulders. For example, in 1946, the first year of Irwin's major staff expansion, 59 of the 293 total articles were written by staff writers, an increase of 5 per cent from 1945. If you included the regular departmental features in this total, staff writers accounted for 179 (or 37 per cent) of the total 485 articles in 1946.[13]

As for the kinds of articles Irwin wanted, news became the touchstone for *Maclean's* in the late 1940s. 'Under the term "news" we include anything and everything that affects the lives of the Canadian reader,' Irwin wrote in his program for 1947. Canadian news was especially important, and 'we will apply the best talent we can command to report the Canadian story, interpret the Canadian scene, dramatize the Canadian way of life.' The individual angle remained important, and Irwin promised to 'continue to search for and develop hard-hitting, no-holds-barred articles on controversial subjects.'[14] He outlined his ideas in an article pattern for 1947:

1) International News
2) National News
3) Canadiana:
    Canadian Achievement Stories
    Enterprise in Action Stories
    Canadian Scene:
        Descriptive
        Inspirational
        Historical.
4) Personalities
5) Controversy, Opinion and Criticism
6) Sport
7) Entertainment, Theatre, Movies, Humor etc.
8) 'You' or Self Interest articles
    Health, Body, Mind
    'How To Do' articles
    Beliefs
9) This Changing World and what it means to You the Reader
10) Science
11) Natural History and Outdoor Interest
12) Life Close-Ups[15]

The primary international development in the late 1940s was, of course, the Cold War, and the *Maclean's* position on international communism was stated clearly in a 1 May 1948 editorial entitled 'Are the Communists Entitled to Liberty?' 'Accept the idea that we are at war – a war no less serious because it is, so far, bloodless,' the editorial began. 'Accept the idea that a period of conflict requires, as it has always required, more than ordinary precautions. But make every effort to see that caution does not mount into panic and prudence into persecution.' Extremism was to be avoided, but not vigilance. 'Let's not develop the frame of mind that classes every man of independent mind or an unorthodox view as a Soviet agent; but let's not be too squeamish in our handling of those people who by their allegiance to Communism have clearly identified themselves as Soviet agents.'

The Cold War was everywhere in *Maclean's* in the late 1940s. Irwin dispatched Blair Fraser to Paris to cover the peace conference and the rapidly deteriorating wartime alliance in 'Battle of the Peacemakers.' Other stories with an international flavour followed: 'Canada – Next Belgium?' historian A.R.M. Lower asked in December 1947. American correspondent Howard K. Smith wrote of the Communist coup in Czechoslovakia in 'Conquest Without Blood.' Roving reporter Lionel Shapiro tramped through Europe and fed back articles on the civil war in Greece, political uncertainty in France, and profiles of European titans like Joseph Stalin. (Shapiro's instincts were not always correct, however. In a January 1945 article entitled 'Last Act for Franco,' he announced: 'Fascism in Spain is dying ... the end cannot be far off, Freedom and Republicanism may come next summer.')

Fashion and political science were brought together by the distinguished historian Liddell Hart in an photo-article entitled 'Do Styles Foretell Wars?' 'Keep your eye on women; there's history in hemline,' the accompanying blurb announced. 'Weird, skimpy clothes portend trouble – grandma's styles mean peace.' Under the collection of fashion photographs were captions such as, 'When bonnets burgeoned, 1914 was coming,' and 'Queer hats meant woe in the 15th century.' In a more serious vein, Irwin contributed a short reflective piece following his 1948 European trip in 'Why Do We Help Those Germans?' His tone was optimistic. Europe was recovering, signs of reconstruction were everywhere, but the job was not yet complete. 'Germany is the crucial front in the struggle between Moscow and the West,' Irwin warned. 'Who wins the power, the mind and soul of Germany wins Europe.'

Irwin ensured that the main focus for *Maclean's* in the late 1940s remained Canada itself. There were the standard features of past decades: political exposes and sports closeups, Backstage at Ottawa, London Letters, and other regular columns, and a steady stream of profiles and interviews of well-known Canadians in the arts, business, and politics. Editorials, meanwhile, focused on contemporary political issues, discussing everything from labour relations to Nazi war crimes.

All aspects of Canadian life were open for examination. Doug MacFarlane provided an article on returning Canadian soldiers and their ability to reintegrate into Canadian life in 'Operation Civvy.' Scott Young examined the discovery of oil in Leduc, Alberta, and the potential ramifications for western Canada in 'Pay Off in Oil.' Irwin commissioned novelist Hugh MacLennan to write several articles for the magazine during the late 1940s, the most significant being 'How We Differ From Americans,' a highly personal look at 'the gulf that sets Canadian apart from American.' And a new generation of talented writers found an audience through the pages of *Maclean's*, including Fred Bodsworth, June Callwood, Trent Frayne, Sydney Katz, and James Gray.

The relative importance of fiction in *Maclean's* was in decline under Irwin's tutelage, and this trend continued. Long extended serials were rare, and the number of short stories per issue was limited to three or even two. Members of the permanent staff, including Ralph Allen, John Clare, Eva-Lis Wuorio, Hal Masson, and Scott Young, all contributed their own stories in these years. The stories of Thomas H. Raddall, W.O. Mitchell, Morley Callaghan, Gabrielle Roy, and W.G. Hardy were published as well.

In addition, there was a constant flow of science, medical, and 'You interest' articles that reflected the changing times and issues (ranging from the ridiculous to the frightening). For example, Dr Clifford Adams asked the question on the lips of all parents of teenagers in his article 'Should Nice Girls Neck?' Charles Neville explained the new medical technique of artificial insemination under the title 'Is It Adultery?' Early in 1948, M.C. Dinberg and Gerald Anglin described a new surgical operation called a 'bilateral frontal lobe leucotomy' in an article entitled 'The Cut That Makes Men Sane.' 'Surgery has a new weapon against madness,' they explained, 'an operation that reaches into the brain to snip the mental knots that cripple it.'

Another area of concern for Irwin was *Maclean's* regional coverage. From his earliest days as associate editor he had recommended bringing in writers from the various regions of the country, or at least approaching journalists around the country for reports on local affairs. Irwin's idea of a national magazine was one that was responsive to the various regions and carried material concerning them, but, more importantly, he believed it was also one that should reflect truly 'national' issues. As Irwin understood them, these issues included federal politics and international affairs, as well as those articles which could be labelled universal themes – the 'You' articles, the science pieces, health, education and other social studies, and so on. There was, in his view, a 'national consciousness' in Canada that was more than the sum of all the parts, which all Canadians – regardless of region – could appreciate. Thus, while there were many articles of a regional nature, the great majority of articles in *Maclean's* focused on what Irwin regarded as national matters.

One conscious step that Irwin took was to fill out his growing staff with writers from the different regions of Canada: Mayse and Berton from British Columbia; Allen, Clare, and Young from the prairies; Anglin, Masson, and himself from Ontario; Marshall from Quebec; and Fraser from the Maritimes (he also included Fraser under Quebec). He hoped each would bring a different perspective to the magazine and a better understanding of the concerns of their particular region. Of less concern was whether these writers would continue to represent their regions after exposure to the Toronto scene, and, in hindsight, it is difficult to look back on Blair Fraser as a Maritime writer, or Pierre Berton as the voice of British Columbia. Nevertheless, it did help broaden the scope of *Maclean's* articles compared to the 1930s.

In addition to the various regional items, a series of five articles on the state of the Canadian regions was begun in 1947. Ralph Allen was dispatched to cover the west; Blair Fraser was given responsibility for the Maritimes. Another important domestic development that Irwin followed closely was the entrance of Newfoundland into Confederation in 1949. Between 1946 and 1949, several articles on Newfoundland themes were published – one was Ewart Young's 'Will Newfoundland Join Canada?' – covering politics, history, and profiles of important Newfoundlanders like Joey Smallwood.

Blair Fraser was particularly concerned with Quebec. He had lived there for many years, was bilingual, and was far more in tune with developments there than most anglophone journalists. In articles such as 'What Now, Jean Baptiste?' and others on the developing social and political scene, Fraser tried to explain developments in postwar French Canada to anglophone readers. Quebec presented a unique problem not only to *Maclean's* but to Irwin's brand of nationalism. Where did French Canadians fit into his vision of the country? He did not know many French Canadians personally, and his experiences in Quebec were few and, as in 1917, not especially enlightening. But he brought to the question a liberal and sensitive mind and, like Fraser, became a staunch supporter of bilingualism. 'Understanding' Quebec was only part of the puzzle for Irwin. It was equally important to acknowledge that French Canada existed alongside English Canada and that both groups had certain rights that had to be defended.[16]

Meanwhile, by 1948 the monthly 'Cross Country' series was being put together by Adam Marshall. Cross Country was a selection of news items furnished by more than a dozen regional correspondents whose job it was to 'dig up the regional news they think all Canadians would want to read yet isn't quite as urgent as the news in your newspaper.' Trivia was out; the goal of Cross Country was 'to cast some light on how the other 8 provinces live.'[17]

It is difficult to measure the success of Irwin's attempts to broaden the range of *Maclean's* as a national magazine, but he did draw a little comfort from knowing that the magazine was not just being read in Toronto or Ontario, but, in fact, was widely popular right across English Canada. An audit report for 1948 revealed that the 15 December issue, for example, sold 338,083 copies; of that total, 39.33 per cent (132,953 copies) went to Ontario subscribers, over 26 per cent went to the Prairies, and 15 per cent to British Columbia. Only in Quebec was the average low (8.28 per cent), which underlines how little appeal *Maclean's* had for a francophone audience.[18] These figures remained relatively stable in the late 1940s and compared favourably with other English general audience magazines like *New Liberty, Time,* and *Reader's Digest.*[19]

To get *Maclean's* covers to match the national scope of its articles, Irwin sent Franklin Arbuckle on a cross-Canada painting trip with no instructions other than to capture on canvas a panorama of Canadian scenes. The CPR agreed to give him free train transportation and *Maclean's* supplied cash for his rooms and pocket expenses. Arbuckle spent three months on his tour, travelling from Montreal to the Pacific and north to the Northwest Territories. He returned to Toronto with some seventy sketches of Canadian scenes, such as a cowboy getting a haircut, Christmas eve at one of Montreal's cathedrals, Vancouver's waterfront, the corner of Portage and Main in Winnipeg, a portrait of a Prairie schoolgirl, a snowy street in Yellowknife, and many more. Of these, ten were used for covers in 1947 and 1948. (Despite Irwin's efforts to diversify *Maclean's* covers, most years the highest newsstand sales were recorded by issues with 'girl covers.')

At their first meeting after his trip, Irwin greeted Arbuckle with a question: 'Well, now you've seen all this country of Canada. What do you think of it?'

Arbuckle was surprised by the question and fumbled for an answer. 'Well, gee,' he said. 'It's big.'[20]

Pierre Berton, meanwhile, churned out dozens of articles and rapidly rose to the forefront of a very talented staff. Hardly a month passed without at least one Berton piece, from investigations into prescription drug abuse in 'Nightmare Pills' and 'Benzy Craze' to several articles on a theme he knew so well – the Klondike. He quickly graduated from the lighter journalist-adventure pieces of his 'Headless Valley' days to serious examinations of racism in Canada, with articles such as 'They're Only Japs,' and 'No Jews Need Apply.' Scott Young recalled meeting with Irwin and Ralph Allen only a few months after Berton's arrival. 'How good is this Pierre Berton?' Irwin asked. 'Are we overrating him?' Allen looked straight at Irwin and replied: 'Arthur, there isn't any job on the magazine that Berton can't do.' And he meant Irwin's job too.[21]

Berton still had plenty of time for adventure. Early in 1949 he accompanied twenty-three prize-winning Canadian Holstein-Friesian cows and one Red Poll bull in a crowded transport airplane bound for Uruguay and lived to tell the tale in 'Git Aloft, Little Dogie.' On his return, Editor's Confidence announced: 'Berton left here with our camera and light meter, half a dozen rolls of film and an English-Spanish dictionary. He returned, two weeks later, with a bad sunburn, a tin of Chilean crab meat and a tendency to pepper his conversation with the word "*manana.*" Of the camera there was not the slightest trace.'

These were exciting times. Today some of the articles appear hackneyed, sophomoric, and sensational, but they also reveal a genuine enthusiasm: enthusiasm for telling a good story and telling it well; enthusiasm for introducing readers to new discoveries and inventions and bringing them to new places around the world (and even in outer space); and, above all, enthusiasm for revealing to Canadians something about themselves. What they learned was not always pretty or comforting. It was a dangerous world and, in addition to the great triumphs and accomplishments, Canadians were equally capable of hypocrisy and hateful activities and were often guilty of racism, nativism, and a narrow nationalism. Perhaps most important, at least for Irwin, many of his fellow citizens were for the first time seeing themselves as Canadians.

◆

No one could question the success of the magazine. At the turn of the decade *Maclean's* circulation surpassed the 400,000 mark for the first time, an increase of almost 25 per cent from the end of the war.[22] By 1945 the Maclean company as a whole could boast of tremendous growth and profits from its more than thirty magazines and newspapers (including five in the United States and the United Kingdom). That same year, in recognition of Horace Hunter's contribution, the company's name was changed to the Maclean Hunter Publishing Company. Two years later construction began on an enormous Maclean Hunter plant in North York. The colonel, already in failing health, died in 1950, and his place as chair of the Maclean Hunter board of directors was assumed by Hunter. At the same time, Floyd Chalmers became the company president.

A few years later Irwin took a little time to reflect on the late 1940s – the time that has come to be recognized as the beginning of *Maclean's* 'golden years.' In article selection, he wrote Ralph Allen in 1955, 'we deliberately concentrated on stories of Canadian achievement in no matter what field – business, the arts, industry, sport, science, farming, finance, government, medicine, the frontier, always with emphasis on the people involved. Along with this we ran a sprinkling of hell-raising pieces – stinkers to you – of this or that aspect of Canadian life rightly or wrongly we felt deserved a prodding.'

It was never an easy task editing Canada's national magazine, but it 'was a thrilling experience to sit at a desk or roam the country and feel the response. We used to get brickbats as well as bouquets, and financially, as Mr. Hunter or Floyd will tell you, it was a tough struggle. But you have only to look at the magazine today to realize it paid off not only in dollars but in values of greater importance than dollars.' And, reflecting on the reasons behind the success of *Maclean's*, he concluded: 'Many times I used to be asked how we managed to meet the competition from the South. My answer always was and still is: Only Canadians can edit a magazine about Canada for Canadians, for success demands particular insights which must be Canadian.'[23]

At the end of 1948 Arthur Irwin was more secure at *Maclean's* than he had ever been in the past. His old antagonist Napier Moore was still in a never-never land as 'editorial director,' his influence in the editorial offices reduced to a shadowy memory. Irwin, meanwhile, knew the business and was comfortable behind his desk: guiding the weekly staff conferences, maintaining a safe distance from the administration, overseeing the production side of things, and assigning duties and responsibilities to a hand-picked staff he had come to trust. At last he could sit back, relax, and confidently look forward to many more years as editor of *Maclean's*. The moment would not last; in little more than a year he was gone.

FOURTEEN

The Last Year

On 30 October 1948, Jean Irwin died in Toronto General Hospital. Her asthma had grown gradually worse, and she had suffered repeated serious attacks in previous years. At times the attacks were so severe she was forced to sleep sitting up. Although it was painful for her and distressing for the family, her asthma was not considered life-threatening. That October a heavy smog hung over Toronto for three days, and her condition rapidly deteriorated. She was rushed to the hospital but died within twenty-four hours. Irwin explained to a friend more than a year later that 'it wasn't until about half an hour before the end that I realized that she might not pull through.' Then he added, in a typically understated way: 'As you can well imagine it was something of a block buster.'[1]

His mother was already in hospital, having suffered a stroke earlier that year. She died three days later, on 2 November, the day of Jean's funeral. Jean was cremated and her ashes were buried at Mount Pleasant Cemetery. Among the friends and colleagues who attended the service was George Drew, who had recently left Queen's Park to assume the leadership of the federal Conservative party. Irwin never forgot Drew's letter of condolence, which arrived addressed 'Dear Bill.'

Not uncharacteristically, Irwin bottled up his feelings inside and revealed them to only a few close friends and associates. Hugh MacLennan later remembered sitting with him, quietly reading the morning newspapers. Irwin let down his paper abruptly, saying 'Did you know that my wife died?'[2] He even seemed reluctant to admit it to himself at first. Except for one afternoon, when he was getting something from the closet and he stumbled on a pair of Jean's shoes which she had worn only a couple of times before her death. He stood over them for a few moments, his eyes transfixed on the newness of the leather. He later recalled how his defences evaporated and all the pent-up emotions surged into his chest and he fell back on the bed, sobbing, his grief flowing over him like waves. But it was not like Irwin to grieve in public; Jean's death was a personal tragedy for him and his family. Their mourning was to be done in private.

He took up painting shortly after Jean's death, and embarked on regular excursions north of the city, where he would sit for hours working on a landscape, or trying out different painting styles. He never became good, but it did help take his mind off recent events. As for the three children, the death of their mother was a great loss, but fortunately they were old enough to cope with the new stresses of managing the family home.

Eva-Lis Wuorio became very important to Irwin after Jean's death. Wuorio, fondly remembered by Irwin's children as outgoing, domineering, and something of a 'bombshell,' became a regular visitor to the Irwin residence. She would not allow Irwin to mope and, despite occasionally passing out on the living-room sofa, she never failed to revive his spirits. Irwin came to rely on her and at one point proposed marriage, but she refused him. Both later came to realize that their marriage would have been doomed to failure.

In the months following Jean's death, work on the magazine continued, but what had been challenging work in the past was becoming routine; what had seemed creative and spontaneous was verging on predictable. Forced to sit back and re-evaluate his life, Irwin for the first time began to think that maybe he had been at the magazine for too many years. He did not actively start looking for a new job, but in retrospect the death of Jean was clearly a turning-point.

There continued to be staff changes at the office. Earlier, in the summer of 1948, John Clare was moved from fiction to articles editor to fill the vacancy created by the resignation of Scott Young, who left the magazine to pursue a career as a freelance writer. To fill the role of fiction editor, Irwin hired W.O. Mitchell, a Saskatchewan native who had already established himself as a short story writer and novelist, with the recent publication of his book *Who Has Seen the Wind*.

A heavier blow was the departure of Ralph Allen near the end of the year. Allen had been promoted to managing editor and Irwin had come to depend on him more than any other person on the staff. But

Allen wanted to write serious fiction and believed he could not be both a novelist and managing editor simultaneously. In December he accepted a post as sports writer for the Toronto *Evening Telegram*, a job, he told Irwin, that would be less time-consuming and would enable him to devote more time and energy to writing. 'Under you I have learned more in this brief time than I had learned under all the editors for whom I had worked previously,' he told Irwin in his letter of resignation. 'Beyond this, it has given me real pride and satisfaction to play a small part in the operation of a magazine which, in my opinion, is one of the most constructive and vital forces in Canadian life.'[3]

Apart from the fact that he had come to rely on Allen, Irwin faced the extra burden of finding a suitable replacement, and hiring new staff was a challenge that he took very seriously. His first choice for Allen's replacement was Blair Fraser, but Fraser was reluctant to leave Ottawa. 'I'd rather stay where I am,' he wrote Irwin on Christmas Eve. 'I have been happier in this job than in any I ever had; liked it from the start, and have been liking it better ever since.'[4]

To fill the vacancy created by the departure of Ralph Allen, John Clare was moved to associate editor and Pierre Berton was given Clare's post as articles editor. That still left a vacancy at the more junior level, and Irwin agonized for weeks to find a suitable writer. Files were opened and dozens of memos written concerning the suitability and availability of a variety of candidates. Friends outside the magazine were approached for their opinions of particular individuals. Staff members were regularly stopped in the hallways and asked for their advice. Irwin was very much interested in Borden Spears, who was with the Toronto *Star* (and, indeed, he later became editor of *Maclean's*). John Clare recalled being asked several times by Irwin: 'What do you know of this fellow Spears?' Irwin's inquiries later became something of a joke between Clare and Jerry Anglin, because it was Clare who had suggested Spears to Irwin in the first place.[5]

Finally, in the spring of 1949, Irwin hired Leslie Hannon as an assistant editor. Hannon was a hard-working, New Zealand-born newspaperman who migrated to Canada after service in the New Zealand forces. His name first appeared on the *Maclean's* masthead on 1 June 1949. Like Borden Spears, he later became editor of the magazine.

◆

In mid-September Irwin received from Floyd Chalmers an extraordinary memorandum written by Horace Hunter. A note or memo from the company president was not unusual in itself, but the one that arrived this day was, for Irwin, nothing less than devastating.

'We are not developing in the minds of our people a sufficient feeling of pride in Canada,' Hunter began. 'There is not a sufficient realization among the people generally of the advantages we possess as citizens of Canada, and of the opportunity that we have here for further development of a great nation. We are so much smaller than the United States that we are apt to get an inferiority complex, and to think that the importance of a country can be sized up accurately by the extent of its population and income.' Hunter came to the point: 'Could we not make this the keynote of a continuous campaign in Maclean's Magazine?'[6]

Chalmers passed the note along to Irwin and attached a few comments of his own. 'It could be argued that the entire editorial program of the magazine is designed to do precisely this. I think what Mr. Hunter has in mind is something in the nature of a more organized campaign capable of being defined and recognized as such and which would embrace picture stories, articles and editorials all linked together with some common slogan or theme.' It would be Irwin's job to implement such a program, but in Chalmer's opinion if 'something can be developed within the editorial program of the magazine I think the idea would have a great deal of merit.'[7]

At first Irwin was stunned. Could it be possible that Hunter had missed everything that he had been trying to do for more than twenty years? He pulled a slip of paper from his desk and twisted it into his typewriter. He started tapping slowly, but in a few moments the flood gates opened and his feelings poured out into a bitter, distressing, and revealing letter to Floyd Chalmers.

Sept. 15, 1949
Dear Floyd:

I don't think I've ever been so crushed as I was when I read H.T.H.'s memo suggesting that we carry on a continuous campaign to inspire a feeling of pride in Canada.

I've put in 24 years of my life trying to do just that and apparently it has made no impression whatever on the president of this company. When the paper was imperialist I sold an English editor on the idea that this was a great country in the making and that only by being Canadian, intuitively, intellectually, and every other way could we build a great periodical.

I fought Englishism for 15 years to bring that about. I've written articles about the country which old ladies said made them cry. [illegible hand-written sentence] I've slaved my guts out over more than a million dollars worth of the printed word in a never ending battle with mediocrity in an effort to get power, and drama, and emotional conviction into the singing of the story of Canada. I've passed through the post-adolescent stage, the impatient stage, the didactic stage – look at some of the See Canada First travel issues we used to get out years ago and now they'd make you puke; the critical stage, the stage of bewilderment and doubt, the navel gazing stage, and so has the magazine; but never for one moment have I lost my belief that this country marched with destiny and that its destiny was great.

I've coddled and wheedled writers by the hundreds to make them reveal this country and its people in singing prose, persuaded artists to hold up the mirror, spewed out ideas for other men to wrestle with and taught them how to wrestle, built a Canadian staff where there was no staff, transformed a tenth-rate American dress into a Canadian dress whose origins are unmistakable, built a great property which is as unmistakably Canadian as the smell of the autumn forest in Timagami and is recognized as such from one end of this country to the other.

And now we are asked to launch a campaign to inspire in Canadians a feeling of pride in Canada complete with slogans.

Doesn't the president see what's been going on under his nose. By God, if he doesn't, the country does. Doesn't he know that you can't do these things with slogans but only with the parable? which reaches the heart?

As you can see you've got me with my emotions down. I'm very tired and at the moment feel like throwing in the sponge and going fishing.

Now tear this up and forget it. I wouldn't send it down unless I felt I knew you well enough to let you know how I feel.

WAI[8]

'Your note is a natural (and not unexpected) reaction,' Chalmers replied in a confidential memo. 'I'll be able, I think, to handle the situation,' he added.⁹ But in many ways the damage had already been done.

♦

A few weeks after receiving Hunter's crushing letter, Irwin received an unexpected visit from Campbell Moodie, the press officer at Canada House in London, the headquarters of the Canadian high commissioner in Great Britain. Irwin had known Moodie for some time, and the two had worked together earlier that year in Geneva, during the UN Conference on Freedom of Information.

'You ought to be in External Affairs,' Moodie said, in a rather casual way at one point in their conversation. Irwin replied that the thought *had* crossed his mind. Clearly he found the suggestion attractive.

'Can I tell them that in Ottawa?' Moodie asked. Irwin protested that he was happy at *Maclean's* and had no wish to leave, but before Moodie left he said: 'Well, if you want to you can say that you ran into me in Toronto and got the impression that I wasn't necessarily wedded to Maclean's for life.'¹⁰

Irwin did not make very much of the conversation – to him it was little more than an informal chat with a visiting friend – he filed it away in the back of his mind and got on with his work. In November, he received a telephone call from Norman Robertson, the clerk of the Privy Council and one of the top Ottawa mandarins. Robertson asked him to come to Ottawa – there was something he wanted to talk to him about – and at that moment his earlier conversation with Moodie must have clicked in his mind. Irwin met Robertson in Ottawa a few days later.

'I hear you might be interested in External Affairs,' Robertson began. 'We want you to take over the National Film Board [NFB].' There were a few positions in External Affairs open, he continued, but he admitted that he had brought Irwin to Ottawa under false pretenses.

'Good God, Norman,' was Irwin's immediate reaction, 'at the moment that's the toughest job in Ottawa.' Irwin was aware of the controversy swirling around the film board; the charges and sensational allegations of Communist infiltration, the public accusations in the House of Commons, and the air of suspicion that hung like a thick black cloud over its operation. What a mess. Who would want to land willingly in the middle of such chaos?

Robertson added that once the job was finished – say in two or three years – then Irwin might be assigned to a position in External Affairs. Robertson 'said that the Government wanted me to take over the Film Board and clean it up,' Irwin wrote a few days later, 'and dangled a foreign post in External affairs as bait.'[11] Irwin nibbled and agreed to speak to the minister responsible for the film board. Robertson whisked Irwin in to see Robert Winters, the minister of reconstruction and supply who had the added responsibility of overseeing the film board. Winters struck Irwin as an intelligent and handsome man, well-spoken and friendly, but inexperienced and less sure of himself when discussing cultural issues.[12] Winters repeated Robertson's invitation to take over the NFB, giving Irwin some of the background leading up to this request. Robertson remained in the room, sitting off to one side and speaking rarely except to insist 'that the Film Board and External Affairs should be considered together.'[13]

Winters informed Irwin that the Toronto consulting firm J.D. Woods and Gordon Ltd. had been hired to investigate the NFB and to make recommendations for its reorganization. Plans were also under way to rewrite the Film Board Act, and the government wanted the right person in charge to implement the recommendations and oversee the writing of a new act. Irwin was to be that person, and Winters made his pitch.

Irwin recalled the conversation in his memoir notes: 'I'm authorized to offer you the job at $8,000 a year,' Winters announced.

'I'm sorry, Mr. Winters,' Irwin responded, 'I appreciate the offer but I'm sorry I can't consider it.'

'Ten?'

'I'm sorry, Mr. Winters, I appreciate your offer but I can't consider it.'

'Twelve?'

'Mr. Winters, with respect, I suggest this is a bit absurd. I don't mind telling you what I'm making. I'm making $15,000 plus expenses.'

Winters could go no further, and there the conversation ended, at least for the moment. As he left, Winters indicated that the matter was not closed and he asked Irwin to keep an open mind. Irwin returned to Toronto, a little bewildered by what had transpired. Obviously Winters had not done his homework, he thought.

It was an attractive offer – especially if they upped the financial side – but Irwin hesitated. Before making any final decision he wrote his thoughts in a confidential letter to his old friend Bruce Hutchison.

Irwin explained that he had been 'playing footsie with the boys in Ottawa,' and then proceeded to describe the events of the preceding days. 'The Film Board is in one godawful mess. The Government regards it as the worst one they've got. They said they wanted someone who could establish the confidence of the government itself in the Film Board, ditto the confidence of the departments and the general public. All very flattering but it didn't really sell me.' His mind still not made up, Irwin continued:

What do you think? My own view is that the Film Board is at least a five-year job and a very tough one at that. They've screened only one department so far and they've already got some thirty people who are under suspicion. Some six or eight of them are known Communists. What the setup is in the other departments they don't yet know. Administration is in a godawful mess. Public confidence is shot. Morale within the organization is near absolute zero. It's a political hot potato. I figure it would take at least a year and a half, perhaps two years, to handle the flushing-out process. They don't want a totalitarian purge but want it all done quietly on a selective basis. This would take time. And once that phase is through you'd have to start building a new staff and this would be extremely difficult in a field where there are few trained technicians in the country. Then, having built an organization, you'd have to produce concrete results. And, as I say, I think this would take five years.

Another factor: I've just been through seven years of the same kind of business here and, frankly, I don't want to do the same thing all over again. Also I'm not thoroughly sold on the Film Board idea itself and I also feel that this job here is perhaps even more important than the Film Board.

External Affairs is a different kettle of fish altogether. The minimum in their talk is Head of Mission. If this happened to be in an interesting spot in Europe I'd be very much tempted. Twenty-four years is a long time to keep whanging away at the magazine business. And from here in I'd like to be able to live as well as to work.[14]

From this letter it is clear that Irwin believed the NFB job to be an enormous challenge, and the thought of taking on such a challenge had its appeal. But there would also be grave risks – he would have to throw over everything he had built at *Maclean's* and gamble with uncertainty. The inclusion of a promise of a foreign service post was the real attraction, and, in the final analysis, the determining factor.

Robertson telephoned Irwin again on 6 December and the following day, after dictating the above letter to Hutchison, he returned once more to Ottawa and the comfortable confines of Parliament Hill. Winters announced that he was prepared to match Irwin's *Maclean's* salary of $15,000 (on a two-year contract) if Irwin took on the NFB commissioner's job.

Irwin brought up two issues concerning the NFB that were on his mind. First, he asked Winters for a verbal commitment that the government intended to support and finance the NFB for the foreseeable future – he had no desire to lord over the destruction of a national cultural institution. Secondly, he wanted to know something about the security question at the board and his perceived role in it. Irwin was reluctant to accept the offer if he then had no freedom to handle the problem as he felt best. He refused to act as a figurehead while the RCMP decimated the staff, and quite likely smeared everyone else in the process. He wanted some input. Winters gave his assurance on both points.

Following the meeting with Winters, Irwin met first Lester Pearson, who had recently become minister of external affairs, and then the prime minister, Louis St Laurent. Pearson and Irwin had known each other casually for many years, and he promised Irwin that, if he were still in office when Irwin's term at the NFB expired, he would do everything in his power to see that he received a posting in External Affairs. The prime minister made a similar pledge although he stopped short of an official commitment. Irwin later recalled the moment. St Laurent went on to say something like, 'I understand you have been talking to Mr. Pearson. You will appreciate, of course, that there can be no formal commitment. For instance, if I were going to appoint a Governor-General tomorrow, I could tell you today that I would appoint a Canadian. But, if sometime in the future, I would have to appoint a Governor General, how could I be certain today that at that time in the future it would be a Canadian. But I think I can go so far as to say that there would be a moral commitment.'

The prime minister added that he felt that the film board was an important job, and he played on Irwin's sense of public duty to accept it. Irwin greatly admired St Laurent and such a request coming from this man was almost irresistible.

Irwin returned to Toronto to ponder his future, and discuss his options with his children. The decision to accept the government's offer was remarkably simple to make. For one thing, the job attracted him. The film board offered challenge and excitement, not to mention controversy, and these qualities would provide a change from the routine of *Maclean's*, where he increasingly believed he was growing stale after twenty-four years. And Hunter's thoughtless memo of a few months earlier only reinforced his deeply held feelings that his work at *Maclean's* was not fully appreciated in the Maclean Hunter Company. He also was secure in the knowledge that the staff he had recruited and trained was quite capable of carrying on without him.

More important in his decision was the death of Jean. In the months since her passing he had lost heart and felt his world go stale. 'The resulting upheaval [following Jean's death] had a good deal to do with my coming down here,' he confessed to a friend a few months later. 'Some of my friends think I have been foolish but as I worked myself through the adjustment period I began to feel that some pretty radical change was indicated if I was going to keep an interest in things. And this job has certainly provided the change.'[15] In addition, his three children had grown up; his youngest child Neal was almost eighteen and would soon be off at college. Whether he took the film board job or not, the family home would likely break up within a year or two. The timing was right for a major upheaval.

On the positive side, the most appealing aspect for Irwin was the people he would be working with, especially in a future foreign service posting, individuals like St Laurent, Pearson, and the others he knew in the public service. He was attracted by their integrity and their devotion to the *idea* of public service – a kind of ambition, yes, but not the kind that was measured in dollars and cents. The Methodist minister's son had heard the call to public duty.

Irwin viewed his impending departure philosophically. The film board was in 'one ungodly mess,' he wrote Beverly Baxter a few days after making his decision. 'It's been accused of harboring Communist spies and our own defence department has refused to allow it to take any of its secret pictures. There has been quite a tizzy about it and I'm in the middle of it. Whether I'm being just a plain damn fool or not, time will tell. But it's at least new and interesting and it should be an adventure.' Irwin anticipated Baxter's disapproval: 'I can see you shaking your head over the business of jumping from John Bayne's frying pan into Louis St. Laurent's fire, but for the time being at least the new bronco is going to be tougher to ride than the old one, and that's probably a good thing for yours truly. Where the thing will end up God alone knows.'[16]

The final arrangements were made and notice of his appointment was released to the press on 16 December. Irwin approached the announcement cautiously. 'My own notion is that during the preliminary stages I should say nothing, if possible, and if that is not possible, as little as possible,' he wrote Winters late in December. At least until he had actually met the board, he felt he should say nothing. 'As I've no doubt you'll agree, the public relations aspect of the job is important and I don't want to start off by creating the impression that we're acting snooty; but on the other hand I'm certainly not going to talk when I don't know what I'm talking about. I do need some guidance on what it would be proper for me to talk about and what not.'[17]

Before he left he ensured that the succession to the editor's chair was settled. There was one obvious choice for the new editor – Ralph Allen. Even though Allen had left the staff a year earlier, Irwin suspected that he would jump at the chance to return to *Maclean's* as editor, and there was no one Irwin would have preferred more to see in his chair. Irwin called Allen, and he immediately accepted the offer, exclaiming: 'I'll be up there in half an hour!'

It did not take long for news of his impending departure to circulate through the Maclean Hunter offices. Staff members stopped him in the hallway to offer their congratulations, or to tell him how much he would be missed. One colleague was Robert Allen, who met Irwin in the office washroom soon after he had announced his decision to accept the NFB post.

'What does the National Film Board do?' Allen asked, as they stood side by side at the urinal.

'I don't know,' Irwin replied. 'That's what I'm going to find out.'[18]

With the announcement in the newspapers, letters flooded in from friends and colleagues in journalism, government, and academe. 'Your crossing of the Rubicon is displayed in tonight's public prints,' Bruce Hutchison wrote. 'I do hope you have protected your flanks and your rear and especially your front. Remember what I told you about sucked oranges landing in gutter or Senate, which are the same place. My experiences ... suggest that in all such matters one should be tough and I hope you have been. The film job will be nothing for you. In six months you'll have cleaned the Augean stables with a ruthless broom, I am sure. What then? Do you propose to go to India and catch sprue or some other distinguished tropical disease; or to Paris to drink champagne; or to Moscow for Vodka? I burn to hear.'[19]

Others – especially writers who worked with Irwin over many years – wrote of their appreciation of his talents as an editor. 'If you do for the Film Board a fraction of what you have done for *Maclean's* this country will be your debtor once more,' wrote Hugh MacLennan from Montreal. 'As a contributor, I'm sorry to see you go from the magazine – more than you can ever guess. I have never worked with another editor who gave me more confidence, and I have never known one who, accepting the realities of popular magazine readership, was not to some extent hypnotized by them. You lifted *Maclean's* into a magazine of which people became proud, and I think I have a fair idea of what it must have cost in strain, stress, judgment, compromise and determination to do so.'[20]

Frank Underhill, an old friend from the history department at the University of Toronto, showed less concern for his leaving *Maclean's*. 'I always thought you were too intelligent for the Maclean-Hunter publications, whose real function is to peddle dope to the Canadian bourgeoisie. It is only in working for a public body like a university or the film board that a man of imagination and intelligence has any chance to express himself in this country. And I hope you manage to do something to make our dead bones rattle.'[21]

Irwin's formal letter of resignation went to Floyd Chalmers, but before he left he went to see Hunter one last time. The meeting was cordial and short, as neither man was given to small talk. 'This is a great compliment, Art,' Hunter said of the invitation into government service. Afterwards Irwin wrote Hunter a short letter, thanking him for 'the confidence you have reposed in me during my association with Maclean's and particularly during my tenure as managing editor.'

The sharpest memories were of a time the two men worked closely together under difficult circumstances. 'I shall never forget the backing you gave me, for instance, during the Bren gun affair, and the downright guts with which you stuck to your guns once the lines of battle were drawn.' There was no lingering trace of anger in Irwin's tone as he praised Hunter as a publisher. 'I suspect there have been times when you wondered whether or not the boys up in our department were going to kick the side out of the building but you've never wavered in your insistence that editorial discretion should rest with the editor. And that's what makes for great publishing and a great publisher and great periodicals.' Now it was time to go. Irwin finished by once more underlining where his priorities had lain for a quarter of a century. 'May the magazine and the company – I'd be less than human if I didn't think of the magazine first – long continue to flourish.'[22]

Irwin did not leave *Maclean's* a wealthy man. He had some savings (he liked to keep an amount equivalent to six months' pay in savings as a kind of insurance policy against sickness or unemployment) and a little equity built up in his house. But not much else. The Maclean Hunter pension plan had not been in operation long enough for him to collect anything above what he had contributed, and years later he began receiving monthly cheques of $69.94. His one paper-security was twenty shares of Maclean Hunter stock which he purchased in 1939, when 6000 shares of common stock were issued. Most staff members were allotted ten shares each (at $120 per share) and one afternoon Victor Tyrrell took Irwin aside and offered him ten more. These twenty shares were the subject of a conversation with Floyd Chalmers after the announcement of his resignation. Chalmers asked if he would be 'turning in' his twenty shares, claiming that he wanted to distribute them to other staff members. Irwin refused and held onto them as his only 'pension' from the company. Over subsequent years Chalmers tried several more times to buy them, but Irwin rejected all offers.

Irwin's last act at *Maclean's* was, ironically, not as an editor but as a writer. On Ralph Allen's insistence *Maclean's* published the text of a speech he delivered to an American audience in Buffalo, New York, the previous June. Fittingly, it was entitled 'The Canadian,' and it served as Irwin's valedictory at *Maclean's*.

'I come here today as a Canadian,' Irwin began, 'to try to tell you something about my country and its people. Who is this Canadian and what makes him act the way he does?' After twenty-five years of writing and talking about Canada at *Maclean's,* Irwin had some experience answering those questions.

The roots of Irwin's Canadian were to be found firmly planted in this continent. 'We are sprung from many sources but the one thing we now have in common as a people is that we are Americans ... North Americans ... just as you are.' But there were unique differences, of course, that separated the Canadian from the American. Irwin focused on two:

> One: We are the northern North American with all that implies in terms of influence of climate and terrain on character and a way of life.
>
> Two: We are the unique American in that we alone among all the Americans of two continents have insisted on maintaining political connection with our parent stem in Europe.

Irwin went on to describe his Canadian as essentially 'two persons in one,' a mixture of what he called the geography man and the history man. Geography played a role in shaping Canadians, forcing them to 'build a way of life suited to a stern and difficult land, in the face of great obstacles both physical and political.' History, too, had left its stamp on the country, with all the struggle and dynamism of a bilingual and multicultural heritage.

History and geography had taught Canadians lessons in compromise: compromise with nature to enable a people to live successfully in a hostile environment; compromise in a duality of language and religion; compromise between the pull of traditional and political ties to Great Britain and the enticing lure of economic and cultural ties to the United States. Canada 'was born of compromise between two races, two languages, two cultures. Inevitably [the Canadian] has had to learn that there are always two sides to a case.' Canadians could now teach others around the world those lessons in compromise.

Irwin described his Canadian as a 'Man in the Middle' both geopolitically and philosophically – a role derived, above all, from the 'unconscious reconciliation of the seemingly opposite poles of nationalism and internationalism.' Less obvious but inherent in such a role was the 'concept of limited national sovereignty,' which Irwin explained.

The Canadian has shown that a nation can be ... can achieve independent identity ... can capture freedom to live its own unique life ... under a sovereignty not unlimited, but a sovereignty limited by organic association with other nations for a common purpose.

And that way lies the only tolerable solution to the great problem of our time ... the problem of achieving order with freedom in a world made anarchic by the unlimited sovereignty of the modern nation state.

The only other way is a universal state dictated from some such power-mad capital as Moscow.

And that way lies an end to freedom.[23]

PART FOUR

1950–

FIFTEEN

'Mad Ministers, Rioting Reds, and Posh Parties'

Irwin joined the National Film Board as film commissioner on 1 February 1950. He took an apartment in Ottawa, leaving his children to look after the house in Toronto until the summer, when it would be sold. His break with Toronto was complete. 'Cheer up, chum,' Eva-Lis Wuorio wrote a few days before his departure, 'all you have is a mere volcanic eruption, mad ministers, rioting reds, and posh parties – whereas I'm really in the slurp with rewrites rewrites rewrites. Would you care to lend me two thousand bucks so I can go to Europe and sin?'[1]

His mandate at the film board was simple: restore government and public confidence in the NFB. But if his goal was clear, the means to achieve it were not. He came to the board under a cloud of suspicion himself. He was not a filmmaker and there was considerable controversy surrounding his appointment. How, many NFB staffers asked, could he be anything but a government hatchet man, appointed by his Liberal friends to do their dirty work?

Irwin was sensitive to these charges, and he was careful to avoid the immediate pitfalls that inexperience and unfamiliarity were sure to throw in his way. But the many problems facing the film board could not be ignored; they would have to be faced. And at the beginning he had far more questions than answers.

◆

The NFB was created by an act of the Canadian parliament in May

1939. Its original purpose was modest: to supervise and coordinate the production and distribution of government films. Government departments were instructed to channel their film needs through the board, which would assume responsibility for seeing that the work was done. From these rather modest beginnings the NFB grew, in a few short years, into a major force in the Canadian film industry and a world leader in the production of documentary films. The outbreak of war a few months after its creation sparked an ever increasing demand for the NFB's output, a ready audience for its product, and a cause to fight for. Overnight the government recognized the unique value of film as a propaganda weapon in the struggle against the Axis nations.

In the vanguard stood John Grierson, the NFB's first film commissioner and Canada's 'Propaganda Maestro' (a name, interestingly, taken from a *Maclean's* article by Thelma Le Cocq). The Scottish-born Grierson was a man of enormous talent and vision who spearheaded the evolution of documentary film in Canada. Under his direction, the NFB had, by 1945, produced several hundred documentaries, short dramas, animated shorts and educational films – many of the highest technical and artistic calibre – that mirrored Canadian life and explored its international dimensions, triumphed the Canadian war effort, and began to look to the world that might emerge after the war.

With the end of the war, however, the opposition of the private film industry, which viewed the NFB as a competitor, became more pronounced. Charges were made that the board (which had ballooned to a staff of almost 800) had become too big, too wasteful, and too expensive. Questions were raised concerning the role of the film board and even over its continued existence. What purpose was there behind maintaining the NFB? Perhaps the board should be limited to the production of educational films and tourism promotion? Did we still need a propaganda maestro?

Opposition to the board intensified in the increasingly hostile atmosphere of distrust and suspicion sparked by the defection of Soviet intelligence officer Igor Gouzenko in September 1945 and the revelation of the existence of a Soviet spy ring in Canada aimed at discovering Canada's atomic secrets. A royal commission was established to investigate, and, thanks to a single unfortunate reference to Grierson in the notebook of Freda Linton, Grierson's former secretary and one of those implicated by Gouzenko's papers, a long shadow was thrown over the NFB and its employees. The Cold War had begun and NFB films were scrutinized for any pro-Soviet messages or for being 'soft on communism,' NFB employees were sufficiently unorthodox – in dress, social behaviour, 'artistic temperament,' and political views – for those opposed to it to uncover all kinds of 'evidence' of, if not subversion, at least 'communistic-like' activities. In an era of rumour, unsubstantiated allegations, and guilt by association, and with the definition of subversion left so deliberately vague, it was relatively easy to smear anyone.

Internationally, the wartime alliance lay in ruins. The international community lurched from one crisis to another in Austria, Hungary, China, Berlin, Prague, and elsewhere, and the fledgling United Nations seemed unable to live up to early hopes and expectations. At home, hardly a day passed without new sensational headlines of spy-rings and espionage right under naïve and unsuspecting Canadian and American noses. Disloyalty seemed to be everywhere. Loyalty became something that one had to be able to prove. And, in the House of Commons, the government found itself under attack and forced to defend the NFB at a time when its own suspicions of the board were increasing.

Screening of government departments for spies, Communists, and fellow-travellers began in 1946 and was carried out by the RCMP and supervised by the civilian Security Panel.[2] Screening usually meant the filling out of a government questionnaire which was then checked against RCMP files for criminal records, fascist activities, membership in the communist party, and so on. In some cases the RCMP investigation included a more expensive and time-consuming 'field investigation' – a process of interviews with neighbours and colleagues. The screening of NFB employees began early in 1949 and by mid-summer the board had been declared a 'vulnerable agency.'[3] Ross McLean, Grierson's successor as film commissioner, agreed that until the screening was finished the Department of National Defence (DND) would have its films dealing with classified material produced by outside commercial film companies.

The muddle at the NFB – charges of Communist infiltration and subversion, public bickering, on-going screening of its employees – continued through most of the year and the board appeared to be drifting in uncharted waters and uncertain winds. On the government side there were suspicions that board employees were feeding information to the opposition to embarrass the government; in Quebec the provincial government began censoring and banning NFB films.[4] Winters responded to the situation in November by appointing J.D. Woods and Gordon Ltd., the Toronto consulting firm, to investigate the state of the film board.

A crisis was temporarily postponed until later that month when an article in *The Financial Post*, written by Ken Wilson and Cyril Basset, brought things crashing down. The thrust of *The Financial Post* article was not – as subsequent legend has it – on the security issue, but rather on the NFB's monopoly over government film production and the rising opposition to the board in the private film industry and from other government departments. But what caught the public's attention was the question asked at the start: 'Is the Film Board a leftist propaganda machine?' and two sentences in the article's first few paragraphs: 'When The Post began probing this situation, it found that the Department of National Defense no longer uses the Film Board on "classified" (i.e. secret) work for security reasons. As a result, films "classified" for security reasons are being placed by the Department of National Defense with outside commercial organizations.'[5]

The explosive nature of such an accusation was not lost on the Conservative opposition in the House of Commons, which for months had been attacking the government on the security issue. Once the government admitted that *The Financial Post's* allegations were true the opposition had a field-day. Everyone knew that the NFB was a hide-out for subversives of every shade of red. When was the government going to take out a broom and sweep the place clean? The RCMP, meanwhile, returned with a list of thirty-six NFB staffers who had not passed their security screening, but McLean refused to dismiss any of them.[6] It appeared that a difficult problem was about to get completely out of hand.

Something had to be done, and done quickly. Clearly McLean was not the one to reorganize the board. He lacked Grierson's creativity and organizational ability, and did not have Grierson's influence or connections with the prime minister and others in the government. And, he no longer had the confidence of the government. At precisely the same moment that the government was fending off attacks in the Commons, Norman Robertson was on the telephone to Irwin asking him to come to Ottawa.

Why Irwin? For one thing he was an outsider and as such was unscathed by the allegations and charges that had been ricocheting around Ottawa and the board for years. And Irwin had the right anti-Communist credentials; this was apparent to anyone who read 'The Canadian' or his *Maclean's* articles from his European trips. As an editor of *Maclean's* for almost twenty-five years he had gained enormous experience dealing with creative people – individuals who, to outsiders, might seem unorthodox in social behaviour – and he had helped to build a successful operation. Perhaps he could do the same for the NFB.

Irwin was also well known to the people in Ottawa. His years at *Maclean's* had earned him a degree of notoriety, and his long years of involvement in the CIIA had produced friendships with many of the top mandarins in the public service – some of those who would have direct input into decisions concerning the film board. If he needed character references in the government itself he did not have to go very far. Lester Pearson, the minister of external affairs, was an acquaintance of many years standing, while Brooke Claxton, a friend from his army days and associate in the CIIA, was minister of national defence and a one-time chair of the NFB. These people knew him as a liberal-democrat with a strong nationalist streak, and as a man who shared the views of most of those in the progressive wing of the Liberal government and its bureaucracy.

The crucial event, however, was that afternoon in October 1949, when Irwin suggested to Cam Moodie that he could be enticed into public service. Irwin had the experience and the ability to do the job; now it appeared that if handled correctly, he could be persuaded to accept a thankless job in Ottawa. The way to 'handle' Irwin was to link the NFB commissioner's job with a 'moral commitment' of a posting in the Department of External Affairs.

It should also be mentioned that a number of persons interviewed for this project suggested that there might be another reason for Irwin's selection: the government feared 'another Bren gun.' The anti-government mudslinging of George Drew, who now led the federal Conservative party, and the muckraking attacks from *The Financial Post* had a familiar ring to government members who remembered the activities of ten years earlier when Drew and the Maclean company linked up for an assault on the Liberal government, an assault based on material gathered by Arthur Irwin. What better way to prevent such a recurrence than to take one of the central protagonists of the earlier affair and place him in charge of cleaning up the mess at the film board? How could Maclean Hunter launch a new campaign with one of its own as the target? It is an intriguing theory, but no evidence has surfaced to support it.

In a similar vein, the *Canadian Film Weekly* openly asked if Irwin was hired to act as the mouthpiece for the private film industry. His ties to *The Financial Post*, which was seen as an organ for big business and free enterprise, was pointed to as evidence that he was despatched to Ottawa to oversee a serious curtailment or even destruction of the film board. 'Might as well make me editor of Maclean's,' one producer was quoted. 'I certainly know as much about editing a magazine as the new commissioner knows about film production.'[7]

With Irwin's acceptance of the government's offer, the board met on 16 December and approved the arrangement and officially recommended that Irwin replace McLean as film commissioner. A press release was issued later that day and the stunning news quickly spread through the film board offices. Marjorie McKay, a long-time staffer described the moment in her unpublished NFB history: 'One of the truck drivers brought the paper into John Street [a NFB location]. A salesman brought the news into Purchasing. A boy going out for a cup of coffee in Distribution saw the news and came running in with a dozen papers. A cameraman on a train picked up a newspaper left lying on a seat and read the story. Stunned by the news, employees rushed to buy papers and Arthur Irwin's face stared back at them from the front page.'[8]

It would be hard to imagine a more perplexing atmosphere to begin a new and difficult job. McLean's removal was effective immediately while Irwin was scheduled to join the board in February 1950, more than a month later. While awaiting Irwin's arrival, rumours of mass firings circulated. Wasn't that, after all, why the government hired Irwin – to decimate the staff and dismantle the board? He could not have been appointed for any film-related reasons; the new commissioner had no film experience and probably could not tell the difference between a camera and a projector.

McLean's resignation was followed by a series of outbursts of complaint from loyal staffers. His assistant, Ralph Foster, tendered his resignation immediately, but others argued against such a step, noting that the continuing existence of the board was far more important than the fate of one employee. There also was some question over the message that resigning would send. As McKay noted, those who resigned immediately would be followed by a cloud of suspicion for the rest of their careers.[9]

Things were not improved by the press's handling of the affair. Robert Winters claimed in the House that he had notified McLean weeks earlier (before the issuance of the press release in December) that his contract as commissioner would not be renewed.[10] But rumours quickly spread that McLean was further insulted by learning of his replacement by Irwin – after the fact – from the evening newspaper. *Time Magazine*, meanwhile, brandished a photograph of a smiling Arthur Irwin – horn-rimmed glasses and polka dot bow tie firmly in place – ready to take on a new challenge. 'I go in there with a virgin mind,' Irwin was quoted. 'I quit a job at 27 to try something else; I'd hate to think I'm too old to do it now.'[11]

Much was made of Irwin's starting salary. Several papers suggested that McLean's dismissal was in part a result of his request for a raise. 'Last month he asked for a raise in his $8,000 salary ... the government decided not to reappoint him. Instead it hired Irwin – at $15,000 a year.'[12] But it was the security issue that dominated. The *Sudbury Daily Star* said it all:

The National Film Board this week was throwing up the bomb-proof shelters in preparation for the 'shakeup' promised with the replacement of Film Commissioner Ross McLean by W. Arthur Irwin ...
   The government gave Irwin the job specifically to clean Reds out of the film board.
   Irwin, unofficially, has let it be known he will do just that.
   One of Irwin's big weapons in his cleanup is the secret list prepared by the RCMP as a result of their recent screening of the board.
   Rather than wait for the tap on the shoulder by Irwin, a lot of senior board officials this week were getting their resignations ready.[13]

A meeting with Norman Robertson was hastily organized by a handful of staff members to vent their protest on the government. 'Why had Ross been fired?' was what they wanted to know. The cerebral Robertson responded to the angry meeting by talking of the Griersonian tradition at the film board – the tradition of trying to anticipate the foreign policy of the country.[14] The crowd left unsatisfied. McLean, meanwhile, did not leave with his head down. He landed a good position as director of the film section of UNESCO. Before he left, a tearful and somber party was thrown in his honour and he was presented with enough money to buy himself a new car. That so few gave so much was a clear indication of the love and respect the other staff members had for him.

Irwin walked straight into a hornet's nest, fully aware of the resentment, distrust, and the outright hostility that awaited him. He had tried to mollify the staff's fears somewhat by announcing that there would be no firing at all until he had arrived. But the security issue would not go away and it would be waiting for him at the top of his agenda.

◆

The presence of Communists or the existence of study groups or 'cells' in the film board is not disputed. There were a number of different groups formed in the 1940s to discuss a wide range of issues, most of which had to do with films rather than politics or revolution. Communists – either card-carrying members or 'fellow travellers' – participated in some of these groups. The conversations might turn to the injustices of unemployment or the inadequate distribution of income in Canadian society. But whether there was anything illegal – let alone subversive – about these groups is another matter.

One individual, who was not a party member, but attended a few meetings of one group, later described the experience. Members were informed of upcoming meetings through silent hand signals from other members as they passed in the hall. The signal was the clasping of hands and the number of times indicated the number of evenings until the meeting. It was all very cloak and dagger, and 'something like we did in high school.' The meetings themselves were less than inspiring.

We sat around ... that night somebody read a long – very dull – section from *The Dialectics of Materialism* and we discussed that. Then we got over onto the question of how ineffective the new head of distribution [at the NFB] was, which had nothing to do with communism or anything, and after having done that we got into a little bit of gossip, which was quite interesting about who was living with who now and whose marriage was breaking up. Then we came back to *The Dialectics of Materialism*. And then we came back to a *thundering* defence of Stalin. This was at the end of the war. And then those of us who didn't like Stalin made our comments about Stalin and the others turned on us and said if we felt like that we had no place in their meetings. We said that we thought that if this was a discussion of Communism this was a key factor. And Stalin was a bastard, and had been all the time. He may have been a great war leader – well, so was Churchill and he was a bastard too. We were not popular.

Marjorie McKay, who was a close associate of Grierson (she took a year's leave of absence after the war to work with Grierson in Great Britain) knew of the meetings of the 'armchair reds' as she called them. She had decidedly left-wing views herself, although she never was a member of a party (Communist, CCF or Liberal), and fully expected to be fired after her RCMP screening. She had already lost a job as a high school teacher when it was discovered that her brother was a prominent Communist (who was killed fighting for the republican cause in the Spanish Civil War). 'When I was cleared by the RCMP,' she later confessed, 'I was probably the most surprised person in Ottawa.'

The only breach of security McKay experienced in all her years at the board occurred during the war. The board produced a short ten-minute, 16 mm film on radar and was preparing to screen it for a handful of military officers at the board. At the same time, another film – this one on five new apple dishes – was produced for the Women's Institute. Somehow the films were placed in the wrong cans and the Women's Institute was exposed to secret material on radar while a room full of generals sat through a lesson on cooking apples. McKay later asked the secretary responsible for sending the films how she could ship the wrong ones, and she replied: 'It was marked secret, so I didn't open it.'[15]

It is clear that there was little if any espionage or subversion going on at the board during these years. No evidence of any has surfaced. There were people on staff with left-wing political views and many staffers might be considered eccentric. But left-wing views and eccentricities do not add up to subversion. And, as Michael Spencer, who served as security officer under Irwin, later suggested, screening employees was unlikely to unearth spies in any event; real spies were not likely to have criminal records or be known members of a subversive group. They tended to be the unlikely ones – the ones you would never suspect. On the NFB being a security risk he was doubtful; as for it being a political risk he was sure.[16]

Canada did, however, have secrets worth stealing, especially (but not exclusively) dealing with atomic energy. There were documents and information in Canada that the Soviets wanted to have and they were willing to use spies to get them. The government decided that it was worth the possible infringement of individual civil liberties to protect Canadian society against what it believed was a serious threat. And most Canadians, according to public opinion polls taken during the Gouzenko enquiry, supported the government in its investigations.[17] Such sacrifices had proven themselves quite valuable during the war;

the fact that the war was over seemed not to deter them, for there was a war of a new kind to be fought. Thus, there were persons on the ministerial and official levels who had for their whole lives defended individual civil liberties now supporting rather Draconian actions against suspected security risks. It is in this context that their actions must be examined.

The film board, as a government agency, automatically fell into a screening category. What made it stand out were the questions raised in parliament and the sensational news stories that swirled around it. The film board presented an easy target and became something of a cause célèbre for the government, a test case on which its ability to deal with subversion would be measured. In this sense the film board security issue was not as much a security as a political problem. Irwin's task was to restore the government's and the public's confidence in the board. But clearly it was the political aspect that dominated; as has been pointed out elsewhere, it is not at all clear that the *public* ever lost confidence in the board.[18]

Irwin did not request or initiate the screening of the board's employees, but it fell to him to deal with its results. On his arrival he was presented with the list of thirty-six names that the RCMP had previously given to Ross McLean, a list of suspected board employees derived from RCMP investigations. It was divided into three sections: security risks, probable risks, and possible risks.

Irwin insisted on the unusual practice of 'cross-examining' the RCMP on their selection. An interview was arranged between Irwin and RCMP Inspector R.A.S. MacNeil, a member of the government's Security Panel. MacNeil would not permit Irwin to see the material in his files, claiming security reasons – protection of sources and the names of undercover agents. As a result, an elaborate process was worked out in which MacNeil read his files aloud to Irwin, witholding the names of the RCMP sources, and his words were recorded by a police stenographer. The censored dossiers were passed on to Irwin, and a day or two later he was given an opportunity to question MacNeil. In perhaps less direct words than he would have used with a novice writer at *Maclean's,* Irwin was asking MacNeil: 'Have you done your homework?' Irwin accepted that there might be security risks in the NFB, but he was unwilling to accept unsubstantiated claims and allegations about past behaviour as proof. Irwin recalled one dossier on a board employee whose only crime appeared to have been that he had heckled James Gardiner, the minister of agriculture, at a political rally in Saskatchewan.

Once the sessions with MacNeil were completed, Irwin was on his own to wrestle with the evidence and make a final decision. Most of those listed he dismissed from consideration immediately – men and women whose names had popped up on obscure files, or who had participated in left-wing activities (and, it appears, support for the CCF was included here) at some time in their lives. These people never posed any risk and should never have appeared on any list to begin with.

He did find three names that he was convinced were potential security risks. He found no evidence of subversion or any breach of security, but the nature of the investigation was not to unearth past crimes but rather to weed out potential future risks. And these three were 'so close to the communist apparatus' as he later put it, that he believed they posed a genuine security risk.[19]

Before taking any public action, Irwin passed his bundle of dossiers on to Norman Robertson for his perusal – without informing him of the names that he had selected. Robertson disappeared with the files and, when he returned a few days later, he had selected the same three people.[20] Irwin next met with Winters and informed him of his and Robertson's independent selection. Winters accepted his decision without argument (although Irwin later recalled Winters asking about the staffer who heckled Gardiner). Irwin believed that Winters never personally looked at the files.

The next step was the most distasteful of all. 'I had to bring these boys in,' Irwin said later, during an interview for the NFB, 'and all I said was I'm very sorry but as you know this has been declared a vulnerable agency, and I hadn't been able to satisfy myself that you're the kind of person that should be employed in that agency ... and I must say that to their credit they accepted this.'[22] Three NFB employees were 'separated.' No charges were laid, their contracts were not renewed, and their resignations were accepted immediately. Irwin attended the next board meeting and informed the members of his actions, and Winters took the necessary steps to permit the resumption of NFB work on DND material. The decision was made public by Winters in the House of Commons on 29 March.

The announcement that the board was again open for DND business effectively ended the 'red scare' at the film board. Irwin still faced an enormous task of reorganization, but the political air had been cleared. The questioning in the House of Commons continued for a brief time, but with the appointment of a new commissioner and subsequent 'cleanup,' the blustery wind in the opposition's sails petered out. In the Security Panel and DND a few lingering concerns persisted over the board's security status, and in American military circles there remained a reluctance to pass on sensitive films to the DND 'in view of the adverse publicity on the National Film Board.' But such concerns could be dealt with quietly, and Robertson noted that Irwin 'had taken hold effectively and with a keen sense of responsibility in regard to the security problem.'[22]

Winters's announcement, of course, did not end the security issue for the staff – and former staffers – at the film board. Once the original screening process was completed, an automatic security check was implemented for all new employees. This arrangement was not unique to the NFB, however. And, for those who were fired there was no recourse. They accepted their fates without a public fuss, but they had no alternatives in any event. Public protest would only have made it far more difficult to find other jobs.

Other staffers resigned from the board before and after Irwin's arrival. It is impossible to put a figure on the number involved because most employees were on three-month renewable contracts and people were leaving all the time, for a variety of reasons. Some resigned because they believed that they would be fired on security grounds (whether they would have been is unclear); others believed that the atmosphere of distrust and suspicion during this period made it impossible to go on with their jobs. Others left to pursue their careers elsewhere. Still others were dismissed because they were bad filmmakers and could not do their jobs – as in any ordinary government or private organization.

The legacy of this episode – and its apparent infringement of civil rights – lives on and has spawned a small cottage industry of books and magazine articles. The government acted in an arbitrary fashion and justified its actions by pointing to the real risks of espionage and by concluding that strong measures were necessary to combat so devilish a foe. But as others have pointed out, 'it is difficult to avoid the conclusion that the Canadian government, confronted with an extraordinary situation, reacted with arbitrary and harsh measures that threatened to ape the standards of the society that the Soviet spies were serving.'[23] That it is unlikely that such an episode would ever be repeated today is small comfort to those who lost their jobs or lived and worked in fear.

Inevitably, comparisons are made between the NFB red scare and

'Mad Ministers, Rioting Reds, and Posh Parties'   241

similar happenings in the United States that soon followed. The Canadian version was more limited in scope and less vicious in implementation than its American counterpart, and Canadians can find some comfort in these facts. It was also far quieter. No public trials and blacklisting, no vindictive witch-hunts. Security risks were to be removed from sensitive areas quietly, not hounded for the rest of their lives. As one NFB historian put it, 'Canada had cast a net of suspicion far and wide over its government agencies, but, ironically, the Liberals' attitude was that security risks should be given jobs in less sensitive areas so they could still feed their families and pay their mortgages.'[24]

Irwin did not create the security problem at the National Film Board, but he was obliged to deal with it. In the end he acted decisively, doing what he thought was right, under very trying circumstances. Yet, he was never completely at ease with the way things were handled in the security cases. He later confessed to an NFB interviewer: 'I was never really easy ... I'm not sure this is the way to handle the security problems ... should these fellows [have] had a chance to defend themselves in public ... should they have been charged in public ... or should it be handled in this way without any publicity at all ... I'm not sure what was the right way ... at any rate that's the way it was done.'[25]

Any regret he may have felt was directed not at the decisions that he was forced to make – because he stood by them – but rather at having to take distasteful measures against a few film board employees. Irwin's liberalism made him unwilling to dismiss people indiscriminately, but, like many of his public service colleagues, he believed that the security question was an issue that had to be addressed. He could have avoided the whole affair by refusing the government's original offer, but he accepted the job clear in his own mind on the necessity of protecting the state from potential subversion. He wrestled with the civil rights aspect but concluded that if he could justify in his own mind that if an employee was a genuine security risk he or she should be dismissed. It was a classic no-win situation.

A few years after he had left the NFB Irwin returned to the board and, during a private lunch with a few producers who had been colleagues during his years as commissioner, he attempted to explain his actions and the difficult and complex situation he inherited at the board in 1950. Now, with the suspicion and anger gone and the atmosphere much improved, he was able to reveal a few of the details and untangle a few of the mysteries surrounding his appointment. Tom Daly, one of the senior producers who attended the lunch, later put

Irwin's role in perspective: 'Irwin turned out to be exactly the necessary person who could have led us – at that time. And he turned out ... to be the person who left us in a perfect condition to go on positively after that, with, of all things, the public press satisfied that we were okay – because one of their own people had come in and [had] done what was necessary, and we were left with a clean sheet.'[26]

SIXTEEN

'Going to Bat' for the NFB

The security issue dominated Irwin's first few weeks at the film board, but within two months of his arrival the matter was closed, at least as far as he was concerned. At the same time, he began to work on what he perceived to be his greatest task: the physical and administrative reorganization of the board.

The physical problems were obvious. The NFB was divided into a number of divisions which were spread out in more than half a dozen buildings around Ottawa. Technical operations and the production department were housed in the largest building on John Street, the distribution department was located in the Sovereign Building on Sparks Street. Photo services, camera stores, the filmstrip section, and displays and publication design were situated in other buildings along Sparks. The purchasing department, stores department, and a few additional small groups were scattered in other locations. Administratively it was a geographical nightmare.

Irwin toured each of the buildings, which gave him a chance to meet some of the staff and to see the kinds of things they were doing. He was impressed by the board's activities but appalled by the conditions under which the staff was forced to work. At least one of the sites quite clearly should have been condemned as a fire-trap; some departments worked without heat and were forced to rely on small space heaters.[1] In one building he found staffers working with their coats and gloves on. In Irwin's mind a new home was necessary for two reasons: to give an administrative coherence to the board's operations, and to raise the standard of working conditions to a level comparable to other government agencies.

Irwin's initial problems with his new staff were compounded by the sour atmosphere which engulfed the board during the security screening. He was blamed for what had happened to Ross McLean, and the remaining staff feared that he would merely oversee the destruction of the board. Such emotions made an already onerous task far more difficult. Irwin also brought his own style to the board and in many ways he was a different person than either John Grierson or Ross McLean.

Under Grierson and McLean the board was an informal place to work. Small production groups worked relatively freely. Days were not regulated by lunch breaks, time clocks, or closing hours – projects dictated such things. It was not unusual for staff members to work late into the evening, and then all – including Grierson – would continue in an Ottawa restaurant or bar. Grierson and McLean were known as friends, colleagues, and co-workers. They knew all about films, they understood the film business, and they (especially Grierson) made films themselves. Grierson was 'totally accessible by anybody at the Board,' producer Tom Daly recalled. 'He came around and was among people. He came to all the parties, and he would hole up, maybe in the kitchen, and get into any kind of argument or philosophical discussion that you might want.'[2] This style was not Irwin's. While Grierson and McLean were regulars at the frequent office parties, Irwin was not. In fact, he was rarely invited.

Irwin was more difficult to read, his emotions rarely showed through his reserved and rather austere demeanour. 'We practically never heard directly from him,' Daly remembered; 'everything was done through somebody else. And there was a feeling of being totally cut off.' No longer could a staffer walk into the commissioner's office because he wanted to chat about some news item in the paper or a movie he had seen the night before. With Irwin one needed an appointment. As Marjorie McKay wrote in her NFB history, 'art lovers and music lovers, French intellectuals and English book enthusiasts could not bring themselves to face Irwin's battery of secretaries to ask for an appointment to discuss their latest enthusiasm. A breadth and depth of perception was lost.'[3]

Others remembered Irwin as a 'telephone man,' someone who would spend half an hour or forty-five minutes talking on the telephone trying to make a point or sway an opinion. It was a technique, Michael Spencer recalled, that Irwin used to considerable effect. But it was not the kind of arrangement that produced strong bonds of friendship. There was always an air of formality around him. Marjorie

McKay recalled how it took Irwin two years before he called her Marj – she never called him anything but Mr Irwin (compared to John and Ross).[4]

Irwin made a valiant effort to overcome a situation that to him was a mixture of confusion and misunderstanding. He made a point of getting out as much as possible, to wander the halls meeting people, seeing what was being done. He tried to get to know his senior people on a more informal basis. Sydney Newman, a future film commissioner, remembered coming to Ottawa and Irwin cooking him dinner in his apartment. For desert Irwin prepared a home-made peach melba and then sat – 'salivating' – while Newman ate it. Irwin's stomach problems still forbad such delicacies.[5]

It took time to dismantle barriers built upon suspicion and fear, and Irwin's occasional use of the term 'reds' in conversation was a little jarring to those around him. And he continued for many months to expose his non-film background by using the magazine word 'circulation' when he meant film 'distribution.' Minor things, of course, but they left an enduring impression on his staff and colleagues.

As commissioner, Irwin was given two offices, the main one in the Sovereign Building on Bank Street, and a smaller one in the John Street Building. His reorganization began here, as he brought together a hand-picked staff to help with the daily running of his office. One of the key people was Reta Kilpatrick, a bright and capable aide who joined the NFB in 1945 and worked under Ralph Foster until he resigned. Following the resignation of his first assistant, Irwin made her his administrative assistant and transferred her to his Bank Street office. Kilpatrick later described the board that first year as a madhouse, where everyone regularly worked until midnight and on the weekends. Kilpatrick herself came down with whooping cough but worked right through it, except for a few days, thinking it was merely a bad cold.[6]

The closest thing Irwin had for a blueprint for his planned reorganization was the Woods and Gordon report. Appointed the previous autumn, the Woods and Gordon consultants – headed by Walter Gordon – worked all through the security scare and submitted their report in March 1950.[7] The report recommended separating the board from direct government supervision, by removing the government ministers and appointing in their place the film commissioner as chair and increasing the public representatives to five. More concretely, the report advocated the centralizing of the board's activities in a suitable location. The report also toyed with the idea of turning the board into a crown corporation, suggesting that it would be a 'logical solution' to the problem of efficiency. In the interim, the report suggested a handful of amendments to the Film Board Act (dealing with control of costs, revenues, contracting) to help it operate more effectively.

On the suggestion of the consultants, Irwin undertook a survey of the various board operations with an eye to shifting some of the board's duties to other government departments and agencies. For example, the board's microfilming activities were discontinued, the displays section was transferred to the Department of Trade and Commerce, while the three-person posters and publication design section was shifted to the King's Printer.[8] Within the board itself, the skeleton of a firm administrative structure was established with the creation of five directorates: production, distribution, administration, planning, and technical services. Filmstrip and still photo production was transferred to the production branch. Each section was headed by an appointed director.

Irwin's choice for director of production caused a minor ruckus. During the Grierson and McLean eras each of the production units acted as independent fiefs under the charge of an executive producer who was personally responsible to the commissioner. But Irwin was not a hands-on commissioner in the Grierson mould, and he wanted one single producer to oversee the activities of the various production units. There were two likely candidates for the job. The first and most favoured was James Beveridge, a talented and popular producer, who had chaired the producer's committee (and who was also Norman Robertson's cousin). Beveridge developed his abilities as a filmmaker under Grierson's tutelage during the war, and, interestingly, had been Grierson's choice as his own successor.[9] The second was Donald Mulholland, an American-born producer, who arrived at the board in 1946 after serving in the RCAF. Mulholland could be abrasive and was known for his sharp (and often vulgar) tongue, and he lacked Beveridge's connection with the Grierson tradition.

Irwin was concerned less with popularity than he was in selecting someone suited to administration. He chose Mulholland for his administrative and organizational abilities, but his decision provoked a storm of protest.[10] To some, Mulholland's selection was further proof of Irwin's hidden agenda to destroy the board. Others rebelled against the establishment of any kind of hierarchy; there had been none in the past, and the choice of Beveridge at least would have meant a looser and easier control over production. From Irwin's perspective it was the 'Grierson phalanx' rising once again, this time with Jim Beveridge as figurehead. Once the initial storm passed, Mulholland became an effective director of production, but the episode served as a reminder of the lingering tensions left in the wake of Irwin's arrival.[11]

In addition to the structural and administrative changes, Irwin focused a good deal of energy on the National Film Board Act. The problem, as he saw it, was rooted in the NFB's original design. The board had no firm legal basis for its activities, it had only limited control over its own finances, and the system of temporary staff contracts was awkward and inefficient. (Irwin later complained that one staffer worked full time doing nothing but the paperwork for contract renewals.) And now that the board was deeply involved in film production and distribution, Irwin believed that the act must be modified to reflect these changes. At first he hoped that the original act could be amended but it quickly became apparent that a whole new act was necessary. With the help of colleagues in the NFB and from officials in the Justice Department, and using the Woods and Gordon report as a guide, a new film act was written by June 1950. It passed through the House of Commons in July and came into effect on 14 October.

As recommended by the Woods and Gordon report, the new act revamped the board's composition by removing the two government ministers and giving the chair of the board to the film commissioner. Thus the film commissioner was granted status akin to a deputy minister, who reported to a minister in the government, and through the minister to parliament. Of the other eight board members, three were to come from the public service (or Canadian forces), and the remaining five from outside.

For Irwin the key aspect of the new act was that it clearly set out the board's role – something that was missing in the 1939 act – and, as Irwin later noted, it 'firmly nailed down the fact that the Government was going to stay in the film business.' The final wording bore Irwin's imprint, and read, in part:

The Board is established to initiate and promote the production and distribution of films in the national interest and in particular
    (a) to produce and distribute and to promote the production and distribution of films designed to interpret Canada to Canadians and to other nations;
    (b) to represent the Government of Canada in its relations with persons

engaged in commercial motion pictures film activity in connection with motion picture films for the Government or department thereof;

(c) to engage in research in film activity and to make available the results thereof to persons engaged in the production of films.

The act continued with a description of the board's powers; it set out the financial provisions under which it would operate, and redefined the role of film commissioner. The thrust of the act was to make some sense from what was seen as administrative chaos at the board, and the solution was to remodel it along the lines of any other government agency. Critics later charged that such changes damaged the board's vitality by making it bureaucratically top-heavy, but for Irwin the changes were long overdue and merely recognized the fact that the board had grown from a small loose collection of filmmakers and production units into a substantial *government* institution.[12]

With Irwin's structural reorganization complete and with the passage of the new Film Board Act, the charges that Irwin had been sent by the government to destroy the NFB all but disappeared. From the financial and administrative side, the board was in a stronger position than it had ever been before. The long arm of government, meanwhile, had been pushed a little farther away with the removal of ministerial involvement. The NFB was clearly a permanent institution.

As he had at *MacLean's*, Irwin directed a good deal of his efforts towards recruiting new staff. 'On the administrative side, the Board is still weak and the objective here is to build an organization of young, first-rate people who if necessary could take over the operation within a relatively short time,' he wrote Vincent Massey, in words reminiscent of earlier letters to Napier Moore and Horace Hunter. 'So far the difficulty has been to lure first-rate people away from private industry at salaries we can afford to pay and to lure first-class people from other government services to the Film Board. This is one of the most difficult management tasks that lies immediately ahead but it must be solved.'[13]

One area that struck Irwin as particularly weak was the francophone side of the board, especially in the administrative branch. He therefore made an effort to recruit and promote talented francophones within the organization. One young employee that attracted his attention was Pierre Juneau. Juneau was born in Verdun, Quebec, in 1922 and was a graduate of Montreal's Collège Sainte-Marie and the Sorbonne. He joined the NFB in 1949, serving as Montreal district supervisor, before transferring to Ottawa as director of international distribution.[14] Irwin saw in Juneau a young man of energy and ability – just the kind of individual he wanted for the film board. In 1952 he approved Juneau's appointment to London as assistant head of the European office under Jim Beveridge. In 1954 Juneau returned to Ottawa as secretary of the NFB, a post he held for eleven years.

Irwin became involved in a different kind of recruiting after he met P.K. Page, a young scriptwriter in the filmstrip unit. Page, who was born in Great Britain and had come to Canada at the age of two, had lived in Calgary, Halifax, Montreal, and Victoria before joining the film board at the end of the war. During the war she began publishing her poetry in literary journals and wrote a novel entitled *The Sun and the Moon*. A book of poetry, *As Ten as Twenty*, followed in 1946.

At the time the security issue flared up in 1949 Page had already decided to leave the film board. But, like many others on staff, she decided that it would be best to wait until the storm blew over. In the summer of 1950, when the mood was much improved, she again contemplated resignation. But before she left for another job, Irwin telephoned and asked her out to dinner, the reason being to discuss her resignation.[15]

Irwin persuaded Page to stay with the board – for the time being at least – and the two began seeing each other socially. Within a few months the couple announced their engagement and Page gave up her job at the board. They were married in Ottawa on 16 December. 'Let me say at once that your judgement in matters of the heart seems to rival your judgement in matters of the pen,' Pierre Berton wrote to Irwin when he heard the news.

I heard of PK. Page long before I heard of W.A. Irwin. Indeed she and I once shared a spot between the covers of a little magazine called Reading (which I heard of long before I heard of Maclean's). I have admired her poetry ever since, although for some time, because of the by-line, I thought she was a man.

In the circle in which I move people are always paying tribute to P.K. Page's poetry. Regrettably, many of these same people, on hearing your name mentioned, turn with a snarl and cry: 'Irwin? That's the sonofabitch that turned down my article on The Dichotomy of Emmanuel Kant – that guy has no understanding of the finer things.' Obviously, these people are wrong.

I have of course your own appreciation of the situation when, last spring, I mentioned that you had one of Canada's best poets in your employ. 'Yes' you said, 'and she's a good looker, too.'[16]

'Where for the honeymoon?' Pat wrote Arthur in October. 'It is hard to know. I'm not overly enthusiastic about Banff – I don't much like being surrounded by mountains and I *hate* climbing them.'[17] The newlyweds settled on the St Moritz Hotel in New York City.

◆

Irwin is perhaps best remembered as film commissioner as the man who moved the National Film Board from Ottawa to Montreal. Nobody argued with the need for a new locale to centralize board activities, and Irwin was clear in his own mind on the need for a single building. The Woods and Gordon report recognized and acknowledged the need as well.

Irwin asked what really was an obvious question, Why should the National Film Board be in Ottawa? The growth of the NFB during the war had been haphazard and unplanned; did this development necessarily wed the board to the city forever? When he could not answer his own question satisfactorily he launched a personal investigation to find some answers. And the more he looked at the issue the harder it became for him to justify in his own mind keeping the board in Ottawa.

Irwin embodied a recommendation that the NFB be moved in a detailed memorandum which he prepared for the board in May 1950. His arguments were rooted in the fact that the board's present facilities were unsuitable and that it would be moving *somewhere*. A new site in Ottawa's Tunney's Pasture was under consideration, but Irwin was not at all sure that this was the appropriate location. Ottawa was a 'relatively small community,' he wrote. 'a highly homogeneous community which is definitely stereotyped and the stereotype is not one which takes kindly to the non-conformity of creative people.'[18]

But from Irwin's perspective, a proposal to move the board out of Ottawa in no way suggested the possibility of dismantling or decentralizing its operations. Despite the sprawling locations around the city, the NFB was a centralized federal operation when Irwin arrived in 1950 and he was neither asked nor desired to alter that fundamental relationship during his tenure. Irwin shared with many others of his generation a strong federalist and centralist streak, and he believed that the state could play an important and beneficial role in Canadian life, including in the cultural field. Like his friend Brooke Claxton, who later became the first chair of the Canada Council, he favoured 'an Ottawa-centred activist role for the support of culture.'[19]

In Irwin's mind it was more important to find a metropolitan environment, where the board would be neither conspicuous nor self-conscious and where there would be a greater cross-section of creative people. A major city offered a greater variety and higher level of expertise in almost every aspect of filmmaking – actors, musicians, technicians, equipment suppliers, and production and recording facilities. A major city would offer everything, it seemed, except government ministers and bureaucrats. Most important, a metropolitan area would provide the creative atmosphere within which the board could flourish, 'where it will be in immediate contact with other creative people as good or better than the members of the group, people who can kick it around aesthetically and intellectually.'[20]

There were disadvantages to leaving Ottawa, and Irwin was fully aware that such a decision could spark a controversy. The board was, after all, a government agency and much of its business dealt directly with other government departments in Ottawa. Clearly, even if the board left the city, some presence would have to be maintained in Ottawa, if only to sustain the connection with the responsible minister. For Irwin this was not a crucial factor; indeed, he saw the greater separation from the government apparatus as a positive reason for removing the board in the first place.

A more significant concern was the dislocation that moving the board would have on its employees. He estimated that some 350 staffers would be forced to leave their homes to start new lives in another city. But, he reasoned, such dislocation was temporary in nature and in the overall context should not be permitted to halt the move.[21]

For Irwin the question was not whether the board should move, but rather should it be moved to Toronto or Montreal, the only two significant metropolitan centres within a few hours of Ottawa. In several ways Toronto was the obvious choice and, if the country were unilingual English, it would be the prime location. 'The Board's operations, however, are bilingual,' Irwin argued, 'and, if it were to locate in Toronto, it would not have the immediate contact with French Canada which is necessary to operate effectively in the French language.'

As a cosmopolitan city, Montreal had a lot to offer – culturally, creatively, and aesthetically – and Irwin pointed out these aspects. But the key factor was the bicultural dimension. 'The English language community in Montreal offers the advantages of a metropolitan area,' he continued, 'and the desirability of the Board being in immediate contact with both English-speaking and French-speaking talent would seem to be a determining factor.' Looming in the background throughout these discussions was the role of the NFB in the development of the new medium of television. In these early stages it was still not clear what role either the CBC or the NFB would play. But Montreal was seen as a future television centre and this was another factor in the decision to locate the board there.

Irwin took his ideas and his memo first to the board members for their consideration. At the same time he undertook a little arm-twisting of notable Ottawa mandarins to gather some support for his plan. Winters was an easy convert; he quickly saw the advantages of moving the board to Montreal, but, equally, he was alive to potential roadblocks thrown up by the Quebec government, which had already placed restrictions on NFB films. Winters discussed the NFB 'ban' with Quebec's Premier Duplessis and received a hint that the restrictions would be lifted. Winters recommended that the prime minister have a private talk with Duplessis to iron out any remaining difficulties.[22]

In the meantime, Winters prepared a cabinet document based on Irwin's memo. St Laurent had received and read a copy of Irwin's original memo as well. Like Irwin, St Laurent supported the move because he hoped it would lead to the expansion of the francophone side of the board.[23] The new document was submitted to cabinet on 30 September, and, after Winters presented the case, cabinet approved the plan for the move in principle.[24]

The next step was to find a suitable location in the Montreal area, and a small committee was established within the board of governors to oversee the project. For months this committee (which was chaired by C.S. Band), in conjunction with the Department of Public Works, reviewed more than a dozen prospective sites for a new building. Consideration was given to purchasing the building and assets of a bankrupt film studio not far from downtown, and to a vacant lot in Montreal's south shore. The choices were eventually narrowed down to three: an available downtown site near the Forum, a large tract of farmland in suburban Pointe Claire, and a lot in Ville St-Laurent close to Decarie Boulevard.[25]

The St-Laurent site was the final selection for a number of reasons. A large tract of land was available, and it was close to mixed French/English residential areas. The site was close to a highway, which was considered an advantage in that it gave relatively good access to

Ottawa and permitted easy commuting downtown. Less spectacular although equally important factors included moderate land costs, a good power supply, and a water capacity which needed only a little upgrading.[26] In addition, early plans for the site included the need for storing millions of feet of aging and highly explosive nitrate stocks which, for safety reasons alone, precluded utilizing a downtown location. Ironically, this nitrate stock was never housed in the new building.

The announcement of the board's intention to move to Montreal sparked another storm of protest, first within the board and later in the public. People complained and circulated petitions in opposition, citing personal and professional reasons for keeping the board in Ottawa (including the silly charge that Irwin had decided to move the NFB to Montreal because his new wife wanted to live there). Irwin countered with a personal telephone campaign, trying to persuade all doubters of the benefits of going to Montreal, usually with mixed results. Many staffers opposed the move right up until the end.

The controversy swirled long after Irwin left the board. Prominent Ottawa citizens who had never given the board a second thought in the past became staunch defenders of this cultural institution. Mayor Charlotte Whitton took up the cause, announcing to the Ottawa *Citizen* (3 March 1954): 'I've been looking through my history books and I can only find two other cases where a group of people was forcibly removed and relocated. These were the expulsion of the Acadians and the moving of the Japanese away from the coast in World War II.'

Don Mulholland gave Irwin a personal commitment to support the move (against his personal feelings) but that commitment was not extended to Irwin's successors. When Irwin left the board in 1953 Mulholland came out in opposition to the move and prepared a long memorandum arguing against virtually every point Irwin had made in support. The new film commissioner, Albert Trueman, passed the memo to Walter Harris, the minister of citizenship and immigration, who had assumed the responsibility for the film board.[27] Ultimately Prime Minister St Laurent intervened, stating that a *final* decision had been made and there would be no turning back. There the controversy ended.

By the time the film board building on Côte-de-Liesse Road was completed in 1956, it had been three years since Irwin vacated the film commissioner's chair. His hopes that the move would spark francophone film production were fully realized. Many talented francophones were attracted to the NFB in the following decades and the formation of an NFB French unit contributed to the development of a significant French-Canadian film industry. They also brought their own political, cultural, and intellectual concerns, and the francophone input eventually changed the entire face of the NFB. Pierre Juneau later was emphatic that such a development could not have occurred in Ottawa. 'It would have been impossible,' he stated, 'to develop a French side to the Film Board if the Film Board had not moved to Montreal.'[28]

Still, there were difficulties. Noise was never a serious problem, but the location of the building did prove unpopular. Working next to a busy highway produced a few anticipated headaches, but nobody expected the traffic nightmare that emerged when the trans-Canada highway was expanded into an elevated multilane octopus. Visitors and staffers alike complained of driving along the highway, within a hundred yards of the NFB, but somehow still finding themselves on the autoroute to the Laurentians, north of the city. Others were astounded by the cab fares for rides even short distances from the NFB building.

More serious criticisms were leveled at the impact of the move on the board's film production. Some critics wondered aloud if the price paid for the development of francophone film production was too high. Most of the incoming anglophone staff adapted well, but there were some who never adjusted to the move and floundered in their new environment. And the English-speaking staff never became involved in the Montreal scene to the degree Irwin had hoped; they tended to move farther out in the suburbs and away from downtown. Other critics charged that the board lost all sense of direction in the fifties and sixties and became bureaucratically top-heavy – just another fat government institution, with more secretaries, administrators, and memo pads than films or filmmakers. Perhaps there was no justification to continue funding the board at all. Couldn't the private film industry do everything as well and cheaper?

Irwin had to live with his decisions too. He never questioned the wisdom of moving to Montreal, although he would often shrug with dismay when discussing the building site. (In 1976, Irwin wrote one colleague: 'Had I had the imagination to visualize what the Trans-Canada Highway was going to do to the environment I wouldn't have gone along with the selection.')[29] But there was comfort in the knowledge that the National Film Board went on to make many of its greatest films – in English and in French – from these unhappy headquarters that were drowning in traffic and industrial soot, and nestled under a direct flightpath from Dorval airport. That the board should be preserved and maintained he was equally convinced. But after 1953 such issues were for others to contemplate.

◆

There has been an unfortunate tendency when examining Irwin's years as film commissioner to focus on the issues surrounding his arrival, the security issue and subsequent reorganization, and the move to Montreal. All important events indeed, but they tend to overshadow the most significant role of the NFB – producing and distributing films for Canadian and international audiences. Despite the internal turmoil of the early 1950s, the film board produced a number of extraordinary films during Irwin's tenure as commissioner.

In terms of total film footage, viewing audience, and the number and variety of films made, 1950–3 were very productive years. Well over 100 films, plus newsreels and films for continuing series such as *Canada Carries On* and *Eye Witness*, were produced in each of Irwin's three years as commissioner. Dozens of NFB films won national and international awards and honours. Theatrical bookings for NFB productions numbered in the thousands and the productions had total annual worldwide audiences of close to 25 million.[30] The kinds of films produced ran the gamut from animated shorts, to newsreels and documentaries, to non-theatrical films produced for government departments, to four-reel documentaries prepared for theatrical release.[31] Without question, the two outstanding films of these years were *Royal Journey* and *Neighbours,* films of radically different natures. Irwin played a small but important role in the success of both.

The visit to Canada of Princess Elizabeth and her new husband the Duke of Edinburgh in the autumn of 1951 was the occasion for a film following the royal couple as they made their way across the country. Originally the plan was to shoot a two-reel documentary tracing the royal couple but, because it was a rather special event, Irwin approved the use of a new 35 mm Eastman colour stock film, which had not been used commercially before this time. It was a terrific gamble, especially on the processing side which was still at the experimental stage, but Irwin felt the risk worth taking.

Shooting began on 8 October 1951 and continued through until 12 November. Tom Daly was producer, David Bairstow was director, and more than one hundred full- and part-time NFB employees worked on the filming. The decision to use the new Eastman stock paid off, because on twenty-six of the thirty-seven days the weather was bad enough to make shooting extremely difficult, and it may have been impossible to shoot with normal commercial stock. As Tom Daly recalled, the final parting of the royal couple from St John's was to be the film's big finale, but the couple left in a 'dark and dismal' storm. Using regular stock would have made it impossible to shoot. Instead, *Royal Journey* was able to capture some terrific unexpected moments in less than desirable weather.[32]

When the first rushes came in everyone involved with the filming was astounded by the quality of the film. Original plans for two reels were expanded to five, and Irwin called in people from distribution and private industry, including J.J. Fitzgibbons, the president of Famous Players Canadian Corporation, which owned the largest theatre chain in the country. The film was shown – without narration or sound, and before final editing – to a packed and silently anxious crowd. Fitzgibbons was impressed and insisted that the film not be cut at all, and he promised to play it in his theatres as a feature film providing the final product could be ready for Christmas – barely a month away. The crew accepted the challenge and for the next four weeks worked non-stop to complete the film.

The final product was a spectacular fifty-four-minute colour documentary, one of the NFB's first feature-length films. It ran in dozens of theatres in Canada, to an audience estimated at over two million, and in crowded theatres in the United States, Great Britain, Australia, and New Zealand. Everywhere the film was shown it opened to long line-ups and rave reviews. In 1952, *Royal Journey* won a British Film Academy Award for best documentary film.

Irwin was instrumental in the success of *Royal Journey*, although he played no part in the actual production of the film. As film commissioner he made the decision to approve the project and set the ball in motion, and then had the good sense to leave the production to Tom Daly and his team of filmmakers. 'It has been a pleasure to have you going to bat for us all along the line,' Daly wrote early in 1952. 'And I hope we may have other such films for you before long.'[33] Irwin did too, because in his mind *Royal Journey* probably did more than anything else to improve the tarnished image of the National Film Board.

The film *Neighbours* was much more the product of one mind, that of Norman McLaren, the brilliant and innovative director who had joined the NFB in 1941. The film was described as 'a simple parable about two people who, after living side by side with mutual friendliness and respect, come to blows over the possession of a flower that one day grows where their properties meet.' Eventually the two characters kill each other and the pantomime film ends showing two graves (each with a flower and picket fence) with 'Love Your Neighbour' printed in a dozen languages.[34]

Not long before his death in 1987, McLaren described the genesis of *Neighbours* in a letter to Irwin. In 1950, after returning to Canada from China, where he had 'witnessed the "revolution."' McLaren, together with Grant Munro, a colleague at the NFB, began investigating the possibilities of a new film technique which came to be called 'pixillation,' essentially the use of live actors rather than cartoons with an animation camera. 'I had animated drawings, flat-cutouts, solid objects,' McLaren wrote, 'but why not, I asked myself, animate live human beings?'

McLaren graciously credited Irwin for providing a spark, by prompting him to turn his thoughts for his next film 'to a topic of some international significance.' McLaren recalled being 'subconsciously stirred' by Irwin's suggestion,

but I couldn't imagine how I could possibly use our new 'pixillation' technique for a theme of international value: one was frivolous, the other serious. I mulled it over, and a few days later Grant [Munro] and I rescreened all our test rushes. Amongst them was a brief sequence (about 30 seconds) of two men exchanging supernaturally violent fist-blows. The moment I saw it the idea for 'Neighbours' lept into my mind ...[35]

Neighbours played across Canada and to international audiences in the United States, Europe, and Australia, and in 1953 won an Oscar for best documentary short. 'In its last few minutes, *Love Your Neighbours* gets rather ugly and may prove too strong for squeamish audiences,' one reviewer warned, and indeed Australian censors did cut out a short bit.[36] Nevertheless, *Neighbours* was universally acclaimed as a brilliant and powerful motion picture.

Irwin had his share of failures as well, especially with his proposed series of films – dubbed the 'Freedom Speaks' program – designed to promote and defend freedom and democracy (although he would have bristled at the suggestion that he was fashioning himself a second propaganda maestro). 'Freedom Speaks' was an imaginative and expensive project that was quickly scuttled by the Treasury Board. A few films were put into production, but the plans for a large well-organized program evaporated.[37]

The area where Irwin had more success was in defending the film board against its enemies, critics, and inquisitors. He had plenty of opportunities. 'The Board had now in the space of two years,' Marjorie McKay wrote, 'been investigated unofficially by the Financial Post, officially from the aspect of business management by the Woods Gordon team; had been reported on by a multitude of agencies and private individuals to the Royal Commission on the Development of Arts, Letters and Sciences in every respect of its operations.'[38] And, there was more to come. In March 1952 Robert Winters announced in the House of Commons that a parliamentary special committee would be established to investigate the workings of the NFB in light of its recently published annual report (for 1950–1). The twenty-six-member committee was established at the end of April and held its first meeting on 8 May.

The creation of this new special committee was not perceived as a threatening gesture by the members of the film board as it might have been in 1949 or 1950. The board was firmly on its feet again and was operating smoothly; consequently there were few fears of a new round of public controversy and debate. Indeed, even the board's sharpest critics in the past now seemed to want to say nice things about the NFB.[39] Nevertheless, it was important that the gains of the past two years not be lost as a result of unfortunate publicity surrounding the committee or through the creation of a bad impression on its members. Irwin was scheduled to appear before the committee – to be held accountable in a sense for the activities of the board – and he was determined not to destroy the government confidence that he had worked so hard to establish.

Irwin began an exhaustive process of gathering together all the information he could concerning board activities and then cramming his head full of facts and statistics – ready to answer any question the committee might think of. He called a meeting of senior staffers in his office and set up a mock committee room with the staffers grilling him on any possible topic. These meetings lasted for several days in Irwin's office atop the Sovereign Building (where the elevators stopped at 5:00 P.M. and the staff had to climb the seven stories on foot).

In the process, Irwin established a bond with those staff members present. 'I think we were all impressed,' Michael Spencer later noted, 'with his ability to retain the information and give it out in a coherent and effective way. He was very good at that.'[40] For really the first time Irwin was seen as a protector of the board, as someone who could stand up to the government and beat them at their own game, rather than as the hatchet-man with a hidden agenda to destroy it. 'To those working on the project,' Marjorie McKay wrote, 'the Commissioner seemed to take on the mantle of Grierson ... warm, encouraging, inspiring, demanding, absolutely tireless, and always two jumps ahead of everyone else. A new respect and a new bond was created.'[41] Comparison to Grierson from a long-time board staffer was high praise indeed.

Irwin appeared before the special committee at its first meeting and gave an extended history of the film board and a review of its activities. He made no reference to the more recent sensationalism but spoke in glowing terms of the efforts of Canadian filmmakers to document their country and its people. 'To fulfill the belief which is Canada,' he said, in words reminiscent of 'The Canadian,'

we must steadily nourish the paradox of unity with diversity which characterizes our life as a people. The Board's films, I believe, contribute substantially to that nourishment by stimulating in Canadians pride in their achievements, by projecting their growing sense of oneness while portraying their diversities, by interpreting the parts of the whole and the whole to the parts, by holding up images of the Canadian past, the present and the long road that leads to the future.[42]

Irwin ended his testimony with an invitation to the committee to come to the film board offices and see for themselves. 'We will show you the cameras, the rushes, the processing, the editing, the sound cutting, the mixing of the sound and the visuals; and you will see at the end the finished product on the screen.' It was an inspired move. When the committee members arrived at the John Street building, they were met by whirling cameras that followed them as they moved through the building. At the end of the day they sat and watched themselves on the screen. How could they not be impressed?

The report of the committee was issued in June and it put to rest any lingering doubts concerning the government's commitment to the film board. In a brief two pages the committee pronounced that 'the production and distribution of films and other visual aids by the National Film Board are playing vital roles in developing a national consciousness in Canada and in protecting the image of Canada abroad, and commends the Board on its adherence to the principle of producing films designed primarily to interpret Canada to Canadians and to other nations.'[43]

Irwin was immensely pleased that the film board had passed this one last test with ease. The government stamp of approval had not been sought, but it did seem to vindicate all his efforts of the past two years – many of which had sparked heavy fire from his critics. The administrative structure of the NFB had been reorganized from top to bottom, the security issue had begun to fade in the minds of all but a few, the new Film Act was in operation, and the move to Montreal was approved and work was well under way. Most important, he was convinced that over time these changes would only enhance the creative atmosphere in which truly talented filmmakers could produce films of the highest calibre. What else was there for him to do?

◆

After three years at the film board Irwin was proud of his accomplishments. He could list the notable achievements or discuss the relevant merits of his more controversial decisions, but, interestingly, the most noteworthy developments were noticeable primarily by their absence. When Irwin arrived in 1950 the board was in turmoil and under attack from the government and in the press. The buildings were dilapidated, the administration chaotic, the film act out of date. By 1953 these problems – with the exception of the move – were distant unpleasant memories. The board was at peace with itself and its government. When Irwin passed the responsibility to Albert Trueman, the board was focused on one thing – films.

Less satisfying was the personal side of the job. After three years he still could not understand why that wall between him and his staff had not come crashing down. He had spent most of his adult life working with artistic people, and he wanted nothing more than to feel a part of the creative process at the film board. But he never achieved a sufficiently close bond with his producers that might have helped foster such a relationship.

Tom Daly, for example, recalled having real difficulty at first relating to and understanding Irwin. At one point he was motivated to such a degree that he pulled out two sheets of paper and wrote 'a list of all the things that bothered me about Irwin' – to see if any patterns emerged or if there was anything he could do to improve the situation. If nothing else, he wanted to be clear in his own mind about the man. Daly returned to the list after a few hours. 'It came into my head to ask myself: How would I rate myself on the same points toward the people under me? Then my face got longer and longer and *longer* as I went through this.' On fifteen of the seventeen points he found distinct similarities between himself and Irwin ('and I wasn't even sure about the other two').[44]

In the end there was only a greater understanding of Irwin – his motives, his personality, his ambitions. There was trust more than friendship, respect rather than love. To the NFB staffers, Irwin arrived as an unknown quantity and he never opened up enough to let others get to know him, or to disprove the allegations and rumours. In this way he shared the responsibility with those who mistrusted him. Interestingly, his marriage to P.K. Page, while it filled the void left in his life following the death of his first wife, also helped bring people in the NFB around to him. Page was well known and admired by her co-workers at the board, and, as one producer put it, 'if P.K. Page would marry him, he really had to have something.'[45] Others recalled the way he had defended the board to the government, or the way he had demanded improvements to the buildings – these actions won him much respect. Perhaps the greatest compliment came when he announced that he was leaving the board. Colleagues and staffers were stunned at his decision. As Michael Spencer put it, working for the board was the best job in the world. Why would anyone leave? With an ironical twist, some of those who had suspected him on his arrival and resented his presence now were saddest to see him go. For Irwin there was little solace in knowing that he had made some progress on the personal level after all.

Arthur Irwin's tenure at the NFB came at a time of great change. The wartime era of challenge, enthusiasm, and an almost evangelical commitment to film had waned but had not totally disappeared, as Canada slid into the comfortable 1950s. But the coming of the television age virtually ensured that the film board would be pushed towards the periphery. Such dramatic changes were not easy to bear for many NFB staffers, and for some Irwin would always be held responsible for those changes. He would never be anything but a man without vision, a Toronto businessman imported to Ottawa to tatoo the government's imprint across the face of the National Film Board.

Years later, in Rio de Janeiro, Irwin and Grierson met for lunch in the Brazilian Bankers' Club. The talk of two ex–film commissioners naturally turned to the NFB. 'I don't know whether you realize it or not,' Grierson told him, 'but you saved the Board.' Irwin rightly dismissed Grierson's words, at the time and later, as hyperbole. Irwin did not *save* the film board because the government never intended to destroy it. The board did not have to be saved, but it needed the restoration of that illusive government 'confidence' which followed in the wake of Irwin's restructuring and stabilization. And, thanks to Irwin, the National Film Board was set on course for some of its most productive and prosperous years.

SEVENTEEN

◆

'The Canadian Was Simpatico'

Late in the afternoon of 15 January 1953, on a typically cold Ottawa winter day, Irwin walked into Robert Winter's office in the House of Commons and informed his minister that he would be leaving the NFB to accept a post as Canadian high commissioner to Australia. The decision was not a hasty one; he had thought it over for some time before concluding that he had accomplished what he set out to do at the film board.

He could have stayed on at the board if he wished. But Irwin was the first to admit that he had developed a long-term interest in international affairs and the conduct of foreign policy, and it was here that he wanted to finish his career.[1] If nothing else, he wanted to spend his remaining years before retirement doing something that he enjoyed, and here was a new challenge. After all, he had devoted his career to telling Canadians about themselves; now he wanted to try his hand at interpreting his own people to others.

He had met with Lester Pearson, the secretary of state for external affairs, on several occasions concerning a diplomatic posting, and Pearson had not forgotten his 1949 commitment. Pearson offered three postings – Mexico, Australia, or consul general in Seattle – and left it for Irwin to choose. Seattle did not interest him at all, and that left Australia and Mexico. He chose the former for two reasons: first it was a commonwealth nation and that attracted him, and, second, Australians spoke English and he would get his diplomatic feet wet without having to learn another language.'[2]

It would take a few weeks to get cabinet approval for his appointment and to secure the approval of the Australian government, and it was hoped that the announcement of his resignation could be held off for some time, at least until a successor was found for the NFB. Winters agreed, but was less than optimistic. Only a few individuals in Ottawa were privy to the information concerning his pending appointment to Australia, but the night before he had heard Mrs Pearson discussing it in public with her husband.[3]

Despite their efforts to keep the news quiet, rumours spread over the following weeks and the official announcement was made in February. 'He is not an extrovert,' *Saturday Night* magazine described Irwin, following the announcement, 'and it may be a little while before the Australians get to know him well. When they do, they will find this grey-haired, balding Canadian a man with a wide range of interests ... He will look quietly at the Australians through his horn-rimmed glasses, and when they look back at him they will see a man whose sharp mind is controlled by a well-developed sense of what is right and what is wrong.'[4]

Irwin's appointment to Australia was the beginning of an eleven-year service in the diplomatic corps. After three years in Australia, he was appointed ambassador first to Brazil (1956–9), and then to Mexico (and Guatemala) 1960–4. At the age of fifty-five, his life was about to take another dramatic turn.

◆

Like most Canadians, Irwin knew very little about Australia or Australians. The shared traditions and membership in the British Commonwealth was the stuff of breezy after-dinner speeches, but on closer examination Canada's relations with the commonwealth were really conducted one-on-one with Great Britain and not with the other members of the group. The same was true for Australia. Things were beginning to change, but in 1953 Australians looked to the Pacific and north to Asia; Canadians looked to the Atlantic and south to the United States.

Irwin received the usual post report on the Australian mission, outlining the conditions he might expect to find there and containing some background information on relations between the two countries and an indication of the direction of government policy. He talked to others in the Department of External Affairs who knew something about the country. Further help came from C.J. Burchell, the first

Canadian high commissioner in Australia, who informed him of year-round golf and recommended lawn-bowling as the best way to meet the right people.

The high commissioner's residence in Canberra was modest by diplomatic standards, but, as Australian Prime Minister Menzies had been heard to say, it had 'an atmosphere of its own.'[5] A comfortable two-storey house with a large kitchen and extra bedrooms downstairs, it was suitable for living purposes but a tight squeeze for entertaining. 'The house is rather comic and too small for proper entertaining,' Irwin wrote his youngest daughter soon after arriving, 'but in many ways it is quite attractive.'[6]

The major domestic problem was the cold; there was no furnace in the house and only a fireplace in the living-room and small electric heaters in the bedrooms. Canberra was not Sydney, where the temperature rarely dropped to anywhere near what he had been used to in Canada. But in the capital during the winter months the mercury often dipped below the freezing mark. Irwin heard rumours that on especially wintry evenings the previous residents abandoned the dining-room table to eat their meals on card tables by the living-room fire. Not much had changed by the time he and Pat arrived. 'It is cold as billy-be-damned,' he complained, 'as are most of the offices and we will have to try to do something about this.'

Irwin took a broad approach to his job, defining his role liberally as Canada's representative in Australia, Canada's eyes and ears as it were. He was also to serve as a conduit for the exchange of information between capitals. Despite the vast technological improvements in international communications (and the growing cynicism over the potential role of the diplomat in a shrinking world), Irwin believed that it was still possible for an ambassador to have an impact – however small – on the conduct of foreign policy. The individual on the spot always has a unique perspective on developments in any country and through immediate and intelligent reporting to Ottawa a diplomat could hope to have some influence on government decision makers.

Most of his days, however, were taken up with routine office matters: handling outgoing diplomatic mail and other correspondence, dealing with the regular stream of visitors and meetings, establishing and maintaining contacts with important politicians and business people, and learning what he could on social, economic, and political matters from various sources. In addition, there were the wide consular functions of looking after Canadians abroad – Canadians with health problems, or those who got themselves lost or in trouble. Irwin did not handle all these cases personally, of course, but occasionally he was roused from bed by an urgent telephone call to find a lost husband or to help spring a fellow Canadian from the local jail. There were also the more formal occasions, and in all posts there was a steady procession of dinner parties to attend or host. Protocol and red tape came with the job.

Occasionally as high commissioner or ambassador Irwin became directly involved in diplomatic negotiations – concerning international air agreements in Australia and later in Mexico, for example – but for the most part these negotiations were left to the teams of officials despatched from Ottawa for the specific occasion. Similarly, trade matters, other than in a general way, were left to the various trade commissioners and other officials. The head of post was always there, nevertheless, to open a few previously closed doors, or to whisper soothing words into the right ear. And in some tricky sets of negotiations, such an intervention could be crucial.

Irwin devoted considerable time to travelling within the countries he was posted to, meeting provincial governors or state premiers, local officials and politicians, launching a ceremonial kick at the odd football match, hosting various exhibits of Canadian cultural output, and representing his government at state functions. Following each trip Irwin prepared lengthy reports for Ottawa, describing in detail what he saw and the people that he met.

Irwin took great – perhaps too great – care to write articulate and interesting reports that sometimes read more like travel narratives than diplomatic accounts of his travels. 'Despite all one reads and hears about Australia's Empty North,' one draft began, 'it is impossible to appreciate how empty – and how isolated – this particular emptiness can be without experiencing it.'[7] Lingering at the back of his mind was the fear that few – indeed perhaps no one – in Ottawa would read his reports. But it was a job he had to do, and he insisted on doing it as best he could.

In many aspects of character and temperament, Irwin was more suited to being a diplomat than to any other occupation he had had. His interest in international affairs stretched back for decades. For almost twenty years he had been a contributing member of the CIIA, and he had written on and studied foreign policy issues extensively. His experience as a member of the 1945 Commonwealth Conference and the 1948 Conference on the Freedom of Information exposed him to the subtleties of negotiation and mediation. He brought to the job those qualities that he had displayed on numerous occasions over the years: he was a hard worker, conscientious and insightful, and he could throw himself into a new subject and within a few days discuss it with experts without embarrassing himself. He was not given to self-pity, or to complaining about the various tasks he was expected to perform, and he was able to concentrate his energy on doing what had to be done at a particular moment, without his other duties suffering.[8]

Other of Irwin's characteristics epitomized the able public servant. He was rational, discreet, direct, cogent, and fair in judgment – someone who could see both sides in a dispute. He also was a modest man, who had shown over the years his ability to submerge his own feelings in a larger cause and to work with other people. He could take orders and carry them out, even if he questioned the judgment on which they were based. And to him public service was a high calling.

Irwin was also a good listener, he had a sponge-like quality for soaking up information and understanding nuance. When he met foreign diplomats and politicians he really listened to what they had to say, much as he had with his staff at *Maclean's*. They often responded by taking him into their confidence. His personal integrity was never questioned, and he was able to establish relationships of trust with the foreigners with whom he had to deal. His reports to Ottawa were thus thorough and informative, well-written, and based on long hours of personal observation and of gleanings from an extensive range of contacts and sources.

His main weakness as a diplomat was on the social side: Irwin was never good at small talk or idle chatter, and he tended to be uncomfortable at social functions, in particular when he was called upon to make a speech. When Irwin 'is confronted with Sydney Harbor Bridge, the pride of Australia,' one columnist chimed in 1953, 'he will probably say: "Ug!" That is, if he is feeling comparatively talkative. When not absolutely mute, Irwin usually employs Eskimo-like monosyllables, though occasionally when unbending in private he talks a blue streak, interestingly, pithily, and with wit.'[9] For a private citizen it was no serious drawback, but the world of the diplomat is a public one, filled with social demands and responsibilities.

Irwin admittedly found the social demands of the job tiring and uninspiring, and he recognized his own shortcomings. But he accepted the responsibilities and, when it came his turn to play the host, he worked hard at making people feel comfortable. Fortunately he was complemented by Pat, who was very interested in people and good at remembering names and faces. Friends and colleagues later recalled how much she aided her husband at social affairs. In this respect, she became an indispensable colleague.

To career foreign service officers, Irwin – and others like him – were often viewed as usurpers, individuals parachuted into foreign posts as heads of mission, without working their way up through the ranks. To career diplomats, such appointments were distasteful but not unexpected, and they were greeted with a degree of resentment or, more correctly, resignation. The complaint was that the new heads arrived unskilled in the art of diplomacy and interested in the larger, more exciting issues and not the daily administrative grind of operating an embassy or high commission.

Geoffrey Pearson, who served under Irwin in Mexico, remembered him as an individual interested in the 'big picture,' and as someone who would delegate authority to those under him. Irwin struck him as a reflective man who seemed to find the office routine boring. And a bit of a perfectionist, too, who took enormous interest in writing – Pearson's as well as his own. The old editor in Irwin punched through the diplomatic calm, and he frequently pencilled in changes on the margins of Pearson's drafts.[10]

More profoundly, Irwin had always been in the forefront of his profession, in charge and able to get things done. Now, as a diplomat, he felt that he had been relegated to the periphery, where few listened and no one really cared about what he had to say. Despite the pleasure and pride he derived from doing the job well, it was hard for him to accept a secondary role. He later mused with regret that he had started in External Affairs too late in life. Had he joined in 1930s he might have been in line for one of the senior posts, but as it was, starting in his mid-fifties, his chances of reaching the top were small. That shift – from participant to observer – was the hardest adjustment to make.

Still, he believed he could have an impact through his reporting, and his Australian dispatches gave Ottawa full coverage of the political situation, particularly as it geared up for the 1954 election. And it became the focus of much of his attention to learn about Australian politics and society, through a mixture of background reading, the establishment of close friendships with influential Australians, such as R.G. Casey, the minister for external affairs, and by making a special effort to maintain good relations with the host government.

It was this part of the job that Irwin loved the most: informal discussion with knowledgeable people, wrestling with important ideas, and gauging the correct Canadian response. Through his close friendship with Casey, for example, Irwin gained a firsthand look at the evolution of Australian policy towards the developing Suez Crisis in the summer of 1956. Irwin passed on Casey's confidential thoughts – and included many of his own ideas – in private letters to Lester Pearson in Ottawa. 'I am delighted that you have established this kind of relationship with [Casey],' Pearson wrote 'because it is particularly good for Canadian-Australian relations that they should be conducted to a considerable extent in easy chairs.'[11]

Irwin was never bored in Australia. His three years were busy ones indeed; in addition to his consular and diplomatic duties and his and Pat's wide travels across the continent they managed a few vacations, the most notable being a month's trip to New Zealand. Visitors from home were less frequent, but there were some. Floyd Chalmers and his wife visited, and, in 1955, Irwin's youngest daughter came for an extended stay. News from Canada was gathered from various sources, and Irwin was never really out of touch. And of course, there were the late – but always welcome – issues of *Maclean's* shipped out from home.

Near the end of his tour, when Irwin received word that he had been posted to Rio de Janeiro, as Canadian ambassador to Brazil, he was a little disappointed. 'As to Rio itself,' he wrote the department soon after being notified of his new assignment 'my knowledge of the nature of the job there is sketchy but my impression, subject to correction, is that the emphasis is rather on the representational side than on substantive political work. Since my primary interest is in ideas and my main experience has been in their handling and development I would not be frank if I did not confess to a feeling that I might be most useful at some location where the emphasis runs in this direction.' Irwin added that he was prepared to take the assignment without hesitation, but, 'in the light of the considerations raised above you might wish to consider whether an alternative might be desirable.'[12]

Unlike his appointment to Australia, however, Irwin was not given a choice with respect to Brazil. He was, after all, a public *servant*, and he would go where he was needed. Still, the news came so suddenly, and it all seemed so strange.

That Brazil and Australia are both south of the equator is one of the few things that they have in common. Otherwise, they are worlds apart. The one is English and dry, the other is Portuguese and lush; the differences in terms of tradition, history, culture, and economy are evident. Even when one stretches for similarities – both, for instance, are continental nations with large undeveloped interiors – it serves, ironically, only to emphasize the differences between Amazonian jungle and Australian outback.

Irwin described Rio as 'tropical, easy-going, disorganized and luxury loving.'[13] The Canadian residence was situated in a Rio suburb, not far from downtown, on a large lot that backed on the slope of a large hill. 'The lot extends back from the street to a distance of approximately 500 metres to the crest of the hill behind the house,' Irwin reported to Ottawa. 'The layout is such that I should think considerably more than half of its area is made up of mountainside forest and jungle. Where our boundaries lie in this jungle, I gather no one at the moment really knows.'[14] The house itself was magnificent, a pink palace of marble, glass, and stone with a half-dozen bedrooms and elegant living quarters. There also were rooms for a handful of servants – chauffeur, cook and assistant, upstairs maid, houseman, cleaners – above the garage and in the basement.

Irwin arrived with a long post report and letter from Jules Léger, who had replaced Norman Robertson as the under-secretary in the department.[15] Irwin could expect that relations with the Brazilians would not be as smooth as they had been with the Australians. There was the language problem, and Brazilian politics could baffle even the most well-informed. The challenge for Irwin would be to see his way through the mysteries in order to assess the truly important issues. For Léger there were two prime matters that needed careful watching: the first was the rise in Communist activities; the second dealt with trade and business. The focus of Canadian business investment in Brazil was the Brazilian Traction, Light and Power Company, an important player in the Brazilian economy. Irwin was not directly concerned with the company but if a crisis arose it would be impossible for him to remain aloof. Be careful, Léger warned. Watch and listen. 'The Light' usually looked after itself – quite successfully – but if 'a major issue should arise during your tour you will naturally be closely concerned with it; in such a circumstance you should seek instructions from the department, if this is possible, before making formal representations to the Brazilian Government to assist the company.'

More generally, Léger asked for quarterly reports on the political situation. Brazil was recognized as a leader in Latin America and its views and actions were of interest to Ottawa. In particular, Brazilian influence in Latin America could have a dramatic effect on voting patterns in the United Nations. Thus, anything Irwin could learn about the direction of Brazilian foreign policy and potential shifts in views would be welcomed by the department.

Following the initial round of protocol calls, Irwin fell into the diplomatic routine without noticeable difficulty. His correspondence to Ottawa reveals his growing interest in the work and his sense of its importance, as well as his love for Brazil. 'The job here continues to be interesting although at times frustrating,' he wrote after his first year, 'because there is so much to be done and we seem to accomplish relatively little in terms of what might be done. I'm beginning to get the feel of the place ...'[16] Later that year he noted: 'both Pat and I are thoroughly enjoying this assignment and the longer we are here the more we feel that for the long term there is a real job to be done here, despite the obvious difficulties of the moment.'[17]

Irwin liked the Brazilians, and he sensed that they liked and respected Canadians. After one trip away from Rio he wrote that he and Pat had been 'conscious of what appeared to be a pro-Canadian bias. To some extent I suspect this may be due to a combination of respect for North American achievement and dislike of Americans.' Nevertheless, he continued, 'there seems to be a genuine liking for Canadians as such. We were told that the Canadian was "simpatico," that he was capable but modest and did not throw his weight around. Discounting the oil which is poured on such occasions we came away with the impression that in some curious way there does seem to be a natural affinity between the Brazilian and Canadian.'[18]

As in Australia, Arthur and Pat spent considerable time travelling in the country, taking official visits to Sao Paulo and other major centres, and trips to the various states and regions of Brazil, the most memorable being a two-week trek through the Amazon region. Every trip included the obligatory tours, inspections, and state dinners. And there were many speeches to be delivered. On most occasions Irwin carried three or four speeches in his jacket pocket, and, depending on the occasion or the feel of the moment, he would select one and deliver it in precarious Portuguese.

One report concerning a trip to Sao Paulo gives some indication of the kind and extent of their activities:

2. In addition to such protocolaire activities as being received by, and addressing, the State Assembly and meeting the highly controversial Mayor, Adhemar de Barros, complete with claque and band, my wife and I, either separately or together, visited the Canadian Brazilian School of the Fathers of the Holy Cross (speech), lunched with the British Commonwealth Community Council (speech), met the press (speech), met the Canadian colony, lunched with the British and Commonwealth Chamber of Commerce (speech), presented thirteen Norman MacLaren [sic] films to the Museum of Modem Art (speech), visited the Museum of Fine Arts, appeared on television (speech), saw the spectacular hydro-electric installations of the Brazilian Traction Company, visited a coffee fasenda and dairy farm, inspected an electric motor plant (Brazilian), had group interviews with representatives of three commercial and industrial and two agricultural associations, saw a snake farm, inspected the State orchid farm, saw the fabricating plant operated by a subsidiary of Aluminum Company of Canada, visited four textile and chemical plants belonging to the Matarazzo family, leading industrialists of South America, caught a glimpse of the coffee port of Santos and surrounding country, visited the University of Sao Paulo Law School (speech), entertained and were entertained by local dignitaries and kicked off at a football match before 50,000 spectators.

3. Strenuous, but interesting.[19]

Irwin never became fluent in Portuguese, but he made a determined effort to speak it as much as he could. ('More than a few times I had to bluff my way through a barrage of Portuguese delivered by people who simply would not accept my remonstrance that my ability to converse in Portuguese was limited,' he wrote on one occasion.) And for the Brazilians – accustomed to speaking with foreigners through an interpreter or in *their* language – making the effort was appreciated.

'We have been reading with interest, not unmixed with respectful astonishment,' Léger wrote from Ottawa after receiving reports of Irwin's speech following the ceremonial soccer kick-off. 'Everybody from the members of the State Assembly to the television watchers, captured by your interest in them, your "futebal" prowess, and especially your able use of Portuguese, seems to have decided that you are "simpatico." This is the way to the heart of a Brazilian, and it is a great pleasure to learn that you have found the way so soon and so readily.'

A change from the Latin American world came for Irwin in the form of an appointment as a member of the Canadian delegation to the United Nations for two general assemblies in the autumn of 1959 and 1960. The 14th and 15th sessions of the General Assembly lasted almost three months each (the 14th session, for instance, opened on 13 September 1959 and closed on 13 December and for most of the time Arthur and Pat were in New York. The Canadian delegation was chaired by Howard Green, an old acquaintance from *Maclean's* and Bren gun days, who had followed Sidney Smith as minister for external affairs.

Irwin and the other delegates were each appointed to one or more UN committees. In 1959, for example, Irwin was the Canadian representative on the Fifth Committee (administration and budgetary questions). Part of the committee's duties were to assess the costs of the United Nations Emergency Force (UNEF), which helped maintain the peace in the Middle East. Irwin co-sponsored a draft seven-power resolution in support of continued financing for UNEF. The following year he participated in the Second Committee (economic and financial) and delivered a lengthy statement on the distribution of world food surpluses via UN agencies to needy countries.

The work was unspectacular but essential to the smooth operation of the United Nations, an organization Irwin fully supported. It also brought him close to the centre of things on an international scale. Being in the UN and seeing Nikita Khrushchev yelling in Russian and slamming his shoe on his desk (while British Prime Minister Harold Macmillan stood emotionless, coolly asking for a translation); seeing Khrushchev and Fidel Castro – dressed in fatigues – embrace in a giant bear-hug in the aisles, only a few feet from his desk,[20] huddling with small groups of officials in the corridors and twisting arms on important matters of detail; anxiously waiting for an overdue call from Ottawa on a policy matter; these were the things that Irwin had joined the service for.

If anything, his experience at the United Nations only whetted his appetite for a posting to a more influential capital. His years in Brazil were entrancing and enjoyable, but Brazilian-Canadian relations were not of sufficient importance to satisfy that part of him which longed to make a contribution to the policy side of things. There just wasn't enough to do beyond the routine of representation, administration, and reporting.

A few months before his term in Rio expired Irwin wrote to Norman Robertson (who had returned to his old post as under-secretary) to enquire what the department had in mind for him. Of course he would take whatever External Affairs wished to give him, he wrote. 'You know my background, my interests and capabilities, and my record in the Department to date; and you are vastly more aware of the Department's requirements than I.' Still, he continued, there were 'one or two generalizations I would make. I would prefer not to have a sinecure, and I would hope that I might end up somewhere in, or close to, the main stream of events where such capabilities as I may have will be fully stretched. As you know, I have spent most of my working life dealing with ideas as springboards to action in fields which seemed significant; and I would hope that the future might bring situations offering similar scope.'[21]

It was not to be. The 1957 and 1958 elections and the massive victory of John Diefenbaker and the Conservative party ensured that most of Irwin's contacts would be out of power for at least four years. Howe, St Laurent, Pickersgill, Robert Winters, Pearson – the people he had dealt with on one basis or another for decades – were all forced into retirement or left scrambling to pick up the pieces of the Liberal party. Worse, the new government mistrusted the top levels of its inherited bureaucracy – labelling them the 'Personalities' – and Irwin himself later confessed to fearing for his own job. His fears were unjustified; in August 1959 he learned that he had been posted to Mexico. (The next year he was cross-appointed as ambassador to Guatemala.)

His hopes for a European posting after Brazil were never realized. Without many years seniority in the service or close contacts in the Conservative party he was offered what could only be considered a lateral move to Mexico. There, despite his efforts to earn another assignment, he stayed until past retirement age.

◆

Irwin never stopped being amazed at how different Brazil and Mexico were. There were the obvious differences, Portuguese as opposed to Spanish, for example. And Rio and Mexico City were remarkably dissimilar, the former tropical, hot, and humid, the latter temperate, resting on a plateau some 7500 feet above sea level. The Mexicans were also more reserved and less receptive to foreigners – their long history of foreign intervention (and the ever-increasing influx of tourists) explained such anxieties – and it took longer for Arthur and Pat to feel at home.

Their new home as of March 1960 was a three-storey house in

suburban Mexico City. The house and grounds were small compared to what they had in Rio, but the stone-faced building had its own appeal. Inside, there was a reception hall, small library and music rooms, a dining-room and living-room with high cathedral ceilings and large black pillars (dubbed the 'elephant legs') by the entrance of the dining-room. The post report estimated that 500 guests could be accommodated comfortably at a reception.

Irwin's arrival in Mexico was followed closely by an official visit of Prime Minister Diefenbaker. Diefenbaker was the first Canadian prime minister to visit the Mexican capital, and his three-day visit was a hectic whirlwind of state dinners and receptions, meeting the press, visits to museums and exhibits (including a display of Canadian books at the university), and a trip to observe a charreada (Mexican rodeo).[22]

Once the prime minister returned to Ottawa Irwin quickly fell into the routine of ambassadorial duties. Mexico has twenty-nine states and Arthur and Pat visited most of them; there were official visits to Yucatan, Campeche, Chiapas, and Tabasco (and detailed reports on each followed) and family tourist trips to the historic cities and ruins of ancient Mexico. In Mexico City there were the increasing consular duties dealing with Canadian tourists and official visitors and delegations, and the latter took many hours of preparation.

There were great moments: the visit to Mexico of Indian Prime Minister Nehru late in 1961 was a particularly exhilarating time for Irwin, who attended the state dinner and, as a commonwealth diplomat, was invited to a private breakfast with Nehru (and his daughter Indira Gandhi). But there were disappointments, too. Irwin strongly believed that Canadians and Mexicans had much in common, in particular a shared history of dealing with the United States, and he strove – with only mixed success – to foster closer relations between the two countries.

Equally, Mexican-Canadian relations was not a topic that inspired much interest in Ottawa. Duties were carried out without a sense of urgency, and rarely would the embassy be asked for its appraisal of particular Mexican issues. As Geoffrey Pearson explained, those in the embassy had to go out and find their own issues, 'invent them' essentially. Pearson added that, at the time, he suspected that Irwin was disappointed at being sent to Mexico, yet he still devoted enormous energy to questions of demographics, economic development, Mexican politics, and border issues with the United States.[23]

In addition to his regular ambassadorial duties, Irwin became a staunch supporter of Canadian membership in the Organization of American States (OAS), which was established in 1948 to act as a coordinating agency for the many bodies operating within the Pan American Union. Following a personal investigation into the pros and cons of the matter, Irwin quickly came to see membership as a way to enhance relations with Latin America and to increase Canadian influence in the region. He was not convinced that Canada would be dragged into endless disputes between the United States and Latin America; indeed, as a member, Canada could hope to play a constructive role in the Western Hemisphere.

Irwin sent his proposals off to the department but received no positive feedback; he also took his idea directly to Diefenbaker and later to Pearson, via his external affairs minister, Paul Martin. But, although he found general support for the idea of membership, few endorsed immediate action. In the months leading up to the 1963 election, for example, Irwin learned from Bruce Hutchison, who was closely following the campaign, that the Liberals were toying with the idea of supporting Canadian entrance into the OAS. Pearson 'was rushed, exhausted, harassed and lying down when I saw him in the hotel,' Hutchison wrote from Victoria just prior to the election. 'We talked briefly of many things. He says he will definitely join the O.A.S. He says he intends to announce this in the election campaign but I don't think he will and I don't think he should – no votes in it and the chance of losing some.'[24] After the election, however, the Pearson government proved unwilling to take the plunge.

Irwin did not give up hope, and he maintained an interest in the OAS long after he retired from public service. In the summer of 1964 he delivered a paper on the OAS to the Second Conference on World Development in Banff. The paper was published in *Queen's Quarterly* the following year, under the title 'Should Canada Join the Organization of American States?' Early in 1966 he delivered a similar paper to the Canadian Club of Victoria, and he mailed the speech in pamphlet form to more than two dozen friends and colleagues.

He quickly discovered how little support there was for his views, and was a little surprised by the virulence of some of his critics. From his years of experience in the region Irwin had come to see the OAS as a large group of individual states, each with their own history, culture, and politics. His critics saw it as an American-dominated organization. There was a fundamental difference in emphasis and perspective. The most bizarre reaction came following a television interview in which

Irwin aired his views on the OAS. 'You said that Canada should join the organization of the United States of America,' one confused viewer wrote. 'If you are that anxious to become an American then WHY NOT LEAVE CANADA AND MOVE TO THE UNITED STATES. In my opinion anyone who would make a statement such as the one you were suppose to have made is a traitor to CANADA.' It was signed: 'A LOYAL MEMBER OF THE ROYAL *CANADIAN* NAVY.'[25] Irwin's goal was eventually realized, but not until 1990 when Canada finally became a member of the OAS.

◆

By early 1962 Irwin had begun thinking about his own future again. He was approaching sixty-five. Would he be able to secure one last posting to carry him through retirement age? 'As to my own immediate future,' he wrote Bruce Hutchison in January, 'I simply don't know what the score is. If the Department sticks to the rules – as I think it will – I will be due for the ashcan in May '63, at age 65. And what then? I really don't know. I want to do something interesting and reasonably remunerative, of course. But what does an ex-editor, ex-film producer, ex-Ambassador, ex-etc., etc., do? Have you got any ideas?'[26]

Repeated letters and phone calls to Ottawa failed to resolve the issue, until January 1963. 'I find there is a serious obstacle to proposing your appointment to a new post,' Robertson wrote from Ottawa, 'since you will reach your sixty-fifth birthday in May of this year.' Such were the rules, and they must be obeyed. Robertson then cushioned the blow with an offer to extend his stay in Mexico, a move that would not be resisted in Ottawa. 'If you agree to such an arrangement, I would be glad to recommend to the Minister that you stay on in Mexico for, say another year. I think in view of the value of your services in your present post the Minister would readily approve a recommendation of this kind.'[27]

Irwin talked the matter over with Pat, and, realizing that his time as a diplomat was running out, agreed to the one-year extension. It was not the way he had hoped to end his diplomatic career. But he enjoyed Mexico and believed there was still a job there for him to do.

In addition to his regular duties as ambassador, Irwin spent his last year in Mexico pondering his future and looking for job opportunities for after he and Pat returned to Canada. A government position of one sort or another might be a possibility, and he asked Robertson to inform him if anything looked promising. He could always write, a syndicated newspaper column perhaps, on international affairs, and Bruce Hutchison was after him with ideas for two or three books: memoirs, or a study of Canada and the problems it faced, for a start. He might also lecture on Latin America or take a part-time position at a university if one were interested. He didn't know just what opportunities there would be, and he started writing letters to friends to find out.

The defeat of the Diefenbaker government in April 1963 raised his hopes somewhat. 'Despite the lack of a clear majority I thought the election results encouraging,' he wrote Hutchison. 'At least it now seems clearly established that the prophet without a prophecy has been sunk without a trace, which would indicate that the country would seem to be seeing things a little more clearly that [sic] it has been in the past.'[28]

Any hopes he may have had that the new Pearson government might prove more generous with jobs were quickly shattered. In November, Hutchison wrote, following a dinner with Pearson at the new prime minister's residence, that he had raised Irwin's name during the meal.

I was determined to put in a word on your behalf and did. What, I asked, is happening to Irwin? Surely I said, he has still some useful work to do. Our friend [Pearson] replied that he had an idea to put you on the Bicultural Commission, but found you were not sufficiently bilingual. You had Spanish and Portuguese but, alas, not French. Then he mumbled something to the effect that you were a most able man.

But what did all this mean for Irwin? 'I feel bound to say,' Hutchison continued, 'that I would not count on our friend if I were you. I no longer count on him for anything ... Unless you have other assurances you would be wise, I believe, to make your plans independently of the government. I am sure you will find work to interest and nourish you.'[29]

In April 1964 Arthur and Pat packed a few things in the car and left the ambassadorial residence in Mexico City for the last time. They had decided on a long leisurely drive through the United States before finally returning home. His diplomatic career was over, he would return briefly to Ottawa to wrap things up officially, and then he would be free. But as he drove northwards through the Mexican countryside he was forced to ask himself: after eleven years in Australia, Brazil, and Mexico, where was home now?

EIGHTEEN

Pax Victoria

At an age when many Canadians are concerned with improving their golf swings or planning winter Florida vacations, Arthur Irwin was concerned with starting a new career. He was not a wealthy man. His Maclean Hunter and future civil service pensions together did not amount to much – certainly not enough to live on – and he had built up no equity in Canadian property while he had been abroad. His sole financial stake rested on his modest financial investments and his twenty Maclean shares, purchased in 1939, which had grown in value. Floyd Chalmers had made several offers to buy them, and early in 1963 he offered $750 a piece. Irwin demurred. Chalmers was no fool, he reasoned, and if he wanted them that badly they might be worth even more before too long. In any event, he had to support himself and his wife, and prepare for old age. The only way was to find a job.

Physically, he was well and strong, although on any given day he was likely to express concern for his health or complain that he was not feeling well. He suffered a gastric haemorrhage in 1960, which briefly hospitalized him for a few days after Christmas. Over previous years he complained on and off of dizziness, weakness, headaches, and some facial numbness, but a series of examinations discovered nothing. He had blood tests, X-rays of his skull and neck, his gall bladder checked for stones, and his stomach for ulcers and cancer, and he sent the test results to medical friends back home just to be sure. In Mexico City he blamed his medical problems on the altitude.

Intellectually, he was quite probably at the height of his powers. He had mellowed with age and had become a better friend to his children and grandchildren, but he had not lost his intellectual curiosity, his penetrating analytical skills, or his profound nationalism. And he had gained tremendous experience from his years abroad, having had an opportunity to view his country from the outside.

If he had not changed significantly, he wondered, what about the country? When he left for Australia the Liberals under St Laurent were comfortably in power, and it looked like they might be there forever. Now, after seven turbulent years under John Diefenbaker and Lester Pearson, the country seemed to be racked by petty scandals concerning German prostitutes and escaped criminals. Unable to rise above their own ignominy, the politicians were threatening to drag the tone of political life down with them into the gutter.

'Like you,' he wrote Bruce Hutchison a few months before returning to Canada, 'I am worried about the long-term future of our great and glorious country, and I think what worries me most is that we seem to be treading the materialist path to hell and damnation. If this is actually the case and the trend continues, a viable political future and the maintenance of a Canadian identity, in my opinion, are down the drain.' Could it be as bad as all that? he wondered. Were Canadians 'really losing our grip on the realities which brought us into being. I can't know, of course, what is going on in the country, as I have been away from it for almost ten years, but some of the symptoms are disturbing.'' In any event, it was no time to retire.

◆

On their way home from Mexico, Arthur and Pat stopped in Washington, D.C. to see Bruce Hutchison, who was on one of his regular junkets to the American capital. Irwin lunched with Hutchison and R.S. 'Dick' Malone, the president of Winnipeg's F.P. Publications Limited. F.P. Publications owned a handful of newspapers across the country, and controlled Victoria Press Limited, which in turn owned the two dailies in Victoria, B.C., the *Colonist* and the *Times*.

Irwin received a message from Malone later that day inviting him to a meeting in his hotel. 'How would you like to be publisher of the Victoria *Times*?' Malone asked when Irwin arrived. The present publisher was leaving for another position and Malone believed Irwin was the right person for the job. He explained some of the details and Irwin left, promising to think it over.

Irwin had never before considered moving to the West Coast. He was a confirmed easterner, and would have wished to return there. But he needed a job, and when he had exhausted the list of people to see on his return – and no better offers had turned up – he and Pat travelled to Victoria to investigate for themselves. Then he called Dick Malone and said: 'Thank you very much, I would be happy to take the job.'

A little negotiation followed and in October 1964 Arthur and Pat moved to Victoria and bought a home with the proceeds from selling some of his Maclean shares (although not to Floyd Chalmers). His official title was publisher of the Victoria *Times* and vice-president of Victoria Press Limited. The former gave him overall responsibility for the editorial direction of the paper; the latter made him responsible to F.P. Publications for the administration of Victoria Press Limited. The subtle irony was that as publisher of the *Times* he was a competitor of the *Colonist,* but as vice-president of Victoria Press he was responsible for *both* papers.

One of the benefits of being publisher of the *Times* was that it permitted Irwin to make annual treks to the east, to feel the pulse of the country and nose around Ottawa for scuttlebutt. It also provided an opportunity to meet old friends and make new contacts. Bruce Hutchinson had proven indestructible and remained a wealth of information. Peter C. Newman, a rising member of the Parliamentary Press Gallery and later the editor of *Maclean's,* became a good friend in Ottawa, and eventually almost a neighbour in Victoria. His rekindled friendship with Blair Fraser grew in strength until Fraser's death in 1968.

Of particular interest was the rise of Pierre Trudeau to the leadership of the Liberal party. The 'flowering' of Pierre in 1968 essentially signified the end of Irwin's generation in politics. The new leader brought new men and women to the centre of the political process, while those that Irwin knew so well either retired or were relegated to the margins.

'Trudeau's impressiveness grows with each exposure,' Irwin had written Peter Newman, and, as the Liberal convention approached, he was forced to consider the possible impact of a Trudeau prime ministership. 'Like you I find myself attracted to Trudeau,' he wrote Newman in February 1968, 'but I also have reservations. I can't help feeling he is pushing his hard line vis a vis Quebec too far and this could lead to trouble. I may, however, be doing the man an injustice since he may not really intend to drive intellectual logic as far as some of his recent statements would seem to suggest.'² His initial reservations over Trudeau evaporated after 1968.

Irwin stayed with Victoria Press for more than six years, retiring finally in the spring of 1971. In May of that year he turned seventy-three. A large dinner was held in his honour,[3] and in his farewell speech he brought some of his fifty years of experience in journalism and communications to a consideration of the future of journalism. 'The simple fact is that in contemporary society the journalistic process is indispensable to the functioning of any self government,' he noted at one stage. 'In its own vague way the public understands this truth. It senses, too, that the general health of society is directly related to the adequacy of the flow of information within it. Journalism is not the only great information system – education and the arts fall in the same category – but the challenge to journalism is unmistakable. Society has both the necessity and the right to demand that journalism illumine the realities of the contemporary world. Here lies the newspaper's essential responsibility and its basic function. Its rise or fall as a medium of mass communication, in my view, will depend on the skill and wisdom with which it meets this challenge.'[4]

His retirement from Victoria Press enabled Irwin to turn his attention to other projects. 'As to a book,' he wrote Peter Newman in 1967 responding to his suggestion that he write memoirs, 'I have thought about it. Had I not taken this job I might have taken a whirl at it but I confess that I have trouble in taking myself that seriously.' But Irwin *had* been giving the idea some serious thought, and would for many years. 'At one time I thought of attempting something under the heading "Education of a Canadian" but suspect that my kind of Canadian is at least obsolescent if not obsolete. Which is rather an inhibiting thought. However, we'll see.'[5]

He gathered his papers together into a dozen file boxes and spread them out in the basement. He took research trips east, particularly to the Public (now National) Archives in Ottawa (where he learned for the first time of Hector McKinnon's efforts to entice the Mackenzie King Liberals into purchasing the *Globe* in 1925) and the Maclean Hunter papers in the Archives of Ontario. At home he began putting together a few short draft chapters and read through the contents sheets for his more than twenty-four years at *Maclean's,* noting articles of interest and jotting down any important items he could recall. Later he began thinking of recruiting a researcher / writer to help him put the book together. But the memoirs were never written.

There were other interests and a constant stream of his and Pat's friends to Victoria, but increasingly his activities were focused on the house and his garden. In 1970 he suffered a mild heart attack and, a few years later, a stroke. But his mind was not affected and he maintained his active interest in politics and international affairs.

More difficult to shake than his health problems was a growing pessimism concerning the future of the country. 'Philosophically, man's actions are motivated by two sets of emotions,' he explained in a 1983 interview with a Victoria newspaper. 'One might be described as the self-regarding emotion, which is absolutely essential to the survival of the individual, and the other is the other-regarding emotion, which is absolutely essential for the viability of the society. To have a viable society you must have the two in balance.' In his view the former was in the ascendancy. 'It seems to me,' he continued, 'in recent decades we've been moving over, way over, to the self-regarding emotion and the self-regarding intellect. This poses a fundamental problem, not only for our society, but for the West generally.'

'We have had to be an outward looking people,' he added, with a flash of his buoyant and positive Canadianism. 'We are the only Americans who insisted during a century and three quarters of a hemispheric American revolution in not cutting our ties. All the colonists cut their political roots with Europe, except one. Who? The Canadians.'[6]

◆

Arthur Irwin did not make *Maclean's* a Canadian magazine. It already was primarily Canadian when he joined the staff in 1925. 'Canadianization' was not his idea, but it did provide him with the opportunity to mould the magazine in his own way and to leave his personal stamp upon it. It was not enough to have Canadians writing the articles and stories in *Maclean's;* it was important that they wrote with a strong 'feel' for the country, seeing it through their own eyes, and speaking with their own voices.

In the end, Irwin recalls the long years of rivalry with Napier Moore less for any personal animosity or petty squabbles and more as a clash between two differing views of what it meant to be Canadian. Moore was the archetypical Englishman who viewed Canada through imperial glasses, and believed that Canada would find its place in the sun as a British nation. His and Colonel Maclean's generation was fast disappearing between the world wars, when Canadians, scarred by the horrors of the first war, lived in fear of a second one, and began looking more to their own neighbourhood for security. Irwin was a part of the generation that saw Canada as a North American nation, with unsevered ties to Europe but with its roots planted firmly in this continent.

As an editor, Irwin brought an insatiable curiosity to the world around him and an ability to draw the best out of the people who worked with him. He enjoyed participating in the creative process and, more important for an editor, derived a real satisfaction from helping others to express their own ideas. He was an observant man, with a talent for discovering people with potential and for being able to establish relationships of trust with them. He quietly and steadily enlarged and upgraded his editorial staff and created an environment in which, together, they produced a quality Canadian magazine that thousands of Canadians turned to regularly for entertainment, information, and insight. In this way he had a profound effect on the development of *Maclean's* and, in turn, on the country and the way Canadians looked at themselves.

It is difficult to measure the worth or influence of such an individual for he left no monuments, great statues or buildings; he established no records. His contribution was more in the realm of ideas and in the determined way that he used the pages of *Maclean's* to tell Canadians something about themselves. Such achievements are less tangible than others perhaps, but no less profound, and their reverberations can still be felt today. Pierre Berton, one of those whose career was influenced by Irwin, later wrote: 'Two generations of Canadian writers in the non-fiction field owe much of their reputation to the schooling they received first on Macleans under your guidance and later from others who had received that schooling. The ripples of your influence are still widening.'[7]

The key to his success was not founded on any statistical abstraction, and he never relied on readers' surveys or polls for editorial guidance. It was more a genuine sympathy with his audience, a quality that was essentially intuitive. Simply put, Irwin succeeded at *Maclean's* in the 1930s and 1940s because his view and understanding of the country was shared by an ever-increasing number of Canadians. If there had been no common chord or mutual sympathy between audience and editor, the magazine surely would have floundered or he would have been replaced by someone else.

Irwin spent a lifetime questioning and searching for a greater understanding of his country and his age. Now, when he looks back over more than ninety-four years, he remembers less the specific achievements and more the enduring faith he shared with other Canadians in the ultimate evolution of Canada as an independent nation. If asked for a common theme running through his life, he would say that he had devoted himself to explaining Canadians to themselves: in print as a journalist, as an editor at *Maclean's*, and through sound and pictures at the National Film Board. As a diplomat he continued to preach his brand of Canadianism, but this time to a foreign audience.

The minister's son rejected the faith of his father but found a new secular faith in Canada. Like others of his generation, Irwin came to hold a special view of his country – a staunchly federalist and pan-Canadian nationalist view – one not shared by all Canadians and today, he worries, in danger of disappearing altogether. His Canada was a transcontinental and bilingual nation, tied together by a strong national government, by common bonds of history, climate, and geography, and by a shared national spirit.

There is a time for everything. But can the country look after itself in the years to come? He is not as sure as he once was. He is probably there today, looking out over his garden, where for so long the human hand has mingled with the hand of nature. As he watches, the sun radiates intensely for a brief moment – filling the world with brilliant shafts of crimson light – before sinking slowly into the pale Pacific sky. Others will have to speak for Canada now.

Abbreviations

AO	Archives of Ontario
DND	Department of National Defence
FP	*The Financial Post*
IP	Irwin Papers
MM	*Maclean's Magazine*
NA	National Archives, Ottawa
NFB	National Film Board
OAS	Organization of American States
PCO	Privy Council Office

Notes

Preface

1 Robert Gittings, *The Nature of Biography* (London 1978), 23

Chapter 1 'From Darkness to Light'

1 Irwin Papers (IP), 'Boyhood Notes.' Unless otherwise specified, the material in this section was taken from here.
2 IP, file unknown, Alexander Irwin, 'Sixty Years in the Ministry,' 1947
3 IP, file: Manuscript: Family background / Written notes
4 Interview with Arthur Irwin, 20 May 1987
5 Ibid.
6 Ibid.

Chapter 2 Gunner Irwin

1 IP, Glen Allen-Irwin interview transcripts, 80
2 IP, file: Irwin, W.A. University. Gertrude Robson (University of Manitoba) to Irwin, 3 December 1936
3 Quoted in Michael Bliss, 'The Methodist Church and World War I,' *Canadian Historical Review* 49 (1968): 219.
4 A.G. Bedford, *The University of Winnipeg: A History of the Founding Colleges* (Toronto 1976), 123
5 IP, file: War I: Manuscript, 'Off to War,' n.d.
6 Ibid.

7 NA, Claxton Papers, MG32 B5 vol 220, file: Memoirs, 148-9
8 IP, 10th Canadian Siege Battery, *War Diary* (privately printed, n.d.), 9
9 IP, file: War I: Manuscript, 'Armistice and After,' n.d.
10 Ibid.
11 NA, Claxton Papers, MG32 B5 vol 220, file: Memoirs, 172. Claxton added that Ord 'left knowing there would be something like a mutiny the next morning but somehow I felt sorry and liked him better.'
12 IP, file: War I: Manuscript, 'Armistice and After,' n.d.
13 IP, 10th Canadian Siege Battery, *War Diary*, 18

Chapter 3 Cub Reporter

1 IP, file: Fam. letters: Jean 1925, Irwin to Jean Irwin, 10 June 1925
2 Ibid., 28 February 1925
3 Ibid., 26 April 1925
4 Ibid., 28 February 1925
5 John Bird, ' "Tough Canadian" Irwin Goes South,' Vancouver *Province*, 30 May 1953
6 IP, file: Family – Irwin, Harvey, Harvey to Irwin, 5 October 1932
7 IP, file: M. Newspaper Notes, General, Newspaper. 1920-25
8 His research file also reveals a keen sense of organization and indefatigable research. In this particular file there are more than two dozen closely typed pages of notes, filled with names, dates, and places ranging from the Riel Rebellions to the Crimean War. Throughout are short notes and reminders, such as 'Look up Elgin Riots and Rebellion Losses Bill,' and 'Is old stores building on Queen east of Bathurst still standing. If it is get photo.'
9 He could identify with the military theme, and on occasion allowed his own experience to surface: 'Cavalry are not made in a day. In fact, it takes years to train the individual trooper and to develop corporate activity. It was not by chance that in 1885 the Indians and halfbreeds of the Western prairies found themselves in constant peril on all sides from a breed of white riders who could live off the country as they fought. The drudgery of warfare succeeded to the drudgery of drill; only men who were born to the game would have mastered it under the unfavorable conditions obtaining in Canada prior to 1885.' He might just as well have been writing about France in 1918. *Toronto Sunday World*, 16 July 1922
10 IP, file: Fam. Irwin, Arthur: Notes and Sketches, untitled, n.d.
11 Under Irwin's name in *Torontonensis*, the University of Toronto's gradua-

tion book for 1921, was the saying: 'Speech is silver, but silence is golden.' Of Irwin, it was written: 'Though Art does not wear his heart on his sleeve, he is liked best by those who know him best. Wields a wicked pen, may yet be heard from.'

Chapter 4 The 'Smoke' of Liberalism

1 W.H. Kesterton, *A History of Journalism in Canada* (Toronto 1967), 85
2 Henry James Morgan, ed., *The Canadian Men and Women of the Time*, 2nd ed. (Toronto 1912), 672
3 IP, Irwin-Allen transcripts, 172–3; Irwin Sandra Djwa interview transcripts, 5–6
4 Morley Callaghan telephone interview, 13 July 1989
5 IP, file: Fam. letters: Jean 1925, Irwin to Jean, 10 June 1925
6 *Globe*, 15 March 1924
7 IP, file: Fam. letters, Jean 1925, Irwin to Jean, 4 February 1925. All the correspondence between Irwin and Jean in this chapter can be found in this file.
8 Bruce Hutchison, *The Far Side of the Street* (Toronto 1976), 70
9 IP, Irwin-Allen interview transcripts, 193
10 IP, file: V. Retirement 1971, Hutchison speech at retirement dinner for Irwin, Victoria Union Club, 27 May 1971
11 Hutchinson, *Far Side of the Street*, 74–5
12 Sir John Willison, *Reminiscences: Political and Personal* (Toronto 1919), 123
13 IP, Irwin-Allen interview transcripts, 197
14 *Globe*, 2 May 1925
15 NA, King Papers, MG26 J13, Diary (hereafter King diary), 17 August 1925
16 IP, Irwin-Allen transcripts, 203
17 IP, Irwin-Djwa transcripts, 3
18 NA, King Papers, MG26 J1 vol 119, Hector McKinnon to King, 22 June 1925
19 Ibid., 28 June 1925
20 Ibid., King to McKinnon, 8 July 1925
21 See H.B. Neatby, *William Lyon Mackenzie King; vol. II: 1924–1932, The Lonely Heights* (Toronto 1963), 61–3
22 King diary, 5 September 1925
23 See *Globe*, 9 October 1925
24 *Globe*, 13 October, 1925. The editorial had its effect on King. He wrote in his diary for 14 October: '*The Globe* has a contemptible editorial on Forke's manifesto, anything to injure me.'

25 IP, unpublished editorial, 'Misleading the Public,' n.d.
26 IP, Irwin-Djwa transcripts, 8
27 Toronto *Telegram*, 16 October 1925
28 Ibid.
29 King diary, 10 October 1925
30 IP, file: Globe Resignation, King to Irwin, 17 October 1925
31 NA, King Papers, MG26 J1 vol 132, reel C-2277, Irwin to King, 18 October 1925

Chapter 5 Canada's National Magazine

1 IP, MM Contents Notes, 1925, 1
2 Ibid.
3 IP, file: MM Letters, Personal, 1926–1940, Irwin to Tyrrell, 23 February 1926
4 W.S. Wallace, 'The Growth of Canadian National Feeling,' *Canadian Historical Review* 1, no. 2 (June 1920), 138, 151, 162
5 On culture and nationalism in these years, see John Herd Thompson with Allen Seager, *Canada 1922–1939: Decades of Discord* (Toronto 1985), chapter 8; M. Vipond, 'The Canadian Authors' Association in the 1920s: A Case Study in Cultural Nationalism,' *Journal of Canadian Studies* 15, no. 1 (spring 1980), 68–79; and Maria Tippett, *Making Culture: English-Canadian Institutions and the Arts before the Massey Commission* (Toronto 1990), chapter 1.
6 *Saturday Night*, 27 February 1926, 1
7 See Mary Vipond, 'Canadian Nationalism and the Plight of Canadian Magazines in the 1920s,' *Canadian Historical Review* 58, 1 (1977); 43–63. See also Charles Stokes, 'Our Americanized News-stands,' *Saturday Night*, 27 February 1926, 2.
8 Floyd Chalmers, *A Gentleman of the Press* (Toronto 1969), 144
9 Quoted in Glen Allen, 'The Business Side,' MM, 30 December 1985, 34.
10 IP, Irwin-Allen interview transcripts, 655
11 Floyd Chalmers, *Both Sides of the Street: One Man's Life in Business and the Arts in Canada* (Toronto 1983), 40
12 Ibid., 163
13 Quoted in Chalmers, *Gentleman*, 192
14 For more on this controversy, see Fraser Sutherland, *The Monthly Epic: A History of Canadian Magazines, 1789–1989* (Toronto 1989), 146
15 IP, MM Contents Notes, 1926, 2–3
16 Ibid., 1926, 12–13

17 Ibid., 1926, 14

Chapter 6 'The Horse Work'

1 *MM*, 1 April 1926
2 IP, MM Contents Notes, 1926, 15–16
3 Ibid., 16
4 IP, file: MM Writers Club, Irwin, Writers Club Notes, 5 December 1979
5 See Theodore Peterson, *Magazines in the Twentieth Century* (Urbana, Ill. 1956), chapter 1
6 Ibid., 17
7 Ibid., 25, 58. The phrase 'silent partner' is taken from Bea Julian, 'Mass Magazines, 1900–Present: Serious Journalism or Mass Entertainment?' in Wm. David Sloan, ed., *Perspectives on Mass Communication History* (Hillsdale, New Jersey 1991), 259.
8 For background on Canadian magazines, see Sutherland, *Monthly Epic*; Noel Robert Barbour, *Those Amazing People: The Story of the Canadian Magazine Industry, 1778–1967* (Toronto 1982); and F.W. Watt, 'Climate of Unrest: Periodicals in the Twenties and Thirties,' *Canadian Literature* 12 (spring 1962), 15–27.
9 See Graham Carr, 'Design as Content: Foreign Influences and the Identity of English-Canadian Intellectual Magazines, 1919–39,' *American Review of Canadian Studies* XVIII, 2 (1988), 181–93; and ' "All We North Americans": Literary Culture and the Continentalist Ideal, 1919–1939,' *American Review of Canadian Studies* XVII, 2 (1987), 145–57; and Allan Smith, 'The Continental Dimension in the Evolution of the English-Canadian Mind,' *International Journal* 31 (summer 1976): 442–69.
10 *MM*, 15 July 1927 and 15 March 1928, respectively
11 IP, file: MM Budgets and Salaries, Irwin memo, 1931
12 IP, file: MM Notes: 1925–1950, Irwin memo on appointment to *Maclean's*, n.d.
13 IP, file: MM Irwin, Personal Documents; Irwin memo for Tyrrell, 6 March 1928
14 See IP, file: MM Editing Examples, for the original manuscript and Irwin's changes.
15 IP, file: MM Irwin, Personal Documents, Irwin memo for Tyrrell, 6 March 1928
16 IP, file: MM Speeches, Writing & Editing, Irwin's Notes re Talk on Short Stories and Writing Generally, n.d. He gave the same speech two months later to the Toronto branch of the Canadian Authors Association.

17 IP, file: MM Irwin, Personal Documents, Irwin memo for Tyrrell, 6 March 1928
18 Peterson, *Magazines in the Twentieth Century*, 126
19 IP, MM Contents Notes, 1927, 29
20 *MM*, 1 October 1927
21 IP, file: MM Irwin, Personal Documents, Irwin memo for Tyrrell, 6 March 1928
22 Ibid., Irwin to E.B. Ramsay, 12 June 1929
23 This episode is taken from IP, MM Contents Notes, 1927, 14–15.
24 *MM*, 15 May 1927
25 *MM*, 15 August 1927
26 For four recent examples, see J.L. Granatstein and Norman Hillmer, *For Better or for Worse: Canada and the United States to the 1990s* (Toronto 1991), 87; Thompson and Seager, *Decades of Discord*, 90–91; Philip C. Enros, 'The Technical Service Council's Origins: A "Patriotic Experiment" in Selling Engineers,' *Journal of Canadian Studies* 24, no. 4 (winter 1989–90), 90–91; and Robert Bothwell, *Canada and the United States: The Politics of Partnership* (Toronto 1992), 13.
27 IP, MM Contents Notes, 1928, 11
28 *MM*, 1 September 1928. Irwin's concern with the issue resulted in a *Maclean's* article by Grattan O'Leary, entitled 'Yes, We Are Not Canadians' (MM, 15 September 1928).
29 Quoted in Arts and Letters Club of Toronto, *News and Views of Club Programmes & Activities*, December 1985.
30 IP, file: MM Writers Club, Irwin, Writers Club Notes, 5 December 1979
31 R.E. Everson interview, Burlington, Ont., 5 May 1988
32 IP, file: MM Letters, Personal, 1926–1940, Deacon to Irwin, 28 July 1931
33 Ibid., Deacon to Irwin, 24 April 1931
34 *Canadian Writer's Market Survey* (Ottawa 1931), 12–16
35 IP, file: MM Writers Club, Irwin Writers Club Notes, 5 December 1979
36 IP, file: MM Letters, Personal, 1926–1940, Deacon to Irwin, 9 March 1931
37 IP, file: MM Irwin, Personal Documents, Irwin to Moore, February 1931
38 IP, file: MM Circulation Data, Tyndall memo, 4 March 1930
39 IP, MM Contents Notes, 1928, 27
40 IP, file: MM Irwin, Personal Documents, Irwin to Moore, February 1931
41 Ibid.
42 Ibid., Irwin memo for Tyrrell, 6 March 1928
43 Ibid., Irwin to Moore, February 1931

Chapter 7 Getting Down to Brass Tacks

1 IP, file: MM Irwin, Personal Documents, Moore to Irwin, 13 September 1932
2 Irwin prepared another transportation brief in 1937; this time the statement of the Ontario Association of Motor Coach Operators for the Ontario Royal Commission on Transportation.
3 MM, Editor's Confidence, 15 September 1934
4 IP, MM Contents Notes, 1934, 12
5 Norval Bonisteel interview, Toronto, 10 May 1988
6 IP, MM Contents Notes, 1934, 7
7 IP, Irwin to Floyd Chalmers, 1965
8 IP, MM Contents Notes, 1928, 18
9 Neal Irwin interview, Toronto, 27 March 1988
10 IP, MM Contents Notes, 1934, 14
11 IP, file: Machine Ballet, Irwin, 'The Machine,' n.d.
12 Ibid., 'Between You and Me' (clipping, n.d.)
13 For one critic's reaction, see Richard Hapgood, ed., 'The Carnival Merry-Go-Round' *Skating* 65 (April 1938): 19–23. Hapgood noted that it was 'probably not too much to say that "The Machine" will stand out as a signpost pointing the way to the development of figure skating as an art form in its own right' (p. 21).
14 See, for example, Doug Owram, *The Government Generation: Canadian Intellectuals and the State, 1900–1945* (Toronto 1986), chapters 6 and 7.
15 IP, Irwin-Allen interview transcripts, 425
16 John Holmes interview, Toronto, 22 October 1987
17 Howard Ferguson, 'Canada Must Arm,' MM, 15 April 1937
18 Frank Underhill, 'Keep Canada Out of War,' MM 15 May 1937
19 *Maclean's Weekly* (staff magazine), 27 May 1939
20 IP, file: MM Irwin, Personal Documents, draft letter, Irwin to Moore, February 1937
21 IP, file: MM Letters, Personal 1926–1940, Irwin to Tyrrell, 29 May 1937

Chapter 8 The Bren Gun Scandal

1 NA, J.L. Ralston papers, MG27 III B11, vol. 89, file: Bren Gun: Correspondence – General, Minutes of Meeting of the Committee of the Privy Council, 5 March 1937
2 Ibid., file: Bren Gun: Correspondence 1938, Jan.–Mar. Minutes of Meeting of the Committee of the Privy Council, 22 March 1938

3 George Drew, 'Canada's Defense Farce,' *The Financial Post*, 26 March 1938. The article was subtitled: 'No Tanks; Planes, Rifles Obsolete – "Bow and Arrow Army Running Out of Arrows."'
4 IP, file: Bren: Origin of Article, Irwin to Chalmers, 22 October 1965
5 MM, 1 September 1938
6 AO, Maclean Hunter Papers, Series C-1-1, Box 111, file: Bren Gun Enquiry, T.H. Howse, Note re Telephone Conversation with Major Hahn, 12 August 1938
7 Ibid., Series B-1-2-d, Box 63, file: Bren Gun Inquiry 2, Hunter to Maclean, 7 October 1938
8 King diary, 31 August 1938
9 See the testimony in the *Report of the Royal Commission on the Bren Machine Gun Contract* (Ottawa 1939), 28.
10 Mackenzie was 'far too provocative,' King recorded. 'I could see it was the effect of the alcohol which is the most dangerous and treacherous of all guides.' Mackenzie refused to prepare a statement in advance, deciding, instead, to improvise. Unfortunately, he could not speak in the afternoon when his head might have been clear, and rose only in the evening. 'Several of his remarks were wholly unparliamentary and diverted sympathy from him where he might easily have gained considerable sympathy. While he roused up the fighting spirit of the men, I felt that the effect on the country would be far from good.' (King diary, 9 February 1939)
11 AO, Maclean Hunter Papers, Box 63, file: Bren Gun Inquiry 2, Minutes of staff conference, 21 January 1939
12 Ibid., Moore to Hunter, 9 February 1939
13 House of Commons *Debates*, 9 February 1939, 787
14 Ibid., 1 March 1939, 1452
15 AO, Maclean Hunter Papers, Box 63, file: Bren Gun Inquiry 2, Editorial conference minutes, 25 March 1939
16 House of Commons, Standing Committee on Public Accounts, *Minutes of Proceedings and Evidence Respecting the Bren Machine Gun and other Armament Contracts*, 24 May 1939, 764–5
17 AO, Maclean Hunter Papers, Box 73, file: Bren Gun Case, W.A. Fraser to Hunter, 26 May 1939
18 House of Commons, Public Accounts Committee, *Minutes of Proceedings*, 30 May 1939, 878
19 IP, file: Bren: Staff Conferences, Minutes of editorial conference, 3 June 1939

Notes to pages 129-37   295

20 House of Commons, Public Accounts Committee, *Minutes of Proceedings,* 30 May 1939, 925-39
21 IP, file: Bren: Staff Conferences, Editorial meeting minutes, 3 June 1939
22 IP, file: Defence: Policy Memos, Hunter memo, 9 June 1939
23 AO, Maclean Hunter Papers, Box 111, file: Bren Gun (Legal file), Conference of editorial committee, 17 June 1939

Chapter 9 The Campaign

1 H.B. Neatby, *William Lyon Mackenzie King; vol 3: 1932-1939, The Prism of Unity* (Toronto 1976), 311
2 AO, Maclean Hunter Papers, Box 111, file: Bren Gun (Legal File), Minutes of editorial conference, 17 June 1939
3 IP, file: Folder 2, Irwin memo, 19 June 1939
4 IP, Irwin-Allen transcripts 351
5 IP, file: Defence: Policy Memos, Minutes of editorial conference, 4 July 1939
6 Ibid.
7 IP, file: Ross, F.M. Cos, Irwin memo, 10 July 1939
8 IP, file: Folder 2, Irwin memo, 10 July 1939
9 Ibid., Irwin memo on conversation with X, 3-4 August 1939
10 IP, file: Defence Investigation, W.A. Irwin Progress Reports, Memo on editorial conference, 18 August 1939
11 Ibid.
12 *The Financial Post,* 26 August 1939
13 Ibid., 2 September 1939
14 Ibid., 9 September 1939
15 King diary, 15 September 1939
16 J.W. Pickersgill, ed., *The Mackenzie King Record; vol. I: 1939-1944* (Toronto 1960), 26-7
17 *The Financial Post,* 23 September 1939
18 Irwin made the suggestion of writing a letter to the prime minister 'indicating that we had important information that had not been published; we were reluctant to go on with the campaign, but had no alternative unless a new Minister was appointed.' An unsigned letter from Hunter to King along these lines has been found in the Maclean Hunter Papers, but not in the King Papers (nor has a response been found). There is no reason to believe that the letter was ever sent. Even if it had, the letter would have arrived after King had made his decision

on Mackenzie's fate. See AO, Maclean Hunter Papers, Box 73, file: Bren Gun Case, Hunter to King, 16 September 1939.
19 IP, file: Defence: Policy Memos, Minutes of editorial conference, 15 September 1939
20 Overall sales of *The Financial Post* were up by 17 per cent from 29 July to 17 October. This is not to suggest that the campaign against Mackenzie and the DND was solely responsible for the increase (sales of *Maclean's* were rising as well); but knowledge of rising sales would only confirm that the Maclean company was on the right course. IP, file: Defence: Comment on Series, A.A. Stagg memo, 17 October 1939
21 IP, file: Defence: Policy Memos, Chalmers to Hunter, 4 October 1939
22 IP, file: Censorship, Chalmers memo for Hunter #1, 30 October 1939
23 IP, file: Defence: Comments on Series, Hutchison to Irwin, no date, received 13 November 1939
24 IP, file: Folder #2, Memo on conversation with McNaughton, 5 October 1939
25 IP, file: Rogers, Norman, Notes on conversation with Norman Rogers, 8 November 1939
26 AO, Maclean Hunter Papers, Box 63, file: Bren Gun Inquiry 2, Maclean memo for Hunter, 21 November 1939
27 See J.L. Granatstein, *Canada's War: The Politics of the Mackenzie King Government, 1939-1945* (Toronto 1975), 76-80.
28 AO, Maclean Hunter Papers, Box 63, file: Bren Gun Inquiry 1, Minutes of editorial conference, 29 January 1940
29 *The Financial Post*, 3 February 1940
30 Mackenzie prepared a lengthy document in response to the charges in *Maclean's* and *The Financial Post* which he distributed to his colleagues. The responses he received to this fifteen-page single-spaced document make for interesting reading and give an indication of the wide opinions concerning the motives of the Maclean company. One Quebec MP suggested that it was the Conservative party behind the articles, with the *Post* undertaking the 'dirty work' on its behalf. Another explained the *Post* attacks as revenge tactics from the Maclean company because the government had abolished Prime Minister Bennett's tax on American periodicals and 'they suddenly were put back on a less rich diet by the present Govt.' Still another MP blamed the incompetence of those individuals involved. The *Post* had never been right about anything, he noted. 'I know quite well the reasons why the Drew articles were published. Macleans never did have backing for them. The investigation

must have been very humiliating, so the *Post* decided that the attack must be concentrated on you [Mackenzie] and that they must go on iterating and reiterating this stuff until, like German propaganda, the gullible would swallow it.' NA, Mackenzie Papers, MG27 III B5 vol 20, file: 41-8

31 *The Financial Post*, 23 March 1940
32 IP, file: Supply Ministry, Irwin memo, 14 March 1940
33 *Ottawa Journal*, 11 January 1941
34 AO, Maclean Hunter Papers, Box 63, file: Bren Gun Inquiry 2, Hunter to Maclean, 15 January 1941
35 C.P. Stacey, *Six Years of War* (Ottawa 1955), 26
36 *The Financial Post*, 18 January 1941

Chapter 10 The War Years

1 IP, Irwin-Allen interview transcripts, 369
2 E.J. Pratt, 'Dunkirk,' *Ten Selected Poems* (Toronto 1947), 36
3 IP, file: CIIA: N.A. Defence, Immediate Problems of Canadian Defence (the Toronto Memorandum), n.d.
4 Ibid., Claxton to Irwin, 6 July 1940
5 Ibid., Claxton to Irwin, 10 July 1940
6 Ibid., Hackett Memo for Irwin, 26 July 1940
7 IP, file: CIIA: War Policy, A Programme of Immediate Canadian Action, 17-18 July 1940
8 NA, Claxton Papers, MG32 B5 vol. 44, file: 500, Claxton to King, 23 August 1940
9 Hugh Keenleyside, *Memoirs of Hugh L. Keenleyside; Volume 2: On the Bridge of Time* (Toronto 1982), 49
10 NA, Claxton Papers, MG32 B5 vol. 44, file: 500, King to Claxton, 21 September 1940
11 For more on *Saturday Night*, see Sutherland, *Monthly Epic*, 164-79.
12 Tippett, *Making Culture*, 159
13 See correspondence in AO, Maclean Hunter Papers, file: W.A. Irwin – Correspondence, 1941.
14 Ibid., Box 402, file: W.A. Irwin: notes, drafts, speeches, Irwin speech transcript, 15 April 1941
15 *MM*, 1 December 1943
16 Ibid.
17 Mary Vipond, 'The Image of Women in Mass Circulation Magazines in

the 1920s,' in Susan Mann Trofimenkoff and Alison Prentice, eds., *The Neglected Majority: Essays in Canadian Women's History* (Toronto 1977), 117. See also, Susan Nauright, 'Transition and Continuity in Images of Men and Women in American Magazine Advertisements during World War Two,' paper presented in the Canadian Historical Association, Queen's University, Kingston, 5 June 1991.

18 MM, 1 January 1943
19 MM, 1 July 1943
20 IP, file: MM Edit: Article Memos, Irwin memo for Moore, 20 November 1941
21 Ibid., unsigned memo for Navy issue, n.d.
22 IP, MM Contents Notes, 1943, 11
23 IP, file: MM Letters: Hutchison, Bruce Hutchison to Irwin, received 13 December 1944
24 Bruce Hutchison, *The Unknown Country: Canada and her People* (New York 1942), 138–9
25 He was, however, offered a job by John Grierson, then in charge of the Wartime Information Board. Irwin discussed the proposal with Hunter and ultimately refused the offer. IP, file: Grierson, John
26 IP, file: MM Letters, Personal: 1941–1945, Irwin memo on conversation with Moore, 17 November 1941
27 Chalmers, *Both Sides of the Street*, 164
28 Ibid., 182
29 AO, Maclean Hunter Papers, Box 83, file: H.N. Moore, Hunter memo, n.d.
30 Chalmers, *Both Sides of the Street*, 181–2
31 IP, file: MM Edit: Powers of Managing Editor, Responsibilities of Managing Editor, 1 March 1944. It should be noted that Irwin had a hand in preparing this memo outlining the duties of the managing editor.
32 IP, file: MM Irwin, Personal Documents, Chalmers to Irwin, 3 December 1942
33 IP, file: MM Budgets and Salaries, Chalmers to Irwin, 20 December 1943; Chalmers to Irwin, 3 July 1944
34 Jerry Anglin interview, Thornhill, Ontario, 9 June 1988
35 Ibid.
36 IP, Irwin-Allen interview transcripts, 365
37 John Fraser and Graham Fraser, eds., '*Blair Fraser Reports:*' *Selections 1944–1968* (Toronto 1969), xvii
38 This position had been filled on a part-time basis in the past. Grant

Dexter had long been a regular contributor, but he left for Europe in 1938. That same year Floyd Chalmers assigned Kenneth Wilson as Ottawa correspondent for *The Financial Post*. Wilson, a long-time *Post* staffer who had risen to become its managing editor, had contributed to *Maclean's* in the past and now doubled as *Maclean's* Ottawa correspondent. With the hiring of Blair Fraser *Maclean's* at last had its own full-time Ottawa correspondent.

39 IP, file: MM Edit: Article Memos, Irwin memo for Fraser, 27 October 1944
40 AO, Maclean Hunter Papers, Box 405, file: War Coverage, Irwin memos, 16 and 18 June 1943
41 IP, file: MM Edit: Article Memos, Reyburn to Irwin, 19 June 1943
42 Ibid.
43 IP, file: MM Edit: Article Memos, Irwin memo, 15 July 1943
44 Ibid., unsigned memo Invasion Coverage, 18 June 1943
45 *MM*, 1 February 1944, 2
46 IP, MM Contents Notes, 1944, 5
47 AO, Maclean Hunter Papers, Box 402, file: Staff Candidates

Chapter 11 The 'Real Meaning' of Destruction

1 IP, file: MM Irwin. W.A. Publicity, Irwin to Gordon ?, 20 December 1945
2 Ibid.
3 A regular visitor to the cottage was Irwin's father, Alexander, who had been appointed secretary of the Ontario Temperance Federation. He had recently become embroiled in a public dispute with Ontario Premier Hepburn over the possible exclusion of enlisted men from bars and taverns, a dispute that led to Alexander being barred briefly from the premier's office in Queen's Park.
4 IP, file: Family: Letters 1924–1949, Jean to Irwin, 16 February 1939
5 IP, file: CIIA: Commonwealth Conf. 1945, Cavell to Irwin, 27 July 1944
6 Ibid., Chalmers to Moore, 8 August 1944
7 Ibid., Irwin, British Commonwealth Relations Conference, London, 1945, 14 April 1976. Many of the following details were taken from these memoir notes.
8 Roland Michener interview, Toronto, 12 May 1988
9 IP, file: CIIA: Commonwealth Conf. 1945, Irwin, British Commonwealth Relations Conference, London, 1945, 14 April 1976, 8
10 Jerry Anglin interview, Thornhill, Ont., 9 June 1988
11 Irwin, 'The Haunted Ruins of Europe,' *MM*, 15 May 1945

12 Franklin Arbuckle interview, Toronto, 16 June 1989
13 IP, file: CIIA: Commonwealth Conf. 1945, Irwin, British Commonwealth Relations Conference, London, 1945, 14 April 1976, 10
14 IP, file: MM Letters Personal: 1941–1945, Irwin memo to self and Moore, 11 June 1945
15 IP, MM Contents Notes, 1945, n.p.
16 John Clare interview, Toronto, 17 June 1988
17 See, for example, Joseph Marshall, 'How We Kept the Atom Bomb Secret,' *Saturday Evening Post*, 10 November 1945, and George Axelsson, 'Is the Atomic Terror Exaggerated?' *Saturday Evening Post*, 5 January 1946.

Chapter 12 The Man Who Made *Maclean's*

1 IP, file: MM Irwin. W.A. Publicity, Irwin to Gordon ?, 20 December 1945
2 IP, file: MM Editorial Reports & Plans, Patterns for 1946, 2 January 1946
3 Arthur Mayse interview, Campbell River, B.C., 21 May 1988
4 Arthur Mayse column, Victoria *Daily Times*, 8 January 1963
5 IP, file: MM Editorial Reports & Plans, Mayse to Irwin, 27 December 1946
6 Mayse interview, 21 May 1988
7 MM, 15 November 1945
8 MM, 1 December 1945
9 AO, Maclean Hunter Papers, Box 401, file: Administration, Notes on Editorial Routine, n.d.
10 IP, file: MM Editorial Reports & Plans, Annual Report, Editorial Department, 1946 n.d.
11 IP, file: 90th Birthday Comments; Scott Young to Irwin, 12 May 1988
12 Pierre Berton interview, Toronto, 9 August 1988
13 Scott Young interview, Toronto, 24 July 1989
14 Ibid.
15 For a recent reiteration of this view, see Sutherland, *Monthly Epic*, 219.
16 The pattern of their relationship was established soon after Allen's arrival in May of 1946. He later wrote of the experience:

> I had arrived with, to me, fairly impressive credentials as a Boy Wonder of the newspaper game. Since the age of sixteen I had never had a single editor say anything but, 'Great stuff, kid.' It was my impression that saying great stuff, kid, was all editors were made for.
> My first staff-written article came back to me with eighty-eight corrections scribbled on the margins.
> 'Mr. Irwin,' I said, 'one of us is crazy.'

'Very likely,' he said. 'Let's figure out which one it is.'
Three hours later, having lost eighty-eight consecutive rounds, I began rewriting the article. I also began my education in the tradition of hard editing, hard writing and hard publishing that has made this company one of the few truly professional publishing concerns in Canada, indeed of only a very small handful in the world.

IP, file: MM Irwin Personal Documents, Ralph Allen clipping from Anniversary Issue, Maclean Hunter Newsweekly, n.d.
17 IP, file: MM Editorial Reports & Plans, Annual Report, Editorial Department, 1946, n.d.
18 Ibid.
19 IP, file: MM Letters, Personal: 1946–1950, Hutchison to Irwin, 2 April 1947
20 Pierre Berton, *Starting Out: 1920–1947* (Toronto 1987), 328
21 Arthur Mayse column, Victoria *Daily Times*, 8 January 1963; Pierre Berton interview, Toronto, 9 August 1988
22 John Clare interview, Toronto, 17 June 1988
23 IP, file: 90th Birthday Comments, Allen to Irwin, n.d.; Scott Young to Irwin, 12 May 1988; Norval Bonisteel interview, Toronto, 10 May 1988; Arthur Mayse interview, Campbell River, B.C., 21 May 1988; Jerry Anglin interview, Thornhill, Ont., 9 June 1988
24 Jerry Anglin interview, Thornhill, Ont., 9 June 1988; Arthur Mayse interview, Campbell River, B.C., 21 May 1988
25 Pierre Berton interview, Toronto, 9 August 1988
26 Scott Young interview, Toronto, 24 July 1989
27 Pierre Berton interview, Toronto, 9 August 1988
28 Victoria *Daily Times*, 8 January 1963
29 Pierre Berton interview, Toronto, 9 August 1988
30 Arthur Mayse interview, Campbell River, B.C., 21 May 1988
31 IP, MM Contents Notes, 1946, 15
32 IP, file: MM Berton, Pierre; Berton to Irwin, 14 November 1950
33 Jerry Anglin interview, Thornhill, Ont., 9 June 1988
34 AO, Maclean Hunter Papers, Box 401, file: Dress-Maclean's Magazine; Leslie Hannon to Irwin, 14 September 1949; Berton to Irwin, n.d.
35 Ibid., Berton to Irwin, 15 August 1949
36 Peterson, *Magazines in the Twentieth Century*, 120

Chapter 13 'The Editor' and His Magazine

1 Prime Minister King was not pleased with Irwin's appointment. He wrote

in his diary on 24 March 1948: 'I had a talk with Senator Davies who was terribly annoyed at the appointment of Tories like Ford of London, Irwin of McLean's [sic] and other Tories to Commissions abroad. I think he is entirely right. I do not understand why these Tory appointments are proposed.' Obviously Irwin had come a long way since 1925, when King referred to Irwin as one of 'us.'

2 AO Maclean Hunter Papers, Box 402, file: Policy, Allen to Irwin, 15 July 1948
3 Irwin to author, March 1990
4 Pierre Berton interview, Toronto, 9 August 1988
5 AO, Maclean Hunter Papers, Box 83, file: H.N. Moore; Chalmers to Irwin, 16 June 1949
6 Pierre Berton interview, Toronto, 9 August 1988
7 AO, Maclean Hunter Papers, Box 401, file: Editing; Howse to Hunter, 20 October 1949
8 Ibid., Irwin to Hunter, 3 November 1949
9 AO, Maclean Hunter Papers, Box 401, file: Bethune; Berton to Ralph Allen, n.d.
10 IP, file: MM Bethune Article; Chalmers to Allen, 23 March 1948
11 Scott Young interview, Toronto, 24 July 1989
12 AO, Maclean Hunter Papers, Box 401, file: Dress-Maclean's Magazine, Berton to John Clare, 27 April 1949; on another issue (concerning column size), see Adam Marshall to Irwin. 26 September 1949, in the same file.
13 IP, file: MM Editorial Reports and Plans, Year-End Staff Conference, 8 January 1947
14 Ibid., Maclean's Magazine Programme for 1947, n.d.
15 Ibid., Article Pattern, Maclean's 1947, n.d.
16 In all of Irwin's years at *Maclean's* he issued very few formal policy statements on any issue. One was 'A Statement of Policy' on Quebec. In part it reads: 'We accept and support the Canadian idea – which is the development of a nation on the basis of two cultures, two languages and two religions. We defend and have consistently defended the legal and moral right of Quebec to preserve those special institutions and customs which are theirs as a matter, not of sufferance, but of right. This is our only "special policy" towards Quebec.' IP, file: MM Policy Memos and Criticism
17 MM, Editors' Confidence, 15 March 1948
18 AO, Maclean Hunter Papers, Box 410, file: Circulation, Audit Report for

1948, n.d. The breakdown was: Nova Scotia 13,254 (3.93%); P.E.I. 2002 (0.6%); New Brunswick 9193 (2.73%); Quebec 27,963 (8.28%); Ontario 132,953 (39.33%); Manitoba 25,670 (7.60%); Saskatchewan 28,850 (8.54%); Alberta 39,864 (11.8%); B.C. 50,841 (15.04%), plus miscellaneous sales in the UK, U.S., and Newfoundland.

19 See ibid., Box 402, file: Reports on Competitors, Canadian Advertising Research Foundation, Audience Study of 11 Magazines in Canada, 1949
20 Franklin Arbuckle interview, Toronto, 16 June 1989
21 Scott Young interview, Toronto, 24 July 1989
22 IP, file: Circulation Data; memorandum on circulation, n.d.
23 IP, file: Letters: Australia: MM; Irwin to Ralph Allen, 23 September 1955

Chapter 14 The Last Year

1 IP, file: FB Personal Letters I; Irwin to R.K. Burge, 5 May 1950
2 Hugh MacLennan telephone interview, 8 May 1989
3 IP, file: MM Letters, Personal: 1946–1950; Allen to Irwin, 15 December 1948
4 AO, Maclean Hunter Papers, Box 403; file: Staff Prospects; Fraser to Irwin, 24 December 1948
5 John Clare interview, Toronto, 17 June 1988; Jerry Anglin interview, Thornhill, Ont., 9 June 1988
6 IP, file: MM Irwin, Personal Documents; Hunter to Chalmers, 12 September 1949
7 Ibid., Chalmers to Irwin, 14 September 1949
8 Ibid., Irwin to Chalmers, 15 September 1949
9 Ibid., Chalmers to Irwin, n.d.
10 IP, File: Film Board: Manuscript Notes; Irwin, Notes on My Stint at the National Film Board, 8 November 1983
11 IP, file: MM Letters, Personal: 1946–1950; Irwin to Bruce Hutchison, 7 December 1949
12 IP, file: Film Board: Manuscript Notes; Irwin, Notes on my Stint at the National Film Board, 8 November 1983
13 IP, file: MM Letters, Personal: 1946–1950; Irwin to Bruce Hutchison, 7 December 1949
14 Ibid.
15 IP, file: FB Personal Letters I; Irwin to M.R.K. Burge, 5 May 1950
16 IP, file: FB Appointment Comment Letters; Irwin to Baxter, 5 January 1950

17 IP, file: FB Appointment; Irwin to Winters, 29 December 1949
18 IP, file: 90th Birthday Comments, Allen to Irwin, n.d.
19 IP, file: Letters: Marriage; Hutchison to Irwin, n.d.
20 IP, file: FB Appointment Comment Letters; MacLennan to Irwin, 16 December 1949
21 IP, file: FB Appointment Comment Letters; Underhill to Irwin, 20 December 1949. Irwin replied in part: 'I appreciate particularly what you said about my alleged intelligence. I don't know about dead bones, but at least we'll try to rattle – apparently I can't shake that editorial "we." ' Irwin to Underhill, 6 January 1950
22 IP, file: MM Resignation, Irwin to Hunter, 23 December 1949
23 *MM*, 1 February 1950

Chapter 15 'Mad Ministers, Rioting Reds, and Posh Parties'

1 IP, file: MM Letters: Wuorio, Eva-Lis; Wuorio to Irwin, n.d.
2 Reginald Whitaker, 'Origins of the Canadian Government's Internal Security System, 1946–1952,' *Canadian Historical Review* 65 (1984): 154–83
3 NA, St Laurent Papers, MG26 L vol 122, file: M-75-1; Winters to St Laurent, 26 August 1949
4 See Piers Handling, 'National Film Board of Canada, 1940–52: Censorship and Scares,' *Cinema Canada* 56 (June–July 1979): 25–31.
5 *The Financial Post*, 19 November 1949
6 Gary Evans, *John Grierson and the National Film Board: The Politics of Wartime Propaganda* (Toronto 1984), 262
7 *Canadian Film Weekly*, 4 January 1950, 3
8 Marjorie McKay, 'History of the National Film Board of Canada' (typescript n.d.), 72
9 McKay, 'History,' 73
10 NA, Privy Council Office, RG2 18 vol 172; file: N-13; Department of Reconstruction and Supply, Press Release, 16 December 1949
11 *Time Magazine* 26 December 1949, 18; Toronto *Daily Star*, 16 December 1949
12 *Time Magazine* 26 December 1949, 18; Ottawa *Evening Citizen*, 16 December 1949; Montreal *Gazette*, 17 December 1949; Quebec *Chronicle Telegraph*, 19 December 1949
13 *Sudbury Daily Star*, 23 December 1949
14 Michael Spencer interview, Montreal, 5 May 1989
15 Marjorie McKay interview, Victoria, 22 May 1988
16 Michael Spencer interview, Montreal, 5 May 1989

17 Robert Bothwell and J.L. Granatstein, eds., *The Gouzenko Transcripts* (Ottawa n.d.), 17
18 Peter Morris, 'After Grierson: The National Film Board, 1945–1953,' *Journal of Canadian Studies* 16, no. 1 (spring 1981), 3
19 IP, file: Film Board: Manuscript Notes; Notes on my Stint at the National Film Board, n.d., 12
20 Ibid.; Evans, *John Grierson*, 263
21 IP, transcripts of NFB interview, n.d., NFB History roll 16, scene 2, take 1
22 NA, Privy Council Office Papers, RG2 Series 18 vol. 189; file: S-100-M; Security Panel minutes, 27 April 1950
23 Bothwell and Granatstein, *Gouzenko*, 17
24 Evans, *John Grierson*, 263
25 IP, transcripts of NFB interview, n.d., NFB History roll 16, scene 2, take 1
26 Tom Daly interview, Montreal, 18 November 1988

Chapter 16 'Going to Bat' for the NFB

1 The RCMP's Fire Prevention Branch reported in November 1949 concerning the John Street building: 'Conditions are such that were this building operating as private industry, it would be padlocked under the Fire Marshal's order, if not under the Factory Inspector, both of whom would not permit further operation in its present capacity. This Branch has gone on record time without number in condemnation of the occupancy and that stand is reiterated.' Quoted in NA, Privy Council Office Papers, RG2 Series 18, vol. 172, file: n-13; Cabinet Document #223-50, Submission on the Location of the National Film Board, 23 September 1950.
2 Tom Daly interview, Montreal, 18 November 1988
3 McKay, 'History,' 74
4 Marjorie McKay interview, Victoria, 22 May 1988; Michael Spencer interview, Montreal, 5 May 1989
5 IP, file: 90th Birthday Comments; Newman to Irwin, 27 May 1988
6 Reta Kilpatrick interview, Montreal, 4 November 1987
7 NA, Privy Council Office Papers, RG2 Series 18, vol 137; file: C-20-5; Woods and Gordon, *National Film Board: Survey of Organization and Business Administration*, March 1950
8 For an outline of these changes, see IP, file: FB Massey Report; Irwin to Vincent Massey, 30 October 1950; NFB, *Annual Report, 1950–51*
9 Evans, *John Grierson*, 233
10 IP, transcript of NFB interview, n.d., NFB History, roll 17, scene 3, take 1

11 Pierre Juneau interview, Ottawa, 22 June 1988; Michael Spencer interview, Montreal, 5 May 1989.
12 The new National Film Board met for the first time on 18 October 1950. Irwin took the chair and welcomed his new team, which included Albert Trueman, Stuart Keate, Charles Band, A.L. Caldwell, Gratien Gélinas, and, from the public service, A.D.P. Heeney, Charles Stein, and Arthur MacNamara. All the members were chosen for their abilities, of course, but in typically Canadian fashion they also were representative of various regions, genders, and linguistic groups. As Robert Winters explained in a letter to J.W. Pickersgill in the Prime Minister's Office, 'we will need representation from the following areas; the Maritimes, Quebec, Ontario, the prairies, and B.C. At least one of the members of the Board should be a woman and it should be composed of people from the following walks of life: business, academic, arts, labour, and probably somebody from a rural community. I believe that two of the members should be French-Canadian and that in all there should be three Roman Catholics.' NA, Louis St Laurent Papers, MG26 L, vol. 122, file: M-75-1; Winters to Pickersgill, 3 July 1950.
13 IP, file: FB Massey Report; Irwin to Massey, 30 October 1950
14 Pierre Juneau interview, Ottawa, 22 June 1988
15 P.K. Irwin interview, Victoria, 25 May 1987
16 IP, file: MM Berton, Pierre; Berton to Irwin, 14 November 1950
17 IP, file: Family. Letters: Pat 1950–; P.K. to Irwin, n.d., envelope stamped 23 October 1950
18 IP, file: Film Board: Montreal Move; Irwin, A Report on the Location of the National Film Board, 19 May 1950. This memo is attached as appendix 2 to NFB minutes, 18 October 1950.
19 Gary Evans, *In the National Interest: A Chronicle of the National Film Board of Canada from 1949 to 1989* (Toronto 1991), 10; see also J.L. Granatstein, 'Culture and Scholarship: The First Ten Years of the Canada Council,' *Canadian Historical Review* 65 (1984): 441–74.
20 Irwin, Report on the Location of the National Film Board, 19 May 1950. The following quotes are also taken from this memo.
21 'But to the staff, the picture was quite different,' wrote Marjorie McKay, one of those ultimately affected by the move. 'Many were actively engaged in the cultural life of the city [Ottawa] – in the Choral Society, the Symphony, the Bach Choir, the Civil Service Recreational Association's Drama clubs, in the Camera Clubs and other activities. They would lose all this and, in the vastness of Montreal, what would they find to take its place? Many owned their own homes and had spent hours on

their gardens and summer cottages. These they would have to sell, and then begin the hopeless task of finding places they liked as well. Moreover, since they had to sell, they would lose money for sure. Others had children attending school, and the transfer of children from the school system of Ontario to that of Quebec was difficult and frequently the child lost a year in the process. Many liked the peace and quiet of Ottawa, and the thought of trading that for the confusion of the largest city in Canada was unpleasant to contemplate.' McKay, 'History,' 89

22 NA, Privy Council Office Papers, RG2 Series 18, vol 172; file: N-13; Winters to St Laurent, 2 June 1950
23 J.W. Pickersgill interview, Ottawa, 4 November 1987
24 Cabinet conclusions, 30 September 1950; NA, Privy Council Office Papers, RG2 Series 18, vol. 172, file: n-13; Cabinet Document #223-50, Submission on the Location of the National Film Board, 23 September 1950
25 IP, file: Film Board: Montreal Move; C.S. Band, Report of the sub-committee, n.d., attached as appendix 21 to NFB minutes, 16 April 1951; NA, Records of Labour Canada, RG27, vol. 862, file: 8-3-19-3-5-2 pt.3; Pointe Claire: Facts Bearing on the Problem, n.d.
26 The man who oversaw the technical aspects of the move was Gerry Graham, the head of the Board's technical operations. Graham was alive to the potential noise problem at the chosen site, given that it was relatively close to three airports: Cartierville, St.-Hubert, and in particular, Dorval airport in the west. Graham later recalled how he persuaded a Canadair pilot (using Irwin's name without authorization) to fly over the site at 500 feet while he measured the sound levels on the ground. One farmer complained of panicky cows, but Graham also got the specifications he needed for building design. IP, file: FB Graham, Gerry; Graham to Irwin, 31 March 1981
27 NFB Archives, Box A-165, file: 1510, Report by Don Mulholland on Move to Montreal, 4 August 1953; see also Albert Trueman, *A Second View of Things: A Memoir* (Toronto 1982), 114–19
28 Pierre Juneau interview, Ottawa, 22 June 1988
29 IP, Letters Personal – 1971–78; Irwin to Ian MacNeil, 4 February 1976
30 NFB, *Annual Report, 1952–53*, 2
31 For more on the films produced in the early postwar years, see Evans, *In the National Interest*, chapter 1; Chris Whynot, 'The NFB and Labour, 1945–1955,' *Journal of Canadian Studies* 16, no. 1 (spring 1981), 13–22; and Peter Morris, 'After Grierson: The National Film Board 1945–1953,' *Journal of Canadian Studies* 16, no. 1 (spring 1981), 3–12.

32 Tom Daly interview, Montreal, 18 November 1988; NFB Archives, PARC 111942, file: 51-219, Royal Journey vol. 1; memo on *Royal Journey*, n.d.
33 Ibid., file: 51-219, Royal Journey, vol. 2, Daly to Irwin, 9 January 1952
34 Ibid., file: 51-212, Neighbours, memo on *Neighbours*, n.d.; McLaren memo on *Neighbours*, 3 June 1952
35 IP, file: McLaren, Norman, McLaren to Irwin, 26 February 1984
36 *Globe and Mail*, 12 February 1953; NFB archives, PARC 111942, file: 51-212, neighbours, Len Chatwin memo, 22 March 1954
37 NA, Records of Labour Canada, RG27 vol 862, file: 8-3-19-3-5-2 pt.3, Memorandum on the Use of Films in the Conflict with International Communism, 15 December 1950. See also, in the same file, R.B. Bryce to Irwin, 26 January 1951, and Irwin to Arthur MacNamara, 26 January 1951, and Evans, *In the National Interest*, 20–22.
38 McKay, 'History,' 87
39 'Film Board Head Lauded Ere Inquiry Undertaken,' *Globe and Mail*, 1 May 1952
40 Michael Spencer interview, Montreal, 5 May 1989
41 McKay 'History,' 87
42 House of Commons, Special Committee on the National Film Board, *Minutes of Proceedings and Evidence*, 8 May 1952, 21
43 Ibid., *Minutes of Proceedings and Evidence, Including Second and Final Report to the House*, 3 June 1952, 24 June 1952, 77
44 Tom Daly interview, Montreal, 18 November 1988
45 Ibid.

Chapter 17 'The Canadian Was *Simpatico*'

1 Irwin interview, Victoria, 25 May 1987
2 Irwin-Allen interview transcripts, 572
3 IP, file: FB Resignation Clippings; Irwin Conversation with Minister, 15 January 1953
4 *Saturday Night*, 14 March 1953
5 IP, file: Australia: Letters on Appointment; C.J. Burchell to Irwin, 25 March 1953
6 IP, file: Family: letters – 1953–1956; Irwin to Sheila Irwin, 8 July 1953
7 IP, file: Australia: Northern Territory Trip and Draft Report; Irwin, Australia's Empty North, June 1956
8 P.K. Irwin interview, Victoria, 25 May 1987
9 John Bird, '"Tough Canadian" Irwin goes South,' Vancouver *Province*, 30 May 1953

10 Geoffrey Pearson interview, Ottawa, 27 June 1988
11 NA, Lester Pearson Papers, MG26 N1, vol. 2; file: Pearson: Nominal Files; Pearson to Irwin, 25 April 1956
12 IP, file: Brazil: Appointment to; Irwin to under-secretary of state for external affairs, t. 108, 30 July 1956
13 IP, file: Brazil: Trips to States I; Irwin to secretary of state for external affairs, t. 247, 30 May 1957
14 IP, file: Brazil residence; Irwin to under-secretary of state for external affairs, t. 130, 27 March 1957
15 IP, file: Minister's Visit; Leger to Irwin, 22 January 1957
16 IP, file: Brazil: Personal Letters; Irwin to Jules Leger, 2 January 1958
17 Ibid, 26 September 1958
18 IP, file: Brazil: Trips to States I; Irwin to secretary of state for external affairs, t. 247, 30 May 1957
19 Ibid.
20 IP, Irwin-Allen interview transcripts, 800
21 IP, file: Brazil: Personal Letters; Irwin to Norman Robertson, 19 February 1959
22 Another visit of note during Irwin's stay in Mexico, came from Lester Pearson, now leader of the opposition. Pearson was well known and respected in Mexico from his many years as a diplomat. Particularly after winning the Nobel Peace Prize in 1957, Pearson regularly received invitations to speak in Mexico. Moreover, in 1961 his son Geoffrey was posted to Mexico as first secretary in the Canadian embassy, so a visit to Mexico was not out of the ordinary. During his stay, Pearson was the guest of honour at a private luncheon hosted by the Mexican foreign minister, Manuel Tello. Tello stood and welcomed the leader of the opposition to his country, but then added that he hoped that the next time Pearson came he would 'come as prime minister.' Diefenbaker heard of this breach of protocol and, as Irwin later learned, was outraged.
23 Geoffrey Pearson interview, Ottawa, 27 June 1988
24 IP, file: F. Letters, Personal Mexico 1963–64; Hutchison to Irwin, 11 November 1963
25 IP, file: V. Letters, Personal, 1966; unsigned to Irwin, 8 February 1966
26 IP, file: F. Letters. Personal, Mexico 1962; Irwin to Hutchison, 25 January 1962
27 IP, file: Mexico: Personal Correspondence; Robertson to Irwin, 4 January 1963
28 IP, file: F. Letters, Personal Mexico 1963–64; Irwin to Hutchison, 25 April 1963

29 Ibid., Hutchison to Irwin, 11 November 1963

Chapter 18 *Pax* Victoria

1 IP, file: F. Letters, Personal, Mexico 1962; Irwin to Hutchison, 25 January 1962
2 IP, file: V. Letters, Personal 1968; Irwin to Newman, 20 February 1968
3 On Irwin's retirement, Pierre Berton wrote from Toronto:

> Arthur Irwin is the most retiring man I know. Ever since I have known him he has been retiring. When I was a child in knickers he retired from Maclean's ostensibly to spend his golden years at some Senior Citizens Home in Tuscaloosa. He immediately took a job as commissioner of the National Film Board of Canada. As soon as he reached retirement age he retired from the film board, ostensibly to spend his golden years at the Tired Old Journalists Home in Mimico. He immediately took a job as a senior diplomat, moving at once to Canberra, Australia, retiring after three or four years and going on to Rio de Janeiro and then retiring again to another stint in Mexico City. After several decades of mastering foreign tongues (including Australian) he was again retired, ostensibly to spend his golden years at Rockabella, the well known Vancouver Island hippy haven. He immediately took a job as publisher of the Victoria Times. Now I understand he is retiring once more. Well, good luck to him. I will believe it when I see it.

IP, file: V. Retirement 1971; Berton to Gordon Bell, n.d.
4 Victoria *Daily Times*, 1 June 1971. Irwin's words were distilled from an earlier statement he made to the Special Senate Committee on Mass Media, which was printed as a pamphlet in 1970 under the title 'The Challenge to Journalism.'
5 IP, file: Newman, Peter; Irwin to Newman, 29 May 1967
6 Irwin quoted in Victoria *Monday* vol 9, n. 27 (July 1–7 1983)
7 Berton earlier dedicated his book *The National Dream* to Irwin, 'since you were the first guy that taught me what facts really were and I've always been grateful for it.' IP, file: MM Berton, Pierre; Berton to Irwin, 14 August 1970

A Note on Sources

In the spring of 1992 Arthur Irwin's papers were transferred to the National Archives in Ottawa. At the time of the transfer they consisted of thirteen filing cabinet-size boxes, one filing cabinet of recent correspondence and financial records, plus a few miscellaneous files, photographs, tapes and Irwin's collection of old issues of *Maclean's Magazine*. I was also given access to the tapes and/or transcripts of interviews of Irwin conducted by other scholars, including: Glen Allen, Peter Desbarats, Sandra Djwa, Walter Young, and the National Film Board. Irwin gave me access to his own memoir notes which cover his early years and a few specific episodes of his later career. More importantly, he made available the hundreds of pages of notes he made concerning the actual articles in *Maclean's*. After his retirement, Irwin went through every issue of his almost twenty-five years at the magazine and wrote extensively on article selection, why a particular author was chosen, office politics, editorial content, and the process of editing a magazine. These notes were especially valuable.

The strengths and weaknesses of Irwin's papers inevitably affected the nature of this biography. The papers boast a comprehensive collection of material on Irwin and his dealings with *Maclean's Magazine*: articles, letters, notes, and memos on issues ranging from pay raises and budgets to the overall editorial direction of the magazine; correspondence concerning his relations with Napier Moore and the Maclean company administration; drafts and research notes for his own articles; files on various other articles that reveal his editorial style; plans for staff improvement and office routine; personal material on his career advancement; forecasts and outlines for upcoming issues; in short, all the things that deal with an editor's role in

A Note on Sources

the production of a mass-circulation magazine. Taken together with his voluminous contents notes and the several boxes of Irwin material in the Maclean Hunter papers in the Archives of Ontario, this material furnishes a unique perspective on Irwin's role and impact on the evolution of *Maclean's*, and it is here that much of this biography is focused.

Irwin's papers on his years at the NFB are equally full, at least concerning the issues that confronted him as film commissioner. Irwin was not a filmmaker and he came to the NFB without long-range plans to radically change the nature of filmmaking in Canada, and his papers reflect this reality. They are good for official correspondence, copies of government reports and documents, and background information dealing with Irwin's actions in the three areas that most concerned him during his short stay at the NFB: his efforts to end the security issue and to restore the government's confidence in the board, his revision of the Film Board Act to set the NFB on a more permanent footing, and his decision to move the board to Montreal.

The documents covering his diplomatic career are also plentiful and include lengthy descriptions of his many travels and bulging files on the daily routine of life in a Canadian embassy, but they were of less direct value for this study. Where possible I augmented Irwin's papers with additional research in the National Archives in Ottawa, the Archives of Ontario in Toronto, at the NFB headquarters in Montreal, and several other locations. A complete list of primary sources follows.

Unfortunately, there is a relative shortage of personal letters in Irwin's papers; he rarely travelled for extended periods away from his wife and family, and he was not a prolific letter writer in any event. The letters that do survive are by and large recent ones, are mundane by any standard, and reveal little of Irwin's private thoughts. The one minor exception is a group of letters written to his first wife while Irwin was posted to Ottawa as the *Globe*'s member of the Parliamentary Press Gallery in 1925; these letters survive and give a good look into his personality in his mid-twenties. I do not believe there is any extant document in Irwin's hand before that time, and for Irwin's early life I have been forced to rely on interviews and a variety of secondary sources such as Irwin's memoir notes and Brooke Claxton's unpublished memoirs and war diary. A more serious problem is the small number of personal documents covering his adult life. In particular, Irwin never kept a diary, and so much of the personal material in this book has been drawn from interviews with Irwin and those who knew him, and from what could be found in other archival sources.

Archival Sources

Victoria, B.C.
    Arthur Irwin Papers (now held in the National Archives, Ottawa, MG31, E97)

National Archives, Ottawa
    Brooke Claxton Papers (MG32 B5)
    Howard Green Papers (MG32 B13)
    A.D.P. Heeney Papers (MG30 E144)
    William Lyon Mackenzie King Papers (MG26 J)
    Ian Mackenzie Papers (MG27 III B5)
    A.G.L. McNaughton Papers (MG30 E133)
    P.K. Page Papers (MG30 D311)
    Lester B. Pearson Papers (MG26 N)
    J.L. Ralston Papers (MG27 III B11)
    Norman Robertson Papers (MG30 E163)
    Louis St Laurent Papers (MG26 L)
    Robert Winters Papers (MG32 B24)
    Department of External Affairs (RG25)
    Department of National Defence (RG24)
    National Film Board (RG53)
    Privy Council Office (RG2)
    Records of Labour Canada (RG27)
    RCMP Records (RG18)

Archives of Ontario, Toronto
    Maclean Hunter Papers
    George Drew Scrapbooks

National Film Board, Montreal
    NFB records
    Tom Daly Papers

McGill University Archives
    John Grierson Papers

Queen's University Archives
    Grant Dexter Papers

Thomas Fisher Rare Book Library, University of Toronto
    William Arthur Deacon Papers

Directorate of History, Ottawa
  Department of National Defence records

Interviews

Hector Alexander, Victoria, B.C., 31 May 1988
Jerry Anglin, Thornhill, Ont., 9 June 1988
Louis Applebaum, Toronto, Ont., 9 May 1988
Franklin Arbuckle, Toronto, Ont., 16 June 1989
J.R. Baldwin, Kingston, Ont., 21 August 1987
Pierre Berton, Toronto, Ont., 9 August 1988
Norval Bonisteel, Toronto, Ont., 10 May 1988
Morley Callaghan, telephone interview, 13 July 1988
Floyd Chalmers, Toronto, Ont., 2 May 1988
John Clare, Toronto, Ont., 17 June 1988
Tom Daly, Montreal, Qué., 18 November 1988
R.G. Everson, Burlington, Ont., 5 May 1988
John Holmes, Toronto, Ont., 22 October 1987
Bruce Hutchison, Victoria, B.C., 26 May 1987
Sheila Irving, Victoria, B.C., 1 June 1988
Arthur Irwin, Victoria, B.C.
Neal Irwin, Toronto, Ont., 27 March, 10 April 1988
P.K. Irwin, Victoria, B.C., 25 May 1987
Pierre Juneau, Ottawa, Ont., 22 June 1988
Yousuf Karsh, telephone interview, 28 September 1989
Hugh Keenleyside, Victoria, B.C., 21 May 1987
Reta Kilpatrick, Montreal, Qué., 4 November 1987
Henry Langford, Toronto, Ont., 11 August 1987
Arthur Mayse, Campbell River, B.C., 21 May 1988
Hugh MacLennan, telephone interview, 8 May 1989
Marjorie McKay, Victoria, B.C., 22 May 1988
Roland Michener, Toronto, Ont., 12 May 1988
Grant Munro, St-Laurent, Qué., 6 October 1989
Peter C. Newman, Victoria, B.C., 27 May 1987
Geoffrey Pearson, Ottawa, Ont., 27 June 1988
J.W. Pickersgill, Ottawa, Ont., 4 November 1987
Escott Reid, Ste-Cécile-de-Masham, Qué., 4 November 1987
Michael Spencer, Montreal, Qué., 5 May 1989
Scott Young, Toronto, Ont., 24 July 1989

Index

Adams, Clifford, 207
Allan, Ted, 203
Allen, Ralph, 5, 167–8, 170, 177, 193, 194, 197, 207, 208, 210, 211, 225, 300n16; joins staff of *Maclean's*, 189–90; editorial-management relations, 200–1; and Bethune article, 203; leaves *Maclean's*, 214–15; becomes editor, 223
Allen, Robert, 193, 223
Allison, William Talbot, 18, 36–7
Anderson, Harry, 44, 55, 58–9, 61; relations with Irwin and McKinnon, 58–60
Anglin, Jerry, 177, 187, 193, 197, 207, 208, 215; first meeting with Irwin, 164–5
Arbuckle, Franklin, 178; cross-country tour, 209–10
Arts and Letters Club, 96
Atlantic Monthly, 156
Attlee, Clement, 176

Bairstow, David, 255

Baldwin, John R., 111, 154
Band, C.S., 252
Basset, Cyril, 232
Bassett, John, 48
Battersby, D.M., 185, 197
Baxter, Beverly, 106, 158, 160, 176, 187, 222
Beeman, Colonel, 26–7, 28
Berton, Pierre, 5, 194, 201, 202, 203, 208, 210, 215, 249, 310n3; joins staff of *Maclean's*, 191–3; and changes to the magazine, 197–8, 204
Beveridge, James, 246–7, 249
Bishop, Charlie, 48, 89
Bland, Salem, 18, 30
Bliven, Bruce, 180
Blue, A.W., 83
Bodsworth, Fred, 207
Bonisteel, Norval, 106–7, 164, 185
Borden, Sir Robert, 110
Bren gun contract, 118, 145–7; Royal Commission on, 122–3, 128
Brewin, F.A., 175
Briscoe, R. Laird, 73

Index

British Commonwealth Relations Conference, 174–6
Brown, George, 43
Brunton, Captain Sir Stopford, 21
Bryce, R.B., 154
Burchell, C.J., 264–5
Business Magazine, 69. See also *Maclean's Magazine*
Busy Man's Magazine, 69, 71. See also *Maclean's Magazine*
Byrnes, James, 156

Callaghan, Morley, 45, 89, 157, 207
Callwood, June, 207
'Canada's Armament Mystery,' 4, 120. See also Drew, George
Canadian Forum, 204
Canadian Institute of International Affairs (CIIA), 67, 152, 172, 174, 233, 266; Irwin joins, 110–11, and Toronto memorandum, 153–5. See also British Commonwealth Relations Conference
Canadian Magazine, 69, 72, 88, 114, 156
Casey, R.G., 268–9
Casson, A.J., 90
Castro, Fidel, 273
Cavell, R.G., 154, 174
Chalmers, Floyd S., 71, 75, 76, 104, 125, 128, 165, 170, 174, 183, 211, 269, 279, 281; and defence contract investigation, 131–2, 133, 135, 137, 139, 141–2; on Irwin, 162–3; and editorial-management relations, 200–3; and Hunter memo, 215–18; and Irwin's resignation from *Maclean's*, 224–5
Chatelaine, 158
Charpentier, Fulgence, 48

Churchill, Winston, 157
Clare, John, 5, 169–70, 190, 193, 194, 196, 197–8, 202, 207, 208; joins staff of *Maclean's* 188–9; becomes associate editor, 214–15
Clarke, A.D., 44
Clarke, Harry, 165
Claxton, Brooke, 21, 22, 111, 233, 250; and World War I 'mutiny,' 27–8, 288n11; and CIIA, 153–5
Coldwell, M.J., 160
Collier's Weekly, 82, 99, 156, 191
Cooke, Albert, 22, 28–9, 47; enlists with Irwin, 20–1
Cornish, Frank, 38–40
Cosmopolitan, 63, 74, 86, 89, 99
Costain, Thomas B., 71–2, 88
Coulter, John, 157
Craick, Arnot, 71
Crawford, A.W., 31–2, 33
Crerar, Lieutenant-General H.D.G., 3
Currie, General Sir Arthur, 23

Dafoe, John, 110
Daly, Tom, 244; on Irwin at NFB, 241–2; directs *Royal Journey*, 255–6; relations with Irwin, 260–1
Davis, Henry Hague, 122–3, 124. See also Bren gun contract
Deacon, William Arthur, 97–9
Defence Purchasing Board, 122–3, 124, 133, 136, 145
Dempsey, Lotta, 158–9
Désy, Jean, 199
Dexter, Grant, 48, 50, 89, 105, 159–60, 299n38
Diefenbaker, John, 274, 275, 276, 278, 280, 309n22
Dinberg, M.C., 207

Index

Dinsmore, E.J., 190
Drew, George, 4, 123, 158, 213, 233; first articles for *Maclean's*, 107–8; Bren gun article, 118–21, 125, 126; and Public Accounts Committee, 128–30; attacks Mackenzie King, 141–3
Duplessis, Maurice, 252

Eldridge, Harold, 106, 109
Evans, Maurice, 97
Everson, R.G., 97

Farquharson, R.A., 40–1, 44, 45, 46
Ferguson, Howard, 113
Ferguson, Hugh, 44
Financial Post, 4, 70, 71, 118, 119, 232, 233–4; and defence contract investigation, 130, 135–40, 143–5
Fitzgibbons, J.J., 256
Ford, Arthur, 199
Forke, Robert, 49, 59
Foster, Ralph, 234, 245
Fraser, Blair, 5, 180, 187, 189, 201, 202, 206, 208, 215, 281; hired at *Maclean's*, 165–6, 299n38
Frayne, Trent, 207

Gadsby, H.F., 48
Gandhi, Indira, 275
Gardiner, James, 238–9
Glazebrook, G.P. de T., 110, 111
Globe (Toronto), 36, 37, 46, 63; background and staff, 43–4; editorial controversy at, 54–62
Gordon, Walter, 245
Gouzenko, Igor, 230
Graham, Gerry, 307n26
Grahame, Gordon Hill, 72
Gray, James, 207

Green, Howard, 158, 273
Grierson, John, 157, 232, 236–7, 244, 246, 259, 298n25; and security issue, 230–1; meeting with Irwin, 261–2
Grove, Frederick Philip, 89

Hackett, W.T.G., 154
Hahn, James, 119, 130; plan to manufacture Bren guns, 117–18; and Bren gun article, 121–3
Halton, Matthew, 167–8
Hannon, Leslie, 215
Hardy, W.G., 89, 207
Harper's, 156
Harris, Walter, 253
Hart, Liddell, 206
Hassard, Rev. Richard, 10
Hassel, Hilton, 185
Heming, Arthur, 90
Hepburn, Mitch, 142–3, 157
Hewelcke, Geoffrey, 165, 188
Holmes, John, 111
House of Commons, Standing Committee on Public Accounts. *See* Public Accounts Committee
Howe, C.D., 145, 274
Howse, T.H., 162, 202–3
Hutchison, Bruce, 50, 89, 139, 191, 223, 276–7, 281; first meeting with Irwin, 49; relations with Irwin, 160–1; visits the *Maclean's* office, 196–7; and Irwin's *Maclean's* resignation, 219–20; correspondence with Irwin in Mexico, 276–8, 280
Hunter, Horace T., 76, 100, 104, 162–3, 183, 211, 224, 248; background, 70–1; and Bren gun article, 119, 121, 124–6; and Pub-

lic Accounts Committee, 128–30; and defence contract investigation, 131, 134, 137, 139, 140–3, 145–7; on editorial- management relations, 200–1; and memo to Chalmers, 216–18, 222

Ickes, Harold, 156
Irwin, Rev. Alexander James, 9–10, 11, 12, 15, 16, 30, 34, 35, 299n3; and Methodism, 13–14
Irwin, Amelia Jane (née Hassard), 10, 13, 34, 213
Irwin, Arnold, 10
Irwin, Gordon, 10
Irwin, Harold, 10
Irwin, Harvey, 10, 34–5
Irwin, Helen, 10, 34, 35
Irwin, Jean Olive (née Smith), 45, 46, 50, 95, 153; marriage to Irwin, 41–2; correspondence from Irwin, 51–3; family life, 108–9, 172–4; death of, 213–14, 222
Irwin, Neal Alexander, 95, 172, 222
Irwin, Patricia Jean, 95
Irwin, Patricia Kathleen. *See* Page, P.K.
Irwin, Sheila Ann, 95, 269
Irwin, William, 9
Irwin, William Arthur, 70, 71, 83, 84; nationalism of, 3–4; character of, 5–6, 30–1; early life, 7–8, 10, 11–16; and Methodism, 13–14; in Winnipeg, 17; at Wesley College, 18–19; enlists, 20–1; war experience, 22–9; discusses future with father, 30; and Winnipeg General Strike, 32–3; and brother Harvey, 34–5; looking for first job, 36–7; at *Mail and Empire*, 37–42; at *Globe*, 43–7; as member of Parliamentary Press Gallery, 47–53; and election of 1925, 53–62; is hired at *Maclean's*, 63–6; early days at *Maclean's*, 72–6; first meeting with Napier Moore, 80–1; editorial activities and article selection, 85–90; early articles at *Maclean's*, 90–5; joins Toronto Writers Club, 96–7; relations with W.A. Deacon, 97–9; and salary and editorial problems, 99–102; work during the Depression, 104–8; and Machine Ballet, 109–10; joins CIIA, 110–11; article for *The Round Table*, 111–12, 114; plans for *Maclean's*, 114–15; and Bren gun article, 118–20, 123–4; and Public Accounts Committee, 128–30; and defence contract investigation, 131–47; and defence issues, 151–6; and war coverage, 157–61, 167–70; promotion to managing editor, 163–4; relations with Blair Fraser, 165–6; home life, 171–3; wartime trip to Europe, 174–8; theme issue on atomic energy, 179–81; promotion to editor, 182–3; staff changes, 184–93; editorial activities, 194–8, 204–12; editorial-management relations, 199–204; death of Jean, 213–14; and resignation, 215–26; joins NFB, 229–36; and NFB security issue, 236–42; and reorganization of the NFB, 243–9; marries P.K. Page, 249–50; and move of NFB to Montreal, 250–5; and film production,

255–7; defends the NFB, 258–62; appointed to Australia, 263–4; in Australia, 264–9; in Brazil, 270–4; in Mexico, 274–8; moves to Victoria, 279–81; retirement, 282–5

Jackson, Gilbert, 89
Jaffray, Senator Robert, 43
Jaffray, William Gladstone, 43–4, 54, 55, 56; and election of 1925, 57–62
James, Jane, 9
Jeffers, Wellington, 98
Jenkins, Charles, 83
Jennings, Claude, 37
Johnston, Franz, 90
Juneau, Pierre, 248–9, 254

Katz, Sydney, 207
Keenleyside, Hugh, 155
Khrushchev, Nikita, 273
Kilpatrick, Reta, 245
King, William Lyon Mackenzie, 15, 51, 64, 89, 108, 117, 131, 136, 151, 301n1; meeting with Irwin, 49–50, 54; and possible purchase of the *Globe*, 55–7; letter to Irwin, 61–2; and Bren gun scandal, 121–3, 125–6; attacked by Maclean company, 140–2, 144, 146; and defence memo, 155
Knister, Raymond, 89

Ladies Home Journal, 99
LaFlèche, Colonel L.R., 117, 118, 122–3, 132, 136, 146; and Public Accounts Committee, 126–7, 128, 130
Lambert, Norman, 16
Lapointe, Ernest, 57, 143

Larkin, Peter, 57
Lash, Herb, 38, 40
Laurier, Sir Wilfrid, 15
Le Cocq, Thelma, 157, 230
Léger, Jules, 270–2
Lewis, John, 54, 62
Life, 156
Linton, Freda, 230
Lipsett–Skinner, G., 48
Lloyd, E.A., 85–6
Lloyd, Trevor, 159
Lloyd George, David, 47
Lower, A.R.M., 206
Lyon, T. Stewart, 43–4, 47, 57, 59, 61; gives Irwin editorial position, 54–5

McArthur, Dan, 199
McCall's, 82
McCulloch, J.H., 98
Macdonald, Angus, 160
Macdonald, Sir John A., 37
Macdonald, Murdoch, 36–7
MacFarlane, Doug, 207
McGeer, Gerald, 129
McGill Draft (10th Canadian Siege Battery), 22–3; Irwin joins, 21–2
MacInnis, Angus, 158
MacKay, Isabel Ecclestone, 89
McKay, Marjorie, 234, 258–9; and NFB security issue, 236–7; relations with Irwin, 244–5
McKenzie, J. Vernon, 63–4, 65, 72, 73, 96; relations with Irwin, 74–6
Mackenzie, Ian, 130; and Bren gun contract, 118–24, 126; under attack from the Maclean company, 131–8, 140–1, 143–4, 146
McKinnon, Hector, 44–5, 46, 47, 74, 200, 282; brings Irwin to the

Globe, 41–2; becomes editorial writer, 54–5; letters to Mackenzie King, 55–7, and 1925 election, 57–62; recommends Irwin for job at *Maclean's*, 63–5
McLaren, Norman, 256–7
MacLean, Hugh, 88
Maclean, Colonel John Bayne, 71–2, 75–6, 80, 88, 100, 108, 140, 162, 200–1, 211, 283; first meeting with Irwin, 64–5; background, 68–70; and Bren gun scandal, 119, 121; and campaign against the government, 140–1, 145–6
McLean, Ross, 231–2, 238, 244, 246, 272; removed as NFB film commissioner, 234–5
McLean, William, 38
Maclean Publishing Company, 70–1, 84, 104, 201; and Bren gun scandal, 123, 130; and its campaign against the government, 131–2, 138–9, 142–6; reorganized, 162–3, 165, 211
Maclean's Magazine, 3, 4, 64–5, 66, 76, 82; early years, 69, 71–2; editorial office, 73; design and production, 83–8; changes during Depression, 104–6; Bren gun article, 20–1, 124–5, 130, 145; compared to *Saturday Night*, 156–7; wartime articles, 157–60, 167–9, 179–81; changes in late 1940s, 204–10
MacLennan, Hugh, 207; on the death of Irwin's first wife, 213–14; on Irwin's resignation from *Maclean's*, 223–4
Macmillan, Harold, 273

McNaughton, General A.G.L., 133, 134, 139; meeting with Irwin, 131–2
MacNeil, Inspector R.A.S., 238–9
Mail and Empire (Toronto), 36, 37, 41, 45, 63
Malone, R.S., 280–1
Marshall, Adam, 185, 188, 208, 209
Martin, Paul, 154, 276
Massey, Vincent, 176, 248
Masson, Hal, 187, 188, 191, 207, 208
Mayse, Arthur, 5, 208; hired by Irwin, 185–7; resigns, 191–2; and editorial conferences, 194–5
Mears, Fred, 48, 49, 50
Meighen, Arthur, 48, 51, 59, 61; meeting with Irwin, 49–50
Menzies, Sir Robert, 265
Michener, Roland, 175
Mitchell, W.O., 5, 157, 207, 214
Moodie, Campbell, 199, 218, 233
Moore, Napier, 3–4, 83, 84, 88, 89, 90, 96, 99, 119, 159, 162, 164–5, 169–70, 172, 174, 179, 187, 190, 193, 200, 211, 248, 283; comes to *Maclean's*, 75–6; background, 79–81; and Irwin's emigration articles, 93–4; relations with Irwin, 99–101; and Depression economy measures, 103–8; and Bren gun scandal, 121, 124, 128, 130; and defence contract investigation, 131, 137, 142; leaves editorial chair, 182–3; later dealings with *Maclean's*, 200–2
Moorhouse, Hopkins, 89
Mulholland, Donald, 246–7, 253
Munro, Grant, 257
Munro, Ross, 167–9

National Film Board, 5, 235; background, 229–32; and J.D. Woods and Gordon report, 219, 231–2, 245–7, 250; and security issue, 236–42; reorganization of, 243–8; move to Montreal, 250–5; early 1950s film production, 256–8; parliamentary review, 259–60
Nehru, Jawaharlal, 275
Nelles, Vice-Admiral Percy, 160
Neville, Charles, 207
New Liberty, 204, 209
Newman, Peter C., 281, 282
Newman, Sydney, 245
New Republic, 180
Newton, B.G., 162

Ogdensburg Declaration, 155–6
O'Leary, Grattan, 48, 89, 105, 106
Ord, Major L.C., 22, 24, 25, 27
Organization of American States, 276–7

Packard, Frank L., 89
Page, Patricia Kathleen, 261; marriage to Irwin, 249–50; in Australia, 265, 268, 269; in Brazil, 271–2; in New York City, 273; in Mexico, 274–5, 277–8; in Victoria, 280–1, 283
Paré, Lorenzo, 199
Parliamentary Press Gallery, 47–8
Pearson, Geoffrey, 268, 275
Pearson, Lester B., 233, 269, 274, 276, 278, 280, 309n22; on Irwin's diplomatic appointment, 263–4
Pickersgill, J.W., 154, 274
Plaxton, Hugh, 120–1, 122
Porter, Mackenzie, 196
Pratt, E.J., 97, 178

Public Accounts Committee, 126–7, 130, 134, 163

Racey, A.G., 90
Raddall, Thomas H., 89, 157, 160, 207
Raine, Norman Reilly, 73
Ralston, J.L., 143
Rawlings, Charles, 160
Readers' Digest, 204, 209
Red Book, 82
Reeves, Wilfred, 99
Reid, Escott, 111
Reyburn, Wallace, 157–8, 167–9
Riegger, Walingford, 109
Roberts, Sir Charles G.D., 50, 97
Roberts, Leslie, 159
Roberts, Lloyd, 50, 89
Robertson, Norman, 232, 235, 246, 270, 277; discusses Irwin's appointment to NFB, 218–20; and NFB security issue, 239–40; and Irwin's appointment to Mexico, 273–4
Rogers, Norman, 136, 141; meeting with Irwin, 139–40
Roosevelt, Eleanor, 150
Roosevelt, Franklin D., 155
Ross, C.E., 158
Roy, Gabrielle, 207
Rutledge, Joseph Lister, 72, 88

St Laurent, Louis, 199, 221–2, 252, 274, 280; and NFB move to Montreal, 252–3
Sandwell, B.K., 175
Salverson, Laura Goodman, 89
Saturday Evening Post, 72, 82, 83, 99, 156, 180, 191, 204
Saturday Night, 68, 69, 156, 204, 264

Scott, F.R., 154
Scott, Jack, 191–2
Seymour, Jane, 73
Shapiro, Lionel, 167–9, 187, 206
Shumiatcher, Morris, 158
Sifton, Victor, 175
Sinclair, Bertrand, 89
Sinclair, Gordon, 97, 158, 202
Skelton, O.D., 155
Smith, Dora, 41, 108
Smith, Howard K., 206
Smith, Sidney, 273
Smyth Report, 180, 188
Spears, Borden, 215
Spencer, Michael, 237, 244, 258–9, 261
Star (Toronto), 36
Stead, Robert, 90, 105
Stettinius, Edward, 156
Stringer, Arthur, 89
Stursberg, Peter, 167
Sullivan, Alan, 89
Sunday World (Toronto), 38, 40

Tarr, Edgar J., 154, 175
Thomas, Lillian Beyon, 90
Thompson, Walter S., 139
Time, 209, 235
Tippett, Maria, 157
Toronto Memorandum, 153–4, 156. *See also* Canadian Institute of International Affairs
Toronto Skating Club, 109–10
Toronto Writers Club, 96–7, 98, 108, 111; and Writer's Market Survey, 98–9
Trotter, R.G., 175
Trudeau, Pierre, 281–2
Trueman, Albert, 253, 260

Truman, Harry, 156
Tupper, Sir Charles, 50
Tyrrell, H.V., 64, 65, 66, 70, 75–6, 91, 100–1, 104, 114, 162–3, 225; background, 70–1; and defence contract investigation, 131, 137, 142, 145

Underhill, Frank, 113, 224
United Nations Conference on Freedom of Information, 199, 203, 218
University of Manitoba, 16, 17, 19

Van Passen, Pierre, 44
Van Valkenburg, Lucinda Ann, 10
Vaughan, R.C., 133
Victoria College, 9, 10, 34, 41
Vimy Ridge, 23, 24

Wallace, Henry, 156
Wallace, W.S., 67
War Supply Board. *See* Defence Purchasing Board
Werner, Max, 180
Wesley College, 16, 30; background, 17–18; and World War I, 19–20
Whitton, Charlotte, 253
Willison, J.S., 50, 54
Wilson, Ken, 160, 232, 299n38
Winters, Robert, 223, 231, 234, 239, 258, 274; and Irwin's NFB appointment, 219–21; and NFB move to Montreal, 252; on Irwin's resignation from the NFB, 263–4
Woods, Rex, 90
Woodsworth, J.S., 97, 118, 151
Wrong, George, 35

Wuorio, Eva-Lis, 5, 191, 207, 214, 229

'X,' 134

Young, Ewart, 208
Young, Scott, 5, 187, 188, 189–90, 192, 194, 203, 207, 208, 210, 214